GENDER IN THE PREMODERN MEDITERRANEAN

Medieval & Renaissance
Texts and Studies

Volume 539

GENDER IN THE PREMODERN MEDITERRANEAN

Edited by
Megan Moore
University of Missouri

Arizona Center for Medieval & Renaissance Studies
Tempe, Arizona
2019

Arizona Center
for Medieval &
Renaissance Studies

Published by ACMRS (Arizona Center for Medieval and Renaissance Studies)
Tempe, Arizona
© 2019 Arizona Board of Regents for Arizona State University.
All Rights Reserved.

Cover Image:
Codex Manesse f. 319r
Zurich ca. 1305–1340
Heidelberg University Library, Cpg 848
CC-BY-SA 4.0

∞
This book is made to last. It is set in Adobe Caslon Pro,
smyth-sewn and printed on acid-free paper to library specifications.
Printed in the United States of America

TABLE OF CONTENTS

Acknowledgments

The expansion of recent scholarly interest in the Mediterranean has come through the dedication and curiosity of many, in particular the group of scholars who founded the Mediterranean Seminar. I would like to express gratitude to Sharon Kinoshita and Brian Catlos, its founders, whose time and dedication in gathering together scholars from near and far to discuss the Mediterranean has formed a vibrant critical community in which ideas such as those expressed in this volume can thrive and even be interrogated. The Seminar has been a welcoming and stimulating experience for many of us and has not only helped to sharpen the critical tools with which we approach premodern Mediterranean studies but also permitted participants to forge new relationships and exchange work.

In addition, forums and panels organized at meetings of the Renaissance Society of America, the Modern Language Association, the International Medieval Congress, the New Chaucer Society, the Medieval Academy, and the Shakespeare Association of America, among others, have provided many of us with important critical discussion of our work among others interested in gender studies and in Mediterranean studies. I am, as always, grateful for the support of the University of Missouri and its Department of Romance Languages in preparing this volume.

Chapter 1
GENDER IN THE PREMODERN MEDITERRANEAN

MEGAN MOORE, UNIVERSITY OF MISSOURI

> Here it thunders now over the Mediterranean, high and lonely,
> this anachronism in primal red, in yellow purer
> than can be found anywhere today, a purity
> begging to be polluted . . . of course Empire took its way
> westward, what other way was there but into those
> virgin sunsets to penetrate and to foul?
> — Thomas Pynchon, *Gravity's Rainbow*

Thomas Pynchon's brief reflection on the power of "a nineteenth-century wilderness" sunset thundering over the Mediterranean in *Gravity's Rainbow* imagines war-torn identities as constructed through fluid connections between self and place. In this short passage, gender and geography collide, as the Mediterranean metonymizes empire, with its attendant dynamics of despoiling and befouling, situating the process of expansion as the destruction of virginity, the corruption of a mythical, perfected femininity in the service of patriarchy. Perhaps a tongue-in-cheek reflection on the perfection of an era that never existed, Pynchon's corrupted "virgin sunsets" nonetheless build upon a long tradition of Mediterranean contact and conquest that relies on gender politics as an integral way of figuring power, where desecration of gender norms announces power and victory.

Pynchon's play on gender and empire resonates with academic discussions of identity, although, unlike him, we are mostly unwilling to combine the long story of the Mediterranean with nineteenth-century romanticism. Although area studies such as Mediterranean Studies have become insightful tools for approaching intersectionality, we still tend to conceptualize gender practices as highly localized. Indeed, incredibly careful and thorough studies of the intricacies of local practices of gender, race, and class have lent credibility to burgeoning studies of identity politics, describing the personal in ways that are both intellectual and political. Intersectional work from the past two decades, such as that of Anne McClintock (*Imperial Leather*) or Kathleen Brown (*Good Wives, Nasty Wenches, and Anxious Patriarchs*), exemplifies how reading a panoply of sources in order to isolate highly specific cultural locales may help us to better understand the identities constructed there.[1] Because of this careful work on intersectionality, scholarship now seeks to explore the nuances of conflicting identity categories to contextualize our discussions, thereby avoiding essentialist categories such as "feminist" or "woman" or "masculine." However, discussions of gender remain essentially tied to a highly localized space — either ideological, socio-economical, or even geographical. Yet, if we look to Pynchon's highly successful mashup of WWII, the Mediterranean, and the gender politics of romanticism, we might inquire, should they be?

In this volume we try to respond to the question: what happens when we take a step back from the highly *local*, or the highly individual, to explore the ways in which an *area* and its constraints interlace with practices of gender? In Antonio Benitez-Rojo's *The Repeating Island*, for example, the Caribbean island is a structure unto itself, with constants that expand beyond borders of language or empire; likewise, the essays in *Gender in the Premodern Mediterranean* explore how the culture of the sea interfaces with gender performance. One of the tenets of this volume is that cross-culturalism affects the possibilities of gender: whereas reading from the perspective of a highly nationalized culture might produce one set of gender norms, the premodern Mediterranean, with its normalization of hybridity and cross-cultural exchange, represents a unique vantage point for understanding how cultural melding impacts gendered performances. The sirens of this volume invite us to better understand how the premodern Mediterranean, in all its fluidity, permitted and even embraced gender practices that are at turns hegemonic (imperial princess), despondent (impoverished widow), lucrative (savvy sea-faring traders), and surprising (ferocious Saracen women in blackface).

We are by no means the first to read premodern gender in its larger cultural context. Critical studies of premodern gender have recently addressed gender and authority, liturgy, aging, narration, piety, and affect, as in Eric Dursteler's recent investigation of Mediterranean women who used religious conversion to acquire power in his *Renegade Women* or Jutta Sperling and Shona Kelly Wray's collection *Across the Religious Divide*, among many others.[2] While there are many important anthologies and monographs that explore gender in a premodern context,[3] to my knowledge, no major studies have systematically sought to compare the practices of gender in the Mediterranean across boundaries of religion, culture, language, and geography within the premodern period. The prevalence

---

[1] K. Brown, *Good Wives, Nasty Wenches, and Anxious Patriarchs*; McClintock, *Imperial Leather*.

[2] Dursteler, *Renegade Women*; Sperling and Wray, *Across the Religious Divide*.

[3] Stafford and Mulder-Bakker, *Gendering the Middle Ages*; Brubaker and Smith, *Gender in the Early Medieval World*; Fenster and Lees, *Gender in Debate*. Woodacre, *Queenship in the Mediterranean*; Brubaker and Smith, *Gender in the early medieval world: east and west, 300–900*.

and importance of gender studies in almost all disciplines means that there are several fundamental studies of a more localized nature, yet none have focused on the ways that gender and area studies coalesce in the premodern period. As a site of unusually widespread economic, cultural, and agrarian exchange for the premodern period, the Mediterranean provides a unique vantage point for understanding how cultural contact and gender practices were co-constitutive and deployed for specific purposes. We begin here with the premise that the exchange facilitated by the Mediterranean made possible the gender positions that negotiated a spectrum of identities upon its shores.

This volume explores the ways in which gender was performed in the Mediterranean as well as how gender practices helped to shape Mediterranean cultural practices. In the interest of representing a spectrum of positions, the volume contains essays spanning gender practices from the early medieval to the late Renaissance. While this time frame is certainly almost as expansive as the sea itself, the volume is not meant to represent every culture or gender practice in the Mediterranean but, rather, to show a nebulous and complex web of gender performances, the very variety of which is made possible through the mixing on its coasts. The essays in this collection both situate gender performances within their particular cultural context, and respond to the comparative focus of this volume, in which we seek to determine to what extent the Mediterranean impacted gender performances and permitted new kinds of gendered possibilities.

The field of Mediterranean Studies has gained traction, but to date, few monographs have considered gender in a cross-cultural Mediterranean construct.[4] Many of the essays in the past ten years have rightly sought to elucidate gender in Muslim or Jewish contexts, but few studies seek to contextualize these practices (or even those of Christians) within a broader premodern Mediterranean context. Our research tools themselves reflect this paucity. Even many of the most refined databases offer geographical divisions that divide the Mediterranean and resist thinking with it: Brepols' IMDB, for example, offers "Eastern Mediterranean," "Iberia," "Italy," and "Africa" as limiters. Likewise Early English Books Online offers geographical limiters based on nationalized borders (presumably relating to place of publication). While the digital humanities—in their most basic form as databases detailing publications within premodern studies and in their more complex form as tools such as GIS software, N-gram, and Wordle—offer us many advantages in researching premodern identities, they also limit and constrain our research choices by seeking to normalize modern political paradigms by mapping them onto medieval and early modern geopolitical constructs. The practice of limiting inquiry by nationalized linguistic paradigms—essentially mapping them to current geopolitical paradigms—under-

---

[4] See, for example, Moore, *Exchanges in Exoticism*. Winer, *Women, and Community in Perpignan*; Burns, *Sea of Silk*; Rosen, *Unveiling Eve: reading gender in medieval Hebrew literature.*

scores the concerns expressed in recent digital humanities scholarship on the cultural practices embedded in cartography.[5] The geocultural and digital limitations imposed on Mediterranean research resonate with earlier scholarship about identity, which largely obscured non-canonical races, classes, and genders, if not on purpose then by omission.[6] In service of recognizing, recovering, and analyzing non-canonical identity positions — permitted precisely by the premodern and through its Mediterranean — we have written essays designed to begin scholarly dialogue about gender practices that efface borders and bridge cultures. Moreover, while gender is constructed through the Mediterranean Sea, our essays here argue in part that the fluidity of gender practices helps produce some of the most visible facets of the premodern Mediterranean itself, its power structures.

Mediterranean Studies

As the explosion of scholarship in area studies would suggest, it is no surprise that scholars have turned to the Mediterranean as a promising site of analysis, a place not only with its own history (a "history *of* the Mediterranean") but also one that itself affects cultural practices, one that produces "history *in* the Mediterranean." To that end, it is worthwhile understanding the particularities of the premodern Mediterranean, not only to see what it offers as a scholarly framework but also to recognize its limitations in functioning as a site that produces identity.

As the fundamental works by Fernand Braudel and by Nicholas Purcell and Peregrine Horden tell us, the Mediterranean is a fully functional category through which to read cultural history.[7] Starting with the ancient Greeks, the region has had a thoroughly annotated and deliberated history replete with documentation of its cross-cultural philosophy, economy, art making, and war mongering. For some of today's scholars, thinking with the Mediterranean has helped break down disciplinary and nationalist constraints on scholarship. As Sharon Kinoshita and Brian Catlos, co-founders of the Mediterranean Seminar, have explained,

---

[5] Harley, "Deconstructing the Map"; Harley, "Cartography, Ethics and Social Theory"; Belyea, "Images of Power"; Crampton, "Maps as Social Constructions." See also Summerhayes, "Embodied Space in Google Earth."

[6] We have only to turn to the Hereford *mappamundi* to see the ways in which the scientific idea of mapping is directly tied to cultural constructions of racial and gendered hegemony; this volume highlights these kinds of constructs as deeply tied to cultural geography.

[7] Braudel, *The Mediterranean and the Mediterranean World in the Age of Philip II*; Horden and Purcell, *The Corrupting Sea*. See also Harris, *Rethinking the Mediterranean*.

Though because of the dominance of modern national paradigms, the weight of teleological historical traditions, and assumptions about the rigidity of ecumenical divisions, the premodern Mediterranean is frequently regarded as an anomaly, it was central to the historical developments and cultural transformations that produced Modernity.[8]

For premodern purposes, the Mediterranean is a way of exploring cultural exchange in a time better known in the popular eye for its associations with warfare (the Crusades, civil wars, and Ottoman invasions), disease (the Plague), and archaic political systems based upon violent physical retribution (fictionalized in *The Game of Thrones*). Yet paying attention to the particularities of this region reveal its importance — not in figuring the archaic but in constructing the modern. As a site of analysis, the Mediterranean offers an escape from common assumptions about power and nation (as in studies of the courts of Aragon, the Medici, or the Komnenoi, to name but a few).

While scholarship on specialized locales has offered us a much fuller picture of daily life in the premodern period — and in many instances has offered us a clearer vision of gender practices in those locales — exploring Mediterranean dynamics offers us a chance to think with diaspora and emigration as the norm, even in a period reputed for its lack of mobility — geographic, social, or otherwise. We can then ask how localized paradigms function on a larger scale and depend on our knowledge of highly localized practices and also how they are made possible precisely through the cultural slippage that is the hybridity of the Mediterranean contact zone. We may think of the Mediterranean as a band of nebulous interactions, instead of as a neat body of water or a particular geopolitical space; it is a zone that produces particular identities unique to the kinds of contact on which it depends, such as the African merchant who negotiates customs along the Spanish coast.

There is, of course, much work on the Mediterranean from fields as disparate as premodern medicine, history, geography, art history, archaeology, math, astronomy, and literature; the diversity attests to the draw of the approach and the recognition of its value in providing a valuable framework for analysis. The work in this volume draws on constructions of the Mediterranean first proposed by Braudel and then refined (and even contradicted) by Horden and Purcell.[9] While Michael Herzfeld has long been a vocal critic of the validity of "Mediterranean" as a construct, others have worked to unpack and refine its utility, focusing in many cases on how individually disparate practices fit into larger

---

[8] http://humweb.ucsc.edu/mediterraneanseminar/info/mission.php. Visited on 14 March 2015.

[9] Braudel, *The Mediterranean and the Mediterranean World in the Age of Philip II*; Horden and Purcell, *The Corrupting Sea*.

paradigms made possible through the sea.[10] Historians such as David Abulafia and Palmira Brummett and cartographers such as Grant Parker have worked to destabilize totalizing definitions of the Mediterranean,[11] seeing instead its diversity, what Brummett has claimed as an area "more often composed of fragments: separate seas, stretches of coast, zones of livelihood, points of departure, and points of arrival."[12] For Brummett, the Mediterranean becomes a tool through which hegemony (both in premodern texts and in the scholarship that examines it) is exposed, analyzed, and rebutted:

> For me, that sea is indelibly fragmented into its ports, islands, coasts, and their attendant interiors. It is divided into a set of city-linking itineraries, routes for the transmission of ideas, goods, and military forces. If I do imagine the Mediterranean as a whole, it is not a space divided into Christian and Muslim "halves" [. . .] It is not marked by ecological zones but by complex, overlapping, ethnolinguistic, commercial, and cultural identities.[13]

For Brummett, the Mediterranean is not only a site where history happens but also a site through which particular histories have been constructed. Her call to consider the Mediterranean as a category of analysis highlights the sometimes divergent purposes of scholars working in this field, but it points to both the flexibility of the construct and its potential to revise received notions of identity, center, and hegemony.[14] Her call resonates with Patrick Geary's scholarly project to clean up the "history of Europe's nations," which he has called a "toxic waste dump, filled with the poison of ethnic nationalism."[15] While not specifically grounded in the Mediterranean, Geary's *The Myth of Nations* questions the integrity of a supposed premodern French nationalism, in the process highlight-

---

[10] Herzfeld, "Practical Mediterraneanism"; Marino, "Mediterranean Studies and the Remaking of Pre-Modern Europe."

[11] Abulafia, "Mediterraneans"; Abulafia, "What Is the Mediterranean?"; Abulafia, *The Western Mediterranean Kingdoms 1250–1500*; Brummett, "Visions of the Mediterranean"; Finucci, *Mapping the Mediterranean*; Parker, "Mapping the Mediterranean."

[12] Brummett, "Visions of the Mediterranean," 9.

[13] Brummett, "Visions of the Mediterranean," 10–11.

[14] In this, the Mediterranean can be understood as a construct that naturally interrogates traditional dialogues about power by redefining centers and peripheries, building off of the work by Homi Bhabha and others in postcolonial studies (for example in his *The Location of Culture*). For intersections of the premodern and postcolonial, see Akbari, "From Due East to True North"; Ingham and Warren, *Postcolonial Moves*; Baker and Fuchs, "The Postcolonial Past"; Davis and Altschul, *Medievalisms in the Postcolonial World*; Gaunt, "Can the Middle Ages Be Postcolonial?"; and Lampert-Weissig, *Medieval Literature and Postcolonial Studies*.

[15] Geary, *The Myth of Nations*, 15.

ing the very dynamics Mediterranean studies seeks to question. Likewise, Sharon Kinoshita advocates a Mediterranean that

> [m]ost obviously . . . displaces the nation as the default category of analysis
> that, even in our purportedly postnational age, continues to "ghost" our lit-
> erary imaginings [. . .] Such a move is indispensable for the Middle Ages,
> a period in which "nation," in the sense of the nation-state, is an unwieldy
> anachronism.[16]

The work conceptualizing the Mediterranean seeks to highlight the ways in which our received notions—of East and West, of Muslims and Christians—rely on deeply seated and clearly unstable binaries, leaving out so many sites of interaction, of hybridity and cross-cultural exchange.[17] While conceived before the explosion of interest in Mediterranean scholarship, economic histories by Angeliki Laiou and Olivia Constable show a complex web of trade and exchange stretching well back into late antiquity and undergirding the Mediterranean as a category of analysis. Their work highlights a set of networks that trouble a consideration of the shoreline predicated uniquely upon a traditional east-west geography, and studies such as those by Avner Greif invite a much more complex formulation of the economic Mediterranean, including its ties to the African slave trade.[18]

Both northern and southern shores are integral to figuring the Mediterranean experience, as scholars of Al-Andalus such as David Wacks and Brian Catlos have most forcefully pointed out.[19] Indeed work on the trading networks in Italian cities, especially in the late Renaissance and early modern periods, shows that north-south exchange was the norm for cities stretched all along the shores and that our intense interest in formulating an east/Muslim and west/Christian dichotomy may be more a legacy of nineteenth- and twentieth-century politics than pertinent to premodern studies.[20] Most recently, Lisa Lampert-Weissig has built off of Mary Louise Pratt's notion of "contact zones" to reconceptualize Iberia as a zone of interaction, a gradient of cross-culturalism, pluralism, and hybridity, rather than a strict division between north and south or even Islam

---

[16] Kinoshita, "Medieval Mediterranean Literature," 602.

[17] See, for example, Mallette, *European Modernity and the Arab Mediterranean*.

[18] Lopez and Raymond, trans., *Medieval Trade in the Mediterranean World*; Abulafia, *The Two Italies*; Abulafia, *The Western Mediterranean Kingdoms 1250–1500*; Day, "The Levant Trade in the Middle Ages"; Laiou, "Exchange and Trade, Seventh–Twelfth Centuries"; Greif, "Reputation and Coalitions in Medieval Trade"; Hunwick, "Black Slaves in the Mediterranean World"; Goitein, *A Mediterranean Society*; Ashtor and Ḳedar, *East-West Trade in the Medieval Mediterranean*.

[19] Catlos, *The Victors and the Vanquished*; Wacks, *Framing Iberia*. See also Menocal, *The Ornament of the World*.

[20] Darling, "The Renaissance and the Middle East"; Arbel, *Trading Nations*.

and Christianity.[21] It is in this vein that we consider the Mediterranean to be both a way of disrupting stark binaries such as East and West, or Muslim and Christian, and a zone for exploring gradients of identity, seen most forcefully in gender practices such as those of Byzantine eunuchs or the premodern Italian stage actors considered by the contributors to this volume.

Contemporary historians' uses of Mediterranean and sea studies to revise nationalized identities resonate with the questions posed by literary scholars, who have advocated for a Mediterranean that encapsulates a diaspora of identity positions and who have most forcefully used the Mediterranean to interrogate received notions about premodern national paradigms. In medieval French studies, one of the first and most widely cited examples is the rereading of the *Song of Roland* within a Mediterranean geopolitical context. Whereas the *Roland* has long been read as a testament to the birth of "French" identity, scholars attentive to the nuances of a Mediterranean methodology have reread that text and the birth of its interpretation in late nineteenth-century France as more enmeshed in modern politics than thoroughly grounded in medieval culture. Sharon Kinoshita, Patrick Geary, and Michelle Warren have separately argued through their Mediterranean readings of the *Roland* and its nineteenth-century century appropriations that we must reconsider the construction of "self" and "other" in this text;[22] their readings reveal not only the ways in which the text is itself a piece of medieval propaganda but also how others — namely, nineteenth-century scholars such as Gaston and Paulin Paris and Joseph Bédier — disregarded the Mediterranean context of the *Roland* in favor of the geopolitics of nineteenth-century France's struggle for cultural and political sovereignty in the face of Prussian power.[23] Kinoshita, for example, writes:

> Disengaging the *Roland* from this colonial context, in which alterity is implicitly or explicitly cast in the taxonomic categories of racialized difference, brings into focus the fluidity characterizing medieval notions of difference. This in turn reveals "France" and "Europe" to be not geographical entities given in advance, but ideological constructs with their own deeply complicated history of conquest, colonization, and acculturation, in ways that continue to resonate, for example, in political debates on multiculturalism in France or in the emergence of the European Community.[24]

---

[21] Lampert-Weissig, *Medieval Literature and Postcolonial Studies*, 50–55; Pratt, *Under Imperial Eyes.*

[22] Kinoshita, "Pagans Are Wrong and Christians Are Right"; Geary, *The Myth of Nations.*

[23] See the analyses of nineteenth-century scholarship, for example, in Warren, *Creole Medievalism.*

[24] Kinoshita, "Pagans Are Wrong and Christians Are Right," 103.

As Kinoshita points out, the Mediterranean is not merely a location in which a text is set; it is a location through which a text constructs identities, sometimes to the detriment of highly specific and localized identities. The Mediterranean is not only a zone of interaction but also a weapon of representation, sometimes deployed to blur localized constructs.

The methodology of Mediterranean studies has become so useful that it seeps into many analyses that are not intentionally focused by geocultural specificity; we take this to be a testament to its utility. In a literary study, Jane Burns has carefully traced the path of textiles that make their appearance in medieval French romance, a genre traditionally more closely aligned with northern Celtic myth than with the ebb and flow of the Mediterranean. Though not intentionally invoking the Mediterranean, her methodology and work in *Sea of Silk* and *Courtly Love Undressed* reveal the Mediterranean as integral to imagining and fashioning community—in this case, the community of nobility—in literature of the medieval period.[25] Similarly, studies by Karla Malette, Lynn Ramey, Marla Segol, Nina Zhiri, Lisa Lampert-Weissig, and myself in French;[26] Jeffrey Jerome Cohen and Suzanne Akbari in English;[27] Krijna Ciggaar in Byzantine studies;[28] Eric Dursteler, Marie Kelleher, María Rosa Menocal, David Wacks, and David Wasserstein in Spanish,[29] to name but a few, have all advocated for not only recognizing the importance of the Mediterranean in premodern cultural studies but also for reconceptualizing our commonplaces—east and west, north and south, other and self.

Pervasive within early modern studies, the Mediterranean has become integral to figuring the premodern self, for example in recent scholarship tying English theater to the Mediterranean; exploring the expansive role of Ottoman contact and rule; and examining the impacts of trade networks and printing

---

[25] Burns, *Sea of Silk*; Burns, *Medieval Fabrications*; Burns, *Courtly Love Undressed*.

[26] Mallette, *European Modernity and the Arab Mediterranean*; Mallette, *The Kingdom of Sicily*; Ramey, *Christian, Saracen and Genre in Medieval French Literature*; Segol, "Floire et Blancheflor'"; Segol, "Medieval Cosmopolitanism and the Saracen-Christian Ethos"; Stahuljak, *Bloodless Genealogies of the French Middle Ages*; Stahuljak, "Going Global, Getting Medieval"; Lampert-Weissig, *Medieval Literature and Postcolonial Studies*; Moore, *Exchanges in Exoticism*.

[27] Akbari, "From Due East to True North"; J. Cohen, *The Postcolonial Middle Ages*; J. Cohen, *Hybridity, Identity, and Monstrosity in Medieval Britain*.

[28] Ciggaar, *Western Travellers to Constantinople*; Ciggaar, "Encore une fois Chrétien de Troyes et la 'matière Byzantine'"; Ciggaar and Teule, *East and West in the Crusader States*; Ciggaar, "L'émigration anglaise à Byzance après 1066."

[29] Menocal, *The Arabic Role in Medieval Literary History*; Menocal, *The Ornament of the World*; Wacks, *Framing Iberia*; Dodds, Menocal, and Balbale, *The Arts of Intimacy*; Wasserstein, "Byzantium and Al☒Andalus."

technologies.[30] Yet in studies of Mediterranean convergence, if gender has a role, it is often to support a larger argument about the Mediterranean or to delve deeply into highly local practices, not highlighted as a primary way of approaching the Mediterranean rather than functioning. This collection of essays seeks to differ by offering examples of larger Mediterranean paradigms through regional studies of gender practices spanning from late antique and early medieval religious texts to early modern Venetian theatrical performance.

Gender Studies and the Mediterranean

Both early and more contemporary scholars of gender studies share a common desire to explore gender positions from which to articulate and claim identity, while simultaneously exposing the assumptions of patriarchy on which not only society but also scholarship is framed.[31] In the case of the most recent feminist work from the United States, this has resulted in criticism of gender studies itself, which too long ignored how particular identity positions (race, class, religion, ethnicity, disability, etc.) affected the practices of gender. Post-second wave feminist reflections such as *This Bridge Called My Back* sparked a new attention to intersectionality and to the privileges of first-world feminism; the attentiveness of these activists and scholars has proven useful for considering intersectionality in medieval and early modern scholarship, even if we often lack the voice of the repressed in our paucity of sources.[32]

Several excellent edited volumes can help guide the introductory student or scholar through major work in the field; recently, scholarship attentive to the multiple ways identity is constructed in terms of race, class, gender, ethnicity, and

---

[30] Vitkus, *Turning Turk*; Greene, *A Shared World*; Goffman, *The Ottoman Empire and Early Modern Europe*; Rothman, "Interpreting Dragomans"; Hulme and Sherman, *"The Tempest" and Its Travels*; W. Cohen, "The Undiscovered Country"; Gillies, *Shakespeare and the Geography of Difference*; Fuchs, "Conquering Islands."

[31] While the struggle for gender equality is far from over, gender studies themselves have worked their way into public, private, and academic discourse and have become mainstream enough to have departments at many large universities, centers for public policy, and have helped us to rearticulate the look of equality within legal and social structures. As such, it may not be possible to offer an overview of such an expansive field here, but a few markers will help indicate the orientation of this volume's essays. Simone de Beauvoir, Luce Irigaray, and Julia Kristeva first shaped the corners of the field, and since then others such as Judith Butler, Susan Bordo, Chandra Mohanty, Gloria Anzaldúa, and Judith Halberstam have expanded on the questions they asked about the feminine experience, using their questions about hegemony first to theorize and then to interrogate a spectrum of gender positions.

[32] Moraga and Anzaldúa, *This Bridge Called My Back*.

religious and sexual orientations has helped nuance the dialogue.[33] While some of the most strident criticism of white upper-class feminism has been launched in the past few decades by scholars and activists involved with modern (American) culture, medievalists and pre-modernists have by no means ignored the nuances of these identity positions, however hard that may be in a period in which sources remain extremely scarce. In fact, medievalists and early modernists have recently revealed how these conversations about gender are often dominated by assumptions about modernity. Like women of color calling for a reformulation of "women's" experience, scholars whose subject and work were often marginalized or excluded for their lack of relevance have greatly enriched the understanding of gender as a concept. Premodern voices nuance our dialogues about identity, and by recognizing alternate concepts of family, love, sexuality, and power they reveal much about modern assumptions about the hegemony of a singular, "modern" experience of gender.

Perhaps more important to our project, several scholars have already worked extensively on gender in the premodern period, with carefully researched scholarship that has fundamentally altered our understanding of the horizons of premodern existence.[34] Work by Jane Burns, Jane Chance, Elizabeth Robertson, Caroline Walker Bynum, Roberta Krueger, Karma Lochrie, and Peggy McCracken helped to propel the importance of gender in a historical period from which sources about non-hegemonic identity positions are relatively scarce.[35] Beyond this foundational scholarship, other collections have expanded our understanding of gender in particular social milieux: some have focused on

---

[33] For a short but by no means exhaustive sample, see Alcoff and Mendieta, *Identities*; Andersen and Collins, *Race, Class, and Gender*; Jordan and Weedon, *Cultural Politics*; and Disch, *Reconstructing Gender*.

[34] Lochrie, McCracken, and Schultz, *Constructing Medieval Sexuality*; Bullough and Brundage, *Handbook of Medieval Sexuality*; Stafford and Mulder-Bakker, *Gendering the Middle Ages*; Karras, *From Boys to Men*; Fenster and Lees, *Gender in Debate*; J. Brown and Davis, *Gender and Society in Renaissance Italy*; Krueger, *Women Readers and the Ideology of Gender*; Hadley, *Masculinity in Medieval Europe*; McCracken, *The Curse of Eve, the Wound of the Hero*; Tougher, "Images of Effeminate Men"; James, *Women, Men, and Eunuchs*; Gaunt, *Gender and Genre in Medieval French Literature*; Hall, *Things of Darkness*; Ferguson, *Dido's Daughters*; Matchinske, *Writing, Gender and State in Early Modern England*; Farmer, *Surviving Poverty in Medieval Paris*; Skinner, "Gender and Poverty in the Medieval Community."

[35] While by no means exhaustive, seminal works include: Burns, *Bodytalk*; Krueger, *Women Readers and the Ideology of Gender*; Lochrie, McCracken, and Schultz, *Constructing Medieval Sexuality*; Gaunt, *Gender and Genre in Medieval French Literature*; and Bynum, *Jesus as Mother*. In addition to this list, see the more extensive surveys offered in Burns, "Medieval Feminist Movement"; and Robertson, "Medieval Feminism in Middle English Studies."

gender and class, with a particular attention to the experience of the poor;[36] others have approached the question of religious difference through gender;[37] still others have looked at gender and exoticism;[38] or gender as an expression of hegemony.[39] As in this study, premodern gender studies have used print sources, architectural features, and cultural artifacts to explore gender in an increasingly expanding world of "texts," in Barthes' sense.[40]

Taken together, we see that both Mediterranean and gender studies are interested in how intersectionality impacts identity; both fields systematically reject monolithic categories of identity, and both invite consideration of how a spectrum, how zones of interaction, construct identity. Rather than focus on a singular performance as representative, both fields seek spectrums of exchange, contact, and fluidity as ways of conceptualizing existence. In the long premodern period of this volume—a time span, of course, naturally prone to societal evolution and change—the Mediterranean is nonetheless useful because it is predicated on a lack of searching for a singular position of geocultural stability; rather, it is constituted through the exchanges it facilitates—its power lies in its base in evolution, rather than its departure from an imaginary, fixed point of nationalized, localized identity. Likewise, while working from the early medieval to the early modern, the essays here join together in showcasing the power of the Mediterranean as a methodological approach that nuances our understanding of identity--and in particular, its interwoven gender structures--in the premodern. The intersection, then, of premodern gender studies and Mediterranean studies is particularly fruitful, and the essays here, while divergent in subject matter and time period, come together around the shores of the sea they take as integral to figuring identity, as they identify how gender and the Mediterranean are co-

---

[36] Hall, *Things of Darkness*; Korda, *Shakespeare's Domestic Economies*.

[37] Aers and Staley, *The Powers of the Holy*; Galatariotou, "Holy Women and Witches."

[38] Kinoshita, *Medieval Boundaries*; Moore, "Boundaries and Byzantines in the Old French *Floire et Blancheflor*."

[39] Hadley, *Masculinity in Medieval Europe*; Fowler, "Mourning, Melancholia, and Masculinity in Medieval Literature"; Tougher, "Images of Effeminate Men"; Matchinske, *Writing, Gender and State in Early Modern England*; McNamara, "Women and Power Through the Family Revisited"; Aers and Staley, *The Powers of the Holy*. See also alternate gender positions researched in James, *Women, Men, and Eunuchs*; Tougher, "Byzantine Eunuchs"; Tougher, "Two Views on the Gender Identity of Byzantine Eunuchs"; Galatariotou, "Holy Women and Witches"; and James, "Goddess, Whore, Wife, or Slave."

[40] Anchored by studies such as those of Beilin, *Redeeming Eve*; Hamlin, "Female Mourning and Tragedy in Medieval and Renaissance English Drama"; Rose, "Where Are the Mothers in Shakespeare?"; Wall, *The Imprint of Gender*; Ferguson, *Dido's Daughters*; Korda, *Shakespeare's Domestic Economies*; Hall, *Things of Darkness*; Matchinske, *Writing, Gender and State in Early Modern England*; Amussen, *An Ordered Society*; Perry, *Gender and Disorder in Early Modern Seville*; Smith, *Entiendes?*; and Fuchs, "Border Crossings."

constructed, not only in times of war but also in spiritual undertakings, cross-cultural trade, and in theatrical depictions.

Contributions to this Volume

This volume stems from an intersection of the latest work on gender studies and a scholarly commitment to retheorizing the medieval and early modern experience as constitutive of, produced by, and contributing to the Mediterranean. The essays here seek to illustrate how these categories are mutually constructive, and though there is a wide variety of geographic, disciplinary, and theoretical approaches used here, hardly any volume of Mediterranean Studies could be totally representative of the plethora of identity positions constructed there; we still would invite further conversation from Byzantinists and Islamists, for example, in order to enrich our understanding of the variety of ways in which gender and the Mediterranean were co-constitutive in the premodern period. Likewise we hope the volume spurs conversation about intersectionality in the Mediterranean among scholars who do not necessarily consider gender as a primary approach to their work.

In Chapter 2, "Ambrose, Augustine, Perpetua: Defining Gender across the Mediterranean," Margaret Cotter-Lynch questions received notions aligning early Christian communities with narratives that reify gender difference, about women that are "overly influenced by later ideological accruals in which gender binaries are in fact re-established through the trope of virtuous women 'becoming male.'" Cotter-Lynch suggests that we should redirect our attention to Mediterranean gender paradigms evident in texts such as the *Passio Perpetuae* that reveal a wider range of gender positions and, she suggests, offer models for later constructions of gender identity in the Mediterranean. According to Cotter-Lynch, the story of St. Perpetua, a twenty-two-year-old early Christian martyr and nursing mother, reveals that although Perpetua's religion is clearly demarcated, her gender is neither clear nor important. Reading the progression of the Perpetua stories reveals the Mediterranean roots of gender paradigms, in particular "an increasing emphasis on gender dichotomy and hierarchy, until Augustine's sermons overwrite Perpetua's story with St. Ambrose's paradigm that '[o] ne who does not believe is a woman and should be designated in the name of that sex, whereas one who believes progresses to perfect manhood.'" Through readings of the Perpetua tradition over time, Cotter-Lynch argues that "this version of Perpetua, who overcomes her femininity to 'become male,' then dominates the medieval tradition and becomes a model for later Christian women. Augustine thus codifies an understanding of gender that, paradoxically, by allowing for the possibility of holy women 'becoming male,' simultaneously asserts the inherent hierarchy of male over female and indelibly yokes gender definitions to sexuality for the next 1600 years."

Bronwen Neil's "Visions, Female Sexuality, and Spiritual Leadership in Byzantine Ascetic Literature of the Sixth and Seventh Centuries" continues the discussion of gender in the ascetic movement, focusing primarily on dreaming within the *Dialogues* of Gregory the Great and the *Sayings* (*Apophthegmata*) of the Egyptian desert elders. Neil's careful analysis explores what these monastic sources reveal of Byzantine and western views of female sexuality and spiritual leadership, especially as this was manifested in visions. She evaluates the differences and similarities between eastern and western Christian perceptions of dreams and their spiritual value to determine in what ways they contribute to what she innovatively constructs as a Mediterranean theory of dreaming.

In "Bearers of Islam: Muslim Women between Assimilation and Resistance in Christian Sicily," Sarah Davis-Secord explores "the intersections between religious identity and gender within cross-confessional environments," in particular by looking at gender roles described in the travel narratives of Ibn Jubayr, a Muslim who visited Sicily in the twelfth century. Building off of—but frequently nuancing—work on intercultural marriage by scholars focused on Jewish, Christian, and Muslim cross-culturalism in the Iberian peninsula, Davis-Secord shows that in medieval Sicily, women were at the heart of the struggle not only—as is commonly thought—for cultural assimilation but also for cultural preservation. Women were key to the preservation of endangered—and sometimes outnumbered—disempowered minorities, and in her readings of Ibn Jubayr she highlights how their public performances of religion and gender coalesced to preserve Muslim heritage. Tying her argument about localized Sicilian practices of gender and religion to a larger Mediterranean context, Davis-Secord reads women's performances of public and private identities as integral to the preservation of Mediterranean religious diversity, even in the face of medieval colonialism.

Anna Akasoy argues in Chapter 5 that the Qur'an permits mystics the opportunity to paint alternate gender paradigms that were scrutinized and targeted by Ibn Taymiyya, revealing not only their alterity but also their power. Akasoy cites Rābiʿa al-ʿAdawiyya as one example of an eighth-century mystic who "used the language of love in order to describe her relationship to God. While filled with intense longing and anxiety over her own piety, Rābiʿa's expressions are neither erotic nor operate with gender as a relational category. It rather appears as if gender dissolved in the sole focus on God." Akasoy continues her study of gender fluidity and mystical conceptualizations of God with the poetics associated with the figure of Laylā among medieval poets, concluding that "the symbol of Laylā functions as a unifying force for diverse allegorical approaches to God and thus as an effective poetic framework for paradox and *coincidentia oppositorum*."

In Chapter 6, "Navigating Gender in the Mediterranean: Exploring Hybrid Identities in *Aucassin et Nicolete*," Mèriem Pagès explores how literary depictions of gender and genre entwine in the Mediterranean text *Aucassin et Nicolette*. Covering a spectrum of gender and racial positions and beginning with Aucassin's utter failure to conform to norms of masculinity, Pagès reads episodes such as the men's childbirth scene in order to conceptualize the Mediterranean as a site for fluidity. In the second part of her essay, Pagès explores these shifting identity positions in terms of performativity, focusing in particular on Nicolete. In this reading of Nicolete's ambiguous gender and racial positions, the Mediterranean was not only a unique site for creating and performing alternate gender roles but also was shaped by the kinds of gender-ethnicity identity politics nobles performed there. Pagès's reading ultimately suggests that the Mediterranean facilitates the expression of different gender possibilities, thereby challenging the generic conventions of literary representation in *Aucassin et Nicolette*.

Elena Woodacre offers an excellent historical overview of Mediterranean women's rule in Chapter 7, "Gender and Authority: The Particularities of Female Rule in the Premodern Mediterranean," claiming that the Mediterranean may have been more amenable to women's rule than northern Europe. She explores women's rules through a series of "case studies from the Byzantine empresses of late antiquity to Aragonese queen-lieutenants in the fifteenth century" designed to highlight mechanisms of gendered access to power unique to the Mediterranean. Her nuanced discussion of Byzantine empresses' power reveals that practices of feminine authority were entwined with alternate constructions of masculinity, in that, as Woodacre argues, empresses' authority depended upon the power and reach of their eunuchs. Using numismatic and other evidence to support her claims, Woodacre admits that while women's power may have been more expansive in the Mediterranean, nonetheless "it has to be acknowledged that these women were later displaced in the line of succession by the birth of brothers [. . .] [T]he fact that women were accepted as potential heirs and viable claimants is important" and, in her analysis, permitted by gender structures unique to the Mediterranean.

In Chapter 8, "Religious Patronage in Byzantium: The Case of Komnenian Imperial Women," Vassiliki Dimitropoulou explores women's contributions to artistic and architectural building programs by focusing on religious patronage by Byzantine imperial women, in particular the Komnenoi. By focusing on the establishment of monastic communities at Kecharitomene, Pantokrator, Pantepoptes, Pammakaristos, and Chora, Dimitropoulou is able to explore how Komnenian imperial women engaged their power and assets to invest in religious establishments. Despite the limitations placed on Byzantine women, she reads Byzantine women's generosity as a kind of compelling exemplarity that created a Mediterranean economy of aristocratic women's gift-giving to monastic communities, in both large- and small-scale donations: "the number of projects in which Komnenian women were involved and the large scale of these projects meant that they set a very high standard that women from other Mediterranean cultures strove to emulate."

Erith Jaffe-Berg explores the role of gender in Jewish community theater in Chapter 9, "Jewish Women and Performance in Early Modern Mantua." Reading archival sources against the commonly accepted work of early modern Jewish dramatist and director Leone de' Sommi, Jaffe-Berg argues that, contrary to scholarly assumptions that women did not participate in public theater, her archival evidence from Mantua suggests that women's participation may have been the very cause for its eventual cessation in 1649. Although de' Sommi's *Quattro dialoghi in material di rappresentazioni sceniche* provided nuanced appreciation of women's work in the theater, scholars have assumed that because there were no mentions of Jewish women working in, attending, or appreciating theater, their participation was nonexistent. Yet the state archives tell a different tale, one that Jaffe-Berg argues depicts women as "active participants, and audience members and perhaps collaborators, in the producing of plays." Continuing the conversation of others in this volume, Jaffe-Berg's work on gender and performance suggests that women had an important role to play in negotiating cross-cultural and cross-confessional confrontation, interactions, and social structures spurred uniquely through Mediterranean trading networks.

Finally, Katarzyna Lecky explores how the gender possibilities others have conceptualized here as proper to the Mediterranean play out in the Renaissance in her chapter entitled "The Politics of Mediterranean Marriage in Chaucer, Shakespeare, and Milton." Lecky focuses on the romance of cross-cultural marriage as a site that "offered a manageable metaphor for thinking through the complex diplomacies of trans-Mediterranean relations." Her readings of Chaucer, Milton, and Shakespeare situate cross-cultural marriage as a microcosm that performs "the dramas of trade and conquest playing out between the yoked societies of the Christian West and the Muslim East." Focusing on the intersection of larger public economic interests and individualized familial love interests, Lecky argues, for example, that in Chaucer, marriage is a site of negotiation employed "in order to draw out the dialectic of coverture and consent, endogamy and exogamy, and enslavement and equity." This dialectic, as she notes, fails in many texts and may metonymize larger concerns about cultural confrontation, as exemplified in her reading of how in Shakespeare the "dissolution of Othello's and Desdemona's cross-cultural union evokes the breakdown of their conjoined bodies politic and stages a concurrent decomposition of their social stature." Yet, despite acknowledging the tensions inherent in negotiating cross-cultural encounters, Lecky's readings convincingly suggest a highly productive Mediterranean in which gender and community are co-constructive, where "cross-cultural unions have the potential to engender [multinational] citizens . . . who maintain their former alliances while embracing their new community."

Taken together, these essays reveal Mediterranean power structures, cross cultural identities, and gender fluidity to be deeply interdependent. From Perpetua's lessons on the transformations of gender ambiguity in the ancient Mediterranean, to medieval Christian dogmatic approaches to model gendering, to the unique historical position of power inhabited by Byzantine eunuchs, to the ways in which the Mediterranean imaginary helped frame Shakespeare's deployment of gender, the essays in this volume explore models of gender constructed in concert not with micro-particulars but with a broad, connected sea. Not only does the Mediterranean permit the articulation of many non-hegemonic gender positions but its very structures—its multilayered identities—are also constituted through them.

Bibliography

Abulafia, David. "Mediterraneans." In *Rethinking the Mediterranean*, ed. W. V. Harris, 64–93. Oxford: Oxford University Press, 2005.

———. *The Two Italies: Economic Relations between the Norman Kingdom of Sicily and the Northern Communes.* Cambridge: Cambridge University Press, 1977.

———. *The Western Mediterranean Kingdoms 1250–1500: The Struggle for Dominion.* London and New York: Longman, 1997.

———. "What Is the Mediterranean?" In *The Mediterranean in History*, ed. David Abulafia, Oliver Rackham, Marlene Suano, and Geoffrey Rickman, 11–29. Los Angeles: Getty Publications, 2011.

Aers, David, and Lynn Staley, eds. *The Powers of the Holy: Religion, Politics, and Gender in Late Medieval English Culture.* Pittsburg: Penn State Press, 1996.

Akbari, Suzanne Conklin. "From Due East to True North: Orientalism and Orientation." In *The Postcolonial Middle Ages*, ed. Jeffrey Jerome Cohen, 19–34. New York: St. Martin's Press, 2000.

Alcoff, Linda, and Eduardo Mendieta, eds. *Identities: Race, Class, Gender, and Nationality.* Oxford: Blackwell, 2003.

Amussen, Susan Dwyer. *An Ordered Society: Gender and Class in Early Modern England.* New York: Columbia University Press, 1988.

Andersen, Margaret L., and Patricia Hill Collins, eds. *Race, Class, and Gender: An Anthology.* Belmont, CA: Wadsworth, 1998.

Arbel, Benjamin. *Trading Nations: Jews and Venetians in the Early Modern Eastern Mediterranean.* Leiden: Brill, 1995.

Ashtor, Eliyahu, and B. Z. Ḳedar, eds. *East-West Trade in the Medieval Mediterranean.* London: Variorum, 1986.

Baker, David J., and Barbara Fuchs. "The Postcolonial Past." *Modern Language Quarterly* 65, no. 3 (2004): 329–40.

Beilin, Elaine V. *Redeeming Eve: Women Writers of the English Renaissance.* Princeton: Princeton University Press, 1987.

Belyea, Barbara. "Images of Power: Derrida/Foucault/Harley." *Cartographica: The International Journal for Geographic Information and Geovisualization* 29, no. 2 (1992): 1–9.

Benítez-Rojo, Antonio. *The Repeating Island: The Caribbean and the Postmodern Perspective.* Trans. James E. Maraniss. Chapel Hill: Duke University Press, 1997.

Bhabha, Homi K. *The Location of Culture*. London and New York: Routledge, 1994.

Braudel, Fernand. *The Mediterranean and the Mediterranean World in the Age of Philip II*. Los Angeles and Berkeley: University of California Press, 1996.

Brown, Judith C., and Robert Charles Davis, eds. *Gender and Society in Renaissance Italy*. London: Longman, 1998.

Brown, Kathleen M. *Good Wives, Nasty Wenches, and Anxious Patriarchs: Gender, Race, and Power in Colonial Virginia*. Chapel Hill: University of North Carolina Press, 1996.

Brubaker, Leslie, and Julia M. H. Smith, eds. *Gender in the Early Medieval World: East and West, 300–900*. Cambridge: Cambridge University Press, 2004.

Brummett, Palmira. "Visions of the Mediterranean: A Classification." *Journal of Medieval and Early Modern Studies* 37, no. 1 (2007): 9–56.

Bullough, Vern L., and James Brundage, eds. *Handbook of Medieval Sexuality*. New York: Routledge, 2013.

Burns, E. Jane. *Bodytalk: When Women Speak in Old French Literature*. Philadelphia: University of Pennsylvania Press, 1993.

———. *Courtly Love Undressed: Reading through Clothes in Medieval French Culture*. Philadelphia: University of Pennsylvania Press, 2002.

———. *Medieval Fabrications: Dress, Textiles, Clothwork, and Other Cultural Imaginings*. New York: Palgrave Macmillan, 2004.

———. "Medieval Feminist Movement." *Medieval Feminist Forum* 42, no. 7 (2006): 29–40.

———. *Sea of Silk: A Textile Geography of Women's Work in Medieval French Literature*. Philadelphia: University of Pennsylvania Press, 2009.

Bynum, Caroline Walker. *Jesus as Mother: Studies in the Spirituality of the High Middle Ages*. Berkeley and Los Angeles: University of California Press, 1982.

Catlos, Brian A. *The Victors and the Vanquished: Christians and Muslims of Catalonia and Aragon, 1050–1300*. Cambridge: Cambridge University Press, 2004.

Ciggaar, Krijna Nelly. "Encore une fois Chrétien de Troyes et la 'matière Byzantine': la révolution des femmes au palais de Constantinople." *Cahiers de Civilisation Médiévale* 38, no. 3 (1995): 267–74.

———. *Western Travellers to Constantinople: The West and Byzantium, 962–1204: Cultural and Political Relations*. Leiden: Brill, 1996.

———, and Herman G. B. Teule, eds. *East and West in the Crusader States: Context, Contacts, Confrontations II: Acta of the Congress Held at Hernen Castle in May 1997*. Leuven: Peeters, 1999.

———. "L'émigration anglaise à Byzance après 1066: un nouveau texte en Latin sur les varangues à Constantinople." *Revue des Études Byzantines* 32, no. 1 (1974): 301–42.

Cohen, Jeffrey Jerome. *Hybridity, Identity, and Monstrosity in Medieval Britain: On Difficult Middles*. New York: Palgrave Macmillan, 2006.

———. *The Postcolonial Middle Ages*. New York: St. Martin's Press, 2000.

Cohen, Walter. "The Undiscovered Country: Shakespeare and Mercantile Geography." In *Marxist Shakespeares*, ed. Jean E. Howard and Scott Cutler Shershow, 128–58. New York: Routledge, 2001.

Crampton, Jeremy W. "Maps as Social Constructions: Power, Communication and Visualization." *Progress in Human Geography* 25, no. 2 (2001): 235–52.

Darling, Linda T. "The Renaissance and the Middle East." In *A Companion to the Worlds of the Renaissance*, ed. Guido Ruggiero, 55–69. Oxford: Blackwell, 2008.

Davis, Kathleen, and Nadia Altschul, eds. *Medievalisms in the Postcolonial World: The Idea of "the Middle Ages" Outside Europe*. Baltimore: Johns Hopkins University Press, 2009.

Day, John. "The Levant Trade in the Middle Ages." In *The Economic History of Byzantium from the Seventh through the Fifteenth Century*, ed. Angeliki Laiou, 807–14. Washington, DC: Dumbarton Oaks, 2002.

Disch, Estelle. *Reconstructing Gender: A Multicultural Anthology*. Boston: McGraw-Hill Higher Education, 2009.

Dodds, Jerrilynn Denise, María Rosa Menocal, and Abigail Krasner Balbale, eds. *The Arts of Intimacy: Christians, Jews, and Muslims in the Making of Castilian Culture*. New Haven: Yale University Press, 2008.

Dursteler, Eric. *Renegade Women: Gender, Identity, and Boundaries in the Early Modern Mediterranean*. Baltimore: Johns Hopkins University Press, 2011.

Farmer, Sharon. *Surviving Poverty in Medieval Paris: Gender, Ideology, and the Daily Lives of the Poor*. Ithaca: Cornell University Press, 2005.

Fenster, Thelma S., and Clare A. Lees, eds. *Gender in Debate from the Early Middle Ages to the Renaissance*. New York: Palgrave, 2002.

Ferguson, Margaret W. *Dido's Daughters: Literacy, Gender, and Empire in Early Modern England and France*. Chicago: University of Chicago Press, 2007.

Finucci, Valeria. *Mapping the Mediterranean*. Durham, NC: Duke University Press, 2007.

Fowler, Rebekah Mary. "Mourning, Melancholia, and Masculinity in Medieval Literature." PhD. diss., Southern University of Illinois–Carbondale, 2011.

Fuchs, Barbara. "Border Crossings: Transvestism and 'Passing' in *Don Quijote*." *Cervantes* 16, no. 2 (1996): 4–28.

———. "Conquering Islands: Contextualizing The Tempest." *Shakespeare Quarterly* 48, no. 1 (1997): 45–62.

Galatariotou, Catia. "Holy Women and Witches: Aspects of Byzantine Conceptions of Gender." *Byzantine and Modern Greek Studies* 9 (1985): 55–96.

Gaunt, Simon. "Can the Middle Ages Be Postcolonial?" *Comparative Literature* 61, no. 2 (2009): 160.

———. *Gender and Genre in Medieval French Literature*. Cambridge: Cambridge University Press, 1995.

Geary, Patrick. *The Myth of Nations: The Medieval Origins of Europe*. Princeton: Princeton University Press, 2003.

Gillies, John. *Shakespeare and the Geography of Difference*. Cambridge: Cambridge University Press, 1994.

Goffman, Daniel. *The Ottoman Empire and Early Modern Europe*. Cambridge: Cambridge University Press, 2002.

Goitein, Shelomo Dov. *A Mediterranean Society: Economic Foundations*. Vol. 1. Berkeley and Los Angeles: University of California Press, 1967.

Greene, Molly. *A Shared World: Christians and Muslims in the Early Modern Mediterranean*. Princeton: Princeton University Press, 2000.

Greif, Avner. "Reputation and Coalitions in Medieval Trade: Evidence on the Maghribi Traders." *The Journal of Economic History* 49, no. 4 (1989): 857–82.

Hadley, D. M. *Masculinity in Medieval Europe*. London: Longman, 1999.

Hall, Kim F. *Things of Darkness: Economies of Race and Gender in Early Modern England*. Ithaca: Cornell University Press, 1995.

Hamlin, William M. "Female Mourning and Tragedy in Medieval and Renaissance English Drama: From the Raising of Lazarus to King Lear." *Renaissance Quarterly* 60, no. 2 (2007): 670–72.

Harley, John B. "Cartography, Ethics and Social Theory." *Cartographica: The International Journal for Geographic Information and Geovisualization* 27, no. 2 (1990): 1–23.

———. "Deconstructing the Map." *Cartographica: The International Journal for Geographic Information and Geovisualization* 26, no. 2 (1989): 1–20.

Harris, William Vernon, ed. *Rethinking the Mediterranean*. Oxford: Oxford University Press, 2005.

Herzfeld, Michael. "Practical Mediterraneanism: Excuses for Everything, from Epistemology to Eating." In William Vernon Harris, *Rethinking the Mediterranean*, 45–63. Oxford: Oxford University Press, 2005.

Horden, Peregrine, and Nicholas Purcell. *The Corrupting Sea: A Study of Mediterranean History*. London: Blackwell, 2000.

Hulme, Peter, and William Howard Sherman, eds. *"The Tempest" and Its Travels*. Philadelphia: University of Pennsylvania Press, 2000.

Hunwick, John O. "Black Slaves in the Mediterranean World: Introduction to a Neglected Aspect of the African Diaspora." *Slavery and Abolition* 13, no. 1 (1992): 5–38.

Ingham, Patricia Clare, and Michelle R. Warren, eds. *Postcolonial Moves: Medieval through Modern*. New York: Palgrave Macmillan, 2003.

James, Liz. "Goddess, Whore, Wife, or Slave: Will the Real Byzantine Empress Please Stand Up?" In *Queens and Queenship in Medieval Europe: Proceedings of a Conference Held at King's College London, April 1995*, ed. Anne J. Duggan, 123–39. London: Boydell, 1997.

———. *Women, Men, and Eunuchs: Gender in Byzantium*. London and New York: Routledge, 1997.

Jordan, Glenn, and Chris Weedon, eds. *Cultural Politics: Class, Gender, Race and the Postmodern World*. Oxford: Blackwell, 1995.

Karras, Ruth Mazo. *From Boys to Men: Formation of Masculinity in Late Medieval Europe.* Philadelphia: University of Pennsylvania Press, 2003.

Kinoshita, Sharon. *Medieval Boundaries: Rethinking Difference in Old French Literature.* Philadelphia: University of Pennsylvania Press, 2006.

———. "Medieval Mediterranean Literature." *PMLA* 124, no. 2 (March 2009): 600–608.

———. "Pagans Are Wrong and Christians Are Right: Alterity, Gender, and Nation in the Chanson de Roland." *Journal of Medieval and Early Modern Studies* 31, no. 1 (2001): 79–111.

Korda, Natasha. *Shakespeare's Domestic Economies: Gender and Property in Early Modern England.* Philadelphia: University of Pennsylvania Press, 2002.

Krueger, Roberta L. *Women Readers and the Ideology of Gender in Old French Verse Romance.* Cambridge: Cambridge University Press, 1993.

Laiou, Angeliki E. "Exchange and Trade, Seventh–Twelfth Centuries." In *The Economic History of Byzantium from the Seventh through the Fifteenth Century,* ed. Laiou, 697–770. Washington, DC: Dumbarton Oaks, 2002.

Lampert-Weissig, Lisa. *Medieval Literature and Postcolonial Studies.* Edinburgh: Edinburgh University Press, 2010.

Lochrie, Karma, Peggy McCracken, and James A. Schultz. *Constructing Medieval Sexuality.* Minneapolis: University of Minnesota Press, 1997.

Lopez, Robert Sabatino, and Irving Woodworth Raymond, trans. *Medieval Trade in the Mediterranean World: Illustrative Documents.* New York: Columbia University Press, 2013.

Mallette, Karla. *European Modernity and the Arab Mediterranean: Toward a New Philology and a Counter-Orientalism.* Philadelphia: University of Pennsylvania Press, 2011.

———. *The Kingdom of Sicily, 1100–1250: A Literary History.* Philadelphia: University of Pennsylvania Press, 2005.

Marino, John A. "Mediterranean Studies and the Remaking of Pre-Modern Europe." *Journal of Early Modern History* 15, no. 5 (2011): 385–412.

Matchinske, Megan. *Writing, Gender and State in Early Modern England: Identity Formation and the Female Subject.* Cambridge: Cambridge University Press, 1998.

McClintock, Anne. *Imperial Leather: Race, Gender, and Sexuality in the Colonial Contest.* New York: Routledge, 1995.

McCracken, Peggy. *The Curse of Eve, the Wound of the Hero: Blood, Gender, and Medieval Literature.* Philadelphia: University of Pennsylvania Press, 2003.

McNamara, Jo Ann. "Women and Power through the Family Revisited." In *Gendering the Master Narrative,* ed. Mary Carpenter Erler and Maryanne Kowaleski, 17–30. Ithaca: Cornell University Press, 2003.

Menocal, María Rosa. *The Arabic Role in Medieval Literary History: A Forgotten Heritage.* Philadelphia: University of Pennsylvania Press, 1987.

————. *The Ornament of the World: How Muslims, Jews, and Christians Created a Culture of Tolerance in Medieval Spain.* Paris: Hachette, 2009.

Moore, Megan. "Boundaries and Byzantines in the Old French *Floire et Blancheflor.*" *Dalhousie French Studies* 29 (2007): 3–20.

————. *Exchanges in Exoticism: Cross-Cultural Marriage and the Making of the Mediterranean in Old French Romance.* Toronto: University of Toronto Press, 2014.

Moraga, Cherrie, and Gloria Anzaldúa, eds. *This Bridge Called My Back: Writings by Radical Women of Color.* Watertown, MA: Persephone Press, 1981.

Parker, Grant. "Mapping the Mediterranean." *Journal of Medieval and Early Modern Studies* 37, no. 1 (2007): 1–8.

Perry, Mary Elizabeth. *Gender and Disorder in Early Modern Seville.* Princeton: Princeton University Press, 1990.

Pratt, Mary Louise. *Under Imperial Eyes: Travel Writing and Transculturation.* London and New York: Routledge, 1992.

Ramey, Lynn Tarte. *Christian, Saracen and Genre in Medieval French Literature: Imagination and Cultural Interaction in the French Middle Ages.* New York: Routledge, 2013.

Robertson, Elizabeth Ann. "Medieval Feminism in Middle English Studies: A Retrospective." *Tulsa Studies in Women's Literature* 1, no. 1 (2007): 67–79.

Rose, Mary Beth. "Where Are the Mothers in Shakespeare? Options for Gender Representation in the English Renaissance." *Shakespeare Quarterly* 42, no. 3 (1991): 291–314.

Rothman, E. Natalie. "Interpreting Dragomans: Boundaries and Crossings in the Early Modern Mediterranean." *Comparative Studies in Society and History* 51, no. 4 (2009): 771–800.

Segol, Marla. "'*Floire et Blancheflor*': Courtly Hagiography or Radical Romance?" *Alif* 23 (2003): 233–75.

————. "Medieval Cosmopolitanism and the Saracen-Christian Ethos." *CLC-Web: Comparative Literature and Culture* 6, no. 2 (2004): 4.

Skinner, Patricia. "Gender and Poverty in the Medieval Community." In *Medieval Women in Their Communities,* ed. Dianne Watt, 204–21. Toronto: University of Toronto Press, 1997.

Smith, Paul Julian. *Entiendes? Queer Readings, Hispanic Writings.* Durham: Duke University Press, 1995.

Sperling, Jutta G., and Shona Kelly Wray, eds. *Across the Religious Divide: Women, Property, and Law in the Wider Mediterranean (ca. 1300–1800).* New York: Routledge, 2009.

Stafford, Pauline, and Anneke B. Mulder-Bakker. *Gendering the Middle Ages: A Gender and History Special Issue.* Oxford: Blackwell, 2001.

Stahuljak, Zrinka. *Bloodless Genealogies of the French Middle Ages: Translatio, Kinship, and Metaphor.* Gainesville: University Press of Florida, 2005.

————. "Going Global, Getting Medieval." *UCLA Center for Medieval and Renaissance Studies Newsletter 2008–2009*, n.d., 3.

Summerhayes, Catherine. "Embodied Space in Google Earth: Crisis in Darfur." *MediaTropes* 3, no. 1 (2011): 113–34.

Tougher, Shaun F. "Byzantine Eunuchs: An Overview, with Special Reference to Their Creation and Origin." In *Women, Men and Eunuchs: Gender in Byzantium*, ed. Liz James, 168–85. New York: Routledge, 1997.

————. "Images of Effeminate Men: The Case of Byzantine Eunuchs." In *Masculinity in Medieval Europe*, ed. Dawn Hadley, 89–100. London: Longman, 1999.

————. "Two Views on the Gender Identity of Byzantine Eunuchs." In *Changing Sex and Bending Gender*, ed. Alison Shaw and Shirley Ardener, 60–73. London and New York: Routledge, 2005.

Vitkus, Daniel. *Turning Turk: English Theater and the Multicultural Mediterranean*. New York: Palgrave Macmillan, 2003.

Wacks, David. *Framing Iberia: Maqāmāt and Frametale Narratives in Medieval Spain*. Leiden: Brill, 2007.

Wall, Wendy. *The Imprint of Gender: Authorship and Publication in the English Renaissance*. Ithaca: Cornell University Press, 1993.

Warren, Michelle R. *Creole Medievalism: Colonial France and Joseph Bédier's Middle Ages*. Minneapolis: University of Minnesota Press, 2011.

Wasserstein, David. "Byzantium and Al⊠Andalus." *Mediterranean Historical Review* 2, no. 1 (1987): 76–101.

Chapter 2
Ambrose, Augustine, Perpetua: Defining Gender across the Mediterranean

Margaret Cotter-Lynch,
Southeastern Oklahoma State University

In the fourth century, St. Ambrose wrote, "One who does not believe is a woman and should be designated in the name of that sex, whereas one who believes progresses to perfect manhood."[1] A few years later, St. Jerome echoed the sentiment when he wrote, "As long as woman is for birth and children, she is different from man as body is from soul. But when she wishes to serve Christ more than the world, then she will cease to be a woman, and will be called man."[2] The trope of particularly virtuous religious women "becoming male" is well established and well studied in medieval feminist circles. As Christianity developed within a deeply patriarchal structure, biblical dictates for the inclusion or even equality of women before the Lord were easily interpreted to imply that virtuous Christian women, by becoming "as good as men," were, in fact, "becoming men." Much scholarship in the past thirty years has examined the phenomenon of early Christian, late antique, and medieval religious women discussed in male terms, their virtue (pun intended) figured as transcendence of their flawed female status in order to achieve the superior spiritual status of a male.[3]

However, while such rhetoric and attitudes did certainly exist (and persist) and arguably became dominant from the late fourth century onward, I would like to suggest that the extant literature from the first four centuries of Christianity offers a much more complex variety of thinking about gender difference than many scholars acknowledge. I argue that many of our contemporary readings of early texts, specifically early texts about women, are overly influenced

---

[1] St. Ambrose, *Expositionis in evangelius secundum Lucum libri X*.161, in PL 15:1844.

[2] St. Jerome, *Commentarius in Epistolam ad Ephesios* III.5 in PL 26:567a.

[3] The scholarly literature on this topic is enormous; see, for example, Brown, *The Body and Society*; Newman, *From Virile Woman to Womanchrist*; and Cobb, *Dying to Be Men*.

by later ideological accruals in which gender binaries are in fact re-established through the trope of virtuous women "becoming male." Such descriptions of medieval religious women reify a clearly hierachized gender binary, in which, paradoxically, sexual difference is absolute, and overcoming or transcending this difference is cause for celebration. An individual is, in the formulations of Ambrose and Jerome, always either male or female. One may, in extraordinary circumstances, transform from one to the other, but these patristic writers do not consider the option of escaping gender categorization entirely, or fully inhabiting both genders at once. In contrast, I suggest that in the Mediterranean of the first four centuries of the Common Era, just such options were considered, if ultimately rejected. Turning our scholarly attention to the representation of gender in early Christian texts such as the *Passio Perpetuae* reveals a wider range of possible formulations of gender identity. By re-examining this range of ways of talking about gender in the late ancient Mediterranean, I hope that we can recuperate the origins of later gender formulations and their implications. In order to do this, I propose to trace the first 200 years of the life of the story of St. Perpetua, starting with her prison diary, the earliest known autobiographical text composed by a woman.

St. Perpetua, a twenty-two-year-old nursing mother, was executed in the arena at Carthage on 7 March 203 CE on charges of being a Christian. We have extant an early composite text, which scholarly consensus has generally accepted as containing her autobiographical account of her time in prison, including four visions that she understood to be divinely inspired; a section written by her fellow-martyr Saturus, recounting a divinely inspired vision that he experienced; and a framing narrative by an anonymous redactor and apparent eye witness to her death in the arena. The story of Perpetua has enjoyed enormous popularity and attention, in the ancient, medieval, and modern worlds; it has been subjected to numerous retellings and commentaries, by both ancient authors and modern scholars.[4] The early dissemination of Perpetua's story demonstrates the religious and cultural networks that connected the early third-century Mediterranean, as Perpetua, a North African woman heavily influenced by the New Prophecy movement from Anatolia, had her story reframed through the theology of St. Ambrose in Italy, Augustine in North Africa, and Jerome in the Holy Land, as it spread throughout the Mediterranean world.[5]

Perpetua's third-century prison diary demonstrates that her status as a Christian is clear and important, while her gender, perhaps, is neither. Or, more

---

[4] Cotter-Lynch, *St. Perpetua across the Middle Ages*, traces the variety of versions and uses of Perpetua's story through approximately 1500 CE.

[5] Jonathan Conant has documented the early dissemination of Perpetua's cult in his "Europe and the African Cult of Saints, circa 350–900." He demonstrates a strong, early, and enduring cult for Perpetua in Spain and Italy, with lesser but still noticeable dissemination of her story in Byzantium, Gaul, and England.

precisely, her gender is not an impediment, or even a clear boundary. In recounting the story of her imprisonment on charges of being a Christian, Perpetua relates her concern for the well-being of her infant son, her complex but clearly affectionate relationship with her parents and brothers, and her role as vocal leader of a group of imprisoned Christians. Her prophetic dreams figure her as a new Jacob and a gladiator fighting Satan in the arena. The same person can both nurse a baby and fight in combat; gender markers can and do mix, and the biblical injunction that there is "neither male nor female for we are all one in Christ Jesus" (Gal. 3:28) is logically extended to imply that one can be both male and female at once. For later Christians, especially St. Augustine, this formulation causes problems. In this paper I trace the first 200 years of the story of St. Perpetua's story, from her self-authored *Passio*, composed in 203 CE, through the anonymous fourth-century *Acta*, in which her story is simplified and rewritten in two different forms, to the three sermons about Perpetua composed by St. Augustine in the early fifth century. I argue that in this progression of stories we see an increasing emphasis on gender dichotomy and hierarchy, until Augustine's sermons overwrite Perpetua's story with St. Ambrose's paradigm that, "[o]ne who does not believe is a woman and should be designated in the name of that sex, whereas one who believes progresses to perfect manhood." This version of Perpetua, who overcomes her femininity to "become male," then dominates the medieval tradition and becomes a model for later Christian women. Augustine thus codifies an understanding of gender that, paradoxically, by allowing for the possibility of holy women "becoming male," simultaneously asserts the inherent hierarchy of male over female and indelibly yokes gender definitions to sexuality for the next 1600 years.

St. Paul, in his letter to the Galatians (3:28), famously states "there is neither male nor female. For you are all one in Christ Jesus."[6] As Barbara Newman explains in *From Virile Woman to WomanChrist*, this exhortation to the transcendence of sex was often understood, as evidenced in the quotes cited above, to mean leaving behind one's female sex in order to become male, as women were seen as defined by their sex in a way that men were not. Dyan Elliott cites the *Passio Perptuae* as an example of this idea of "becoming male"; however, she also describes another possibility suggested by Luke 20:35:

> But they that shall be accounted worthy of that world, and of the resurrection from the dead, shall neither be married, nor take wives. Neither can they die any more: for they are equal to the angels, and are the children of God, being the children of the resurrection.

---

[6] This and all English Bible citations are from the Douay-Rheims translation; Latin translations, unless otherwise noted, are from the Vulgate, with the recognition that Perpetua herself would have known the Vetus Latina.

This passage, in combination with Galatians, led some early Christians to suggest that chastity be understood as leading to the "vita angelica," or a sex/genderless identity equivalent to that of the angels. Tertullian of Carthage, a contemporary of Perpetua's, was one of the early promoters of this interpretation, although he turned away from it in his later writings out of concern for maintaining the clear differentiation between humans and angels.[7] Peter Brown has identified the idea of the eradication of sexual difference through asceticism as especially prominent in late antique Syria, of which he writes, "Of all the restricting boundaries that defined settled society, that between the sexes was the most blatant. Hence, it also could be shown to vanish in a life lived in imitation of the angels."[8] However, as the examples cited by both Elliott and Brown show, in practice, for many male writers and theologians, androgyny ended up looking distinctively male.[9]

However, taken at face value, Paul seems to indicate an eradication of gender classification, not the hierarchical privilege of one gender over another. I offer the proposition that returning to the biblical phrase, rather than the patristic reading of it, can be instructive for understanding the *Passion of St. Perpetua*. Perpetua, I claim, presents herself as "neither male nor female" specifically by presenting herself as *at once* male and female, thus undermining the very idea of gender categories and their relevance in the face of Christianity. Perpetua's *Passio* presents one of the very few extant early Christian documents composed by a woman; as such, it offers us an opportunity to see a possibility for an ancient understanding of Christianity as expressed by a female, rather than male, author.

Most discussions of gender in the *Passio* depend upon readings of the fourth dream Perpetua reports experiencing while in prison awaiting her execution. To briefly summarize the contents of this divinely inspired vision, Perpetua is escorted from prison by the deacon Pomponius, who leads her to the amphitheater where she knows she is to be martyred. Once there, Pomponius reassures her and departs, leaving her in the middle of the arena, watched by the crowd. Then, she tells us, according to Heffernan's translation (emphasis mine):

> And *I was stripped naked*, and *I became a man*. And my supporters began to rub me with oil, as they are accustomed to do for a match. And I saw that Egyptian on the other side rolling in the dust. Next there came out a man of such great size that he exceeded the height of the amphitheater. He was wearing an unbelted robe, a purple garment with two stripes running down the middle of his chest, and decorated shoes made of gold and silver, and carrying a rod or wand as if a gladiator trainer, and a green branch on

---

[7] Elliott, *The Bride of Christ Goes to Hell*. Perpetua's text is cited on pages 11–12; much of the remainder of the chapter explores Tertullian's changing thoughts on the matter.

[8] Brown, *The Body and Society*, 332.

[9] The implicit masculinity of ancient androgyny is explored in more detail by Martin, *The Corinthian Body*.

which there were golden apples. And he asked for silence and said: "This Egyptian, if he defeats *this woman*, will kill *her* with the sword, but if *she* defeats him, *she* shall receive this branch." And he departed. And we drew near to each other and began to throw punches at each other. He kept trying to grab hold of my feet while I kept kicking him in his face with my heels. And *I was raised up* into the air, and I began to strike him stepping on his face, as though I were unable to step on the ground. But when I saw that there was a hesitation, I joined my hands so that my fingers were knit together and I grabbed a hold of his head. And he fell on his face and I stepped on his head. And the crowd began to shout and my supporters began to sing hymns. And I went to the gladiator trainer, and I took the branch. And he kissed me and he said to me: "*Daughter*, peace be with you." And I began to walk in triumph to the Gate of Life. And then *I woke up.* And I knew that *I was going to fight* with the devil and not with the beasts; but I knew that victory was to be mine.

(Et *expoliata sum*, et *facta sum masculus*, et coeperunt me favisores mei oleo defricare, quomodo solent in agone; et illum contra Egyptium video in afa volutantem. Et exivit vir quidam mirae magnitudinis, ut etiam excederet fastigium amphit[h]eatri, discinctatus, purpuram inter duos clavos per medium pectus habens, et galliculas multiformes ex auro et argento factas, et ferens virgam quasi lanista, et ramum viridem in quo erant mala aurea. Et petiit silentium et dixit: "Hic Aegyptius, si *hanc* vicerit, occidet *illam* gladio; *haec*, si hunc vicerit, accipiet ramum istum. Et recessit. Et accessimus ad invicem et coepimus mittere pugnos; ille mihi pedes apprehendere volebat, ego autem illi calcibus faciem caedebam. Et *sublata sum* in aere, et coepi eum sic caedere quasi terram non calcans. At ubi vidi moram fieri, iunxi manus, ut digitos in digitos mitterem, et apprehendi illi caput, et cedidit in faciem, et calcavi illi caput. Et coepit populus clamare et fautores mei psallere. Et accessi ad lanistam et accepi. Et osculatus est me et dixit mihi: "*Filia*, pax tecum." Et coepi ire cum gloria ad portam Sanavivariam. Et *experta sum*. Et intellexi me non ad bestias sed contra diabolum esse *pugnaturam*; sed sciebam mihi esse *victoria[m]*.)[10]

Upon waking, Perpetua explains that she understood the dream to mean that she and her fellow imprisoned Christians were to be martyred, and that by their deaths they would in fact be defeating Satan. There are, obviously, a number of salient points for discussing the allegorical nature of Perpetua's reported dream, but for the purpose of the present argument, we will concentrate on the representation of her gender and whether or how it is transformed both within the dream and through its narration.

---

[10] *Passio Perpetuae* X:7–14. All citations and translations of the *Passio* are from Heffernan, *The Passion of Perpetua and Felicity.*

The scholarly literature on gender in the *Passio* is enormous and has been variously approached with particular attention to questions of literary genre and tradition, the construction of authority, Roman versus Christian family structures, theology, and psychoanalysis, to name but the most prominent approaches.[11] All such readings of gender in the *Passio* must somehow account for the contents of the gladiatorial dream. In the standard modern account of this dream, in order to engage in this contest, the young woman Perpetua is miraculously transformed into a man. Peter Dronke, in the first chapter of his seminal *Women Writers of the Middle Ages*, writes, "She is stripped of her womanly clothes, and becomes masculine [. . .] Perpetua wants to strip herself of all that is weak, or womanish, in her nature."[12] Joyce Salisbury, in *Perpetua's Passion, the Death and Memory of a Young Roman Woman*, writes:

> Certainly there is no more vivid image of personal change than Perpetua's dream image in which she is transformed into a man [. . .] If one is looking for a metaphor of personal change, one cannot do better than a transformation of one's gender, which is at the heart of one's self-identity. In her dream, Perpetua was changed into a man. Led by the deacon of her new community, she was fully transformed from her old self into a new empowered individual who could stand in the arena and fight for what she believed.[13]

Most readings of Perpetua's fourth dream seek to show Perpetua as a young woman empowered by her faith and her impending martyrdom, and they claim that this empowerment is oneirically expressed in essentialized gendered terms — men are more powerful than women, thus becoming powerful means becoming a man. Salisbury even takes for granted that "gender . . . is at the heart of one's self-identity." While certainly Dronke and Salisbury would argue that such gender binaries are cultural constructs, they never seem to question whether this particular construct was essential to Perpetua's view of herself and her world — or, as we can more easily see from a distance of nearly 2000 years, whether such gender binaries are integral to her self-presentation in this autobiographical text.

Thomas Heffernan also discusses this episode in terms of "gender transformation." He writes of the moment when Perpetua's garments are stripped from her:

> She must be naked to wrestle, but more importantly, she must be naked so that her gender transformation stands revealed. Her clothing hides her

---

[11] For a compendium of recent work, see Bremmer and Formisano, *Perpetua's Passions: Multidisciplinary Approaches to the Passio Perpetuae et Felicitatis.*

[12] Dronke, *Women Writers of the Middle Ages*, 14.

[13] Salisbury, *Perpetua's Passion*, 108–9.

femininity, but her nakedness reveals her masculine identity. As soon as she is stripped naked, she is revealed as a man. For the contest to be credible, for her to emerge as the champion of Christ, his *miles Christi*, she must divest herself of her femininity and take on a male persona [. . .]this gender transformation is a projection of her own unconscious desire to seek martyrdom, and as such it exhibits her social understanding that the role of the martyr requires a transformation from the traditional depiction of females as nonagressive and domestic to one of male combativeness. (see Augustine, Sermons 280 and 281)[14]

Heffernan here follows centuries of previous scholars in reading Perpetua's "transformation" as not only metaphorical but also physical (within the dream), implying that she visibly acquires male anatomy (presumably a phallus) within her dream. In his reading of the *Passio*, Heffernan even cites directly, as source of his interpretation, Augustine's explanation of Perpetua's "becoming male." As we will see, it is clear that Augustine interprets Perpetua's dream this way, but such an interpretation is not self-evident in the early text itself. Rather, I propose that Perpetua's account of her dream expressly *denies* that she becomes physically and essentially male, instead suggesting that martyrs such as herself simultaneously inhabit both genders, perhaps even eradicating the relevance of gender as a category in the face of Christian eschatology.

    I argue that reading this vision as the one in which Perpetua "becomes male" misreads the inherent ambiguity of the Latin. In modern English translation, part of this misreading is linguistic—English does not attach gender to adjectives and participles, as Latin does, and so the initial phrase signaling Perpetua's transformation—"facta sum masculus"—loses its gendered difficulty. As Maud Burnett McInerney has explained, this phrase is inherently and necessarily problematic in Latin, since the subject of the sentence is marked as female, and the adjective is marked as male.[15] The sentence thus effectively says, "I, as a woman, was made male." McInerney reads this sentence as a vector: Perpetua begins the sentence as a female (indicated by the feminine participle *facta*) and undergoes a transformation in order to end the sentence as a male (indicated by the masculine adjective *masculus*). I, however, read this sentence differently. Grammatically, in Latin as well as English, the verb *to be* or *esse/sum* functions as an equal sign. In Latin, the nouns or adjectives on each side of this verb are to agree in gender, number, and case; thus, *masculus* is in the nominative case, equal to the (unstated) subject of the sentence. Therefore, instead of reading this sentence as a vector in which Perpetua becomes male, I read this sentence as an equation, in which she is *at once* male *and* female. Thus I argue that the sentence effectively dismantles conventional gender dichotomies, to mark Perpetua as *simul-*

---

[14] Heffernan, *Passion of Perpetua*, 251–52.
[15] McInerney, *Eloquent Virgins from Thecla to Joan of Arc*, 26.

taneously male and female. While I agree that Perpetua undergoes an oneiric transformation that allows her to fight as a gladiator in the arena, in my view, she does not become male. Rather, she transcends the binary gender categories that dictate that women cannot be gladiators by redefining the categories themselves: as a woman, she becomes male, inhabiting both genders at once. This reading is further supported by the sentence's diction: *masculus* is translated by Heffernan (and most other English translators of the *Passio*) as a substantive, an adjective that grammatically functions as a noun within the sentence. The effect here is to say "I, as a woman, was made a thing which is male." This word choice is important because the substantive maintains some of its adjectival quality; the sentence does not say, for instance, "facta sum vir," or even "factus sum vir," which would most directly and unambiguously portray a transformation into a man. Instead, this sentence, in both its grammar and diction, indicates the simultaneity of two genders within the oneiric Perpetua.

My reading of this sentence is supported by the gender markers attached to Perpetua through the rest of her vision: Perpetua, while engaging in gladiatorial combat, is repeatedly addressed by the trainer using feminine pronouns. When referring to her own actions in the oneiric combat, Perpetua uses the feminine form of the past participle (*sublata sum*). At the conclusion of the fight, the trainer addresses the victorious Perpetua as "filia"/"daughter." When Perpetua awakes, she again uses a feminine participle in the phrase "experta sum," signaling a gender continuity between the oneiric Perpetua who fought in gladiatorial combat and the Perpetua who awakens in the prison cell. Finally, in her interpretation of the dream's significance, Perpetua again uses the feminine participle in the phrase "esse pugnaturam." We thus see a continuity in gender markers attached to the dream-character Perpetua, the Perpetua who experiences the dream in the prison cell, and the Perpetua who will die in the arena. In fact, the only marker of her male gender in the narration of the dream is the single word *masculus*–unless we assume, as so many interpreters have, that women cannot fight. But such an argument from Perpetua's oneiric actions is a clear reification of traditional gender expectations based upon cultural assumptions, rather than Perpetua's text itself. What Perpetua's text actually tells us is that, as a woman, she also became male, and as a woman (thus the feminine pronouns) with this acquired masculinity, she (and the pronoun is significant here) fought as a gladiator (within the dream) and against the devil (in the prophetic fulfillment of the allegory of the dream). In view of all of this, I argue that Perpetua clearly and explicitly *does not* become male but, rather, is *at once* male and female, figuring Paul's exhortation to be "neither male nor female" in an entirely different light than Augustine. She does not cross gender boundaries; she eradicates them.

The ambiguity of Perpetua's gender identification in this fourth dream has been recently discussed by both Barbara Gold and Craig Williams. While Gold follows many previous readers in understanding "facta sum masculus" as indicating a physical change within the dream, she describes a pervasive destabilization of gender categories throughout the narrative that allows her to identify gender as an inherently ambiguous category in the *Passio*. In reference to the juxtaposition of *facta* and *masculus*, Gold writes, "Thus in this moment she was both male and female."[16] She reads the use of the word *masculus*, as opposed to *vir* or *mas*, within the context of classical examples in which the word *masculus* is used in combination with the word *femina* to describe intersex individuals. She concludes, "The word *masculus* seems to signal, then, both by its form and its semantic connotation and associations, a sexual ambiguity in Perpetua's transformation into a male body."[17] Gold summarizes two dominant strains in the reading of Perpetua's gender. The first, which I associated with McInerny above and which she identifies with Mieke Bal, views Perpetua as undergoing a substantive and permanent gender transformation.[18] The other interpretive possibility, with which Gold identifies, "calls Perpetua's fixed gender identity into question, revealing a woman who often behaves in a determinedly masculine way and yet firmly identifies with her corporeality, her female relationships, and her sexuality throughout the story."[19]

Craig Williams, meanwhile, elegantly reads both the grammar and the rhetoric of Perpetua's fourth dream to demonstrate that the word *masculus* represents neither a permanent physical change in the Perpetua within the dream nor a fundamental transformation of Perpetua the dreamer's gender identity. He identifies ample classical precedent for the rhetorical ambiguity of Perpetua's gender, thus offering this oneiric moment as the deployment of a well-established trope of the exceptional-but-not-unique woman.[20] In his discussion of the grammar used to describe Perpetua's dream, he points out not only the feminine pronouns and participles noted above but also a grammatical balancing of male and female identifications and images throughout the dream narrative. He objects to readings that identify the word *masculus* as designating a physical change in Perpetua, noting "I find neither surprise nor a hint at genital transformation in Perpetua's narration of her dream."[21] While Williams identifies the gender ambiguity as a narratological and oneiric effect, rather than a statement of destabilized gender categories, his careful dissection of the Latin grammar amply demonstrates the insufficiency of readings that identify in the *Passio* a clear change of Perpetua's gender from entirely female to entirely male.

---

[16] Gold, "Gender Fluidity," 245.

[17] Gold, "Gender Fluidity," 246.

[18] Gold cites Bal, "Perpetual Contest." An "updated and corrected" version appears as "Perpetual Contest," in Bremmer and Formisano, *Perpetua's Passions: Multidisciplinary Approaches*.

[19] Gold, "Gender Fluidity," 249.

[20] Williams, "Perpetua's Gender."

[21] Williams, "Perpetua's Gender," 65.

The refusal of clear binaries and obvious contrasts that I see in her fourth dream is also characteristic of Perpetua's narrative as a whole. The mixing of male and female in the oneiric representation of Perpetua's martyrdom shows that this dream is not about a simple change of gender in order for this Christian woman to fit into a male ideal of sanctity. Rather, Perpetua seems to adopt the Pauline verse in earnest, questioning the very relevance of categorization based upon gender amongst Christians. As J. Louis Martyn explains in his analysis of Galatians 3:28 within its original context, "Religious, social, and sexual pairs of opposites are not replaced by equality, but rather by a newly created unity."[22] Perpetua's fourth dream thus offers an instantiation of this unity of genders, as the oneiric Perpetua unifies male and female within herself.

Perpetua's rhetorical formulation of her gender identity caused discomfort almost immediately. As Barbara Gold has noted, the gender ambiguity of the autobiographical portion of the *Passio* stands in stark contrast to the efforts of the anonymous redactor to clearly feminize Perpetua both in the introduction to the text and the eyewitness account of her martyrdom. Taking the redactor's text alone, we get a picture of an honorable Roman matron maintaining the traditional feminine virtues of modesty and decorum.[23] The immediate reception, insofar as we can reconstruct it, reveals a similar discomfort with the gendered implications of Perpetua's story as she tells it.

The next important text in the diffusion of Perpetua's story is the *Acta*, extant in two versions, both shorter versions of the story likely meant for liturgical use. The *Acta* were long thought to date from the fifth century,[24] but the discovery in 2007 of a longer version of Augustine's sermon 282, previously known only in summary, implies that the *Acta* were known to Augustine and therefore may date to the fourth century.[25] While the *Acta* can in general be characterized

---

[22] Martyn, *The Anchor Bible 33a*, 377. Martyn continues on to offer three different possibilities for understanding Paul's collapsing of dichotomies in this verse, with a view to the ancient baptismal formula on which the passage is based: "There are three major possibilities as regards the conceptual background of the baptismal formula: (1) It can be seen as a development of a Stoic and Neoplatonic tradition that speaks of a spiritual and mental freedom from distinctions, and that even looks forward, in a sort of liberal state of mind, to the possibility that the marks of ethnic differentiation will one day disappear. (2) It might have been built on the basis of the proto-gnostic thought that humanity was originally androgynous, thus declaring that baptism returns one to that lost state of undifferentiation. (3) Finally, it might have been drawn from apocalyptic conceptions in which sexual differentiation is expected to be terminated at the resurrection," 379.

[23] Gold, "Gender Fluidity," 247.

[24] Amat, *Passion de Perpétue et de Félicité Suivi des Actes*.

[25] Bremmer and Formisano, "Perpetua's Passions: A Brief Introduction," 5. There remain many questions about the date, place, and conditions of production of these texts, about which very little is known. For a more detailed discussion of possible dating of the

as a summary of the *Passio*, several additions, as well as strategic subtractions, are significant in how we read gender in the story.

The *Acta* are extant in two distinct forms, designated as I and II by Jacqueline Amat in her 1996 edition.[26] The differences between these two versions, as well as the ways in which they are distinct from the *Passio*, have been catalogued by J. W. Halporn,[27] and I agree with him that these three texts—the *Passio*, *Acta* I, and *Acta* II—should be considered as distinct works intended for distinct audiences, each with a distinct "horizon of expectation."[28] As Halporn has noted, both versions of the *Acta* concentrate more on the group of martyrs as a whole and less on Perpetua as an individual; this alone makes the texts less about a woman and more about martyrdom as a category. *Acta* I is recounted in the first person, *Acta* II in the third; in *Acta* I, the story is told in the perfect tense, while *Acta* II uses the imperfect.[29] While both texts are shorter than the *Passio* (and II is still shorter than I), both versions add, to differing degrees, a detailed account of the interrogation of Perpetua and her companions, indicating that the author(s) of the texts was(were) either working from legal transcripts no longer extant or interpolated and adapted the interrogation scene from the *Acts of the Scillitan Martyrs*, to which the scenes in the *Acta* bear a notable resemblance. In any case, the other Christians martyred with Perpetua, including Felicity, get much more attention in the *Acta* than in the *Passio*. As Aviad Kleinberg has noted, in general the *Acta* flatten and simplify Perpetua's story, eliminating psychological depth and conflict.[30]

Both versions of the *Acta* give considerably less attention to Perpetua's fourth dream than does the *Passio*, and both completely elide Perpetua's purported gender transformation. *Acta* I, for example, summarizes the entire dream as follows:

And when they were in prison, once more Perpetua saw a dream: an Egyptian utterly hideous and black, thrown down and rolling under their feet, and she recounted this to her holy brothers and fellow martyrs.

(Et cum essent in carcere, iterum uidit uisionem Perpetua: Aegyptium quendam horridum et nigrum, iacentem et uolatantem se sub pedibus eorum, retulitque sanctis fratribus et conmartyribus suis.)[31]

Acta, see Cotter-Lynch, *St. Perpetua across the Middle Ages*, 45–46. Despite the enormous interest in the *Passio*, the *Acta* have received scant scholarly attention.

[26] Amat, *Passion de Perpétue et de Félicité Suivi des Actes*. I and II correspond to A and B in Van Beek's 1936 edition; Halporn uses Van Beek's designations. Van Beek, *Passio Sanctarum Perpetuae et Felicitatis*.

[27] Halporn, "Literary History and Generic Expectations."

[28] Halporn, "Literary History and Generic Expectations," 235.

[29] Halporn, "Literary History and Generic Expectations," 227.

[30] Kleinberg, *Flesh Made Word*, 78–80.

[31] *Acta I* 7:2.

Acta II reads:

> Once more Perpetua was inspired by visions. She saw an Egyptian, dread-
> fully and blackly foul, rolling under their feet.
>
> (Iterum Perpetua uisionibus animatur. Vidit Aegyptium horrore et nigred-
> ine taetrum, sub eorum pedibus uolutantem.)[32]

These summaries of the dream completely elide the gladiatorial aspect and Perpetua's purported gender transformation. In addition, both versions, while maintaining the image of the Egyptian being kicked or stepped on, change the actors;
instead of Perpetua as an individual stepping on the symbolic devil, in both
versions of the *Acta*, the martyrs as a group trample the Egyptian under *their*
feet—"eorum pedibus."[33] I suggest that the gender-bending recounted in the
Passio was omitted because it was uncomfortable to the author and/or audience
of the *Acta*. While the *Passio* is characterized by gender ambiguity on a variety
of levels (structural, narrative, metaphorical, grammatical), both versions of the
Acta "rectify" these slippages. Most noticeable to the casual reader is the addition
of a husband for Perpetua. While the introduction to the *Passio* tells us that Perpetua was "matronaliter nupta," this single mention only underlines the glaring
absence of her husband from the rest of the text. In the *Passio* he does not figure
in the court proceedings, as her father does, and we are explicitly told that her
parents care for her infant son in her absence, a situation that would have been
surprising in a Roman legal system that normally viewed children as belonging
to the father's family.[34] In both versions of the *Acta*, in contrast, Perpetua's husband accompanies her parents and infant son to visit her in prison.

At this moment, we get a striking scene that departs dramatically from both
the content and mood of the *Passio*. The *Passio* devotes considerable attention
to the clearly affectionate but nonetheless complex relationship between Perpetua, her father, and her family as a whole. The familial love is evident, as are
the internal ruptures within the family unit caused by the religious difference
between her father, on the one hand, and her (apparently Christian) mother and

---

[32] *Acta II* 7:2.

[33] In addition, we see here an elaboration of the symbolism of the Egyptian within
the narration of the dream; in both cases, Perpetua's adversary is described as particularly
ugly and odious, associated with blackness or darkness. This seems a further example of
the ways in which both versions of the *Acta* emphasize clear binary categories, such as
white versus black, good versus evil, and male versus female. For a thorough reading of
both versions of the *Acta*, see Cotter-Lynch, *St. Perpetua across the Middle Ages*, chap. 2.

[34] Heffernan discusses the implications of Perpetua's marriage and the absence of
the husband on pages 147–48; alternately, Kate Cooper suggests that Perpetua may have
been a concubine, a status that the redactor would have tried to obfuscate. Cooper, "A
Father, a Daughter and a Procurator."

brother, on the other. In addition, Perpetua dwells repeatedly on the conflicting emotions caused by her simultaneous love and concern for her still-nursing infant son and her desire for martyrdom. In the *Acta*, however, these complexities are simplified into a clear conflict between pagan family obligations, which must be rejected, and love of Christ, which must be embraced. Implicitly, this conflict between paganism and Christianity is also a conflict between the traditional role of a woman (mother, daughter, and wife), which must be rejected, and a "new" Christian identity, which, while not yet explicitly male, *is* explicitly *not* female. In response to the pleas of her father, mother, and husband to recant her faith and the attempt by her father to place her infant son in her arms, Perpetua responds:

> The truly blessed Perpetua threw off the infant, and repulsed her family saying: "Depart from me workers of iniquity, for I know you not. Not without reason I consider strangers those whom I see separated from the redemption of Christ."

> (Beata vero Perpetua proiciens infantem, ac parentes repellens dixit: "Discedite a me operarii iniquitatis, quia non noui vos. Ego non inmerito alienos aestimo quos a redemptione Christi uideo separatos.")[35]

Both versions of the *Acta* thus demonstrate at least three major differences from the *Passio* that have direct implications for how we read gender in Perpetua's story. First, by radically abbreviating the gladiatorial dream, they erase the part of the story that most directly undermines the gender binary. Second, by shifting the focus from Perpetua as an individual to the martyrs as a group, both *Acta* subsume gendered elements of the story under the broader umbrella of all martyrs. And third, the *Acta* elide the complexity and subtlety inherent in Perpetua's familial relationships, re-writing the story of Perpetua and her family into a clear and unambiguous demonstration of the biblical injunction "If any man come to me, and hate not his father, and mother, and wife, and children, and brethren, and sisters, yea and his own life also, he cannot be my disciple" (Luke 14:26). This transformation of the story from one about the complexity of competing categories and concepts (in the *Passio*) into one about clear binaries has the effect of reifying a binary gender system—in which one can be male or female but not both—and opens up the way for Augustine's interpretation of the story.

As Bishop of Hippo, St. Augustine could not help but be acquainted with Perpetua, who was, in the fourth century, the focus of a vibrant cult in North Africa. We have three extant sermons from Augustine about St. Perpetua and her companion, St. Felicitas—sermons 280, 281, and 282, this last one of the "new" Augustine sermons discovered in 2007. I locate the genesis of the tradition

---

[35] *Acta* II VI:6; cf. *Acta* I VI:6. Both versions recall Matthew 7:23, Luke 13:27, and Psalm 6:9.

of viewing Perpetua as a saint who "becomes male" to the first of these sermons, in which Augustine applies the Pauline verse to the two female saints. As John Kitchen has persuasively shown in his analysis of the relationship between the rhetoric of Augustine's sermons on Perpetua and the spatial relationships of the amphitheater at Carthage, all three of these sermons are constructed around a system of contrasts and dichotomies.[36] For Augustine, the primary and recurring dichotomy in Perpetua and Felicitas's story (for he consistently refers to the two together) is a dichotomy of gender. In Augustine's retelling, the miracle of Perpetua is her gender transformation. The martyrdom story serves as an example of God's continuing agency in the world specifically because two young women became manly. As Augustine says in sermon 280:

> What indeed is more glorious than these women, who are more easily admired by men than imitated? But this is glory to Him most powerful, in Whom they that believe, and in Whose name the faithful assemble with zeal, are found to be according to the inward man neither male nor female;[37] so that even in those that are female in body the virtue/strength/ manliness of their soul hides the sex of their flesh, and one is hard pressed to discern in their bodies what does not appear in their actions.[38]

> (Quid enim gloriosius his feminis, quas viri mirantur facilius, quam imi- tantur? Sed hoc illius potissimum laus est, in quem credentes, et in cujus nomine fideli studio concurrentes, secundum interiorem hominem, nec masculus, nec femina inveniuntur; ut etiam in his quae sunt feminae cor- pore, virtus mentis sexum carnis abscondat, et in membris pigeat cogitare, quod in factis non potuit apparere.)[39]

Or similarly, in Sermon 281:

> Outshining and excelling among the companion martyrs are the merits and names of Perpetua and Felicity, holy handmaids of God. For there is the crown more glorious, where the sex is weaker. Because indeed in these women a manly soul did a greater thing, when under such a weight of femi- nine frailty it was not defeated. Well that they clung to one Husband, to

---

[36] Kitchen, "Going to the Gate of Life." Writing in 2004, Kitchen is working from the summary version of sermon 282, but his conclusions are only strengthened by con- sideration of the full text.

[37] Cf. Gal. 3:28 and Eph. 3:16.

[38] Translations of Augustine are my own.

[39] St. Augustine of Hippo, Sermon 280, chap. 1. The full Latin text of Sermons 280 and 281, as well as the abbreviated version of 282 known prior to 2007, can be found in PL vol. 38, cols. 1280–1286.

Whom the unparelled chaste virgin Church is presented.[40] Well, indeed, that they clung to that Husband from Whom they drew virtue/strength/ manliness to resist the devil; so that women should fell that enemy who by a woman did make man fall.

(Refulget et praeeminet inter comites martyres et meritum et nomen Perpetuae et Felicitatis, sanctarum Dei famularum. Nam ibi est corona gloriosior, ubi sexus infirmior. Quia profecto virilis animus in feminas majus aliquid fecit, quando sub tanto pondere fragilitas feminea non defecit. Bene inhaeserant uni viro, cui virgo casta unica exhibetur Ecclesia. Bene, inquam, inhaeserant illi viro, a quo virtutem traxerant, qua resisterent diabolo: ut feminae prosternerent inimicum, qui per feminam prostraverat virum.)[41]

In both of these examples, the praise of the two female saints is amplified on the basis of their gender; the miraculous nature of the narrative, according to Augustine, rests upon the profound contrast between the saints' status as women and their courage and strength in martyrdom, explicitly figured as manly through the repeated use of the adjective *virtus*. This contrast between womanly frailty and manly strength is consistently emphasized throughout the sermons as the very basis of Perpetua's sanctity. Augustine cites as an example Perpetua's final vision, in which he claims "she was made a man ("virum se factam") and strove with the devil."[42] He glosses Perpetua's first vision, in which she steps on a dragon's head to access the ladder to heaven, through comparison to Eve, claiming that Perpetua crushed the head of the serpent by which Eve was tempted. For Augustine, Perpetua's (and Felicitas's) sanctity is predicated upon clear sexual difference; only through the manifest power of God could such profound difference be overcome in the ways he claims for the two female martyrs.

Sermon 282 repeats many of these themes of the "manly woman," this time directly discussing Perpetua's fourth dream:

In this contest Perpetua, just as was revealed to her in a vision, changed into a man, defeated the devil, having stripped off the world and put on Christ, in the unity of faith and knowledge of the son of God running to meet Him in perfect strength and made in the particular member of His body, in which of the whole body, not one member had been cast aside.

(In hoc agone Perpetua, sicut ei per visionem revelatum fuerat, in virum conversa diabolum vicit, exspoliata saeculo et induta Christo, in unitatem fidei et agnitionem filii dei occurrens in virum perfectum et in eius corpore

---

[40] Augustine here echoes 2 Cor. 11:2, "Despondi enim vos uni viro virginem castam exhibere Christo." The "husband" is thus Christ.

[41] Augustine, Sermon 281, chap. 1.

[42] Augustine, Sermon 281, chap. 2.

membrum facta praecipuum, pro quo totum corpus, non unum abiecerat
membrum.)[43]

The explicit corporeality of this explication of Perpetua's fourth vision exemplifies the reading of Augustine's sermons presented by Gertrude Gillette, who
argues that the martyr here is not *just* "putting on" Christ but is putting on
a particularly and explicitly male Christ—thus, in becoming Christ-like, the
martyr becomes male.[44] It is Augustine, I therefore argue, who inaugurates the
idea that Perpetua unambiguously "becomes male." In contrast to the *Passio*'s
"facta sum masculus," Augustine repeatedly uses the word *vir* ("in virum conversa") to describe Perpetua's oneiric transformation: whereas the *Passio* says she
becomes male, Augustine says she becomes a man. We also see, through the
double-entendre of *membrum*, the birth of the implication that, at the moment
when her clothes are stripped off in the dream, Perpetua looks down to see a
phallus—a reading, as we have seen, not supported by the *Passio* itself but widely
assumed by numerous readers. I thus assert that, for the past 1600 years, most
readers and scholars have been understanding the story of St. Perpetua as told by
St. Augustine, not as told by the martyr herself.

It has become axiomatic that, with the legalization of Christianity in the
early fourth century, what was once a diffuse faith with diverse practices became
codified and institutionalized; in the process it also established as Church doctrine many of the patriarchal assumptions of the Roman culture it inherited.
As a result, many of our assumptions about how gender was understood in the
earliest Christian centuries have, I argue, been unduly influenced by the arguments that eventually won in the fourth and fifth centuries. For example, recent
work on the misnaming of Montanism, due to late antique sexist assumptions
about the relative importance of Priscilla, Maximilla, and Montanus in this
early Christian religious movement, also shows that later theological assumptions about the binary and hierarchical nature of gender are not always accurate
representations of the gender assumptions held by early Christians themselves.[45]
Perpetua's own text and the later rewritings of her story demonstrate the het-
erogeneity of conceptions of gender circulating in the ancient and late antique
Mediterranean—including the privileging of women's prophesy in Montanism
from Anatolia, the ideas of angelic androgyny in Syria, the Gnostic conceptions
of primordial androgyny current in the eastern Mediterranean and Egypt, and
Paul's and Mark's suggestions of an apocalyptic eradication of gender. In addi-

---

[43] Augustine, Sermon 282, chap. 4: Schiller, Weber, and Weidmann, "Sechs Neue
Augustinuspredigten."

[44] Gillette, "Augustine and the Significance of Perpetua's Words." It is worth keeping in mind that Gillette, writing in 2001, did not have access to this particular portion
of Sermon 282, as only an abridged version was known before 2007.

[45] Trevett, *Montanism*.

tion, the dissemination of the multiple versions of Perpetua's story across the Mediterranean and throughout the Middle Ages shows the continued circulation of ideas about gender during this period.[46] While it is certainly true that the classical cultures within which Christianity first appeared were often themselves deeply patriarchal and misogynist, Christians in the first centuries often defined themselves precisely by their difference from and rejection of the surrounding cultures; we should not, therefore, necessarily assume the rejection of patriarchal norms and gender categories was immediately more improbable than, for instance, the rejection of a polytheistic world view.

Rather, the incorporation of the ideals of a patriarchal, hierarchized binary gender system in the Christian Mediterranean was, I argue, the result of several centuries of development and debate amongst the men (and they were men) who would ultimately come to be seen as "The Fathers of the Church." At the time, however, they were prominent but not unique men, exerting considerable effort to swim upstream against several currents of early Christian thought that offered other possibilities for configuring the sex/gender system.

Bibliography

Amat, Jacqueline, ed. *Passion de Perpétue et de Félicité suivi des Actes.* Sources Chrétiennes 417. Paris: Éditions du Cerf, 1996.

Ambrose, St. *Expositionis in evangelius secundum Lucum libri,* in *Patrologiae cursus completus, Series Latina,* ed. J.-P. Migne. 221 vols. Paris, 1841–1885. 15:1844.

Bal, Mieke. "Perpetual Contest." In *On Story-Telling: Essays in Narratology,* ed. Mieke Bal and David Jobling, 227–41. Sonoma, CA: Polebridge Press, 1991.

———. "Perpetual Contest." In *Perpetua's Passions: Multidisciplinary Approaches to the Passio Perpetuae et Felicitatis,* ed. Jan Bremmer and Marco Formisano, 134–49. New York: Oxford University Press, 2012.

Bremmer, Jan N., and Marco Formisano, eds. *Perpetua's Passions: Multidisciplinary Approaches to the Passio Perpetuae et Felicitatis.* New York: Oxford University Press, 2012.

———. "Perpetua's Passions: A Brief Introduction." In *Perpetua's Passions: Pluridisciplinary Approaches to the Passio Perpetuae et Felicitatis,* ed. Jan N. Bremmer and Marco Formisano, 1–13. New York: Oxford University Press, 2012.

---

[46] The *Passio* comes to us in nine extant Latin manuscripts and one Greek, with provenances ranging from Jerusalem to England; see Heffernan, *The Passion of Perpetua and Felicity,* 370 and following. The *Acta* were apparently far more popular in the Middle Ages and survive in forty-one manuscripts (Heffernan, 442). Augustine's sermons, of course, would have circulated widely. In addition, there were numerous other later retellings and adaptations of Perpetua's story, which I survey in Cotter-Lynch, *St. Perpetua across the Middle Ages.*

Brown, Peter. *The Body and Society: Men, Women, and Sexual Renunciation in Early Christianity*, Lectures on the History of Religions 13. New York: Columbia University Press, 1988.

Cobb, L. Stephanie. *Dying to Be Men: Gender and Language in Early Christian Martyr Texts*. New York: Columbia University Press, 2008.

Conant, Jonathan P. "Europe and the African Cult of Saints, circa 350–900: An Essay in Mediterranean Communications." *Speculum* 85, no. 1 (2010): 1–46.

Cooper, Kate. "A Father, a Daughter and a Procurator: Authority and Resistance in the Prison Memoir of Perpetua of Carthage." *Gender & History* 23, no. 3 (2011): 685–702.

Cotter-Lynch, Margaret. *St. Perpetua across the Middle Ages: Mother, Gladiator, Saint*. New York: Palgrave MacMillan, 2016.

Dronke, Peter. *Women Writers of the Middle Ages: A Critical Study of Texts from Perpetua to Marguerite Porete*. Cambridge, UK: Cambridge University Press, 1984.

Elliott, Dyan. *The Bride of Christ Goes to Hell: Metaphor and Embodiment in the Lives of Pious Women, 200–1500*. Philadelphia: University of Pennsylvania Press, 2012.

Gillette, Gertrude. "Augustine and the Significance of Perpetua's Words: And I Was a Man." *Augustinian Studies* 32, no. 1 (2001): 115–25.

Gold, Barbara. "Gender Fluidity and Closure in Perpetua's Prison Diary." *EuGeStA* 1 (2011): 237–51.

Halporn, J. W. "Literary History and Generic Expectations in the *Passio* and *Acta Perpetuae*." *Vigiliae Christianae Vigiliae Christianae* 45, no. 3 (1991): 223–41.

Heffernan, Thomas J. *The Passion of Perpetua and Felicity*. New York: Oxford University Press, 2012.

Jerome, St., *Commentarius in Epistolam ad Ephesios*, in *Patrologiae cursus completus, Series Latina*, ed. J-P. Migne. 221 vols. Paris, 1841–1885. 26:567a.

Kitchen, John. "Going to the Gate of Life: The Archaeology of the Carthage Ampitheatre and Augustine's Sermons on Saints Perpetua and Felicitas." In *Speculum Sermonis: Interdisciplinary Reflections on the Medieval Sermon*, ed. Georgiana Donavin, Cary J. Nederman, and Richard Utz, 29–54. Turnhout: Brepols, 2004.

Kleinberg, Aviad. *Flesh Made Word: Saints' Stories and the Western Imagination*. Translated by Jane Marie Todd. Cambridge, MA: Belknap Press of Harvard University Press, 2008.

Martin, Dale B. *The Corinthian Body*. New Haven: Yale University Press, 1995.

Martyn, James Louis. *The Anchor Bible 33a*. Edited by William Foxwell Albright and David Noel Freedman. New York: Doubleday, 1997.

McInerney, Maud Burnett. *Eloquent Virgins from Thecla to Joan of Arc*. New York: Palgrave MacMillan, 2003.

Newman, Barbara. *From Virile Woman to Womanchrist: Studies in Medieval Religion and Literature*. Philadelphia: University of Pennsylvania Press, 1995.

Salisbury, Joyce E. *Perpetua's Passion: The Death and Memory of a Young Roman Woman*. New York: Routledge, 1997.

Schiller, Isabella, Dorothea Weber, and Clemens Weidmann. "Sechs Neue Augustinuspredigten Teil 1 Mit Edition Dreier Sermones." *Weiner Studien* 121 (2008): 227–84.

Trevett, Christine. *Montanism: Gender, Authority, and the New Prophecy*. Cambridge, UK: Cambridge University Press, 1996.

van Beek, Cornelius Johannes Maria Joseph. *Passio Sanctarum Perpetuae et Felicitatis*. Nijmegen: Dekker & Van de Vegt, 1936.

Williams, Craig. "Perpetua's Gender. A Latinist Reads the *Passio Perpetuae Et Felicitatis*." In *Perpetua's Passions: Multidisciplinary Approaches to the Passio Perpetuae et Felicitatis*, ed. Jan N. Bremmer and Marco Formisano, 54–77. New York: Oxford University Press, 2012.

Chapter 3
VISIONS, FEMALE SEXUALITY, AND SPIRITUAL LEADERSHIP IN BYZANTINE ASCETIC LITERATURE OF THE SIXTH AND SEVENTH CENTURIES

BRONWEN NEIL,
MACQUARIE UNIVERSITY

In late antique Christianity, in both halves of the Mediterranean, the Byzantine East and the Roman West, opportunities for female leadership narrowed, as charismatic and domestic churches were replaced by clerical orders from the third century onward. In spite of the flourishing cults of charismatic female leaders such as Jesus' disciple Mary Magdalene,[1] the martyrs Perpetua and Felicity, discussed in Chapter 2 above,[2] and Thecla, legendary companion of the Apostle Paul,[3] the leadership of women in both eastern and western churches never regained the acceptance that it had enjoyed in the earliest centuries of Christianity in the domestic church context.

Instead, in the imperial Church established by Constantine the Great, spiritual leadership was most commonly exercised only by those sanctioned by an official Church order, increasingly institutionalized and hierarchical in nature, and was ultimately governed by the newly converted Christian Byzantine

---

[1] On the early cult of Mary Magdalene, who was first identified with the sinner of Luke 7:37–50 by Gregory the Great (590–604) and also with Mary of Bethany, sister of Martha, see Jansen, "Mary Magdalen," 531–34. The Byzantine church rejected this composite figure. However, a Byzantine story that identified that Mary with Mary of Egypt, the desert eremitic who appears in the *Apophthegmata Patrum*, gained currency in ninth-century Italy: Jansen, "Mary Magdalen," 532.

[2] It is likely that Perpetua, who prophesied her death at the hands of imperial officials in Carthage ca. 203, and her companion Felicity belonged to the New Prophecy movement founded by Montanus in Asia Minor in the 170s, as argued by Butler, *The New Prophecy and "New Visions."*

[3] On the popular cult that grew out of the apocryphal legend, *The Acts of Paul and Thecla*, see Davis, *The Cult of Saint Thecla*.

emperors and those bishops instituted with their approval. Some opportunities for female leadership, however, continued to exist in the monastic milieu across the Mediterranean. Ascetic leaders were less constrained than clerics, since their withdrawal from the world allowed them to focus on pursuit of divine things, but even *abbas* (spiritual fathers) and *ammas* (spiritual mothers) were governed by monastic rules if they lived in communities. Only the solitaries in the Egyptian desert managed to escape hierarchy (Gk. *taxis*) altogether and to live according to the law of the Holy Spirit. This afforded more gender parity, at least theoretically. The monastic milieu offered the most opportunities for women to exercise spiritual authority, although, as we shall see, literary representations of such women were strictly limited by the literary conventions that governed the genre of hagiography.

My concern is with the ascetic dream literature produced in the sixth to seventh centuries, in both the eastern and western churches. As religious leadership roles for ascetic women grew, so too did their representation as prophetic dreamers become more frequent. However, their prophecy was limited to the sphere of the afterlife and was a far cry from that exercised by the early martyrs. This can partially be explained by the extremely strong desire of bishops and monks to limit the expression of female sexuality, even by consecrated virgins and widows, and its impact on the men around them. Only by interrogating the above-mentioned sources on the differences and similarities between eastern and western Christian perceptions of dreams and their spiritual value can we evaluate what they contribute in the way of evidence for a Mediterranean theory of dreaming.

Towards a Gendered Theory of Mediterranean Dreaming

Gender studies usually have an agenda of social reform and point to disparities of power reflected both in gendered dreaming and in the interpretative strategies applied to them. Dream accounts are particularly relevant to the study of gender in any society, since they represent the desires of ordinary men and women, their "social aspirations and anxieties," as Suzanne McAlister observed.[4] The earliest surviving example of the genre of dream-key manuals, the *Oneirocritica* of Artemidorus of Ephesus, was frequently copied, with modifications, by Greek Christian authors in the first millennium and beyond.[5] It was Michel Foucault who famously brought Artemidorus to the attention of scholars of power relations

---

[4] MacAlister, "Gender as Sign."

[5] MacAlister, "Gender as Sign," gives a good introduction to Artemidorus, the second-century writer from Daldis in Asia Minor, who later settled in Ephesus. On Byzantine *oneirocritica* in general, see Oberhelman, "The Dream-Key Manuals of Byzantium."

in the ancient world.[6] Male and female dreamers' dream contents as portrayed in the Byzantine dream-key manuals (*oneirocritica*)—and their ascribed meanings—reveal power relations, and especially power relations between the sexes, in the early medieval Greek world. The enormous impact of Foucauldian analysis was a prequel to the development of the study of dreams in post-modern gender studies, whether social-psychological,[7] psychoanalytical,[8] anthropological,[9] or multi-disciplinary.[10] However, the dreams of Byzantine women have received little attention, compared with Islamic or western studies of the same period.[11] Western Mediterranean female dreamers and visionaries have been particularly well served, as shown by recent studies of Perpetua, Felicity, and the Montanist prophetesses of the New Prophecy movement, which arose in Asia Minor and North Africa in the late second and third centuries,[12] out of the Mediterranean Christian domestic church movement of the first and second centuries. In the early Christian Mediterranean, religious leadership outside the organized Church was based on the charismatic gifts of prophecy, preaching, speaking in tongues, or the interpretation of tongues. This kind of spiritual authority was much more accessible to women than institutional authority, and by its very nature less able to be co-opted by men. Some degree of institutionalization occurred even in the charismatic movements, however. The Montanists seem to have developed their own hierarchy of regional bishops, and they may have

---

[6] Foucault, *Histoire de la sexualité III*. See also Winkler, *The Constraints of Desire*, 23–44, who used the methods of feminist anthropology, combined with close textual analysis of the Greek text of Artemidorus in its historical context, to uncover the public meanings of sexual dreams in second-century Greek culture.

[7] E.g., the gender content analysis of contemporary American women's dreams by Rupprecht, "Sex, Gender, and Dreams." A comparative study of women's and men's dreams in East Africa, by Monroe, Monroe, Brasher et al., "Sex Differences in East African Dreams," showed that women dreamed as often as men of physical aggression and more often of verbal aggression.

[8] Catia Galatariotou offers a Freudian analysis of Michael Psellos' and his mother's dreams of his future, in "Psychoanalysis and Byzantine *Oneirographia*."

[9] See Stewart, "Erotic Dreams and Nightmares from Antiquity to the Present," a diachronic study of the use of ritual artefacts to induce sexual dreams.

[10] See Tedlock, "Gender Ambiguity in Dreams of Conversion, Prophecy and Creativity," a cross-cultural, cross-disciplinary study of gender ambiguity drawing its materials from the ancient Greeks to the indigenous peoples of South Dakota. See also the collected essays edited by Stephen M. Oberhelman, *Dreams, Healing and Medicine in Greece from Antiquity to the Present*.

[11] Maria Mavroudi attributes this to the former's relevance to the contemporary issue of women's status in Islamic societies: "Byzantine and Islamic Dream Interpretation," 163 n. 9.

[12] E.g., Butler, *The New Prophecy*; Trevett, *Montanism*.

allowed female clergy, as Epiphanius of Salamis charged in 375 CE.[13] Epiphanius also objected to their conceptualization of the Holy Spirit in female form. The prophetess Quintilla or Priscilla reported that even Christ came to her "under the appearance of a woman, dressed in a white robe and imbued with wisdom."[14] It is in this context that we find the Church represented as an old woman in the *Shepherd of Hermas*, another apocryphal text of the second century. However, the Montanist movement did not survive the fifth century. In spite of the continuing flourishing of cults of individual holy women, such as Mary Magdalene and St. Thecla, the leadership of women in both eastern and western Mediterranean churches never regained the acceptance that it had enjoyed in the earliest centuries of Christianity.

Methodological Considerations

Today, scholars of gender relations in the Byzantine world, such as Liz James, recognize that the concept of gender goes further than 'male' and 'female' biological sex. James notes that such a fluid concept invites us to see masculinity and femininity as constructions of society rather than biological necessities.[15] Contemporary thinking on the question of sex and gender sees biological sex as a given, albeit one that can be surgically changed, while gender slides on a spectrum that does not correlate with biological sex.[16] The Church Fathers who authored the texts under discussion here would have agreed that gender and sex need not correlate, but for them it was a matter of sublimating sexuality altogether in order to attain 'perfect' male gender. For them, gender was a given; sex was mutable.[17] Whereas bodies could change because they belonged to the transient realm of 'becoming,' gender as the social meaning attributed to the body was eternal, according to early Christian thinkers. To change one's gender status required transformation of the body, usually achieved through ascetic practices, thereby making oneself a "eunuch for the kingdom of God." Some ascetics took this ideal literally and resorted to self-castration, as in the case of Origen of Alexandria (d. ca. 254). Others found themselves spiritually castrated through angelic interventions in visions, as we shall see below.

---

[13] Epiphanius of Salamis, "Anacephalaeosis IV," *Panarion* 49.1: "[Pepuzians, also known as Quintillianists] allow women to rule and act as priests," trans. Frank Williams, *Panarion of Epiphanius of Salamis*, 1; idem, "Montanists," *Panarion* 48.2.1–8 and 48.12.3–5 [on the prophetesses Priscilla and Maximilla], trans. Williams, 7–8 and 17–18.

[14] "Pepuzians or Quintillianists," *Panarion* 49.1.3; trans. Williams, 22; see Trevett, *Montanism*, 185–86.

[15] James, *Women, Men, and Eunuchs*, xvii.

[16] E.g., Casey, "The Spiritual Valency."

[17] Casey, "The Spiritual Valency," 171.

First, a few words on how *visions* were defined in late antiquity may be useful to the reader, as the term was understood in a different sense from its modern usage.[18] Most western patristic writers, including Jerome, Ambrose, and Gregory the Great, used the terms *vision* and *dream* interchangeably, while others, such as the fifth-century pagan Macrobius and the Christian convert Synesius, later bishop of Cyrene, made more precise distinctions between the two.[19] I have used *vision* here to mean a type of dream that can be divinely or demonically inspired and that can occur during sleep or in a waking or semi-waking state.

In what follows, we are dealing with reported, not necessarily real, visions. Given the didactic function of spiritual literature generally, and hagiography in particular, this is to be expected. The reader of Byzantine and western saints' *vitae* was expected to recognize the biblical tropes at play in the lives of its heroes and occasional heroines. The saints were portrayed as examples for imitation, and thus their actions, their conversations, and even their visions were heavily edited or invented to show how their lives conformed to those of Christ and the apostles and those of the Hebrew prophets and patriarchs before them. As a corollary, their misdeeds and shortcomings were also held up as warnings to the reader of what could happen when he or she departed from the spiritual path. It is in this context that visions most frequently appear, as part of the narrative of the winding road to perfection. Sin, in the case of women, is mostly frequently portrayed as sexual sin. It is this basic misogynist understanding of women that informs their representations in both the *Dialogues* of Gregory the Great and the *Sayings* of the Egyptian desert elders. Even the title of the latter, the *Apophthegmata Patrum*, indicates that the very few women who were represented could be conveniently subsumed under the term *fathers*.

Interpreting Byzantine Sources on Dreaming

The collected sayings of the monks and nuns who inhabited the Egyptian desert from the end of the third century onwards constitute a subgenre of hagiography. These sayings have been preserved by unknown sources, in several collections, most notably the *Apophthegmata Patrum*, preserved in Greek, Coptic, Syriac, and later in Latin. First written down ca. 500 but with additions being made into the

---

[18] Further methodological considerations for the study of ancient dreams and their interpretation have been canvassed by Neil in "Studying Dream Interpretation from Early Christianity to the Rise of Islam." See also Perato Rivas, "Dreams in Evagrius of Pontus' Life and Teaching," forthcoming. I am grateful to the author for allowing me to cite his as-yet-unpublished article.

[19] Stroumsa, "Dreams and Visions in Early Christian Discourse," 189–90, insists on the impossibility of distinguishing between dreams and visions in early Christian discourses.

seventh century, they include the sayings of monks and nuns from St. Antony to the sixth-century Abba Phocas. Although the sayings and actions attributed to the desert mothers Sarah, Syncletica, Pelagia, and the ambiguously gendered Athanasia/Athanasios were not necessarily ever uttered or performed by histori-cal women, their inclusion in improving literature for men and women illustrates the wish to present biblical principles of a godly life for women.

Like the *Apophthegmata*, the *Dialogues* attributed to Gregory the Great[20] enjoyed wide distribution through its translation into a number of languages, and first of all into Greek by Zacharias, the last Greek bishop of Rome (741–52).[21] This work properly belongs to a Byzantine ascetic context, since Gregory, although a bishop of Rome for fifteen years, understood himself as a bishop of the Byzantine church, and a loyal subject of the Byzantine emperor;[22] like many Greek bishops, he was more inclined to the life of an ascetic and recluse than to life as a governor and public figure.

We will see below that there are unexpected parallels between these two texts in their portrayal of women in visions. Any conclusions are of course neces-sarily constrained by the paucity of sources now available to us. However, the fact that the *Anonymous Collection of Sayings of the Desert Elders* was compiled over a period of more than a century suggests that it was indicative of early Byzantine views on ascetic women. Similarly, the *Dialogues* of Gregory cite stories, orally transmitted, from several generations of holy men and women of the sixth cen-tury and therefore may be considered an index of what was considered important enough to preserve in Italy. Moreover, the lasting popularity of both works, as witnessed by their translations into many other languages, shows that they were considered formative and useful beyond their immediate contexts of composition.

Since visions lay outside of the usual practices of the mainstream Church of the sixth and seventh centuries, it is almost impossible to access visionary repre-sentations except in hagiography, the lives of the saints. My focus is on a subset of that literature, the lives of ascetics who embraced a celibate life, whether in their own homes, as solitaries in the desert, or in larger communities. It is to ascetic literature that I now turn.

---

[20] On the recent scholarly debate over the attribution of this work to Gregory I, see Lake, "Hagiography and the Cult of Saints," esp. 225–26. Lake defends the attribution to Gregory and dates the work to between 593 and 594 (p. 227). Even those who doubt Gregory's authorship, most conspicuously Francis Clarke, recognize that the work was composed no later than the seventh century.

[21] Medieval translations included Anglo Saxon (9th century); Old French (by the 12th century), and Middle Dutch (13th century). See Mews and Renkin, "The Legacy of Gregory the Great in the Latin West," 316.

[22] Booth, "Gregory and the Greek East," demonstrates the degree to which Gregory became embedded in the Byzantine church and its networks through his years spent as papal emissary (*apocrisiarius*) in Constantinople before he became bishop of Rome in 590.

Byzantine Asceticism and "Dream Women"

"A monk who encountered some nuns on the road withdrew from the road. Their leader said to him: 'If you were a perfect monk you would not have noticed that we are women.'"[23] Reported utterances like this quotation from the *Apophtheg-mata Patrum* show that, in Byzantine Christianity, the ascetic life idealized male bodies and male gender as the spiritual peak of human existence. Similarly, reported visions show what monks really thought or were supposed to think about women: women and girls uniformly appeared in monks' visions as tempters, agents, and provocatrices. What can this reveal to the contemporary reader about how the female gender and women's leadership were viewed in Byzantine monastic spirituality?

Spiritual advisers in Byzantine monastic communities had to deal with the problem that even very advanced monks reported spiritually challenging visions. The most frequently cited teacher on this subject is Evagrius of Pontus (d. 399), who often reminded his readers how easily demons could cause monks (male and, by implication, female) to have erotic visions, which could result in sinful nocturnal emissions.[24] Such apparitions took various forms, including beautiful women, comely youths, and black Africans or Egyptians. The *APanon* even presents an account of a demon who appeared to Abba Apollo, who saw "a tall person, completely naked, with a black face horrible to behold, ... androgynous, black as soot, with thick lips and a woman's breasts and huge testicles and having a body like an ass."[25] The demon then transformed into a very beautiful naked woman who invited him to satisfy his lusts. Lustful fantasies were just one of the ways in which demons could trouble the desiring and irascible parts of the soul, in order to wage war on the monk, as Evagrius warns in *On Thoughts*.[26] However, the *APanon* is more forgiving of such incidents. Wet dreams were, according to

---

[23] *The "Anonymous" Sayings of the Desert Fathers* [hereafter cited as *APanon*] 154/4.75, ed. and trans. Wortley, 104–5 [emendation correct?].

[24] Perato Rivas, "Dreams in Evagrius of Pontus' Life and Teaching," describes the process of the formation of dream images in Evagrian thought, and their close relationship with the workings of the eight *logismoi* or passionate trains of thought. With great psychological insight, Evagrius shows how images, memories, and stories are interwoven in waking dreams when the monk is assailed by *logismoi*. See Evagrius, *Antirrhêtikos* (an introduction to which is found in the translation of David Brakke, *Evagrius of Pontus. Talking Back*); and Evagrius, *Logismoi* [hereafter cited as *On Thoughts*] 27–29, trans. Sinkewicz, *Evagrius of Pontus. The Greek Ascetic Corpus*, 172–74.

[25] *APanon* 729, ed. and trans. Wortley, 582–85.

[26] Evagrius, *On Thoughts* 27, trans. Sinkewicz, 172: "[I]n the night time during sleep they fight with winged asps, are encircled by carnivorous wild beasts, entwined by serpents, and cast down from high mountains. It sometimes happens that even after they awake they are encircled by the same wild beasts, and see their cave all afire and filled with smoke. And when they do not give in to these fantasies nor give in to cowardice,

an anonymous elder, the equivalent of nose-wiping, and they were to be brushed off without any concern, because they did not "impose any defilement on you. If however, the enemy sees you apprehensive, he will attack even more. But take care not to give in to the desire when you return to consciousness."[27]

Augustine of Hippo also used the term *illusion* (*inlusio*) for demonic intrusion in waking dreams, which came to have erotic overtones from then on, creating an automatic link between erotic dreams and nightmares.[28] The appearance of demons in erotic visions was more than a mental representation; it was viewed as an actual intervention from the demonic realm, as Charis Messis points out.[29] Such visions were a barometer of the monk's (or nun's) spiritual state. Males' sexual sins were readily associated with women, and women's sins were most often construed in this literature as sexual.

Women could exert spiritual authority in some ascetic contexts, whether as solitaries or as leaders and members of female communities. Ascetic leadership offered an alternative domain of spiritual authority to the ecclesial orders, and one which was at least theoretically more open to women. The consecration of male and female virgins in the fourth century, especially popular among aristocratic women and girls in Rome, Gaul, and North Africa, was considered "white" martyrdom, compared to the "red martyrdom" of the persecuted Christians in the second to early fourth centuries. These were lay people who consecrated themselves to God's service within the household, through prayer and fasting and chastity, and often remained living at home with their parents. They were usually wealthy aristocratic women whose inherited wealth and property was left to the Church upon their deaths. Consequently, they were extremely valuable to bishops, not just in spiritual terms, and their stories were carefully preserved as examples to other wealthy women in hagiographic texts such as the *Dialogues* and the *Apophthegmata*.

Prophetic Visions in the *Dialogues*

Gregory the Great's *Dialogues*[30] are full of such householder virgins who experience prophetic visions, usually of their own impending death. Prophetic visions are those that convey a divine message, one which can relate to the present or

---

they in turn see the demons immediately transform into women who conduct themselves with wanton indecency and want to play shameful games."

[27] *APanon* 605, ed. and trans. Wortley, 486–87.

[28] Elliott, *Fallen Bodies*, 20.

[29] Messis, "Fluid Dreams, Solid Consciences," 194: "Hence, temptation-filled dreams are usually not described as dream-like but as true experiences."

[30] On the cult of Roman martyrs in Gregory's day, and his desire to rein in its focus on the gore of the martyrs' deaths and portray them rather as models of virtuous living

the future. They are commonly described as being vehicles by which the Holy Spirit speaks or by which angels speak on its behalf. Most of Gregory's prophetic visionaries predict their own deaths, following the example set by the greatest saint of the *Dialogues*, Benedict of Nursia, whose exploits are the subject of Book 2. Benedict also had a vision of the soul of his sister, the saintly Scholastica, ascending to heaven at the time of her death.[31] Most of Gregory's examples of women foretelling their own or their sisters' ends appear in Book 4, which is concerned with the afterlife. Gregory related how a young girl called Musa saw a vision of the Virgin Mary surrounded by "little girls of her own age dressed in white." Mary encouraged Musa to give up the girlish vices of laughter and foolishness and to adopt a life of sobriety and self-restraint, if the girl wanted to join her heavenly court of virgins. Musa did so, and thirty days later, apparently healthy, gave up her life and was taken up to heaven.[32] Similar portents were seen by Romula, a consecrated virgin who was paralyzed and bed-ridden for many years in the home she shared with another unnamed virgin and their leader, an aged woman called Redempta who "lived as a recluse in the mountains of Praeneste." Romula's death, which was foretold in a vision, was accompanied by heavenly music of the psalms and a pleasant odor.[33] Gregory's aunt Tarsilla is said to have seen a vision of her forebear, Pope Felix III (483–492), who summoned her home to heaven. Shortly afterwards, she too died.[34] A curious tale is told of Galla, a young and wealthy widow who eschewed a second marriage in favor of an ascetic life in seclusion in the convent of the Church of St. Peter. A girl of a "very passionate nature," Galla began to grow a beard and was told that her only hope of stopping the hirsuitism was to remarry. Nevertheless she persisted in her life of celibacy, preferring "a spiritual marriage with the Lord" alongside several other women, one of whom was her particular friend. So close was their bond that when she received news from St. Peter in a vision that she would very soon die of breast cancer, she begged for her fellow nun, Benedicta, to be taken to heaven at the same time. St. Peter refused to grant this request instantly, but allowed another sister to die with Galla, promising that Benedicta would soon follow. A month later, Galla's bereaved companion also died and joined her sister in heaven.[35]

---

for emulation in the present, see Leyser, "Roman Martyr Piety in the Age of Gregory the Great."

[31] Gregory I, *Dialogues* [hereafter cited as *Dial.*] 2.34, trans. Zimmerman, *Saint Gregory the Great: Dialogues*, 104.

[32] Gregory I, *Dial.* 4.18, trans. Zimmerman, 211–12.

[33] Gregory I, *Dial.* 4.16, trans. Zimmerman, 208–10.

[34] Gregory I, *Dial.* 4.16, trans. Zimmerman, 211. The same story is told in Gregory's *Homilies on the Gospels*, *Hom. Ev.* 2.38.15.

[35] Gregory I, *Dial.* 4.14, trans. Zimmerman, 205–6.

Not all the visions related by Gregory in this chapter portray such happy outcomes. Several deal with punishments after death, particularly of men and women who had been buried in churches, a mark of their high status in the Christian community. The degree of punishment they receive may seem to us out of all proportion to their faults. Chaste nuns are punished for "foolish talk" and "loose tongues" by hell fire. In such cases the punishment is only part time. In a sacristan's vision, in the church where a nun guilty of foolish talk was buried, she was cut down the middle, with one half burning and the other not. Two other nuns, reported as being of high birth and unable to embrace suitable humility in their lives as consecrated virgins, were seen by their ancient nurse to rise out of their tombs in the church each Sunday at the time when the priest called for non-communicants to leave the church before communion, as if they had been anathematized. This was on account of their insulting and uncharitable remarks to a layman who served them.[36] These stories served as warning to the noble virgins and widows against such lapses.

Other stories of sexual misdemeanors portray the male perpetrators as unable to resist the temptations of beautiful women, even nuns. One such unfortunate nun possessed "the sort of beauty that corrupts with the flesh."[37] A layman who raped a young girl in his home on the night after he had sponsored her baptism was given one more week to live, at which point he went straight to hell, which was obvious to all from the flames that gradually consumed his body in the grave.[38] Although Gregory stops short of blaming the victims of these unwanted attentions and assaults, it is clear that had all women been ugly or absent altogether, life would have been much easier for him and the monks and laymen he sought to govern.

The Desert Mothers and Fathers of the *Apophthegmata*

These stories from Byzantine Italy show uncanny similarities to those of the monks and nuns who inhabited the desert regions of Egypt from the end of the third century onwards, starting with Antony of Egypt (d. 356), and extending to the sixth-century with Abba Phocas. The sayings of the desert hermits are collected in the *Apophthegmata*. Three collections survive from the sixth century, preserved in Greek, Coptic, and Syriac versions and in a sixth-century Latin translation. Ammas Sarah and Syncletica were among the few desert mothers whose sayings were included in the *Alphabetical Collection* translated by Benedicta Ward. The sayings attributed to the desert mothers were not necessarily ever uttered by historical women, but their inclusion in monastic literature for the

---

[36] Gregory I, *Dial.* 2.23, trans. Zimmerman, 91–93.
[37] Gregory I, *Dial.* 1.4, trans. Zimmerman, 16–17.
[38] Gregory I, *Dial.* 4.33, trans. Zimmerman, 230–31.

edification of ascetic men and women tells us much about how early Christians regarded the relationship between gender and spiritual authority.

Also included in the *Apophthegmata* are stories of cenobitic monks and nuns, or those who lived in spiritual communities. In the 320s, under the guidance of the Holy Spirit, the Egyptian monk Pachomius set up chains of monasteries on military lines in upper Egypt, where each monk had his own cell and work to do for the community, such as making mats to sell, gardening, or pottery. The first was located in Tabennisi, north of Thebes. Under Pachomius' aegis, his sister Maria established a community of women, run along the same lines, but under his ultimate governorship. Obedience to the Pachomian rule, celibacy, and poverty were the primary values in these cenobitic communities, which offered an alternative to the solitary pursuit of the ascetic life by hermits, male and female, that had existed until then. Female communities of nuns were governed by an abbess, to whom absolute obedience was owed. The abbess had ultimate authority over every aspect of the lives of the women in her spiritual charge. One of these women, unnamed, was regarded as a drunkard in her community and was punished for it by her sisters in the convent. She slept outside on the ground and wore tattered rags. This ill treatment continued until Abba Daniel visited the monastery and saw the outcast sister keeping an all-night vigil in the courtyard where she slept "next to the toilets."[39] She had deliberately concealed her holiness from her sisters, relishing their scorn and ill treatment. As soon as her true identity was revealed, she slipped away from the monastery, disguised as a monk, and was never seen again. Great spiritual women were most easily recognized in hindsight.

As the inferior sex, women were seen as more subject to the weaknesses of the flesh than were men, and the discipline required for transcendence of the needs and desires of the body was considered to be "a manly virtue."[40] Thus the Egyptian desert mothers who triumphed over their inferior physical status in the solitary ascetic life could be seen as greater athletes than the men who achieved the same goal with fewer handicaps. The harsh conditions of desert life included lack of regular food and water and exposure to predations of wild beasts and to the elements, which together caused most of their outward female characteristics to fall away, such as the menstrual cycle; their breasts to shrivel; their hair to fall out or be shaved off. In a typical example, Abba Bessarion and an old man came upon a brother in a cave, who was engaged in plaiting a rope. The brother ignored their presence and continued with his task. On their return journey they looked for him again and found him dead in the cave. Bessarion and the old man took the body to bury it and discovered to their astonishment that the 'brother' was

---

[39] *APanon* 596, ed. and trans. Wortley, 458–61.
[40] Neil and Casey, "Religious Leaders: Late Antiquity," 804.

a woman.[41] Such female ascetics as the unnamed "brother" could be considered equal in spiritual terms to men, even excelling them in spiritual warfare. Similar was the mother of two who, after her young children died, received an assurance of their safe arrival in heaven from the martyr St. Julian in a vision. She joined a monastery of the Tabbenisiotes, in the Thebaid, and became a monk. Now called Abba Athanasius, her disguise was so complete that even her husband failed to recognize her: "How could he recognize such wasted beauty and one that looked like an Ethiopian?"[42] The pair travelled together to the Holy Places and then shared a cell in silence for twelve years, with the blessing of the elder who had first received Athanasia into his community. "The elder said to him, "Go, devote yourself to silence, and remain with the brother, for he is what a monk ought to be." Only on her death was her sex discovered. Then the entire city of Alexandria congregated to bury "the venerable remains of the blessed Athanasia with boughs and palms, glorifying God who had granted such perseverance to the woman."[43]

Such a manly woman was Candida, the third-century martyr who, refusing to marry the king of Persia, was subjected to sexually degrading tortures, including the removal of both breasts. Through this process of masculinization she became a figure of sexual ripeness, ready to be joined to her bridegroom in heaven, Christ. Strong locates the composition of Candida's *passio* as an intermediate step between the martyrdom of Perpetua, a young mother whose lack of virginity was not an issue (although through it she was joined with her heavenly spouse, according to the author of her *Passion*[44]), and Martha, whose voluntary chastity was the focus of her cult. The chaste "virgin-martyr" of later (sixth-century) east Syrian martyr commemorations was still in the process of being established as a *topos* when the *Passion* of Candida was written, an event that Strong places in the fourth or fifth century.[45] Strong observes that, since some east Syrian patristic writers celebrated God as mother and the Holy Spirit as female,[46] the appearance of a sexually transfigurative martyrdom such as Candida's could be expected, even as he notes that the "intertwining of such disso-

---

[41] *Apophthegmata: The Alphabetical Collection*, "Bessarion," trans. Benedicta Ward, *The Sayings of the Desert Fathers: The Alphabetical Collection*, 41.

[42] *APanon 596*, ed. and trans. Wortley, 450–51.

[43] *APanon 596*, ed. and trans. Wortley, 452–54.

[44] Candida, *Passio Perpetuae et Felicitatis* 18.2: "as a wife of Christ and darling of God" (. . . *ut matrona Christi, ut Dei delicata* . . .); ed. and trans. Heffernan, *The Passion of Perpetua and Felicity*, 119 (Latin) and 133 (Eng. trans.).

[45] Strong, "Candida, an Ante-Nicene Martyr in Persia," 394–95, presents several arguments, following Sebastian Brock, for an "early" date in the fourth century. The events are described as taking place in the third century, although an exact date cannot be determined due to the uncertain identity of the Persian king Shapur (I or II).

[46] E.g., *Odes of Solomon* 19, ed. and trans. Lattke, *Die Oden Salomos*, 78–81. The hymns of Ephrem the Syrian are another rich source of female images for the deity: Strong, "Candida," 407, n. 75.

nant images of feminine and masculine metaphors in martyr and hagiographic literature has long been a noted curiosity and defies a tidy explanation."[47] Certainly this theory would make sense of the portrayal of the few holy heroines of the sixth- and seventh-century *Apophthegmata*, whose martyrdoms are all white, not red. Assuming their record has not been suppressed in surviving sources, visions are conspicuously lacking from the accounts of desert mothers in the *Apophthegmata*.

Many of the women who ended up living as ascetics in the Egyptian desert were ordinary women who were reduced out of penury to a life of prostitution.[48] These cases are usually interpreted in Pauline terms as cautionary tales of falling victim to Satan, or the demon of fornication. Mary of Egypt was perhaps the most famous of these fallen women, whose repentance in the desert involved years of self-denial, wandering around homeless, eating berries and grasses. Through these deprivations her physical appearance became male, as did her spiritual gender. Another was Mary of Aega, a former prostitute who requested conversion, who features in the *Spiritual Meadow* of John Moschus, an early seventh-century collection of improving tales of monks, nuns and solitary seculars whom Moschus met on his travels through Palestine, Syria, and Egypt.[49] These stories, written in Greek, were translated into Latin in the same century and included in Book 10 of the *Vitae Patrum*.[50] They are another valuable witness to the continuity of Byzantine ascetic practices and common attitudes in Italy in this period.

The association between women and sexual sin is most noticeable in the frequent appearance of demons in female guise, in the visions of monks. These demon-women attempted to seduce sleeping monks when their guard was down. The *Anonymous Collection* tells of one monk who was tempted by four demons of *porneia* (fornication) in the shape of "most beautiful women [who] stayed for twenty days, wrestling with him to draw him into shameful intercourse."[51] The monk, having survived without succumbing, was given God's peace "no longer

---

[47] Strong, "Candida," 407.

[48] E.g., the prostitute who begged her brother, a monk, to deliver her from her sinful life in the city and take her with him to the desert. She repented for procuring "the destruction of many souls" and was forgiven posthumously by God, who revealed to one elder: "Because she was totally unconcerned with any matter of the flesh and also despised her own body, making no complaint at her great wound, for this reason I accepted her repentance": *APanon* 43 (BHG 1438h), ed. and trans. Wortley, 38–39.

[49] John Moschus, *Spiritual Meadow*, chap. 31, trans. Wortley, 22–23.

[50] The Latin version of *Vitae patrum* Book 10 is translated by Benedict Baker and can be found online at vitae-patrum.org.uk. Heribert Rosweyde's edition, *Vitae patrum de vita et verbis seniorum sive historiae eremiticae libri X*, has not been superseded by a modern edition.

[51] *APanon* 188/5.41, ed. and trans. Wortley, 132–33.

to burn in the flesh again." Sexual castration, in a non-literal sense, for monks was the happy result of successfully wrestling with the demons of the flesh. A similar tale is told in the *Spiritual Meadow*.[52] Castration was not, however, a state to which the eremitic women in these collections aspired. Such stories are conspicuously absent from the reported visions of nuns or female solitaries. However, even nuns and female hermits could be the unwitting, and unwilling, instigators of fornication. A secular anchoress in Alexandria put out her eyes rather than lead a would-be suitor into sin.[53] The young man was so shocked he went off to Scythia to become a monk. Another consecrated virgin in Jerusalem who was pursued by a man withdrew to the desert for seventeen years to avoid his unwanted attentions, eating only the few soaked beans she had taken with her, a meager supply that miraculously never ran out.[54]

The lack of reciprocity in such stories, and the one-sided desire of men for women, and seldom vice versa,[55] is a curious feature of both the *Apophthegmata* and the *Dialogues*. The women they describe are paragons of virtue. If they unintentionally lead men astray, they are not blamed for it. This may appear to be an improvement on the classical Greco-Roman stereotyping of female sexuality as rapacious and non-discriminating and something that women, as well as men, needed to be protected from. In the monastic literature of the sixth and seventh centuries, it is the men who need to be protected from their own desires, by the close watch of their superiors and continual examination of their consciences. However, such a "high" view of women deprives them of any agency and independent identity. A stunning example is the Alexandrian woman who sought to repel a would-be suitor by gouging out her own eyes, the feature that had first drawn him to her. The cost of gaining spiritual authority for ascetic women was the renunciation of sexual specificity.

---

[52] Presbyter Conon, in the Monastery of Saba, in the desert near Bethlehem, would not baptize women until John the Baptist appeared in a vision and took the battle away from him. Afterward, he never experienced any excitement of the flesh: *Spiritual Meadow*, ch. 3, trans. Wortley, 5–6.

[53] *Spiritual Meadow*, chap. 60, trans. Wortley, 46–47. The seculars discussed in the *Spiritual Meadow* were men and women who lived alone in their city households, in Constantinople, Jerusalem, and Alexandria.

[54] *Spiritual Meadow*, chap. 179, trans. Wortley, 148–49.

[55] A rare exception is *APanon* 37 (BHG 1318r), the tale of a wife who got *logismoi* for a young friend of her husband. Even this wife was virtuous enough to confess her situation to her husband. The desirable young man, who did not reciprocate her feelings, effaced his beauty by rubbing *lamnin* over his face and hair so that he looked like "an old leper." When the tempted wife saw his ugliness, "God removed the affliction from her": ed. and trans. Wortley, 30–33.

Conclusion

Our brief overview of women and gender in ascetic literature of the sixth and seventh centuries shows that the narrowing of roles for the female gender that is evident in the mainstream institutional Church of this period was not as drastic in the monastic sphere, with its prominent female abbesses, spiritual mothers, and consecrated virgins who assumed a white martyrdom. Visions of the afterlife played a powerful part in cementing that authority but also reinforced a view of women that was unbalanced and hyper-sexualized. The widely disseminated *Apophthegmata* and *Dialogues* placed an increased emphasis on the chastity of holy women, whether they were virgins or widows. While this emphasis may be seen from a contemporary perspective as a limiting of female identity, it was also a source of great spiritual power. There appears to be little difference between these Greek and Latin texts in regard to their portrayals of celibate female spiritual leaders.

Throughout this brief survey of the monastic texts of sixth- and seventh-century Byzantine hagiographers, we have seen that images of women in reported visions of holy men were usually negative. Women and girls most often appeared (at least in reported visions) as temptresses and tools of demonic delusion. In waking life, however, ascetic women were paragons of virtue, and stories of their heroic feats of self-deprivation served to shame both monks and nuns and to spur them on to greater heights of spiritual maleness. This ambivalence seems to have characterized both the Byzantine East and Italy under Byzantine rule in the time of Gregory the Great. In the closely guarded, male-dominated domain of spiritual authority that was typical of sixth- and seventh-century monasticism, the gift of female celibacy, constrained as it was, amounted to real spiritual and social power. Such power, it could be argued, was gained at the expense of earlier sources of charismatic authority.

Our analysis suggests that the narrowing of female roles within Mediterranean monasticism was closely associated with the smaller representations of women in the institutional Church leadership generally across the later Roman empire from the fourth century onwards. With the loss of charismatic movements such as the Montanists, female access to spiritual authority by being the recipients and narrators of divine visions also decreased across the Mediterranean. After the brief flourishing of female visionaries from the second century to fifth, the Greek and Latin sources under examination here show that the classical Greco-Roman suspicion of female sexuality won out over the Pauline Christian ideal of gender equality in monastic dreams, as in monastic life.

Bibliography

Primary Sources

Anon., *The Passion of Perpetua and Felicity*
The Passion of Perpetua and Felicity. Edited and translated by Thomas J. Heffernan. Oxford: Oxford University Press, 2012.

Apophthegmata: The Alphabetical Collection
The Sayings of the Desert Fathers: The Alphabetical Collection. Translated by Benedicta Ward. Rev. ed. London: Mowbray, 1981.

Apophthegmata: The Anonymous Collection (APanon)
The Anonymous Sayings of the Desert Fathers: A Select Edition and Complete English Translation. Edited and translated by John Wortley. Cambridge: Cambridge University Press, 2013.

Epiphanius of Salamis, *Panarion*
The Panarion of Epiphanius of Salamis: Books II and III. De Fide. Translated by Frank Williams. Rev. ed. Leiden: Brill, 2013.

Evagrius of Pontus, *Antirrhêtikos*
Evagrius of Pontus. Talking Back. Antirrhêtikos. A Monastic Handbook for Combating Demons. Translated by David Brakke. Collegeville, MN: Liturgical Press, 1989.

Evagrius of Pontus, *Logismoi*
On Thoughts. Translated by Robert Sinkewicz as *Evagrius of Pontus. The Greek Ascetic Corpus*. Oxford Early Christian Texts 153–82. Oxford: Oxford University Press, 2003.

Gregory the Great, *Dialogues*
Grégoire le Grand. Dialogues. Edited and translated by Adalbert de Vogüé and Paul Antin. Sources Chrétiennes 251, 260, and 265. Paris: Éditions du Cerf, 1978–1980.
Translated by Odo Zimmerman as *Saint Gregory the Great: Dialogues*. Fathers of the Church 39. Washington, DC: Catholic University of America Press, 1959.

John Moschus, *Pratum Spirituale*. Translated by John Wortley as *The Spiritual Meadow*. Cistercian Studies Series 139. Kalamazoo: Cistercian Publications, 1992.
Odes of Solomon. Edited and translated by Michael Lattke as *Die Oden Salomos. Griechisch-Koptisch-Syrisch mit deutscher Übersetzung*. Darmstadt: Wissenschaftliche Buchgesellschaft, 2011.

Vitae patrum. Edited by Heribert Rosweyde as *Vitae patrum de vita et verbis senio-rum sive historiae eremiticae libri X*. Antwerp: Officina Plantiniana, 1628. *Liber* 10, translated by Benedict Baker at vitae-patrum.org.uk (accessed 20 January 2016).

Secondary Sources

Booth, Phil. "Gregory and the Greek East." In *A Companion to Gregory the Great*, ed. Bronwen Neil and Matthew Dal Santo, 109–31. Leiden: Brill, 2013.

Butler, Rex D. *The New Prophecy and "New Visions": Evidence of Montanism in The Passion of Perpetua and Felicitas*. Patristic Monograph Series 18. Washington, DC: Catholic University of America Press, 2006.

Casey, Damien. "The Spiritual Valency of Gender in Byzantine Society." In *Questions of Gender in Byzantine Society*, ed. Bronwen Neil and Lynda Garland, 166–81. Farnham: Ashgate, 2013.

Davis, Stephen J. *The Cult of Saint Thecla: A Tradition of Women's Piety in Late Antiquity*. Oxford: Oxford University Press, 2001.

Elliott, Dyan. *Fallen Bodies: Pollution, Sexuality and Demonology*. Philadelphia: University of Pennsylvania Press, 1999.

Foucault, Michel. *Histoire de la sexualité III. Le souci de soi*. Paris, 1984. Translated by R. Hurley as *The Care of the Self. The History of Sexuality*, vol. 3. New York: Vintage, 1988.

Galatariotou, Catia. "Psychoanalysis and Byzantine *Oneirographia*." In *Dreaming in Byzantium and Beyond*, ed. Christine Angelidi and George T. Calofonos, 221–32. Farnham: Ashgate, 2014.

James, Liz, ed. *Women, Men, and Eunuchs: Gender in Byzantium*. London and New York: Routledge, 1997.

Jansen, Katherine Ludwig. "Mary Magdalen." In *Women and Gender in Medieval Europe: An Encyclopedia*, ed. Margaret Schaus, 531–34. London and New York: Routledge, 2006.

Lake, Stephen. "Hagiography and the Cult of Saints." In *A Companion to Gregory the Great*, ed. Bronwen Neil and Matthew Dal Santo, 225–46. Leiden: Brill, 2013.

Leyser, Conrad. "Roman Martyr Piety in the Age of Gregory the Great." In *The Roman Martyrs and the Politics of Memory*, ed. Kate Cooper. Special issue of *Early Medieval Europe* 9, no. 3 (2000): 289–307.

MacAlister, Suzanne. "Gender as Sign and Symbolism in Artemidorus' *Oneirokritika*: Social Aspirations and Anxieties." *Helion* 19 (1992): 140–60.

Mavroudi, Maria. "Byzantine and Islamic Dream Interpretation: A Comparative Approach to the Problem of 'Reality' vs 'Literary Tradition.'" In *Dreaming in Byzantium and Beyond*, ed. Christine Angelidi and George T. Calofonos, 161–86. Farnham: Ashgate, 2014.

Messis, Charis. "Fluid Dreams, Solid Consciences: Erotic Dreams in Byzantium." In *Dreaming in Byzantium and Beyond*, ed. Christine Angelidi and George T. Calofonos, 187–205. Farnham: Ashgate, 2014.

Mews, Constant J., and Claire Renkin. "The Legacy of Gregory the Great in the Latin West." In *A Companion to Gregory the Great*, ed. Bronwen Neil and Matthew Dal Santo, 316–42. Leiden: Brill, 2013.

Miller, Patricia Cox. *Dreams in Late Antiquity. Studies in the Imagination of a Culture.* Princeton: Princeton University Press, 1994.

Monroe, R. I., R. G. Monroe, A. Brasher et al. "Sex Differences in East African Dreams." *Journal of Social Psychology* 125 (1985): 405–6.

Neil, Bronwen. "An Introduction to Questions of Gender in Byzantium." In *Questions of Gender in Byzantine Society*, ed. Bronwen Neil and Lynda Garland, 1–10. Farnham: Ashgate, 2013.

———. "Studying Dream Interpretation from Early Christianity to the Rise of Islam." *Journal of Religious History* 40, no. 1 (2016): 44–64.

———, and Casey, Damien. "Religious Leaders: Late Antiquity." In *Oxford Encyclopaedia of the Bible and Gender Studies*, ed. Julia O'Brien, 804–6. New York: Oxford University Press, 2015.

Oberhelman, Stephen M., ed. *Dreams, Healing and Medicine in Greece from Antiquity to the Present.* Farnham: Ashgate, 2013.

———. "The Dream-Key Manuals of Byzantium." In *Dreaming in Byzantium and Beyond*, ed. Christine Angelidi and George T. Calofonos, 145–59. Farnham: Ashgate, 2014.

Perato Rivas, Rubén. "Dreams in Evagrius of Pontus' Life and Teaching." Forthcoming.

Rupprecht, Christine S. "Sex, Gender, and Dreams: From Polarity to Plurality." In *Among All These Dreamers. Essays on Dreaming and Modern Society*, ed. Kelly Bulkeley, 106–35. Albany: State University of New York Press, 1996.

Stewart, Charles. "Erotic Dreams and Nightmares from Antiquity to the Present." *Journal of the Royal Anthropological Institute* 8 (2002): 279–309.

Strong, Justin. "Candida, an Ante-Nicene Martyr in Persia." *Journal of Early Christian Studies* 23, no. 3 (2015): 389–412.

Stroumsa, Guy G. "Dreams and Visions in Early Christian Discourse." In *Dream Cultures: Explorations in the Comparative History of Dreaming*, ed. David D. Shulman and Guy G. Stroumsa, 189–212. New York: Oxford University Press, 1999.

Tedlock, Barbara. "Gender Ambiguity in Dreams of Conversion, Prophecy and Creativity." In *Dreaming in Byzantium and Beyond*, ed. Christine Angelidi and George T. Calofonos, 207–19. Farnham: Ashgate, 2014.

Trevett, Christine. *Montanism: Gender, Authority and the New Prophecy.* Cambridge: Cambridge University Press, 2002.

Winkler, John J. *The Constraints of Desire: The Anthropology of Sex and Gender in Ancient Greece.* New York: Routledge, 1990.

Chapter 4
Bearers of Islam:
Muslim Women between Assimilation
and Resistance in Christian Sicily

Sarah Davis-Secord,
University of New Mexico

The last few decades have seen a rise in interest in Muslim women's and gender history, much of it inspired by political and social concerns in the modern world. The topic of "women and Islam" has been the basis for a great deal of academic and non-academic discussion in recent decades, but many questions remain about women and gender in particular contexts within Muslim societies in the premodern world. In the early years of Muslim women's studies, much of the scholarship asked whether the coming of Islam fostered misogyny or brought about an improvement in the status of women. Therefore, much of the inquiry into the medieval period was directed toward an illumination or correction of the contemporary Muslim world, as when Fatima Mernissi wrote that "medieval religious history is crucial for contemporary Muslim politics."[1] A second strain of scholarship has sought to move away from employing normative categories such as "women" and "Islam" and toward contextualized study of women's lives within various medieval Islamic societies in order to bring to light the wide variety of

---

[1] Mernissi, "Women in Muslim History." See also Spellberg, "History Then, History Now"; and Meisami, "Writing Medieval Women." Foundational works of Islamic feminism include Mernissi, *The Veil and The Male Elite*; Ahmed, *Women and Gender in Islam*; Barlas, *"Believing Women" in Islam*; and Wadud, *Qur'ān and Woman*. Contemporary defenses of feminist readings of the medieval Islamic past include Afsaruddin, "Literature, Scholarship, and Piety"; and the response by Abugideiri, "Revisiting the Islamic Past, Deconstructing Male Authority."

women's roles in history.[2] Of particular interest is the question of women's agency within intellectual, economic, cultural, and religious contexts.[3]

At the same time, and also fueled by contemporary interests within a globalized world, much of the recent scholarship on the medieval Mediterranean world has focused on questions of ethnic identity and the fates of minority populations in multicultural regions. Less scholarship, however, has examined the intersections between religious identity and gender within cross-confessional environments, with many questions remaining about how the people of the multicultural Mediterranean viewed their religio-cultural identities in terms of gender distinctions.[4] What has been written on gender and religion in minority populations has focused on the rich multicultural environment of later medieval Iberia, while virtually none of the scholarship has examined the equally complex multicultural context of Sicily, due in large part to the far smaller number of available sources for the study of medieval Sicily.[5] Although the source base for Sicily is not as deep as that for Iberia, bits of evidence remain that can shed light on how women there participated in the shaping and transmission of distinct religio-cultural identities within Sicily's minority communities. This essay offers one perspective on how gender roles impacted cultural assimilation, or religious conversion, in the multicultural medieval Mediterranean, in particular within the minority Muslim population of twelfth-century Christian Sicily. For one male author,

---

[2] For the argument of why such contextualized study of women is necessary, see Kandiyoti, "Islam and Patriarchy"; and Doumato, "Hearing Other Voices." For contextualized studies of women and gender in a wide swath of times and places, see the various essays in Keddie and Baron, *Women in Middle Eastern History*; and Sonbol, *Beyond the Exotic*. Starting points for the historical study of women in medieval Islam are Berkey, "Women in Medieval Islamic Society"; Hambly, "Becoming Visible"; and Keddie, "The Past and Present of Women in the Muslim World."

[3] For one study of the legal and economic agency of Muslim minority women in Spain, see O'Connor, "Muslim Mudejar Women in Thirteenth-Century Spain." Also relevant are many of the works of David S. Powers on the ways in which Muslim women utilized the legal system to their advantage. For one example, see his "Women and Courts in the Maghrib."

[4] For analysis of this problem, possible avenues into the study of intercultural women's relationships, and references to some of the literature that has been published, see Green, "Conversing with the Minority." Good examples of the small body of literature on this topic for Iberian history include Fuente, "Christian, Muslim and Jewish Women in Late Medieval Iberia"; Melammed, "Crypto-Jewish Women Facing the Spanish Inquisition"; Perry, "Behind the Veil"; Perry, "Moriscas and the Limits of Assimilation"; and the articles in a special journal issue about cultural dialogue between Jewish, Muslim, and Christian women edited by Green.

[5] There exist several comprehensive studies of women in medieval Iberia: Marín, *Mujeres en Al-Ándalus*; López de la Plaza, *Al-Ándalus, mujeres, sociedad y religión*; Viguera, *"Aṣluḥu li'l-Maʿāli"*; and Viguera Molins, *La Mujer en Al-Ándalus*.

Ibn Jubayr, a Muslim traveler who visited Christian Sicily during the late twelfth century, Muslim women played pivotal roles as the bearers and preservers of a minority religious culture that he viewed as threatened with extinction through assimilation or religious conversion.

Ibn Jubayr and the Muslims of Norman Sicily

Muḥammad ibn Aḥmad ibn Jubayr (1145–1217 CE), a traveler and pilgrim from al-Andalus, composed his *Riḥla*, or travelogue, after his return from a two-year-long journey from Granada to Mecca and back.[6] His account purports to be a straightforward narrative of the journey to Mecca and back, but the genre of *riḥla* encompasses both a quest for knowledge and an accounting of the wonders and marvels (*ʿajāʾib*) that a traveler experienced in the world.[7] As such, Ibn Jubayr's travelogue described a world of experiences that were often amazing, strange, and disconcerting, including his encounters with Christians and with Muslims of other sects. Beyond a simple description of sights and encounters, indeed, Ibn Jubayr presented his Andalusi readers with a confirmation that their world, of Almohad-ruled Islam in the western Mediterranean, was the only place where a true practice of Islam was to be found: "Let it be absolutely certain and beyond doubt established that there is no Islam save in the Maghrib [Western] lands . . .There is no justice, right, or religion in His sight except with the Almohades."[8] The rest of the world, both within the *dār al-Islām* and in the recently conquered Christian regions of Sicily and the Levant, he found to be fractured by cultural and political disorder, poor practice of Islam, and a confounding (to him) mixture of religious traditions, all to the detriment of Islam.

The primary cause of this disunity in the world, even within the *dār al-Islām*, according to Ibn Jubayr, was *fitna*—a word that refers to disorder or civil war but also to "seduction" or "temptation" or anything leading to a breakdown in the proper order and unity of the universal Muslim community (*umma*). Inadequate Muslim leadership, which Ibn Jubayr called out in many of the regions he visited,

---

[6] Ibn Jubayr, *Riḥlat Ibn Jubayr*; English translation in Broadhurst, *The Travels of Ibn Jubayr*. The passages concerning Sicily are found in Ibn Jubayr, *Riḥlat Ibn Jubayr*, 292–316; Broadhurst, *The Travels of Ibn Jubayr*, 335–60. Biography and background on Ibn Jubayr the man and his travels can be found in Pellat, "Ibn Djubayr," 755; Netton, "Ibn Jubayr"; and Netton, "Basic Structures and Signs of Alienation in the *Riḥla* of Ibn Jubayr."

[7] For the basic description of *riḥla* as a journey in search of knowledge, see Netton, "Riḥla"; and Beckingham, "The *Riḥla*: Fact or Fiction?" For further elaboration of the development of this genre and its relationship to Islamic epistemology, see Touati, *Islam and Travel in the Middle Ages*. For the concept of "marvels," see Dubler, "ʿAdjāʾib."

[8] Broadhurst, *The Travels of Ibn Jubayr*, 73.

was one prominent source of *fitna* that was just as unsettling to him as unbelief or adherence to incorrect teachings. Conversion of lands or people from Islam to Christianity represented the ultimate chaos and upending of the proper order of things. Ibn Jubayr's text thus reflects anxiety about the breakdown and fracturing of the *dār al-Islām*, arising either from assimilation and conversion or from poor Muslim leadership and lawlessness within.

The final stop on his return journey was the island of Sicily, which had been seized from Muslim rule by the Latin Christian Normans about 100 years earlier. His trip across the northern portion of Sicily, lasting from late 1184 into early 1185, occurred during the reign of King William II (1166–1189), known as "the Good." Despite the fact that King William ruled over formerly Muslim territory, Ibn Jubayr initially thought highly of him as a ruler, having heard several rumors about the king's fondness for Muslim servants and concubines and about the ability of Muslims to live comfortably, if secretly, at court. In comparison to the Crusader Levant, the other region in which Ibn Jubayr encountered subjected Muslim communities, Sicily appeared strange to this traveler as a place where Muslims were free to live and worship as they pleased. Nonetheless, by the end of his three-month-long sojourn in Sicily, Ibn Jubayr came to the conclusion that Muslims there were subject to numerous difficulties, indignities, and pressures to convert to Christianity. The very act of living side by side with Christians was, according to Ibn Jubayr, a source of *fitna*: the upending of the proper order of the world and a temptation for subjected Muslims to convert to Christianity.

After nearly two centuries of inclusion in the Islamic world, Sicily was home to a population that was highly Islamized and Arabicized, with significant minority communities of Greek Christians and non-Arab Berbers (who were religiously Muslim).[9] When the Latin Christian invaders, usually called Normans, began their conquest of the island in the mid-eleventh century, many of the Arabic-speaking Muslims fled to regions that remained under Islamic rule, such as Egypt, Iberia, or North Africa. But, due to financial constraints, missed opportunities, or lack of desire to leave a familiar homeland for the unknown abroad, many Muslims remained in Sicily even after the Christian takeover. These Muslim families lived as a subjected minority community in a Christian land, despite general Islamic legal pronouncements about the necessity of emigration rather than remaining under infidel rule. According to Islamic legal thinking, Muslims were not meant to live in a subjected state, in which they would be cut off from the religious and civil support systems that allowed them to practice Islam fully and to maintain their linguistic, cultural, and religious

---

[9] On the problems with the characterization of these invaders as Normans, see Loud, "The 'Gens Normannorum'—Myth or Reality?"; and Loud, "How 'Norman' Was the Norman Conquest of Southern Italy?" For the Berber contribution to Islamic Sicily, see Chiarelli, *Islamic Sicily*.

customs.[10] The lack of a dominant Islamic culture presumably would leave these subjected Muslims vulnerable to various pressures to convert to Christianity or to lose their unique Muslim religious and cultural identity. These were the very fears expressed by both Ibn Jubayr and many of the Muslims whom he met in Sicily.

Despite these pressures and fears, Muslim communities remained in Sicily until the 1220s, when Frederick II forcibly relocated them to the mainland Italian colony of Lucera.[11] During the late eleventh and twelfth centuries, many of these Arabic-speaking Muslims in Sicily worked within the agricultural system of the island, and some served important roles in the Norman administration in Palermo.[12] The Norman royal court at Palermo also hosted Muslim scholars, poets, and scientists who contributed to a court culture that drew upon elements from both Sicily's Greek and Arabic populations as well as Latin imagery and art.[13] These Muslim intellectuals and their influence on the elite culture of Christian Sicily have made the island famous for its supposed multiculturalism and for the Normans' seemingly "tolerant" or even welcoming approach to the various religious communities in their realm.[14]

Many aspects of minority life in Sicily initially appeared to Ibn Jubayr to support this view of a tolerant Christian society. Under Norman rule, Muslim communities were allowed to practice their religious rituals, retain their local religious and civil leadership, and maintain many aspects of their unique cultural identity. During his time in Sicily, Ibn Jubayr witnessed much about life for the

---

[10] The Islamic legal consensus on this topic was referred to as the "obligation to emigrate." Scholarship on the topic, including medieval juristic debate on its necessity, includes Abou El Fadl, "Islamic Law and Muslim Minorities"; Davis-Secord, "Muslims in Norman Sicily"; Gertz, "Permission to Stay in 'Enemy' Territory?"; Lewis, "Legal and Historical Reflections"; Miller, "Muslim Minorities and the Obligation to Emigrate to Islamic Territory"; and Molénat, "Le problème de la permanence des Musulmans dan les territoires conquis par les Chrétiens."

[11] On this relocation and the colony of Muslims established at Lucera, see Taylor, *Muslims in Medieval Italy*; and Abulafia, "Monarchs and Minorities in the Christian Western Mediterranean around 1300."

[12] The seminal study of the Muslim agricultural workers on the estate of Monreale in western Sicily is found in Bercher, Courteaux, and Mouton, "Une abbaye latine dans la societe musulmane." For more recent work, see Johns, "The Boys from Messoiuso." On the role of Muslims officials, the Arabic language, and Islamic customs in Norman administrative system, see Metcalfe, "The Muslims of Sicily Under Christian Rule," esp. 300–302. A fuller examination of the Norman use of Islamic-style governmental practices is found in Johns, *Arabic Administration in Norman Sicily*.

[13] See, for example, Tronzo, *The Cultures of His Kingdom*; and Tronzo, *Intellectual Life at the Court of Frederick II Hohenstaufen*.

[14] Peyronnet, "Coexistence islamo-chrétienne en Sicile et au Moyen-Orient"; Dalli, "Contriving Coexistence."

native Muslims in this society that he described as good and fair. He noted, for example, that the Christians in one community allowed Muslims to celebrate a loud religious festival at the end of Ramadan. He remarked: "We marveled at this, and at the Christians' tolerance of it."[15] He also claimed that it was in one of these independent Muslim districts that he heard the call of the muezzin for the first time in many months:

> We passed the most pleasing and agreeable night in that mosque, and lis-
> tened to the call to prayer, which long we had not heard. We were shown
> high regard by the residents of the mosque, amongst whom was an imam
> who led them in the obligatory prayers.[16]

Many of the Islamic cultural norms were apparent in Sicily's Muslim community, from mosques and festivals to Muslim merchants' prominence in the marketplace, and Ibn Jubayr summed up in regard to Palermo: "The Muslims of this city preserve the remaining evidence of the faith."[17]

The Muslims of Christian Sicily were also allowed to retain a wide range of community leaders, such as the imam whom Ibn Jubayr mentioned. Like monotheist minority groups living under Muslim dominion (known as *ahl al-dhimma*, or *dhimmī*s, after the pact of protection under which they lived), the Muslims of Christian Sicily were granted the right to both religious and civil leadership. Ibn Jubayr described worship led by imams in the many mosques he visited, reported that there were numerous teachers of the Qur'ān in Palermo and muezzins to call the faithful to prayers.[18] It is also known from other sources that Sicily's Muslims had a *qāḍī* (judge) who would adjudicate civil and religious questions for the community.[19] In addition to these religious leaders, Ibn Jubayr made clear to his readers that there were a number of wealthy and noble families on the island

---

[15] Ibn Jubayr, *Riḥlat Ibn Jubayr*, 309–10; Broadhurst, *The Travels of Ibn Jubayr*, 353. For a general approach to considering aural environments within Islamic history, see Fahmy, "Coming to our Senses." Specifically on the topic of "religious noise" and its regulation within multicultural environments, see Constable, "Regulating Religious Noise."

[16] Ibn Jubayr, *Riḥlat Ibn Jubayr*, 303; Broadhurst, *The Travels of Ibn Jubayr*, 346.

[17] Ibn Jubayr, *Riḥlat Ibn Jubayr*, 305; Broadhurst, *The Travels of Ibn Jubayr*, 348.

[18] For the description of the imam leading Ramadan prayers in the community at Qasr Saʿd, see Ibn Jubayr, *Riḥlat Ibn Jubayr*, 303; Broadhurst, *The Travels of Ibn Jubayr*, 346. It is there that Ibn Jubayr and his companions heard the call to prayer for the first time on the island. Muezzins are also described in Palermo, along with the *qāḍī* and teachers of the Qur'ān. See Ibn Jubayr, *Riḥlat Ibn Jubayr*, 305–6; Broadhurst, *The Travels of Ibn Jubayr*, 348–49.

[19] For example, we hear about the chief judge of the Sicilian Muslims from a *fatwā* in which the North African jurist Imām al-Māzarī (d. 1141) discussed the legality of the judgments of the *qāḍī al-Ṣiqilliya*, who had been appointed by the Christian king. See Davis-Secord, "Muslims in Norman Sicily."

who would be considered the "sheikhs" of the island's Muslim community.[20] This community leadership would have been essential for the correct practice of Islamic life and worship and for the preservation of an intact Muslim community on the island.

By the end of his visit to the island, however, Ibn Jubayr came to believe that these remainders of Islamic faith, culture, and leadership were being threatened by the dominant Latin Christian culture: "But in general these Muslims do not mix with their brethren under infidel patronage, and enjoy no security for their goods, their women, or their children. May God, by His favor, amend their lot with His beneficence."[21] He noted that the Muslims of Palermo could not fully practice their faith, despite the appearance of religious freedom: "They do not congregate for the Friday service, since the *khutbah* [Friday sermon] is forbidden."[22]

Despite the many familiar and friendly aspects of life for Muslims in Christian Sicily, we know that some of the conditions of minority life under this regime—such as the payment of an annual tax modeled on the Islamic *jizya* called in Sicily the *gezia*, and a travel ban restricting movement or communication between the Muslims of the island and those in the *dār al-Islām*— were considered onerous (as they may have been intended).[23] Ibn Jubayr recognized that the freedom of the Muslims in Sicily to own property and govern their own communities came at a price, both in monetary and cultural terms. He stated:

> The Muslims live beside them [Christians] with their property and farms. The Christians treat these Muslims well and "have taken them to themselves as friends" but impose on them a tax to be paid twice yearly, thus taking from them the amplitude of living they had been wont to earn from that land. May Almighty and Glorious God mend their lot . . .[24]

He also learned of various pressures, both subtle and direct, placed on the island's Muslim community by the Norman rulers. For example, some of the Muslim community's leaders had been dismissed from royal favor and had their properties confiscated, and some had converted to Christianity under duress.

Indeed, Ibn Jubayr's account of his experiences and the stories he heard demonstrates the problems with thinking in terms of "tolerance" in the multicultural medieval Mediterranean. By the time he ended his stay on the island, and after learning about the conditions of life for Sicily's Muslim minority,

---

[20] Ibn Jubayr, *Riḥlat Ibn Jubayr*, 313; Broadhurst, *The Travels of Ibn Jubayr*, 357.

[21] Ibn Jubayr, *Riḥlat Ibn Jubayr*, 306; Broadhurst, *The Travels of Ibn Jubayr*, 349.

[22] Ibn Jubayr, *Riḥlat Ibn Jubayr*, 305; Broadhurst, *The Travels of Ibn Jubayr*, 348.

[23] Johns, "The Boys from Messoiuso."

[24] Ibn Jubayr, *Riḥlat Ibn Jubayr*, 297; Broadhurst, *The Travels of Ibn Jubayr*, 339–40.

Ibn Jubayr became convinced that living alongside Christians, no matter how peacefully, was quite harmful to the preservation of a distinct Muslim religious and cultural identity. And it is certainly the case that the population of Sicily's Muslim community was steadily eroded across the twelfth century, at the same time that mosques and Greek churches and monasteries were transformed into Latin churches and monasteries. Exact numbers are difficult to establish, but we know that significant demographic decline within the Muslim population was occurring at the time of Ibn Jubayr's visit to the island. One estimate is that at the time of the deportation of the island's Muslims to Lucera, only about 20,000 individuals remained to be sent to the mainland colony. This represents a reduction in numbers estimated by one scholar to have been as much ninety percent of the Muslim population in only a century and a half.[25] That is, within forty years of Ibn Jubayr's visit to Sicily, the Muslim community was exiled to Lucera after having been radically diminished by either religious conversion or cultural assimilation into the Latin Christian majority on the island.[26]

Religious Identity and the Problem of Assimilation

The possibility of religious and cultural assimilation arose in the medieval Mediterranean whenever a region was conquered by rulers from a different religious group or culture. Christians and Jews lived in Muslim al-Andalus, North Africa, and Sicily, while Muslims and Jews remained in Christian Castile, Aragon, the Crusader States, and Sicily. In each of these cases, minority populations lived as cultural and religious minorities under a foreign dominant culture and either maintained their unique religious and cultural communal identity or lost it through assimilation or conversion (either forced or voluntary). Maintaining a religious and cultural tradition as a minority community was not easy, for in most cases the minority group spoke a different language than the majority,

---

[25] Abulafia, "The End of Muslim Sicily," believes that from a quarter of a million Muslims (representing initially more than half of the total population of the island) who lived there in the mid-eleventh century, only 20,000 were deported to Lucera in the 1220s; see esp. 104. Likewise Taylor, *Muslims in Medieval Italy*, 1, estimates an initial Luceran population of between 15,000 and 20,000 Muslims.

[26] While possible, it is highly unlikely that this population decline was the result of violence or pogroms against the Muslims of Sicily. There were very limited occasions of large-scale violence against the Muslim population of Sicily; for the most part, the Norman rulers and the Latin elite were too invested in the economic services rendered by the significantly Muslim population of agricultural laborers to wish them dead. On the question of the conversion of Sicily's Muslims, see Johns, "The Greek Church and the Conversion of Muslims in Norman Sicily?"; and Metcalfe, *Muslims and Christians in Norman Sicily*. A general overview of some of the historiography on the Christianization of Sicily is provided in Dalli, "From Islam to Christianity."

utilized different religious rituals, buildings, and texts, and needed a distinct set of community leaders in order to maintain and transmit traditions and texts correctly. It was expected, and often the case, that conquered people would eventually assimilate into the religio-cultural identity of the new majority, and at times religious conversion was forced.[27] Indeed, minority religious populations were often subject to a continual tension between efforts to maintain their distinct religio-cultural identities and the benefits that would follow upon conversion or assimilation.

Religious identity for medieval people was both individual and communal, and, above all, it was ideally visible. What is considered personal and private for modern individuals was generally perceived as communal, public, and, if not immediately apparent, at least easily discernible. In locations where different cultural groups lived side by side, neighborhood walls and sumptuary laws were designed to clarify and reinforce the boundaries between the groups and to emphasize the visibility of religious identity. These cultural and religious boundaries were designed to help prevent sexual miscegenation and the problems attendant upon mixed-faith families; they simultaneously prevented confusion about the definition of the community that arose when sexual boundaries were crossed.[28] Anxieties about ambiguous or altered religious identity and the possibility of a "secret" identity also plagued many societies in which cultural mixing was prevalent. To take the most obvious example, the *conversos* of late medieval Iberia were feared by the Christian authorities because of the suspicion that,

---

[27] Cultural assimilation and religious conversion can, of course, be distinct processes, and one can happen without the other, but to many medieval observers they were equally to be feared. Much recent scholarship has examined in more depth the processes of assimilation and conversion in medieval Iberia; for two of the most recent, see Zorgati, *Pluralism in the Middle Ages*; and Safran, *Defining Boundaries in al-Andalus*. For an early discussion of acculturation as a large-scale process in multicultural Spain, see Glick and Pi-Sunyer, "Acculturation as an Explanatory Concept in Spanish History." For a brief discussion of the differences between forced assimilation and multidirectional acculturation, see Perry, "Moriscas and the Limits of Assimilation," 274–77.

[28] It is widely recognized that sexual relations and sexual taboos were common cultural boundary markers in many premodern societies. For examples from the medieval Mediterranean, see, for example, Barton, "Marriage Across Frontiers"; Furst, "Captivity, Conversion, and Communal Identity"; Nirenberg, "Religious and Sexual Boundaries in the Medieval Crown of Aragon"; Nirenberg, "Conversion, Sex, and Segregation"; and Meyerson, "Prostitution of Muslim Women in the Kingdom of Valencia." Nirenberg writes of the system of honor, as expressed through the bodies of women, as preserving the coherence of the corporate Christian body, the Ecclesia: "the sexualized boundaries inscribed on the bodies of women in order to demarcate familial honor could be generalized to heighten the cohesion of larger units of society." Nirenberg, "Conversion, Sex, and Segregation," 1071. See also his *Communities of Violence*, chap. 5: "Sex and Violence between Majority and Minority."

although they appeared to act as Christians, their true "secret" identity remained unchangingly Jewish.[29]

Women's roles within the family and as sexual beings were directly at the center of these cultural and communal definitions of identity. Women lay at the nexus of the tension between preservation of a Muslim identity and its disintegration within Christian Sicily's Muslim population, which was faced in the twelfth century with the prospect of assimilation. Through marriage to Muslim men and raising Muslim children, as well as by appearing in public as identifiably Muslim, these women were central to the preservation of their unique cultural identity, both individually and as a community.

Ibn Jubayr included descriptions of women throughout his text, many of whom played special roles in the expression of cultural identity. He was closely attuned to the spectacle of women's appearances and their visible and public identities. From the glittering processions of princesses on the *ḥajj* to chained and shackled female slaves in the Christian Levant, women do not lack for visibility in the *Riḥla* of Ibn Jubayr. It is not only women themselves, however, on which he remarked. Ibn Jubayr dwelt on their appearances, their dress and adornment, and what public female presence could tell the observer about her identity and that of her community. For instance, he spent long paragraphs on detailed descriptions of the gown of a Christian bride in Tyre, on the sparkling outfits and retinues of the princesses on pilgrimage, and on the very familiar accessories of Christian women in Palermo, and he surmised from these appearances such identifiers as class, religion, social role, and how the larger culture was reflected in these women's external adornments.

Women's public visibility itself presented no obvious problem in the eyes of Ibn Jubayr. He did not remark on the impropriety of women appearing in public but, rather, commented on more complex matters of how women's roles and visible identities marked their communities, especially in religious (Muslim-Christian) terms. While he did explicitly complain about poor Muslim leadership, poor treatment of pilgrims and travelers, the lack of proper Islamic worship, and the dangerous mixing of Muslims with Christians, Ibn Jubayr did not complain about women appearing in public. His larger concerns were focused on the health of Muslim communities and the practice of proper Islam in the world. In Ibn Jubayr's analysis, these issues were being threatened both within and outside the *dār al-Islām*. Women's roles could, in Ibn Jubayr's stories, either help or hinder Muslim community well-being, as we will see below.

---

[29] For more on the intersection of gender and the "secret" identity of *conversos*, see Melammed, "Crypto-Jewish Women Facing the Spanish Inquisition" and below. For the intersection of gender and the Islamic tradition of "taqiyya," or dissimulation about religious identity, among the Moriscos of sixteenth-century Spain, see Perry, "Moriscas and the Limits of Assimilation," 279.

Norman Sicily, with its significant Muslim minority population, was a prime example of a Muslim community under threat. When Ibn Jubayr arrived in Sicily, which had been under Muslim dominion for two centuries ending in the mid-eleventh century CE, he found a Muslim minority community that was feeling pressure to convert to Christianity, despite the overall favorable conditions for Muslims on the island. In this time of transformation, after a political frontier had been breached by foreign conquest, Ibn Jubayr expressed his fears about the breaking down of cultural frontiers, which might ultimately lead to the disintegration of this minority Muslim community. Women were central to his concerns about the preservation of a unique Muslim community identity in a time of stress, acting as key figures in the struggle to retain a distinctive religio-cultural identity. Women in this minority community played roles that were both public and familial, as wives, daughters, marriageable young women, and concubines in the royal harem, who, although hidden from public view within the palace, were the subject of much public conversation and rumor; indeed, gossip about the Muslim women of the harem was the basis for much of Ibn Jubayr's perception of the royal court and of King William's treatment of his Muslim courtiers.

These roles that women played as bearers of Islamic identity and culture are crystallized in three forces that Muslim minority women exerted within their community in Christian Sicily: as sexual partners who formed the boundary between religious groups but also had the capacity to bring Islam physically into the sacred precinct of the royal household; as wives and mothers who preserved the Islamic identity of their families and transmitted religious knowledge and customs; and as publically visible representatives of Islamic culture on the streets of Palermo. All three of these forces had the potential to be either assets or liabilities for group identity. That is, the power of women to shape and exhibit their communal religious identity—to literally bear that identity within and on their bodies in order to ensure its continuation—meant that they could either positively assert a minority identity or be the weak point at which the breakdown—assimilation or conversion—could occur.

Religious conversion, whether of an individual or of larger social units, is nearly impossible to quantify and almost as difficult to explain.[30] Ibn Jubayr's eyewitness account of Sicily's Muslim community points to a variety of pressures acting upon that community that, he feared, might induce them to take on a Christian identity. His fears were founded on the notion that proximity, and especially friendly interaction, might seduce weak or vulnerable Muslims

---

[30] For an introduction to the literature on medieval conversion, see Bulliet, *Conversion to Islam in the Medieval Period*. Responses to and revisions of Bulliet's methodology include Morony, "The Age of Conversions"; Penelas, "Some Remarks on Conversion to Islam in Al-Andalus"; and Harrison, "Behind the Curve."

("ignorant souls," as he calls them) into conversion to Christianity.[31] If the boundaries between Muslim and Christian culture were not maintained, these "weaker" Muslims might fail to recognize the important distinctions between the two religions and the superiority of Islam as a truth claim. These most vulnerable Sicilian Muslims included women and children, whom Ibn Jubayr highlights as among the most important players in this tension between the allure of the majority culture and the effort to maintain traditional Islamic religious practices, language, and customs. Especially for these vulnerable members of society, Ibn Jubayr came to believe that the dangers of living together were too risky to be tolerated, as he asserted in reference to Muslims in the Crusader Levant: "There can be no excuse in the eyes of God for a Muslim to stay in any infidel country, save when passing through it, while the way lies clear in Muslim lands."[32] This was, he says, because in addition to being exposed to disturbing proclamations about Muḥammad, the sight of enslaved and shackled Muslim male and female prisoners, and the filthiness and "mixing with the pigs" in Christian lands, the cultural enticements of Christian society and could lead Muslim women and children to convert to Christianity.[33]

Ibn Jubayr provided an example of the insidiousness of this cultural seduction in the story of a young convert in the Levant. He claimed that the young man first spent time with Christians and learned their customs, and only after that did he convert to their religion. This young man "had mixed with the Christians, and taken on much of their character. The devil increasingly seduced and incited him until he renounced the faith of Islam, turned unbeliever, and became a Christian."[34] It is thus apparent that Ibn Jubayr thought that *cultural* considerations as much as *spiritual* ones could lead a person to abandon his or her religion and religious identity. Cultural assimilation, therefore, preceded religious conversion in his mind and was a threat to the most suggestible members of society, including youth, the enslaved, and women. In situations where assimilation was encouraged or approved, Ibn Jubayr believed that the unique religious and cultural identity of the Muslim community was at risk through a process of seduction, or cultural attraction.

---

[31] Ibn Jubayr, *Riḥlat Ibn Jubayr*, 302; Broadhurst, *The Travels of Ibn Jubayr*, 345.

[32] Ibn Jubayr, *Riḥlat Ibn Jubayr*, 279–80; Broadhurst, *The Travels of Ibn Jubayr*, 321–22. It is perhaps noteworthy that he did not repeat this sentiment in reference to the Muslims of Sicily.

[33] Ibn Jubayr, *Riḥlat Ibn Jubayr*, 279–80; Broadhurst, *The Travels of Ibn Jubayr*, 321–22.

[34] Ibn Jubayr, *Riḥlat Ibn Jubayr*, 281; Broadhurst, *The Travels of Ibn Jubayr*, 323.

Women as Bearers of Islam

Women, in particular, could either succumb to such seduction or play a significant role in resisting it. The association of women with *fitna* or seduction is not uncommon in medieval Arabic sources.[35] Women's presence and physical beauty introduces disorder in many literary sources. Both women themselves—their sexualized bodies—and sexual relations could also define the boundaries of a religious community, and the crossing of such limits created disorder and disruption to the social order of a multicultural environment. Ibn Jubayr himself used the term in that manner, but he also associated *fitna* with any culturally seductive element, such as beautiful churches, that might make Christianity seem appealing. For example, he described one church in Palermo as "beyond dispute the most wonderful edifice in the world," with windows that "bewitch the soul" (lit., "provoke *fitna* in souls"); he then went on to ask for God's protection from this captivating sight.[36] In like manner, beautiful women and ornate buildings could both attract the eye and seduce the soul.

At times, these two uses of *fitna* overlap, as in Ibn Jubayr's elaborate description of the wedding attire of the Christian bride processing through the streets of Tyre. Her captivating appearance, as she marched out between two men and followed by other richly dressed Christian nobles, accompanied by the sounds of trumpets, flutes, and other musical instruments, clearly caught Ibn Jubayr's attention, given the length of his description of this procession. He then added:

> Muslims and other Christian onlookers formed two ranks along the route, and gazed on them without reproof . . .We thus were given the chance of seeing this alluring sight, from the seducement of which God preserve us.[37]

The sights and sounds of Christian culture surrounded the bride, and she carried her Christian identity boldly through the public street, which was populated by both Muslims and Christians. Despite its clear attraction for the multicultural crowd and for Ibn Jubayr himself, the bridal gown was not described in terms of what parts of the woman's body it covered or revealed but, rather, in terms of its sumptuousness as a Christian cultural artifact. He mentioned several times that her outfit was "according to their traditional style" and that her attendants were Christians: "Before her went Christian notables in their finest and most splendid

---

[35] For women as disruptive influences in public and political life, see, for example, Lutfi, "Manners and Customs of Fourteenth-Century Cairene Women"; and Spellberg, *Politics, Gender, and the Islamic Past*. For women inciting *fitna* within the literary tradition, see Kruk, "The Bold and the Beautiful."

[36] Ibn Jubayr, *Riḥlat Ibn Jubayr*, 306; Broadhurst, *The Travels of Ibn Jubayr*, 349.

[37] Ibn Jubayr, *Riḥlat Ibn Jubayr*, 278–79; Broadhurst, *The Travels of Ibn Jubayr*, 320–21.

clothing, their trains falling behind them."[38] He did not refer to the exposed skin or face of the bride but commented on the outfit itself and the spectacle surrounding the event. Ibn Jubayr most notably remarked on the "pride" involved in this exhibition of Christian culture, which was taking place in a once-Muslim land: "Proud she was in her ornaments and dress . . . God protect us from the seduction of the sight."[39] The explicit focus of the text is not the sexual desire aroused by a beautiful woman so much as the cultural jealousy it might inspire Muslim onlookers to feel. This sight was surely sensually alluring, possibly capable of causing the male viewer to feel sexual desire, but it was also, more significantly for Ibn Jubayr, culturally attractive, demonstrating the appeal of the elite Christian culture and its triumph over Muslim culture in the region.

Ibn Jubayr's text demonstrates that women not only participated in the creation and maintenance of cultural boundaries but also were key players in the formation and preservation of a unique minority religious identity in twelfth-century Sicily because they played a special role in demonstrating the superior appeal of Islamic culture. Indeed, women appear at the crux of many crises of religious identity in the multicultural Mediterranean. For instance, *converso* women figure prominently in the records of inquisition trials, as their religious identity was made ambiguous by domestic activities.[40] Likewise, many of the Christian martyrs in ninth-century Cordoba were wives and daughters, for whom both marriage and clothing figure prominently in their stories of altered religious identity.[41] For Ibn Jubayr, the status of Sicily's Muslims hinged on several general factors, among which women were centrally important in large part because of the foundational roles they played in the Muslim family. Women were, in fact, a nodal point upon which the minority Muslim identity either was protected or attacked. Notably absent from Ibn Jubayr's discussion is a concern for the common historiographical conceit of women's seclusion as vital for "male honor." Instead, for him, women's status and position reflected the viability of the entire Muslim community under Christian dominion. The wives and daughters of this community were to be protected not in order to safeguard the males of that culture but to protect the culture itself.

The first mention of Sicily's Muslim women in the *Riḥla* concerns the concubines in King William's harem. Ibn Jubayr noted that he had heard that "The

---

[38] Ibn Jubayr, *Riḥlat Ibn Jubayr*, 278; Broadhurst, *The Travels of Ibn Jubayr*, 320.

[39] Ibn Jubayr, *Riḥlat Ibn Jubayr*, 278; Broadhurst, *The Travels of Ibn Jubayr*, 320.

[40] For example, see Melammed, "Crypto-Jewish Women Facing the Spanish Inquisition."

[41] For the very similar function of marriage and domestic activities among Moriscos (Muslims who had converted to Christianity) in early modern Iberia, see the works of Perry: "Behind the Veil," "Moriscas and the Limits of Assimilation," and *The Handless Maiden*.

handmaidens and concubines in his palace are all Muslims."[42] Women were not alone in carrying Islamic identity into the royal precinct, as William surrounded himself with Muslim courtiers and servants and patronized Arabic scholars, but, for Ibn Jubayr, the presence of Muslim women in the harem seemed especially noteworthy and signified an important presence for Islam within the king's family. These women represented Islam within the private boundaries of the royal court and were said to be maintaining the tenets of their faith with the full knowledge of the king. Ibn Jubayr recounted a story that he had learned about William's court in which, during the panic following an earthquake, William heard himself surrounded by Arabic lamentations calling upon Allah and the Prophet: the king "heard nothing but cries to God and His Prophet from his women and pages." In response to this experience, William is reported to have made a statement about the admissibility of all types of worship and the comfort it brings, rather than an admonition about praying to the Christian God.[43] The religion and language of Islam were thus manifest in the private quarters of the royal household both aurally and physically due to the presence of these women.

While none of these Muslim women was his primary wife and none of their children would inherit William's realm, it appeared significant to Ibn Jubayr that the Christian king maintained a harem of women whom he knew to be practicing their Islamic faith. He praised the steadfastness of these Muslim women and stated that: "Of the good works of these handmaidens there are astonishing stories."[44] Ibn Jubayr even asserted that some Christian women who had been taken into the court household were converted to Islam by the Muslim women there, noting that one of the strangest stories he heard was that "the Frankish Christian women who came to his palace became Muslims, converted by these handmaidens."[45] Ibn Jubayr believed that William's court was a place filled with Muslims and Islamic worship, much of it focused on the activities of these women. These Muslim women had the power not only to represent Islam at court but even to perpetuate it through conversion of Christian women and by giving birth to children whom they could raise in the Islamic faith. They carried Islam into the Christian space of the king's harem vocally, physically, and spiritually. In Ibn Jubayr's view, therefore, women were important as bearers of Islam and links in the perpetuation of religious identity.

In truth, however, these Muslim women at the royal court had been bodily appropriated by the Christian ruler, just as the Muslim community as a whole existed at the whim of the Christian rulers. Ibn Jubayr, shocked by the encouraging stories he had heard about life at court for Muslims and William's pro-Muslim stance, did not directly express concern about this problem. But the

---

[42] Ibn Jubayr, *Riḥlat Ibn Jubayr*, 299; Broadhurst, *The Travels of Ibn Jubayr*, 341.

[43] Ibn Jubayr, *Riḥlat Ibn Jubayr*, 299; Broadhurst, *The Travels of Ibn Jubayr*, 341.

[44] Ibn Jubayr, *Riḥlat Ibn Jubayr*, 299; Broadhurst, *The Travels of Ibn Jubayr*, 341.

[45] Ibn Jubayr, *Riḥlat Ibn Jubayr*, 299; Broadhurst, *The Travels of Ibn Jubayr*, 341.

reality would have been that these Muslim concubines were either slaves taken during raids in North Africa or young women from the native Muslim population appropriated for the king's use and thus removed from the island's population of marriageable Muslim women.[46] These women operated in the private, royal, Christian sphere, not within the public of the many Islamic settlements or the private domestic sphere of a Muslim household. In other words, Muslim women who otherwise would have publicly represented Islamic culture in their families and in the streets had been privatized for the king's personal use. Nonetheless, Ibn Jubayr presented this situation as one that was commendable, showing King William's positive attitude toward his Muslim subjects as well as the positive presence of Islam at his court. Keeping Muslim women was, for Ibn Jubayr, another marker of William's acceptance of Muslim individuals, even though these women's bodies had been co-opted by the Christian elite and were thus unavailable as marriage partners for the island's struggling and demoralized Muslim population. Rather than being dismayed, however, Ibn Jubayr lauded these women for bringing Islamic rituals, the Arabic language, and Muslim children into the Christian court.

A second vital role that women played in preserving Islamic religious culture and identity was as wives and mothers within the Muslim family. Women from Muslim families would have been expected to marry Muslim men and raise their children in Islam. Mixed-faith marriages were not unknown in the medieval Mediterranean, but they were often the locus of conflict and tension over religious identity.[47] Muslim men, in both religious law and practice, at times married women from among subject *dhimmī* populations, with the common assumption that the children of those unions would be raised as Muslims.[48] According

---

[46] For a study of enslaved Muslim women in a different Mediterranean Christian context, see Winer, *Women, Wealth, and Community in Perpignan, c.1250–1300*.

[47] The Cordoban Mozarabs of ninth-century al-Andalus are just one example of the tension created within communities when Christians and Muslims attempted to negotiate mixed families or when children of one religious culture converted to the other. For the Cordoban martyrs movement as a family issue, see Coope, *The Martyrs of Cordoba*; see also Safran, *Defining Boundaries*, 81–124. For general study of the Mozarabs, see Epalza, "Les mozarabes: État de la question," *Revue du monde musulman et de la Méditerranée* 63 (1992): 39–50; Epalza, "Mozarabs: An Emblematic Christian Minority in Islamic al-Andalus"; and Kassis, "Arabic-speaking Christians in al-Andalus."

[48] Qu'rān 5:5 states: "And lawful are the chaste Muslim women, and the women of the people of the Book who are chaste, (for marriage) and not fornication or liaison, if you give them their dowries." Ali, *al-Qu'rān: A Contemporary Translation*, 98. For the Islamic legal position on marriages between Muslims and non-Muslims, see Schacht, *An Introduction to Islamic Law*, 132; Spectorsky, "Women of the People of the Book"; Yamani, "Cross-Cultural Marriage within Islam"; and Shatzmiller, "Marriage, Family, and the Faith." For the Christian canon legal position on inter-faith marriages, see Brundage, "Intermarriage between Christians and Jews in Medieval Canon Law." For Christian

to common Islamic legal tenets, however, Muslim women would not be allowed to marry outside of the Muslim community. Yet women from distressed minority populations might find themselves pressured to marry men from the dominant group.

The possibility of inter-faith marriage appears to be the very problem faced by some of the young Muslim women in twelfth-century Sicily, as illustrated in a story Ibn Jubayr related from the end of his trip, heard while waiting for a boat from Trapani back to al-Andalus. This anecdote deals with a young Muslim woman desiring to leave Sicily as the wife of one of the Muslim pilgrims returning to Iberia.[49] This young woman's father approached the group of travelers while they were delayed in Trapani, seeking to marry off his daughter to one of them so that she could flee from life as a subjected Muslim in Sicily. The young woman was a virgin approaching marriageable age whom the father wished to send to Spain in order that she might "escape from the temptation (of apostasy)."[50] The young woman herself was complicit in this request: "We were likewise amazed at the girl—may God protect her—and at her willingness to leave her kin for her love of Islam."[51] This comment demonstrates that the problem did not lie with her; she was not a wayward child or one who had demonstrated an interest in converting to Christianity. Ibn Jubayr again related his sense of wonder at the willingness of this family to part from each other in order that she find a marriage partner and life in a Muslim land, noting the pity and compassion that he felt during this experience. He also stated that this young woman was motherless, making her the sole maternal figure in the lives of her three younger siblings, which made the family's sacrifice even more significant.[52] The specific impetus for this request is unknown, as is the outcome, but the implication was that this girl was facing pressures to marry outside of the Islamic community. Perhaps she had already been approached by Christian men seeking her hand in marriage, or she could not find an eligible Muslim man to marry, or maybe the family had witnessed other young women marrying outside the Muslim community. Whatever the case, the overall picture is clear: at least for this one family, the choice to part from each other seemed preferable to the dangers lurking for this woman within Christian Sicily, and the religious identity of her future marital family was in some way more important than living with or near her natal family.

---

cultural considerations about mixed-faith marriages, see Birtwistle, "Daylight and Darkness."

[49] Ibn Jubayr, *Riḥlat Ibn Jubayr*, 315–16; Broadhurst, *The Travels of Ibn Jubayr*, 360.

[50] Ibn Jubayr, *Riḥlat Ibn Jubayr*, 315–16; Broadhurst, *The Travels of Ibn Jubayr*, 360.

[51] Ibn Jubayr, *Riḥlat Ibn Jubayr*, 315–16; Broadhurst, *The Travels of Ibn Jubayr*, 360.

[52] Ibn Jubayr also noted that the family wished to use the woman as an anchor for their own emigration, if the travel ban imposed by the Norman rulers were lifted.

Extrapolated to the larger society, it appears that marriage-age women from the Muslim community of Sicily were struggling to maintain their religious identities within their new families. Young Muslim women forced to marry Christian men would most likely have assumed a Christian religious identity, meaning that the issue of women's marriage became a vital aspect of the preservation of a distinct Muslim religious identity. If married into a Muslim family, these women would have been able to preserve the customs of their natal families, including language, religious practice, and the domestic practices associated with Islamic belief and culture.[53] In addition, in all of the religious cultures of the medieval period, the education of the youngest children and most girls would have occurred at home at the mother's feet. The child's first introduction into the rituals and customs of the family's religious culture occurred in the home, thus giving the mother a vital role to play in the handing down of this knowledge.[54] Muslim women married to Christian men would presumably have had to abandon their faith, at least publically, and raise their children as Christians.[55]

Women served as the primary transmitters of religious knowledge and custom in many at-risk religious communities. Renée Levine Melammed has argued that many late medieval Iberian crypto-Jewish families were able to maintain their secret Jewish rites only because of the mother/wife of the extended family.[56] As the male-dominated, text-based institutions of formal Jewish learning and law disappeared, the transmission of secret Jewish knowledge was left to the informal and oral pathways of the domestic sphere. This is not surprising, given the nature of many of the important rituals of medieval religious life that

---

[53] The importance of marriage for all Muslim youth was further highlighted by Ibn Jubayr when discussing the good works done by the Muslim servants at King William's court: "They redeem prisoners and bring up their young ones, arranging for their marriage and giving them assistance, and doing all the good they can." Ibn Jubayr, *Riḥlat Ibn Jubayr*, 299; Broadhurst, *The Travels of Ibn Jubayr*, 342.

[54] For women as transmitters of religious culture and knowledge in medieval Iberia, see Fuente, "Christian, Muslim and Jewish Women in Late Medieval Iberia"; and Blasco Martínez, "Queen for a Day."

[55] It is interesting, although perhaps irrelevant, to note that during the period of Islamic dominion over Sicily, a tenth-century Muslim observer, Ibn Ḥawqal, criticized the prevalence of mixed-faith families in this frontier region of the *dār al-Islām*. It was common, he claimed, for Muslim men to marry Christian women and for those women to retain their religious identities. The children of these unions were equally mixed: boys were to be raised Muslim, but girls could be baptized as Christians. See Ibn Ḥawqal, *Kitāb ṣūrat al-arḍ*, trans. in Kramers and Wiet, *Configuration de la terre*. If indeed this was true for Muslim Sicily in the tenth century, it does not appear to have been the prevailing custom in Christian Sicily in the twelfth century. For more on Ibn Ḥawqal, see Gabrieli, "Ibn Hawqal e gli Arabi di Sicilia"; and Tlili, "La Sicilia descrita della penna de un autore del X secolo."

[56] Melammed, "Crypto-Jewish Women Facing the Spanish Inquisition."

occurred in or about the home: food preparation, cleanliness, birth and the ritual welcoming of babies, and preparation of the dead for burial.[57] Many of the inquisitorial accusations against suspected *conversos* were based on the domestic activities—sweeping on Fridays, lighting candles on Friday evenings, avoiding pork products and other food-based customs—that supposedly delineated the cultural boundaries between "true" Christians and those in name only.[58] Likewise for Muslim minority women, such domestic activities as food preparation, the education of young children in language, prayers, ablutions, the preparation of halal food or the abstinence from it during periods of fasting, and other particular Islamic religio-cultural practices originated in and were transmitted within the home.[59] A woman forced to marry outside of her natal religious community would need to learn a new set of customs and practices, leaving behind the traditions of her religion.[60] If too many of these Sicilian women married into Christian families, not only would they and their children further diminish the population of the embattled Muslim community but the distinctive customs that define an Islamic society would have been lost as well.

Another aspect of a Muslim family life that Ibn Jubayr encountered in Sicily again highlights the difficulties with thinking of Norman Sicily as a tolerant society and further emphasizes the importance of women and children in maintaining the integrity of the Muslim community as a whole. Ibn Jubayr claimed that:

> The (Muslim) people of this island suffer, amongst other tribulations, one that is very sore. Should a man show anger to his son or his wife, or a woman to her daughter, the one who is the object of displeasure may perversely throw himself into a church, and there be baptised and turn Christian. Then there will be for the father no way of approaching his son, or the mother her daughter . . . The Muslims of Sicily therefore are most watchful of the management of their family, and their children, in case this should happen.[61]

---

[57] For women's roles in various religious rituals and customs, see Melammed, "Noticias sobre los ritos de los nacimientos"; Melammed, "Some Death and Mourning Customs of Castilian Conversas"; and Halevi, "Wailing for the Dead."

[58] For the experiences of women in the Inquisition trials of suspected crypto-Jews in late medieval Iberia, see Melammed, *Heretics or Daughters of Israel?*

[59] Perry, *The Handless Maiden*, esp. 65–87; Fuente, "Christian, Muslim and Jewish Women in Late Medieval Iberia," esp. 321–25.

[60] For the possibility that intermarriage could be used to force assimilation upon a minority population, see Perry, "Moriscas and the Limits of Assimilation," 275.

[61] Ibn Jubayr *Riḥlat Ibn Jubayr*, 315; Broadhurst, *The Travels of Ibn Jubayr*, 359.

Young people and women were again here the weak points on which the well-being of the Muslim community could founder.[62] This practice, which would potentially aid in converting impressionable and angry Muslim youth to Christianity, demonstrated to Ibn Jubayr that the seemingly favorable conditions for Muslims in Sicily were simply a cover for efforts to convert them to Christianity. The most distressing aspect of this situation for Ibn Jubayr, though, extended beyond the possibility of young people converting to Christianity, to the limitations that this fear placed on parental authority.[63] This restriction on parental sovereignty was not limited to mothers, and it in fact included a restraint on the freedom of a husband to discipline his wife. It is instructive, however, to note that Ibn Jubayr considered the mother's authority over daughters a parallel to that of fathers over their sons. This anecdote also reinforces Ibn Jubayr's earlier statement that, despite their apparently free and comfortable lives in Sicily, Muslims there "enjoy no security for their goods, their women, or their children."[64] Property, women, and children—that is, land, home, and family—were the three most important weak points on which the Norman rulers, according to Ibn Jubayr, were putting pressure on the Muslim community in twelfth-century Sicily.

The final aspect of women's agency in maintaining communal religious identity relates to the public visibility of an Islamic cultural presence, as opposed to private, domestic matters. As much as a private or secret religious identity could be preserved before God, without the knowledge of the larger society, the public demonstration of an obviously Muslim community bore witness to the triumph of Islam in the world. This public and visible presence of Islam was clearly of concern to Ibn Jubayr. When Ibn Jubayr first landed on Sicilian soil, he found himself in Messina, a city that he judged negatively due to the absence of a visible Muslim presence: "it is cheerless because of the unbelief, no Muslim being settled there. Teeming with worshippers of the Cross, it chokes its inhabitants, and constricts them almost to strangling."[65] He also noted with dismay that no speakers of Arabic could be found in that city. The presence or absence of a Muslim community was judged on matters both visual and aural. Functioning mosques and madrasas, the sounds (or lack thereof) of the *khutbah* (Friday

---

[62] On the prevalence of young people among voluntary Jewish converts to Christianity in Europe, see Jordan, "Adolescence and Conversion in the Middle Ages." On the topic of women's conversion, in this case to Islam, see Shatzmiller, "Marriage, Family, and the Faith."

[63] I have written elsewhere about the assault on the Muslim family in Norman Sicily, and the utility of the metaphor of family for thinking about the Muslim minority community as a whole. See Davis-Secord, "Focusing on the Family: Ibn Jubayr on The End of Muslim Culture in Norman Sicily."

[64] Ibn Jubayr, *Riḥlat Ibn Jubayr*, 306; Broadhurst, *The Travels of Ibn Jubayr*, 349.

[65] Ibn Jubayr, *Riḥlat Ibn Jubayr*, 296; Broadhurst, *The Travels of Ibn Jubayr*, 338.

sermon) and the *adhān* (call to prayer), and individuals walking in the streets speaking Arabic would all signal to a visitor that he had entered a land with a Muslim population—that is, a land that demonstrated the superiority of Islam. So too, for Ibn Jubayr, did the sight of women dressed in "the fashion of Muslim women," whatever that meant in a particular context.[66] Thus, the elimination or even diminished presence of Muslim women with their overtly Muslim appearance would have signaled the disappearance of Muslim culture for Ibn Jubayr.

One of Ibn Jubayr's most disorienting experiences in Sicily, in fact, arose from the confusion caused by his seeing Christian women dressed like Muslims. Walking to Palermo's main cathedral on Christmas day, he witnessed groups of women wearing silk veils and henna, which Ibn Jubayr associated with the adornments of Muslim, rather than Christian, women:

> The Christian women of this city follow the fashion of Muslim women, are fluent of speech, wrap their cloaks about them, and are veiled. They go forth on this Feast Day dressed in robes of gold-embroidered silk, wrapped in elegant cloaks, concealed by coloured veils, and shod with gilt slippers. Thus they parade to their churches, or rather their dens, bearing all the adornments of Muslim women, including jewellery, henna on the fingers, and perfumes.[67]

He then, again, called upon God to protect the viewer from this seductive sight. In this anecdote women were clearly central to the process of acculturation, although what is less clear is the directionality of this acculturation: it is uncertain in the text—and Ibn Jubayr must not have known—whether these women were Muslim converts to Christianity who had kept their pre-existing clothing style or whether they were Latin women who had adopted the common Mediterranean clothing styles that Ibn Jubayr associated with the lands of Islam.[68] His

---

[66] Ibn Jubayr, *Riḥlat Ibn Jubayr*, 307; Broadhurst, *The Travels of Ibn Jubayr*, 349–50.

[67] Ibn Jubayr, *Riḥlat Ibn Jubayr*, 307; Broadhurst, *The Travels of Ibn Jubayr*, 349–50. One implication of this passage may be that these women were speaking Arabic but were clearly Christians. He was likewise perplexed by Christians who spoke to him and his group in Arabic while passing them in the road.

[68] He did clearly identify them as Christians, not as Muslim women participating in a Christian festival. For women's shared participation in cross-religious rituals, see Cuffel, "From Practice to Polemic," esp. 411–12 on the need for a prohibition on Muslim women entering Christian churches. For an interpretation of this passage as evidence that Muslim and Christian women in Sicily had found ways to dialogue about matters of importance to them as women—in this case, cosmetics and fashion—see Green, "Conversing with the Minority," 106–7. Green suggests "the possibility that religious boundaries may have functioned differently for women than for men" and that "Christian women were looking to their Muslim counterparts as models for gendered concepts of beauty and fashion," 106.

inability to decipher the answer produced confusion and threatened a breakdown in the distinctions that mattered in such a multicultural environment. Ibn Jubayr was confused by his inability to make a clear distinction between these women by looking at their outer dress, and he considered this another incident of cultural seduction. He held the expectation that such visual markers as veils, silk robes, henna, and perfumes should identify these women to him as Muslim, and he reacted with dismay and perplexity when they did not.

The potential of an individual's appearance for confusing cultural boundaries was a common fear among Muslims, Christians, and Jews in the medieval world. So too was the concern about sexual relations between members of different religions that might arise from unclear visual identification of the other. Clothing and other personal adornments lay at the nexus between private, personal identity and the publicly portrayed identity that would be visible and "readable" to passersby. If one could not accurately read another person's identity, the whole range of acceptable social behaviors and relationships would be unclear.[69] Perhaps the most famous medieval Christian expression of the need for identifiable exterior markers of religious identity is found in Canon 68 of the Fourth Lateran Council. It begins:

> In some provinces a difference in dress distinguishes the Jews or Saracens from the Christians, but in others confusion has developed to such a degree that no difference is discernible. Whence it happens sometimes through error that Christians mingle with the women of Jews and Saracens, and, on the other hand, Jews and Saracens mingle with those of the Christians. Therefore, that such ruinous commingling through error of this kind may not serve as a refuge for further excuse for excesses, we decree that such people of both sexes (that is, Jews and Saracens) in every Christian province and at all times be distinguished in public from other people by a difference of dress, since this was also enjoined by Moses.[70]

Women and their bodies were thus the gatekeepers of religious identity, but male dress restrictions were also meant to protect the identity of a community through constraints on sexual border-crossing.[71] These fears of inter-confessional sexual union were shared between Muslims, Jews, and Christians of the Middle Ages,

---

[69] This confusion appears often in cases of prostitution, as when a Christian prostitute accidentally offered her services to a Jewish or Muslim man because she could not read his identity accurately. See Meyerson, "Prostitution of Muslim Women"; Nirenberg, "Religious and Sexual Boundaries"; and Nirenberg, *Communities of Violence*, chap. 5.

[70] Schroeder, *Disciplinary Decrees of the General Councils*, Latin, 584, English trans., 290.

[71] For more on the role of dress and personal appearance in social relationships writ large within the Muslim world, see Hirsch, "Personal Grooming and Outward Appearance."

as were prohibitions against minorities dressing like members of the dominant religion. The ninth-century so-called Pact of ʿUmar, which, perhaps misleadingly, has been used to describe restrictions on Christian *dhimmī*s throughout the Islamic world, also contains rules preventing them from wearing clothes like the Muslims: "We shall not seek to resemble the Muslims by imitating any of their garments."[72] Sartorial distinctiveness allowed everyone in a situation to know exactly with whom they were interacting and was thus a means of preventing unwanted social mixing.

Culturally and religiously distinctive dress was both common and, in some contexts, legislated. At the same time, common Mediterranean styles of adornment were shared between Jews, Muslims, and Christians. The veil, today often viewed as a symbol of Islamic oppression of women, was in fact a common head covering for women of upper classes in many of the cultures of the Mediterranean, whether Christian, Jewish, or Muslim. It is commonly asserted that Muslim societies restrict the public activities of women in order to reduce the possibility of unlawful sexual contact, or unchecked sexual desire and the *fitna* that arises from it.[73] Within the Islamic context, regulation of bodily coverings—particularly, rules on female modesty within public spaces—was directed at controlling sexual desires and actions and at shaping public perception of one's (or one's family members') identity.[74] *Dhimmī* women were not supposed to wear the veil, however, in order that they be clearly marked as non-Muslims. Likewise in Christian contexts, sumptuary laws were promulgated—although not always enforced—as a means of creating or maintaining an easily identified visual distinction between religious cultures or classes.

Other contexts also show that dress could be one of the most significant markers of an individual's religious identification. Some of the women who died among the Cordoban martyrs, the group of Christians (both natal and converted) who sacrificed themselves to the Islamic authorities by publicly denouncing Muḥammad and the Islamic religion in ninth-century Spain, provide an

---

[72] English translation in Marcus, *The Jew in the Medieval World*, 14–16. Cohen, "What Was the Pact of ʿUmar?" For more on the clothing restrictions placed on *dhimmī*s, see Lichtenstadter, "The Distinctive Dress of Non-Muslims in Islamic Countries"; and Cohen, *Under Crescent and Cross*, 62–64.

[73] For an overview of premodern Islamic legal thinking on gendered space, see Tucker, *Women, Family, and Gender in Islamic Law*, 175–217.

[74] Eli Alshech argues against the feminist interpretation of veiling and other modesty regulations as means of male control over a supposedly or potentially disruptive female sexuality. Instead, he argues that these laws and norms were meant to more broadly define one's public image and to delineate a public/private distinction: "Specifically, I maintain that, by regulating physical and visual access to women's bodies and by restricting the flow of sensitive information about them, Islamic law allowed people (primarily the male members of a woman's family) to protect and control their social image and public reputation." Alshech, "Out of Sight and Therefore Out of Mind."

instructive analogue. For example, two secret Christian women from mixed-faith families, named Sabigotho and Liliosa, who were martyred along with their husbands, provoked their arrest by appearing in a Christian church without veils on their faces.[75] They had been living as Muslims and chose to publicly reveal their adherence to Christianity by removing their veils and entering the church. Their revealed faces, as much as their presence in a Christian place of worship, marked them as non-Muslims because of the restrictions on veiling for *dhimmī*s and the use of the veil as a sign of Muslim identity in that context. Another example is Leocritia, a young girl who was born to an elite Muslim family but who converted to Christianity and initially sought to keep her new spiritual identity a secret. In order to appear to her family that she was still a Muslim, she adorned herself with certain clothing and jewels that marked her as Muslim, despite her private Christian faith.[76] Whether this refers to the veil alone or to other distinctive markers of Islamic dress, the lesson is clear: clothing and appearance were meant to be sure signs of a woman's religious identity.

External adornment was supposed to reflect internal identity; it was particularly problematic for Ibn Jubayr when it instead obscured that identity. He made it clear that more was at stake in this matter than simply knowing the religious identity of one's interlocutor. He expressed the fear that if cultural borders were dissolved, then weak-willed Muslims ("ignorant souls") might be tempted to convert to Christianity.

This was also the fear, and the interpretation of contemporary events, in the reverse situation in ninth-century Islamic Cordoba. Eulogius and Paul Albar, writing about the tensions among the Christian community in early Islamic Spain and the Cordoban martyrs movement, focused on problems of cultural assimilation among the Mozarab population. These authors lamented the attractions presented by the dominant Arabo-Islamic culture, language, and styles of dress. In both ninth-century Muslim al-Andalus and twelfth-century Christian Sicily, members of the minority community feared that cultural assimilation would lead to religious conversion, not the opposite—for example, one did not learn the language after converting but converted after recognizing the appeal of speaking the dominant language. Likewise intermarriage, social and sexual mixing, and adoption of the dominant culture's clothing style might lead to religious conversion. As in Ibn Jubayr's anecdote about the young Muslim convert to Islam in Crusader Acre, too much cultural integration with the dominant community was bad for the soul. And, as such, it was bad for the community and its

---

[75] Eulogius, *Memoriale Sanctorum*, b. 2, c. 10, in Gil, *Corpus Scriptorum Muzarabicorum*, 2:416–30. For the particular story of their unveiled visit to the church, see b. 2, c. 27, in Gil, *Corpus Scriptorum Muzarabicorum*, 2:427–28. See also Coope, *The Martyrs of Cordoba*, 27–29.

[76] Paul Albar, *Vita Eulogi*, c. 13–16, in Gil, *Corpus Scriptorum Muzarabicorum*, 1:337–41. See also Coope, *The Martyrs of Cordoba*, 28–31.

prospects for continued existence. As mothers, wives, transmitters of religious customs, and visible performers of a Muslim identity, women in particular had the power to either succumb to these temptations or resist them in order to maintain the unique religious identity of the family and community.

Conclusion

For Ibn Jubayr, encountering the Muslims of Sicily was a true frontier experience. At once familiar and foreign, Norman Sicily retained several of the hallmarks of a Muslim society and population, but the Christian society there also exerted pressure on actual Muslim people to convert or assimilate to Christian culture. The sound of the *adhān* but not of the *khutbah*, the sight of mosques but also of churches that looked like mosques, and the appearance of Christian women dressed like Muslim ones all created the disorienting effect of dislocation for the observer, foregrounding contemporary Muslims' anxieties about living as minorities under Christian rule. The Sicilian Muslim community lived just beyond the edge of the *dār al-Islām*, in a land that had been wrested from Islamic political control and was on the verge of losing all vestiges of its Muslim cultural identity. This was a region that had been recently in the hands of Muslim rulers but was now irrevocably Christian, at least in political terms. Despite Ibn Jubayr's fervent and repeated prayers that Allah return the island to Muslim dominion, Sicily would remain under Christian control. In cultural terms, the minority Muslim community in this Christian-controlled land was likewise at a crossroads between assimilation and resistance. They could either assimilate and convert to Christianity or struggle to maintain their Islamic faith and culture despite pressure and isolation. Women's roles and lives stood at the front line of this tension.

Ibn Jubayr appears less concerned about the personal spiritual impact that conversion might have on an individual soul than with the spiritual and cultural health of the *dār al-Islām* as a whole. His account could be read as a screed against Christians, but his comments seem to have been inspired less by prejudice than by fear. Whenever he expressed a disparaging remark about Christians, or the prayer that God might deliver Sicily back into Muslim hands, he communicated his fears about the dangers associated with lowered social boundaries between religious groups. He wrote not of his hatred for Christians themselves but of his concern for Muslims and the Muslim community; for Sicily he prayed, "May it be that God will soon repair the times for this island, making it again a home for the faith, and by His power delivering it from fear to security."[77] At the same time, whenever he encountered true kindness from Christians, or sound

---

[77] Ibn Jubayr, *Riḥlat Ibn Jubayr*, 305; Broadhurst, *The Travels of Ibn Jubayr*, 348.

leadership by Christian rulers, he praised them sincerely. But the problem, as he came to see it, was that this kindness was potentially destructive to the unity of the Muslim community, eroding boundaries and threatening to dissolve the unique religious identity of this minority group.

Rather than being a source of disruptive or seductive allure, women were especially equipped to resist these destructive tendencies by providing the foundation for strong Muslim families and by carrying an Islamic identity into society or into the royal household. We can imagine the fear a Muslim male observer might feel about female co-religionists mixing freely in public with men of a different religious community, and the anxiety about sexual boundaries this might inspire. For Ibn Jubayr, though, the fear was broader than the individual honor attached to a particular Muslim woman or family. He feared, indeed rightfully, for the continued existence of the entire Muslim community on the island, which would outlast his visit by less than a half-century. As in stories like that of the young Trapanese woman seeking marriage to a stranger in Iberia, women played a pivotal role in this question. Women, in their functions as mothers, wives, sexual partners, and publicly visible representatives of Islamic culture, literally embodied Islam within the majority Christian society of Sicily. In positive terms, these women demonstrated and transmitted the faith of Islam into a Christian culture. In negative terms, if those women disappeared—as wives or concubines to Christian men instead of Muslims, as émigrés from the island, or because there was no visible distinction between Christian and Muslim women's appearances—so too might the presence of a distinctive Muslim minority community disappear from the majority Christian society.

Bibliography

Abou El Fadl, Khaled. "Islamic Law and Muslim Minorities: The Juristic Discourse on Muslim Minorities from the Second/Eighth to the Eleventh/Seventeenth Centuries." *Islamic Law and Society* 1 (1994): 141–87.

Abugideiri, Hibba. "Revisiting the Islamic Past, Deconstructing Male Authority: The Project of Islamic Feminism." *Religion and Literature* 42, no. 1–2 (2010): 133–39.

Abulafia, David. "The End of Muslim Sicily." In *Muslims Under Latin Rule, 1100–1300*, ed. James M. Powell, 103–33. Princeton: Princeton University Press, 1990.

———. "Monarchs and Minorities in the Christian Western Mediterranean around 1300: Lucera and its Analogues." In *Christendom and its Discontents: Exclusion, Persecution and Rebellion, 1000–1500*, ed. S. L Waugh and P. D. Diehl, 234–63. Cambridge: Cambridge University Press, 1996.

Afsaruddin, Asma. "Literature, Scholarship, and Piety: Negotiating Gender and Authority in the Medieval Muslim World." *Religion and Literature* 42, no. 1–2 (2010): 111–31.

Ahmed, Leila. *Women and Gender in Islam: Historical Roots of a Modern Debate.* New Haven: Yale University Press, 1992.

Ali, Ahmed. *al-Qu'rān: A Contemporary Translation.* Princeton: Princeton University Press, 1988.

Alshech, Eli. "Out of Sight and Therefore Out of Mind: Early Sunnī Islamic Modesty Regulations and the Creation of Spheres of Privacy." *Journal of Near Eastern Studies* 66, no. 4 (2007): 267–90.

Barlas, Asma. *"Believing Women" in Islam: Unreading Patriarchal Interpretations of the Qur'ān.* Austin: University of Texas Press, 2002.

Barton, Simon. "Marriage Across Frontiers: Sexual Mixing, Power and Identity in Medieval Iberia." *Journal of Medieval Iberian Studies* 3, no. 1 (2011): 1–25.

Baumgarten, Elisheva. "'A Separate People'? Some Directions for Comparative Research on Medieval Women." *Journal of Medieval History* 34 (2008): 212–28.

Beckingham, C. F. "The *Riḥla*: Fact or Fiction?" In *Golden Roads: Migration, Pilgrimage and Travel in Medieval and Modern Islam*, ed. Ian Richard Netton, 86–94. Richmond, UK: Curzon Press, 1993.

Bercher, Henri, Annie Courteaux, and Jean Mouton. "Une abbaye latine dans la societe musulmane: Monreale au XIIe siècle." *Annales* 34 (1979): 525–47.

Berkey, Jonathan. "Women in Medieval Islamic Society." In *Women and Medieval Culture*, ed. Linda Mitchell, 95–111. New York: Garland, 1999.

Birtwistle, Rosalind. "Daylight and Darkness: Images of Christians in Mixed Marriages." *Islam and Christian–Muslim Relations* 17 (2006): 331–42.

Blasco Martínez, Asunción. "Queen for a Day: The Exclusion of Jewish Women from Public Life in the Middle Ages." In *Late Medieval Jewish Identities, Iberia and Beyond*, ed. Carmen Caballero-Navas and Esperanza Alfonso, 91–105. New York: Palgrave Macmillan, 2010.

Bresc, Henri. "Mudejars des pays de la Couronne d'Aragón et sarrasins de la Sicile normande: le problème de l'acculturation." In *Jaime I y su época*, ed. Charles-Emmanuel Dufourcq, 51–60. Zaragoza: Institución Fernando el Católico, 1979.

Broadhurst, R. J. C. *The Travels of Ibn Jubayr.* London: Jonathan Cape, 1952.

Brundage, James. "Intermarriage between Christians and Jews in Medieval Canon Law." *Jewish History* 3, no. 1 (1988): 25–40.

Bulliet, Richard W. *Conversion to Islam in the Medieval Period.* Cambridge, MA: Harvard University Press, 1979.

Chiarelli, Leonard C. *Islamic Sicily: A History of Muslim Sicily.* Venera, Malta: Midsea Books, 2011.

Cohen, Mark R. *Under Crescent and Cross: The Jews in the Middle Ages.* Princeton: Princeton University Press, 1994.

————. "What Was the Pact of 'Umar? A Literary-Historical Study." *Jerusalem Studies in Arabic and Islam* 23 (1999): 100–157.

Constable, Olivia Remie. "Regulating Religious Noise: The Council of Vienne, the Mosque Call and Muslim Pilgrimage in the Late Medieval Mediterranean World." *Medieval Encounters* 16 (2010): 64–95.

Coope, Jessica A. *The Martyrs of Cordoba: Community and Family Conflict in an Age of Mass Conversion*. Lincoln: University of Nebraska Press, 1995.

Cuffel, Alexandra. "From Practice to Polemic: Shared Saints and Festivals as 'Women's Religion' in the Medieval Mediterranean." *Bulletin of the School of Oriental and African Studies* 68, no. 3 (2005): 401–19.

Dalli, Charles. "From Islam to Christianity: The Case of Sicily." In *Religion, Ritual and Mythology: Aspects of Identity Formation in Europe*, ed. Joaquim Carvalho, 151–69. Pisa: Pisa University Press, 2006.

————. "Contriving Coexistence: Muslims and Christians in the Unmaking of Norman Sicily." In *Routines of Existence: Time, Life and After Life in Society and Religion*, ed. Elena Brambilla, 30–43. Pisa: Plus-Pisa University Press, 2009.

Davis-Secord, Sarah. "Focusing on the Family: Ibn Jubayr on the End of Muslim Culture in Norman Sicily," in "Muslims, Christians, and Jews in the Medieval Mediterranean," ed. Sarah Davis-Secord and Elisabeth Cawthon (Texas A&M University Press, forthcoming).

————. "Muslims in Norman Sicily: The Evidence of Imām al-Māzarī's *Fatwā*s." *Mediterranean Studies* 16 (2007): 46–66.

Doumato, Eleanor A. "Hearing Other Voices: Christian Women and the Coming of Islam." *International Journal of Middle East Studies* 23 (1991): 177–99.

Dubler, C. E. "'Adjā'ib." In *Encyclopaedia of Islam*. 2nd ed., vol. 1, 203–4. Leiden: Brill, 1995.

Epalza, Mikel de. "Mozarabs: An Emblematic Christian Minority in Islamic al-Andalus." In *The Legacy of Muslim Spain*, ed. Salma Khadra Jayyusi and Manuela Marín, 148–70. Leiden: Brill, 1992.

————. "Les mozarabes: État de la question." *Revue du monde musulman et de la Méditerranée* 63 (1992): 39–50.

Fahmy, Ziad. "Coming to our Senses: Historicizing Sound and Noise in the Middle East." *History Compass* 11 (2013): 305–15.

Fuente, María Jesús. "Christian, Muslim and Jewish Women in Late Medieval Iberia." *Medieval Encounters* 15 (2009): 319–33.

Furst, Rachel. "Captivity, Conversion, and Communal Identity: Sexual Angst and Religious Crisis in Frankfurt, 1241." *Jewish History* (2008) 22: 179–221.

Gabrieli, Francesco. "Ibn Hawqal e gli Arabi di Sicilia," in Gabrieli, *L'Islam nella storia: saggi di storia e storiografia musulmana*, 57–67. Bari: Dedalo Libri, 1966.

Gertz, Steven. "Permission to Stay in 'Enemy' Territory? Ḥanbalī Juristic Thinking on Whether Muslims Must Emigrate From Non-Muslim Lands." *The Muslim World* 103, no. 1 (2013): 94–106.

Gil, Juan, ed. *Corpus Scriptorum Muzarabicorum.* 2 vols. Madrid: Instituto Antonio de Nebrija, 1973.

Glick, Thomas F., and Oriol Pi-Sunyer. "Acculturation as an Explanatory Concept in Spanish History." *Comparative Studies in Society and History* 11, no. 2 (1969): 136–54.

Green, Monica. "Conversing with the Minority: Relations among Christian, Jewish, and Muslim Women in the High Middle Ages." *Journal of Medieval History* 34 (2008): 105–18.

———, ed. Special issue, *Journal of Medieval History* 34, no. 2 (2008).

Halevi, Leor. "Wailing for the Dead: The Role of Women in Early Islamic Funerals." *Past and Present* 183 (2004): 3–39.

Hambly, Gavin R. G. "Becoming Visible: Medieval Islamic Women in Historiography and History." In *Women in the Medieval Islamic World,* ed. Gavin R. G. Hambly, 3–27. New York: St. Martin's Press, 1998.

Harrison, Alwyn. "Behind the Curve: Bulliet and Conversion to Islam in al-Andalus Revisited." *Al-Masāq* 24, no. 1 (2012): 35–51.

Hirsch, Hadas. "Personal Grooming and Outward Appearance in Early Muslim Societies." *Al-Masāq* 23, no. 2 (2011): 99–116.

Ibn Ḥawqal, Muḥammad. *Kitāb ṣūrat al-arḍ.* Edited by J. H. Kramers. BGA 2. Leiden: Brill, 1967.

Ibn Jubayr, Muḥammad ibn Aḥmad. *Riḥlat Ibn Jubayr.* Beirut: Dār Ṣādir, 1964.

Johns, Jeremy. "The Greek Church and the Conversion of Muslims in Norman Sicily?" *Byzantinische Forschungen* 21 (1995): 133–57.

———. *Arabic Administration in Norman Sicily.* Cambridge: Cambridge University Press, 2002.

———. "The Boys from Messoiuso: Muslim *jizya*-payers in Christian Sicily." In *Islamic Reflections, Arabic Musings: Studies in Honor of Professor Alan Jones,* ed. Robert G. Hoyland and Philip F. Kennedy, 234–55. Oxford: Gibb Memorial Trust, 2004.

Jordan, William Chester. "Adolescence and Conversion in the Middle Ages: A Research Agenda." In *Jews and Christians in Twelfth-Century Europe,* ed. Michael A. Signer and John Van Engen, 77–93. Notre Dame: University of Notre Dame Press, 2001.

Kandiyoti, Deniz. "Islam and Patriarchy: A Comparative Perspective." In *Women in Middle Eastern History: Shifting Boundaries in Sex and Gender,* ed. Nikki R. Keddie and Beth Baron, 23–42. New Haven: Yale University Press, 1991.

Kassis, Hanna. "Arabic-speaking Christians in al-Andalus in an Age of Turmoil (fifth/eleventh century until AH 478/AD 1085)." *Al-Qanṭara* 15 (1994): 401–50.

Keddie, Nikki R. "The Past and Present of Women in the Muslim World." In *Women And Islam*, vol. 1: *Images and Realities*, ed. Haideh Moghissi, 53–79. Abingdon: Routledge, 2005.

——, and Beth Baron, eds. *Women in Middle Eastern History: Shifting Boundaries in Sex and Gender*. New Haven: Yale University Press, 1991.

Kramers, J. H., and Gaston Wiet, trans. *Configuration de la terre*. Beirut: Commission internationale pour la traduction des chefs-d'œuvre, 1964.

Kruk, Remke. "The Bold and the Beautiful: Women and 'Fitna' in the 'Sirat Dhat al-Himma': The Story of Nura." In *Women in the Medieval Islamic World: Power, Patronage and Piety*, ed. Gavin R. G. Hambly, 99–116. New York: St. Martin's Press, 1998.

Lewis, Bernard. "Legal and Historical Reflections on the Position of Muslim Populations under Non-Muslim Rule." *Journal of the Institute of Muslim Minority Affairs* 13 (1992): 1–16.

Lichtenstadter, Ilse. "The Distinctive Dress of Non-Muslims in Islamic Countries." *Historia Judaica* 5 (1943): 35–52.

López de la Plaza, Gloria. *Al-Andalus, mujeres, sociedad y religión*. Málaga: Universidad de Málaga, Secretariado de publicaciones, 1992.

Loud, G. A. "The 'Gens Normannorum' – Myth or Reality?" *Anglo-Norman Studies* 4 (1981): 104–16, 205–9.

——. "How 'Norman' Was the Norman Conquest of Southern Italy?" *Nottingham Medieval Studies* 25 (1981): 13–34.

Lutfi, Huda. "Manners and Customs of Fourteenth-Century Cairene Women: Female Anarchy versus Male Shar'i Order in Muslim Prescriptive Treatises." In *Women in Middle Eastern History: Shifting Boundaries in Sex and Gender*, ed. Nikki R. Keddie and Beth Baron, 99–121. New Haven: Yale University Press, 1991.

Marcus, Jacob Rader. *The Jew in the Medieval World: A Source Book, 315–1791*. Cincinnati: The Union of American Hebrew Congregations, 1938.

Marín, Manuela. *Mujeres en Al-Ándalus*. Madrid: Consejo Superior de Investigaciones Científicas, 2000.

Meisami, Julie Scott. "Writing Medieval Women: Representations and Misrepresentations." In *Writing and Representation in Medieval Islam: Muslim Representation*, ed. Julia Bray, 47–87. London: Routledge, 2006.

Melammed, Renée Levine. "Noticias sobre los ritos de los nacimientos y de la pureza de las judeo-conversas castellanas del siglo XVI." *El Olivo* 13 (1989): 235–43.

——. "Some Death and Mourning Customs of Castilian Conversas." In *Exile and Diaspora: Studies in the History of the Jewish People Presented to Professor Haim Beinart*, ed. Aaron Mirsky, Avraham Grossman, and Yosef Kaplan, 157–67. Jerusalem: Hebrew University of Jerusalem, 1991.

——. "Crypto-Jewish Women Facing the Spanish Inquisition: Transmitting Religious Practices, Beliefs, and Attitudes." In *Christians, Muslims and Jews* in *Medieval and Early Modern Spain: Interaction and Cultural Change*, ed. Mark D. Meyerson and Edward D. English, 197–219. Notre Dame: University of Notre Dame Press, 1999.

———. *Heretics or Daughters of Israel? The Crypto-Jewish Women of Castile*. New York: Oxford University Press, 1999.

Mernissi, Fatima. "Women in Muslim History: Traditional Perspectives and New Strategies." In *Women's History: Changing Perceptions of the Role of Women in Politics and Society*, ed. S. Jay Kleinberg, 338–55. Oxford: Berg, 1988.

———. *The Veil and The Male Elite: A Feminist Interpretation Of Women's Rights In Islam*. Reading, MA: Addison-Wesley, 1991.

Metcalfe, Alex. "The Muslims of Sicily Under Christian Rule." In *The Society of Norman Italy*, ed. G. A. Loud and Alex Metcalfe, 289–317. Leiden: Brill, 2002.

———. *Muslims and Christians in Norman Sicily: Arabic Speakers and the End of Islam*. London: RoutledgeCurzon, 2005.

Meyerson, Mark. "Prostitution of Muslim Women in the Kingdom of Valencia: Religious and Sexual Discrimination in a Medieval Plural Society." In *The Medieval Mediterranean: Cross-Cultural Contacts*, ed. Marilyn J. Chiat and Kathryn L. Reyerson, 87–95. St. Cloud, MN: North Star Press, 1988.

Miller, Kathryn A. "Muslim Minorities and the Obligation to Emigrate to Islamic Territory: Two *fatwā*s from Fifteenth-Century Granada." *Islamic Law and Society* 7, no. 2 (2000): 256–88.

Molénat, Jean-Pierre. "Le problème de la permanence des Musulmans dan les territoires conquis par les Chrétiens, du point de vue de la loi Islamique." *Arabica* 48 (2001): 392–400.

Morony, Michael G. "The Age of Conversions: A Reassessment." In *Conversion and Continuity: Indigenous Christian Communities in Islamic Lands, Eighth to Eighteenth Centuries*, ed. Michael Gervers and Ramzi Jibran Bikhazi, 135–50. Toronto: Pontifical Institute of Mediaeval Studies, 1990.

Netton, Ian Richard. "Basic Structures and Signs of Alienation in the *Riḥla* of Ibn Jubayr." In *Golden Roads: Migration, Pilgrimage and Travel in Medieval and Modern Islam*, ed. Ian Richard Netton, 57–74. Richmond, UK: Curzon Press, 1993.

———. "Riḥla." In *Encyclopaedia of Islam*. 2nd ed., vol. 8, 328. Leiden: Brill, 1995.

———. "Ibn Jubayr: Penitent Pilgrim and Observant Traveler." In Ian Richard Netton, *Seek Knowledge: Thought and Travel in the House of Islam*, 95–101. Richmond, UK: Curzon Press, 1996.

Nirenberg, David. *Communities of Violence: Persecution of Minorities in the Middle Ages*. Princeton: Princeton University Press, 1996.

———. "Religious and Sexual Boundaries in the Medieval Crown of Aragon." In *Christians, Muslims and Jews in Medieval and Early Modern Spain: Interaction*

and Cultural Change, ed. Mark D. Meyerson and Edward D. English, 141–
60. Notre Dame: University of Notre Dame Press, 1999.

———. "Conversion, Sex, and Segregation: Jews and Christians in Medieval
Spain." *American Historical Review* 107, no. 4 (2002), 1065–93.

O'Connor, Isabel A. "Muslim Mudejar Women in Thirteenth-Century Spain:
Dispelling the Stereotypes." *Journal of Muslim Minority Affairs* 27 (2007):
55–70.

Pellat, Charles. "Ibn Djubayr." *Encyclopaedia of Islam*. 2nd ed., vol. 3, 755. Leiden:
Brill, 1995.

Penelas, Mayte. "Some Remarks on Conversion to Islam in Al-Andalus."
Al-Qanṭara 23, no. 1 (2002): 193–200.

Perry, Mary Elizabeth. "Behind the Veil: Moriscas and the Politics of Resistance
and Survival." In *Spanish Women in the Golden Age*, ed. Magdalena S. Sán-
chez and Alain Saint-Saëns, 37–53. Westport, CT: Greenwood Press, 1996.

———. "Moriscas and the Limits of Assimilation." In *Christians, Muslims and
Jews in Medieval and Early Modern Spain: Interaction and Cultural Change*,
ed. Mark D. Meyerson and Edward D. English, 274–89. Notre Dame: University of Notre Dame Press, 1999.

———. *The Handless Maiden: Moriscos and the Politics of Religion in Early Modern
Spain*. Princeton: Princeton University Press, 2005.

Peyronnet, Georges. "Coexistence islamo-chrétienne en Sicile et au Moyen-
Orient: à travers le récit de voyage d'Ibn Jubayr voyageur andalou et pèlerin
musulman (fin du XIIème siècle)." *Islamochristiana* 19 (1993): 55–73.

Powers, David S. "Women and Courts in the Maghrib, 1100–1500." In *Dispens-
ing Justice in Muslim Courts: Qāḍīs and their Courts*, ed. M. Khalid Masud,
Rudolph Peters, and David S. Powers, 383–410. (Leiden: Brill, 2006).

Safran, Janina M. *Defining Boundaries in al-Andalus: Muslims, Christians, and
Jews in Islamic Iberia*. Ithaca: Cornell University Press, 2013.

Schacht, Joseph. *An Introduction to Islamic Law*. Oxford: Clarendon, 1964.

Schroeder, H. J. *Disciplinary Decrees of the General Councils: Text, Translation and
Commentary*. St. Louis, MO: B. Herder, 1937.

Shatzmiller, Maya. "Marriage, Family, and the Faith: Women's Conversion to
Islam." *Journal of Family History* 21, no. 3 (1996): 235–66.

Sonbol, Amira El Azhary, ed. *Beyond the Exotic: Women's Histories in Islamic Societies*. Syracuse: Syracuse University Press, 2005.

Spectorsky, Susan A. "Women of the People of the Book: Intermarriage in Early
Fiqh Texts." In *Judaism and Islam: Boundaries, Communication, and Interac-
tion: Essays in Honor of William M. Brinner*, ed. Benjamin H. Hary, John L.
Hayes, and Fred Astren, 269–78. Leiden: Brill, 2000.

Spellberg, Denise A. *Politics, Gender, and the Islamic Past: The Legacy of 'A'isha
bint Abi Bakr*. New York: Columbia University Press, 1994.

———. "History Then, History Now: The Role of Medieval Islamic Religio-
Political Sources in Shaping the Modern Debate on Gender." In *Beyond the*

Exotic: Women's Histories in Islamic Societies, ed. Amira El Azhary Sonbol, 3–14. Syracuse: Syracuse University Press, 2005.

Taylor, Julie Anne. *Muslims in Medieval Italy: The Colony at Lucera*. Lanham, MD: Lexington Books, 2003.

Tlili, Abderrahman. "La Sicilia descrita della penna de un autore del X secolo: Ibn Hawqal." *Sharq al-Andalus* 6 (1989): 23–32.

Touati, Houari. *Islam and Travel in the Middle Ages*. Chicago: University of Chicago Press, 2010.

Tronzo, William, ed. *Intellectual Life at the Court of Frederick II Hohenstaufen*. Washington, DC: National Gallery of Art, 1994.

——. *The Cultures of His Kingdom: Roger II and the Cappella Palatina in Palermo*. Princeton: Princeton University Press, 1997.

Tucker, Judith E. *Women, Family, and Gender in Islamic Law*. Cambridge: Cambridge University Press, 2008.

Viguera, María Jesús. *"Aṣluḥu li'l-Ma'ālī*: On the Social Status of Andalusī Women." In *The Legacy of Muslim Spain*, ed. Salma Khadra Jayyusi and Manuela Marín, 709–24. Leiden: Brill, 1992.

Viguera Molins, María Jesús. *La Mujer en Al-Andalus: reflejos históricos de su actividad y categorias sociales*. Madrid: Universidad Autónoma de Madrid, 1989.

Wadud, Amina. *Qur'ān and Woman: Rereading the Sacred Text from a Woman's Perspective*. Oxford: Oxford University Press, 1999.

Winer, Rebecca. *Women, Wealth, and Community in Perpignan, c.1250–1300: Christians, Jews, and Enslaved Muslims in a Medieval Mediterranean Town*. Aldershot: Ashgate, 2006.

Yamani, Mai. "Cross-Cultural Marriage within Islam." In *Cross-Cultural Marriage: Identity and Choice*, ed. Rosemary Breger and Rosanna Hill, 153–69. Oxford: Berg, 1998.

Zorgati, Ragnhild Johnsrud. *Pluralism in the Middle Ages: Hybrid Identities, Conversion, and Mixed Marriages in Medieval Iberia*. New York: Routledge, 2012.

Chapter 5
GENDER AND THE POETICS OF GOD'S ALTERITY
IN ANDALUSI MYSTICISM

ANNA AKASOY,
GRADUATE CENTER,
CITY UNIVERSITY OF NEW YORK

While God is described as Other throughout the history of Islamic religious literature, the language employed to conceptualize and describe God's alterity varies widely. In about the twelfth century CE, mystics in different parts of the Islamic world developed an elaborate poetics of love to write about their relationship to the divine whom they associated in a variety of ways with the literary figure of the beloved. As mystics in places as distant as al-Andalus and Persia referred to themselves as lovers of the sublime Beloved, they also occasionally tapped into the centuries-old Arabic traditions of love poetry with its iconic couples of lovers, foremost Qays/Majnūn and Laylā.[1] This essay discusses how the conventional assignations of gender in the context of love poetry were mapped on descriptions of God's alterity. Following a short survey of approaches to God's alterity in the Qur'an and its hermeneutics during the formative period of Islamic history (ca. eighth and ninth centuries CE), the main focus will be on the Andalusi poets Ibn 'Arabī (1165–1240) and Abū 'l-Ḥasan al-Shushtarī (1212–1269), who traveled the southern and eastern shores of the Mediterranean world.

God's Alterity: The Qur'an and Intellectual History
in the Formative Period

In terms of its literary structure, the Qur'an is a heterogeneous text. Part prophetic narrative and salvation history, part normative ethics and legislation, part highly evocative mythology and apocalyptic, one of its distinctive features is its dichotomies. Believers listen to the divine revelation and are saved; non-believers ignore the obvious truth and are doomed. Dichotomies also mark references to

---

[1] For surveys of scholarship and bibliography, see Sharma, "Love: Premodern Discourses"; and Chittick, "Love in Islamic Thought."

the divine. The Qur'an emphasizes that nothing is like God and nothing should be "associated" with God. Those who do so are the "associators" (*mushrikūn*). It is only God who can intercede on the Day of Judgment. God is unlike the deities of the polytheists, but God is also unlike angels, prophets, monks, and scholars. The relationship between God and humankind, too, is determined by alterity. God is eternal, humans mortal; God is the Creator, humans created.

In the centuries following the rise of Islam, Muslim scholars developed their own accounts of God's alterity to interpret and supplement the language of the Qur'an. Since the Qur'an was understood to be God's own word, it also provided believers with a self-description of the deity, in the Islamic tradition mostly associated with the "attributes" of God.[2] The relationship between divine speech and human language, however, was controversial. The Qur'an itself became part of these debates, which were at times politically charged. In the early ninth century, for example, the Abbasid caliph al-Ma'mūn forced scholars to accept the doctrine that the Qur'an was created, just like humankind, a doctrine favored by the rationalist theological school of the Mu'tazilites but rejected by most other scholars. Whatever else this conflict involved, it concerned in large part the matter of God's alterity and the extent to which other entities could be said to partake in characteristics that were considered exclusively divine.

Some scholars promoted a literal interpretation of God's self-description in the Qur'an. The Hanbalis, a community nowadays mostly known for their rigorous doctrines and practices in the area of Islamic law, held anthropomorphic views.[3] Other scholars preferred allegorical interpretations—what in the hermeneutical tradition would be associated with the term *ta'wīl*—in order to deal with Qur'anic references to what appears to be an embodied deity, such as God sitting on a throne. Over the long run, the allegorical interpretations were associated with mystics and certain Shiite groups. Yet others developed approaches that can be classified as apophatic or negative theology, stating that while we cannot describe what God is, we can at least affirm what God is not.

Muslim scholars indebted to the Greek philosophical tradition, Aristotelian and Neoplatonic, used the language of ontology and existence to describe God's alterity. Philosophers such as Ibn Sīnā (ca. 980–1037) spoke of God as necessary or necessarily existent (*wājib al-wujūd*), as opposed to the possible being of the created world. Ibn Sīnā's expression found its way as *necesse esse* into the Latin West, where the scholar became widely known as Avicenna.

While conceptualizing God's transcendence in these different ways, many authors also sought to account for God's immanence. There were those who believed that God had created the world and then left it to work according to its own principles, whereas others envisaged a deity much more actively involved. These questions were relevant too for the existence and nature of religious

---

[2] Böwering, "God and His Attributes."
[3] Williams, "Aspects of the Creed of Imam Ahmad ibn Hanbal."

guidance, contested in the Muslim community since the death of Muhammad. According to a general agreement, God had not left the world without guidance, but Muslims disagreed about where this guidance could be found. Most notably, Shiites came to believe that the imams provided such guidance, whereas Sunnis looked not only to the caliphs but also increasingly to the scholars. Some Sufis saw individual mystics distinguished by divine inspiration. The controversial scholar Ibn Taymiyya (1263–1328) composed extensive polemical works against those who believed in such forms of divine immanence, targeting Shiites as well as certain communities of Sufis and comparing them to Christians who believe in incarnation.[4]

The frictions arising from these different hermeneutical and theological dispositions thus lasted well beyond Islam's formative period. In a performance of anthropomorphic hermeneutics, Ibn Taymiyya is reported to have demonstrated physically the act of God's descent by descending himself from a pulpit. This embodiment of divine activity led to some turmoil, if we are to believe the traveler Ibn Baṭṭūṭa (1304–1369), who claims to have witnessed the scene himself during his stay in Damascus.[5] (Incidentally, Ibn Taymiyya was one of the harshest critics of the Andalusi mystics who are the focus of this essay.)[6]

Love and the Gendered God in Medieval Arabic Mystical Poetry

As much as the Qur'an emphasizes the Otherness of God, it also paints a picture of proximity, indeed intimacy, and these passages became popular among mystics. God is closer to a human being than his jugular vein (50:16). "To God belongs the east and the west; wherever you turn, there is the face of God" (2:115). Verse 54 of sura 5 speaks of mutual love ("He loves them and they love Him") between God and humans. Mystics expressed these themes of intimacy, longing, passion, and separation and the underlying alterity of God in terms of a human lover who has tasted proximity to the divine Beloved but remains apart. It is hard to cut through the layers of legend, but Rābiʿa al-ʿAdawiyya in the eighth century may have been an early example of those who used the language of love in order to describe her relationship to God.[7] While filled with intense longing and anxiety over her own piety, Rābiʿa's expressions are not erotic, nor do they operate with gender as a relational category. It rather appears as if gender dis-

---

[4] Knysh, *Ibn ʿArabi in the Later Islamic Tradition*.

[5] Little, "Did Ibn Taymiyya Have a Screw Loose?"

[6] See note 4.

[7] Baldick, "The Legend of Rābiʿa of Basra." For a skeptical view of the origins of Rābiʿa's iconic verses in the Sufi milieu, see van Gelder, "Rābiʿa's Poem on the Two Kinds of Love."

solved in the sole focus on God. Much of the biographical detail that circulates about her, however, stems from a Persian work on the lives of the saints (*Tadhkirat al-awliyā'*) composed by Farīd al-Dīn 'Aṭṭār (ca. 1145–ca. 1221) and is thus likely to be legendary in nature.

By about the ninth century, Muslim mystics had started to develop more elaborate concepts and terminology to build on these ideas of proximity. Some, such as Sahl al-Tustarī (ca. 818–ca. 896), used a language of metaphysics and cosmological theory,[8] whereas others relied on poetry and its intensely expressive emotional force. Among those who used poetry, the Iraqi al-Niffarī (d. 965) deserves to be singled out. The mystic who produced original poetry was held in high regard by the Sufis whose works are explored in this essay. Another figure who merits mention in our context, if mostly for his legendary position, is al-Ḥallāj, whose execution in 922 was connected in the mystical tradition with his supposed revelation of mystical secrets, notably the union with the divine.

The events and controversies of this formative period of Islam left a lasting legacy in Islamic intellectual, religious, and literary history. Ibn Taymiyya cherished Ibn Ḥanbal and decried Sufis of his own time for adhering to the views of al-Ḥallāj. It seems, however, as if Ibn Taymiyya had nothing to say about Rābi'a. To a large extent this should not come as a surprise. In and of itself, love for God is not objectionable. Furthermore, it was mostly among Persian-speaking, mystically inclined Muslims that Rābi'a's ideas became more popular. We have no reason to believe that Ibn Taymiyya would have been able to read 'Aṭṭār's lives of the saints. Indeed, the most famous examples of mystical poetry that put God in the position of the Beloved in the Middle Ages come from Persian literature. Reynold A. Nicholson recites the pantheon of Persian mystical poets whose works had become known early to a western European readership: the abovementioned hagiographer Farīd al-Dīn 'Aṭṭār, mostly known for his *Conference of the Birds*; Ḥāfiẓ (1325–1389), whose poems inspired Goethe; Jāmī (1414–1492), who adapted classical narratives such as *Majnūn and Laylā* or the exploits of Alexander the Great in his mystical *Seven Thrones* (*Haft Awrang*); but above all Jalāl al-Dīn Rūmī (1207–1273), who is unrivalled in the West as a representative of the Islamic mystical tradition. One might add to that Niẓāmī (1141–1209), whose reworking of the Laylā and Majnūn legend marks a milestone in the story's transition into religious poetry.[9] Originally composed in Arabic, the legend tells the story of Qays, who becomes "mad" (Arabic: *majnūn*) over his love for Laylā, a childhood beloved kept away by her family. Majnūn becomes a poet who lives amidst non-human animals in the desert. His verses reach Laylā through the wind, and while she loves Qays too, their love remains socially and physically unfulfilled until their death. In the history of Arabic literature, this type of story belongs to the category of 'Udhrī love poetry, which is marked by chastity. While

---

[8] Böwering, *The Mystical Vision of Existence in Classical Islam.*

[9] For a recent interpretation, see Seyed-Gohrab, *Laylī and Majnūn.*

it lends itself easily to mystical readings, it can also be read in a more this-worldly sense. It conveys more clearly the idea of a gendered love as well, by framing spiritual love in terms of a story of a man and a woman whose respective genders are critical to the plot, which relies on socially regulated interactions between men and women and marriage as the only accepted form of intimacy. In a mystical reading, the duality of human lover and divine Beloved is supplemented by a gendered binary.

According to Nicholson, authors of Arabic mystical literature may have excelled in the area of prose, but the Persian poets were "much superior to their Arab rivals."[10] And yet the Persian mystical adaptation of classical Arabic love poetry was not unprecedented in Arabic mystical literature itself. As'ad Khairallah made a case for mystical interpretations of the Majnūn and Laylā legend before Niẓāmī.[11] Furthermore, the topic of mystical love, and gendered mystical love, found original and prominent contemporaneous expression in the works of twelfth- and thirteenth-century Andalusi poets, notably Ibn 'Arabī and al-Shushtarī.[12] As mentioned above, both belonged to a group of mystics targeted by Ibn Taymiyya for their metaphysical views. Most of them—such as, apart from the two writers themselves, Ibn Sab'īn (ca. 1217–ca. 1270) and 'Afīf al-Dīn al-Tilimsānī (d. 1291)—were of western Mediterranean extraction but had ended up in the eastern Mediterranean from where another person associated with this group hailed: Ibn al-Fāriḍ (1181–1235), known as the "Prince of Lovers,'" was Egyptian.[13] The degree to which these Sufis were indeed a community with shared doctrines remains to be determined. To a certain extent, they may have been the creation of the polemical response, but only Ibn 'Arabī's work has been the subject of a substantial scholarly exploration, and the extent and complexity of his oeuvre also leaves room for further exploration. Either way, these individuals had personal connections, and some features of their thought were also clearly similar, in part because they were inspired by an older mystical tradition. Louis Massignon spoke of a "conspiration Ḥallāgienne,"[14] a suspicion Ibn Taymiyya had, but as mentioned above, there was also a certain interest in

---

[10] Nicholson, preface to his edition and translation of Ibn 'Arabī's *The Tarjumán al-Ashwáq*, iii.

[11] Khairallah, *Love, Madness, and Poetry*.

[12] For an introduction to al-Shushtarī's life and work, see al-Shushtarī, *Songs of Love and Devotion*.

[13] Homerin, *From Arab Poet to Muslim Saint;* Homerin, *Passion before Me, My Fate behind*. Another easterner associated with this group was al-Qūnawī, who distinguished himself as a theoretical author rather than as a poet.

[14] Massignon, "Ibn Sab'īn et la 'conspiration Ḥallāgienne.'"

the works of al-Niffarī, who may himself have been influenced by al-Ḥallāj.[15] The poetic endeavors explored in this essay appear to be another common trend, albeit not one in which all mystics associated with the group partook. While the parallels between the Andalusi mystics and Ibn al-Fāriḍ suggest that certain religious and literary trends were present along all the southern shores of the Mediterranean, the prominence of those hailing from the Iberian Peninsula illustrates regional diversities within the Arabic-speaking areas of the Mediterranean ruled by Muslims. This challenges binary views of the Mediterranean that divide the region in simple terms: Christian areas, Latin and Romance in the north and Muslim areas with Arabic in the south. It also illustrates that Arabic-speaking Muslims who lived predominantly on the southern shores of the Mediterranean were much more besides Muslims and speakers of Arabic. In the present example, they were, at the very least, Andalusis, mystics, male, poets, emigrants and had enjoyed some exposure to philosophy. Although coined in a different area, the concept of intersectionality helps us understand in just how many ways past individuals differed from those we tend to categorize in the same way and just how many features they shared with those we conventionally categorize in other ways. An exploration of parallels and connections between Muslim and Jewish mystics and philosophers in the Arabic-speaking parts of the Mediterranean for instance is beyond the scope of this article, but such relationships have received some attention in recent academic literature.[16]

Ibn al-Fāriḍ: Prince and Master

Th. Emil Homerin, the author of some of the most comprehensive studies of Ibn al-Fāriḍ's works, leaves little doubt as to the standing of his subject: "Umar Ibn al-Fāriḍ is the most famous Arab poet within Islamic mysticism."[17] While mystical inflections of tropes of love poetry can be traced back as far as the ninth century if not earlier and in more elaborate form to the eleventh century,[18] Ibn al-Fāriḍ produced especially poetically refined and innovative pieces. Some of these are adaptations of poems by the famous al-Mutanabbī (915–965), re-sung

---

[15] For the interest among Mediterranean mystics of the twelfth and thirteenth centuries in the work of al-Niffarī, see al-Shushtarī, *Songs of Love and Devotion*, 21; and Akasoy, "Niffarī: A Sufi Mahdi of the Fourth/Tenth Century?"

[16] Examples include Stroumsa, *Maimonides in his World*; and Ebstein, *Mysticism and Philosophy in al-Andalus*.

[17] Homerin, *Passion before Me*, 1.

[18] For an account of the evolution of this tradition, see Homerin, *Passion before Me*, 1–30. Among western Mediterranean authors, the Andalusi Abū Madyan (1126–1198) also deserves mention (Homerin, *Passion before Me*, 25).

according to mystical tunes. This indebtedness as well as Ibn al-Fāriḍ's outstanding talent for word play explain some forms of expression in his mystical poems.

In his adaptations of the poetic traditions of early medieval Arabic literature, Ibn al-Fāriḍ availed himself of a large reservoir of themes and tropes. He composed six mystical *ghazal*s, a category of love poems with a distinctive poetic form and content.[19] *Ghazal*s had developed out of the *nasīb*, the first section of the tripartite *qaṣīda*. According to a common pattern, at the beginning of these formalized poems of pre- and early Islamic Arabia the caravan of the poet's beloved has just departed and all that is left for her heart-broken lover are the traces of their camp and his memories of past bliss, an emotional disposition which resonated well with the common nostalgic sentiment in mystical poetry. The other elements of the *qaṣīda* include a solitary journey through the desert (*raḥīl*) and a poetic target, frequently panegyrics (*madīḥ*).

As so often in mystical poetry, the identity of the Beloved in Ibn al-Fāriḍ's verses permits much speculation. How do we know who Ibn al-Fāriḍ's Beloved is? As far as modern readers are concerned, much seems to hinge on an interpreter's disposition vis-à-vis polyvalence. In a reference to Niẓāmī and al-Shushtarī, Alvarez describes the extent to which a religious and mystical reading of a poem can depend on the reader: "it is basically the willingness of the reader to apply a mystical hermeneutic that makes this a religious poem."[20] Then again, a mystical hermeneutic with its predilection for complexity, multi-layeredness and paradox is also bound to lead to various and coexisting interpretations.

Homerin highlights select expressions in some of Ibn al-Fāriḍ's poems in order to establish the identity of the Beloved, who can be Muhammad, but who can also be God, depending on the contexts in which these expressions are commonly used in religious literature. Homerin challenged both an Ottoman commentator of Ibn al-Fāriḍ, al-Nābulusī (1641–1731), and a modern translator, Arthur Arberry, who had both assumed that in a number of places the Egyptian poet had referred to God as the Beloved. Clues to a divine Beloved, however, can be fairly specific, if we follow Homerin, and are derived from the Qur'an or mystical theology. The following verse from Ibn al-Fāriḍ's *Lāmiyya* (so called after the Arabic character *lām* which stands at the end of each verse) may serve as an example:

> Ancient is my tale of love for her;
> It has, she knows, no beginning, no end,

---

[19] Kuntze, "Love and God." For the place of the *ghazal*s in Ibn al-Fāriḍ's work, see Homerin, *Passion before Me*, 70, where he identifies six of the fifteen core poems of the *Dīwān* as *ghazal*s.

[20] Al-Shushtarī, *Songs of Love and Devotion*, 27.

> And there is none like me in passion for her,
>   While her enchanting beauty has no equal![21]

If read in a religious context, as Homerin argues, the 'ancient tale' can bring to mind a popular Sufi theme rooted in the Qur'an. According to this myth, God and as yet uncreated humankind agreed on a pact on the conditions of creation and createdness. In the mystical tradition, this encounter represents a moment of great intimacy to which mystics strive to return. (Approached with a different frame of mind, the antiquity of the tale is also reminiscent of its literary function as an age-old archetype.) Remarkably, the *Lāmiyya* is the only *ghazal* in which Ibn al-Fāriḍ speaks of a female beloved, although we don't hear much about her bodily features.[22]

Ibn al-Fāriḍ's *Dhāliyya* (named after the Arabic character *dhāl*) features a fairly detailed physical description of the male beloved, some of the elements stemming from a pool of tropes that are also commonly applied to women. The balance of gender references need not reflect any homoerotic disposition of the poet. The male beloved appears to have emerged from the figure of the male patron, object of panegyrical treatment.[23] Moreover, in general, the figure of the beloved does not occupy a lot of space in Ibn al-Fāriḍ's *qaṣīda*s. As the poet foregrounds his own emotional and psychological state, the description of the Beloved/beloved appears to have primarily the function of allowing the poet to write about his love.

Ibn ʿArabī: Poetic Interpreter and Subversive Theorist

Much better known as a mystic than as a poet, indeed one of the most influential Muslim mystics of all times, Ibn ʿArabī too used similar tropes of classical Arabic love poetry to render mystical ideas. These tropes are prominent in his collection *The Interpreter of Desires* (*Tarjumān al-ashwāq*). As in Ibn al-Fāriḍ's works, a number of poems evoke the setting of the desert, the environment that typically served as a stage for the poetic and heroic exploits of pre- and early Islamic poets. Geographical references such as Najd and Tihāma point to the natural landscape of the desert, as do camels and tents. The traditional setting and plot of the *nasīb* are apparent, for example, in the first half of the short eighth poem in the *Tarjumān*, which reads in Nicholson's translation:

> (1) Their abodes have become decayed, but desire of them is ever new in my heart and decayeth not.

---

[21] Homerin, *Passion before Me*, 35. See the same page for Homerin's interpretation.

[22] Homerin, *Passion before Me*, 77.

[23] Homerin, *Passion before Me*, 77.

(2) These tears are shed over their ruined dwellings, but souls are ever melted at the memory of them.

(3) Through love of them I called out behind their riding-camels, 'O ye who are rich in beauty, here am I, a beggar!'

Likewise, like a poet of the older tradition, Ibn ʿArabī describes the female beloved, or rather beloveds, as in poem XXII:

(4) Who murder with their black eyes and bend their supple necks.

(5) Among them is she who loves and assails with glances like arrows and Indian swords every frenzied heart that loves the fair.

(6) She takes with a hand soft and delicate, like pure silk, anointed with *nadd* and shredded musk.

(7) When she looks, she gazes with the deep eye of a young gazelle; to her eye belongs the blackness of antimony.

Although dating of his writings can be difficult, Ibn ʿArabī appears to have completed the work on the *Tarjumān* in around 1215, that is, well into his career as a famed mystic. Ibn ʿArabī suggests that a particular woman inspired his lyrics. He met young and beautiful Niẓām, daughter of a Persian scholar, during his pilgrimage to Mecca. She approached him as he was composing mystical verses. He recounts:

All I felt was a light tap on my shoulder, made by the gentlest of hands. I turned round and saw a young woman, one of the daughters of Rūm. Never have I witnessed a face that was more graceful, or speech that was so pleasant, intelligent, subtle and spiritual. She surpassed the people of her age in her discernment, her erudition, her beauty and her knowledge.[24]

Although Ibn ʿArabī's love for Niẓām appears to have remained chaste in practice, the ancient poetic traditions of desire may have captured his emotional response to her. We cannot tell to what extent his attraction to Niẓām was spiritual or erotic, but Ibn ʿArabī emphasized the former in the preface to the first recension of the *Tarjumān al-ashwāq* collection, where he declared that he had chosen the erotic style because of its popularity to refer to themes of piety and spiritual discovery. Even so, though, the poems seem to have raised some eyebrows on account of their erotic content. (The "erotic content" here consists of descriptions of the physical appearance of women and the poet's passion for them. Elsewhere in the Arabic tradition one finds more explicit accounts of erotic encounters.) This response demonstrates how critical an author's reputation was for the interpretation of his poetry and how compelling the assumption of consistency and

---

[24] Quoted according to the biography by Addas, *Quest for the Red Sulphur*, 209. See also 208–11 for further discussion of Niẓām.

uniformity. An author whom we know had mystical tendencies is not expected to have composed erotic poetry without mystical undercurrents. In the second recension of his *Tarjumān*, Ibn ʿArabī therefore included a commentary in order to decipher and to some extent depersonalize his poetic efforts. Paraphrasing the mystic, Nicholson comments on the classical formula "Halt at the abodes" for example, as follows: "He says to the voice of God . . . calling from his heart, 'Halt at the abodes,' i.e. the stations where gnostics alight in the course of their journey to infinite knowledge of their object of worship."[25] "A girl enclosed in a howdah" is decoded as "the Essential Knowledge contained in the hearts of some gnostics," and "the damsels bright and fair" are glossed as "the knowledge derived from the manifestations of His Beautiful Name."[26] Nicholson's verdict on the literary quality of the *Tarjumān* is fairly critical, especially, it seems, in the light of Ibn ʿArabī's own interpretation of it:

> The obscurity of its style and the strangeness of its imagery will satisfy those austere spirits for whom literature provides a refined and arduous form of intellectual exercise, but the sphere in which the author moves is too abstract and remote from common experience to give pleasure to others who do not share his visionary temper or have not themselves drawn inspiration from the same order of ideas.[27]

The Andalusi mystic may have failed precisely because of the popularity of the style he chose. Furthermore, as Alvarez remarks, by explaining his references, the commentary restricted the reader's imagination by identifying very specific equivalents in a highly technical world of mystical thought.[28] Indeed much of the ambiguity that lends mystical poetry its strength—who is the beloved/Beloved? God's beauty? God? What does union with the beloved/Beloved mean? What do we see when she lifts Her veil or he lifts His?—is thus reduced and dissolved into a much more cerebral and technical exercise. Jaroslav Stetkevych too was unimpressed by Ibn ʿArabī's efforts in his commentary.[29]

Others disagree with this critical view. Cyrus Ali Zargar, for instance, argued that Ibn ʿArabī's commentary was not meant to be exhaustive; rather, it demonstrated how his verses of love poetry could be read in a mystical sense.[30] The poetic tradition rendered effectively the experience of the lover, worldly as well as gnostic. The shift from the description of external elements towards the interior mystical experience and exercise in the commentary, however, confirms the impression that, not unlike Ibn al-Fāriḍ in the account above, Ibn ʿArabī may

[25] Ibn ʿArabī, *Tarjumān*, 82–83.
[26] Ibn ʿArabī, *Tarjumān*, 135 and 145.
[27] Ibn ʿArabī, *Tarjumān*, iii.
[28] Al-Shushtarī, *Songs of Love and Devotion*, 51.
[29] Stetkevych, *The Zephyrs of Najd*, 93–95.
[30] Zargar, *Sufi Aesthetics*, 120–50, on mystical readings of love poetry.

have used the classical Arabic tradition primarily for the purpose of describing his own state rather than for a description of the beloved/Beloved. Likewise in a mystical *muwashshaḥ*, a more vernacular form of poetry than the *qaṣīda* or *ghazal* and typical of Andalusi poetry, the mystic refers to the traditional male lovers Ghaylān and Qays as experiencing love but does not mention explicitly their female counterparts Mayya and Laylā.[31]

Nicholson may have had a point with his contrast between superior Arabic prose and superior Persian poetry, at least insofar as this was occasioned by his subject Ibn ʿArabī, given his mixed reviews as a poet. As Saʿdiyya Shaikh has recently argued in some detail, however, Ibn ʿArabī's technical prose writings reveal a subtle and complex albeit heterogeneous application of gender binaries to an understanding of God and the relationship between God and humankind.[32] On the one hand, Shaikh identifies gendered categories that are in keeping with the patriarchal society in which Ibn ʿArabī lived. The archetypal seeker, for instance, is described as male, "maleness" (*rujūliyya*) denoting spiritual fulfillment.[33] In the relationship of teacher and disciple, gender functions as a relational category: independent of their gender, the teacher is active and male, the disciple receptive and female. Likewise God's creation is the active act of the male, while the created world is receptive and occupies the role of the female. On the other hand, Shaikh argues that the mystic displayed subversive tendencies in various areas that could even make him a suitable reference point for modern feminist interpretations. Among the latter, Ibn ʿArabī's support for the female imamate stands out.[34] Unlike most scholars of his time, indeed our own time as well, he believed that because men and women are both created in the image of God and have the same spiritual potential, women should be allowed to lead a mixed-gender prayer.

More importantly in the present context, Ibn ʿArabī used gendered categories in the cosmological context of divine creation in surprising ways. Apophatic tendencies are complemented by the popular mystical concept of the "coincidence of opposites," frequently referred to in scholarship by its Latin name *coincidentia oppositorum* because it is widely associated with Nicholas of Cusa (1401–1464).[35] Since the process of creation starts within God, God's active and male part interacts with another part of God that is receptive and female. Such feminine and gender-inclusive images of God stand in contrast to, but alongside, male images and "present radical shifts in the Muslim symbolic economy

---

[31] For an analysis of this particular *muwashshaḥ*, see Bachmann, "Manifestations of the Divine," 79.

[32] Shaikh, *Sufi Narratives of Intimacy.*

[33] Shaikh, *Sufi Narratives of Intimacy,* 51.

[34] Shaikh, *Sufi Narratives of Intimacy,* 91.

[35] For the *coincidentia oppositorum*, see Sviri, "Between Fear and Hope."

of the divine."[36] The gender-inclusive notion of God has repercussions for the idea of humankind being created in the image of God, especially if we take the creation myth of Adam and Eve into consideration. The relationship between the mythical woman and man mirrors that between human and cosmos. Apart from serving as an epitome, women "provide the most perfect locus of witnessing God because men can see in the female form both God's activity and reception of activity . . . in women, men witness this *coincidentia oppositorum* as the most complete theophany of God."[37]

Al-Shushtarī: The Multiple Layers of Laylā

Abū 'l-Ḥasan al-Shushtarī seems to have succeeded where the earlier Andalusi mystic left some contemporaneous and modern readers confused, irritated, or dissatisfied: in his use of poetry to popularize mystical ideas. Many of the strategies that al-Shushtarī used in order to adapt the classical Arabic tradition of love poetry into mystical contexts are very similar to what we have already seen in the cases of the two authors of the previous generation, Ibn al-Fāriḍ and Ibn ʿArabī. Al-Shushtarī too composed *qaṣīda*s and *ghazal*s, transforming the desert of the pre-Islamic Bedouin poet into the sacred topography of the Muslim pilgrim and projecting his spiritual love onto a human beloved. Like Ibn al-Fāriḍ, he composed wine poetry in which the reader is exposed to the interplay between spiritual intoxication and transgressive drunkenness. Al-Shushtarī was clearly part of a larger mystical and poetic movement, and he may have been inspired by the works of the locally celebrated Ibn al-Fāriḍ and Ibn ʿArabī, the latter also sharing al-Shushtarī's fate as an Andalusi emigrant.

It is worth mentioning here that both authors were part of what must have been a significant number of Andalusis who left the peninsula for a variety of reasons and were in the eastern lands of the Arabic-speaking world as the Christian armies of the so-called *reconquistadores* took control over several important cities—Cordoba in 1236, Valencia in 1238, Seville in 1248, etc. What a modern writer might with some likelihood and justification represent as a great personal tragedy has left only very few explicit traces in the writings of medieval Andalusis. For our purposes, this long-lasting displacement is significant since it is likely to have contributed to the cultural dynamics reflected in the mystical poetry discussed here and also in adaptations of philosophical elements by mystics, a trend that, although it may have not been entirely imported from al-

---

[36] Shaikh, *Sufi Narratives of Intimacy*, 126. See also 175, where Shaikh argues that ʿArabī's choice of grammatically feminine words underscores his case for a female aspect of the divine.

[37] Shaikh, *Sufi Narratives of Intimacy*, 158 for the epitome, 177 for women embodying the *coincidentia oppositorum*.

Andalus, at least fed into intellectual and religious developments in the eastern Mediterranean.[38] Such cultural dynamics, inspired by regional diversity within the Arabic-speaking parts of the Mediterranean where Muslims constituted the majority of the population, illustrates once again some of the shortcomings of binary views of the Mediterranean. The migration of Andalusis to specific parts of the Muslim world — notably North Africa, Egypt, and Syria, where we know of communities in exile — must have had a lot to do with the fact that Arabic was spoken here too, but the established routes along the Mediterranean also account for the choices displaced Muslims from the Iberian Peninsula made with regard to their future homes. Then again, these choices support binary views of the Mediterranean as well, since it was invariably to lands under Muslim rule that Andalusis fled.

While al-Shushtarī's poems conform to trends attested to elsewhere, it is not clear to what extent he was familiar with the works of Ibn al-Fāriḍ and Ibn ʿArabī. He "composed a series of short odes (*qaṣāʾid*) apparently in response to poems in al-Shaykh al-Akbar's [i.e., Ibn ʿArabī's, A.A.] *Interpreter of Desires*,"[39] but al-Shushtarī gained a reputation for his poetic achievements quite independent of the older mystic. Unlike Ibn ʿArabī, al-Shushtarī excelled in composing vernacular poetry, a form he seems to have employed deliberately in order to communicate his mystical insights to a wider audience. Ibn ʿArabī too chose erotic poetry because of its popularity, but al-Shushtarī appears to have been significantly more successful with his formal choice.[40] Another explanation for the rapid and profound popularization of al-Shushtarī's poetry is the fact that his verses were — and still are — sung to music.

A peculiarity of al-Shushtarī's poems is that some of them are set in Christian monasteries.[41] Even though the Islamic tradition is somewhat critical of monasticism and the celibacy of monks (not unlikely an effort to draw clear distinctions between Christians and Muslims), Muslims had been visiting monasteries for centuries when traveling. At the same time, these places enjoyed a dubious reputation for the presence of wine and loose morals. In line with

---

[38] For a longer version of these observations, see Akasoy, "Andalusi Exceptionalism."

[39] Al-Shushtarī, *Songs of Love and Devotion*, 20–21. The editor Alvarez also notes "aesthetic affinities with the work of Ibn Quzmān" (28). Ibn Quzmān (1078–1160) is known for his poetry.

[40] Al-Shushtarī, *Songs of Love and Devotion*, 24–25. Distinctly Andalusi forms of vernacular poetry, *muwashshaḥāt* and *zajal*s, became popular in the eastern Mediterranean during the late twelfth and early thirteenth centuries, precisely at the time that the mysticism of Ibn ʿArabī and the following generation gained attention. Both kinds of vernacular Arabic poetry were widely used for profane poetry.

[41] Al-Shushtarī, *Songs of Love and Devotion*, 111–25; Abou-Bakr, "The Religious Other."

al-Shushtarī's mystical interest in wine, he presents monasteries as a place for intoxication and illumination.

If we take both settings—the desert from the pre-Islamic ode and the monastery—jointly into consideration, it becomes obvious that in both cases the poet locates his mystical experience in an environment that was Other. Both historically and environmentally, the desert was mostly Other for Ibn al-Fāriḍ, for Ibn ʿArabī, and for al-Shushtarī as well. In fact, it had already been Other for the urban poets of the Abbasid period. They may have been exposed to deserts during their journeys, but they did not spend their lives there.

Whether al-Shushtarī's poetic references to monasteries correspond to actual social interactions with Christians is unclear, just as there is some ambiguity in the relationship between the symbolic and the real in Ibn ʿArabī's gendered categories.[42] The topographic alterity that is derived in both cases from the poetic tradition opens a space for the effective communication of mystical insights. As much as the vernacular poetic forms and colloquial song locate the mystical experience in everyday life,[43] the setting of desert and monastery create a distance and thus reflect the exceptional character of the mystical experience. There is a paradox in the choice of settings that the poet has never experienced in order to convey an authentic experience, although one could argue that as poetic spaces they are in their discursive function familiar locations for a mystical experience. (The same might be said about the function of gender—the female poetic beloved is both a gendered Other and poetically familiar.)

Maria Lourdes Alvarez argued that al-Shushtarī's poems are more accessible because it is more obvious if they are written in a religious register. The confusion that led Ibn ʿArabī to the inclusion of a disambiguating commentary in his *Tarjumān al-ashwāq* does not plague al-Shushtarī's oeuvre.[44] Alvarez notes one exception to this principle: five poems that follow the classical style (rather than the vernacular) and that can easily be read as religious and mystical, but do not contain the otherwise typical explicit clues.

Among these five poems, one stands out that is especially relevant for our present interest in the function of gender in descriptions of God. The poem, titled "Layla" by its English translator, Alvarez, describes in the typical paradox manner of mystics the ineffable being of the same name.[45] The first verse already

---

[42] This is a more general problem; see Behloul, "The Testimony of Reason and the Historical Reality."

[43] Al-Shushtarī, *Songs of Love and Devotion*, 27.

[44] Al-Shushtarī, *Songs of Love and Devotion*, 51: "While his poems are steeped in pre-Islamic or secular Andalusian poetic traditions, they are rather clearly marked as religious either through the use of Qurʾanic vocabulary or mystical terminology or through rhetorical techniques . . ."

[45] Al-Shushtarī, *Songs of Love and Devotion*, 54–55. For the Arabic text, see al-Shushtarī, *Dīwān*, 81–82.

establishes Laylā as utterly unique in the nature of her existence. "Apart from Laylā, nothing in the vicinity (*al-ḥayy*) is alive (*ḥayy*)," states the first hemistich. The assignation of real life already suggests that Laylā stands in one way or another for God who is called "the Living" in the Qur'an (2:255; 3:2), life standing in contrast to mortality as well as to dependent existence of created beings whose aliveness depends on what is truly alive. (Indeed, one might read the words as "Apart from Laylā, there nothing is alive in the Living." The reading might violate the poetic principle that the same word can only be used a second time if it has a different meaning, but theologically speaking, the divine Living is different from any other living being.) Although Alvarez's rendering of the first hemistich brings the Islamic concept of God even more obviously to mind (her "There is no life but Laylā" being reminiscent of the Islamic profession of faith, "There is no god but God," which in terms of its underlying grammatical principles supports my reading of "There is nothing alive in the Living"), in her comments the translator and scholar glosses Layla as "a symbol for divine Beauty,"[46] i.e., as something that is one or two steps removed from God. The following description establishes Laylā — again in paradoxical terms — as ubiquitous, but transcendent as well. The seeker is held to pursue Laylā, to know and to admire her, but the description also states that she cannot be grasped and that full union with her is impossible. The poem ends on a note both optimistic and paradox: Laylā is inside of Qays, and their identities are interchangeable.

Laylā's ubiquity is expressed prominently throughout the poem. "Her mystery emanates in everything" (verse 2), "her beauty is widespread" (verse 3), "in her meadows, there is none but her" (verse 9). Al-Shushtarī uses two images that are popular in the Islamic intellectual tradition. Verse 4 establishes that Laylā "is like the sun, its light radiant." Inspired by Neoplatonism and Plotinus, Muslim philosophers sometimes used the imagery of the sun and its rays in order to express the complex relationship between God's immanence and transcendence and to explain how God could be the source of all being, yet never decrease in existence. The rays of sunlight also helped to account for the ways in which the created world reflected its creator but was so much inferior. The language used by the translator in verse two ("her mystery *emanates*") also brings the technical terminology of Neoplatonism to mind, even more than the Arabic.

A second popular image is the mirror, an image often associated with Ibn ʿArabī's cosmology. The model of the mirror allows mystics to explain in what sense the created world reflects God's nature and is parallel to God, but not identical. Depending on the quality of the mirror (i.e., whether polished or unpolished), the reflection of the divine creator can be better or worse. Ibn ʿArabī has discussed this in great detail in his writings about the human being as a mirror of the divine. The imagery corresponds to the common idea that God created

---

[46] Al-Shushtarī, *Songs of Love and Devotion*, 52.

humans in his own image.[47] In al-Shushtarī's poem, Laylā "is like the mirror in which images appear reflected, yet nothing resides there" (verse 5). "In her raiment, her ambiguity is displayed, for everything is mirrored in her" (verse 13). The mirror allows for some reflection of the fullness of God's being, but it is a reflection only and not an independent source of being, of creation and essences.

Al-Shushtarī mixes images and models here. It is plausible to assume that he was familiar with these cosmological images and the contexts in which they often appeared. The legacy of Ibn ʿArabī must have been very present, and that the younger mystic had some awareness of the philosophical tradition is suggested by his poem rhyming on the letter *nūn*, the *Nūniyya*. Al-Shushtarī does not say the same thing in two different conceptual languages. While the comparison of Laylā and the sun suggests that Laylā is God, the comparison of Laylā and the mirror suggests that Laylā is a manifestation or projection of God. The source of the images that are reflected in her is different from Laylā herself. The dual nature of Laylā, whom I read as a cosmological and metaphysical element designated as feminine, corresponds here to the dual function of the feminine in Shaikh's interpretation of Ibn ʿArabī. While Laylā facilitates creation, she is part of the process of creation herself and does not remain entirely passive.

While the references to Laylā's "mystery" (verse 2) and "beauty" (verse 3) work well with the gloss of Laylā as a symbol for divine Beauty, the references to Laylā as the sun or mirror, indeed the representation of Laylā as omnipresent, suggest that the symbol named Laylā involves much more. Not only God's beauty is manifest in the created world but other aspects of the divine as well. Cosmological femininity here involves more than the conventional elements of beauty and, perhaps, motherhood. In verse 8, al-Shushtarī declares "Her injustice is just. As for her justice, it is grace." Among God's attributes, justice figures prominently in the Islamic tradition. As we can see here, the nature of divine justice is hard or even impossible to grasp for humans, as far as al-Shushtarī was concerned. If we follow widespread theological and hermeneutical views, the statement that Laylā's—or God's—injustice is just might imply that God's justice (just like the other attributes) cannot be measured in human terms. If we understand "God is just" according to our human understanding of the concept of justice, we impose restrictions on the divine. At the same time, however, al-Shushtarī contrasts Laylā's injustice and her justice. While the former is justice, the latter is her grace. The statement reflects the utterly perplexing experience of trying to grasp the nature of God with our human limitations. It reflects the mystical concept of *coincidentia oppositorum* but also the variety within the human experience of the divine. The inability of humans to grasp Laylā is expressed in a variety of ways in the poem, which also reflect the variety of ways in which humans may try to approach her. "Her beauty is widespread,

---

[47] Sells, "Ibn ʿArabī's Polished Mirror."

its fullness, concealed" (verse 3) suggests that while humans can be aware of her existence wherever they are and perceive some of her essential features (such as her beauty or, below in the poem, her justice or grace), they cannot fully perceive or understand her. Even if God's beauty is only one aspect of the divine, a human is not going to be fully exposed to this aspect.

Two verses refer to an orientation of the created world towards Laylā: "everything praises her" (verse 2) and "she alone is invoked" (verse 9). The last phrase too supports the assumption that at least sometimes Laylā symbolizes God rather than God's beauty, since it is more likely that God alone is invoked rather than God's beauty alone. Many of the verses state clearly that the quest for Laylā is to some extent futile, since she remains elusive. Speaking about the light of Laylā the sun, al-Shushtarī explains: "when you seek it, (it) turns to shadow" (verse 4). "A wonder, she remains distant, nowhere" (verse 10). Despite its frustrations, the quest for Layla ought to be pursued: "Hers is the right course, even if I suffer" (verse 7). "And union with her brings us fullness, distance from her, division; both are mine" (verse 11). The promise of full union and unmitigated encounter is a threat as well: "she unveiled one day for Qays and he turned away, saying: O people, I loved no other" (verse 14). The "unveiling" works both literally, if we think about the human lovers Qays and Laylā, and allegorically. The Qur'an too refers to God's veils (42:51), a tradition that gained some popularity in mysticism such as in Ibn 'Arabī's work or in al-Ghazālī's mystical Qur'anic commentary, *The Niche of Lights* (*Mishkāt al-anwār*).[48] According to the Islamic tradition, the created world cannot bear direct exposure to God. Mountains crumble when exposed to their creator (7:143). And yet the mystical tradition in particular affirms the possibility of such contacts, or at least their approximation.

The poem ends with another perplexing paradox and on a note of optimism regarding the quest for Laylā: "I am Layla and she is Qays. What a wonder! How is that what I seek comes to me from me?'"(verse 15) The verses reflects common mystical tropes across different cultures that to understand God one must understand oneself and that the quest of the gnostic is always an internal quest. The reversal of gender roles relates to the idea of a mystical union alluded to in verses 10 and 11. The fact that the reversal of lover and beloved involves assignations of gender, however, points to a potentially subversive dimension of the poem. The lover becomes female, and it is therefore the woman who assumes the active part whereas Qays, the conventional lover, now becomes the beloved — or rather, the Beloved — and the male character assumes a passive role.

Once again we can see a parallel here between al-Shushtarī's cosmology as extrapolated from the poem and Ibn 'Arabī's gendered cosmology as analyzed by Shaikh. The feminine is mostly assigned a passive role, but that does not exhaust her character. Shaikh identifies active elements, and the dual Laylā — active

---

[48] Shaikh, *Sufi Narratives of Intimacy*, 69–70.

creator, passive beloved, Laylā as Qays—too has such different functions at the same time. In terms of cosmology, al-Shushtarī's verses may not be extraordinary, but what distinguishes the poem from many others in the *ghazal* tradition is that it foregrounds the description of the Beloved and offers a sustained description of the Beloved in feminine terms. The symbol of Laylā functions as a unifying force for diverse allegorical approaches to God and thus as an effective poetic framework for paradox and *coincidentia oppositorum*. Laylā allows the gnostic lover to approach God, but since al-Shushtarī maintains the gender binary that is fundamental to the image of Laylā, the female figure also allows al-Shushtarī to express God's alterity. Even at the moment of union the two gendered characters—Qays and Laylā—are separate not just as lover and beloved but also by way of their respective genders.

Conclusions and an Afterthought: Feminist Hermeneutics of the Qur'an

While medieval Muslim scholars were hardly oblivious to issues of gender in their Qur'anic hermeneutics, whether their deliberations were theological in nature or juridical, it is also fair to say that these issues have gained much significance in the modern period. Among those who promote a reading of the holy text that gives greater prominence to the interests and experience of women, Amina Wadud enjoys a particularly high profile.[49] As part of feminist approaches to the Qur'an, some authors point out that apart from the effect of the grammatical gender of God, the divine voice in the text is conventionally perceived as a male voice, not least because public recitations of the Qur'an are mostly conducted by men.

In a similar vein to Shaikh's analysis of Ibn 'Arabī, one can argue that the poetry of al-Shushtarī presents opportunities for disrupting these conventions, opportunities that are derived from the legacy of the Islamic world itself. While most poems referred to here use the Arabic tradition of love poetry in order to account for the internal state of the gnostic lover, al-Shushtarī's verses about Laylā use the female character as a mythological and poetic framework for a complex cosmology as well as in a relational function to uphold the divide between the lover and the transcendent God.

Some final comments too are in order concerning the framework of this volume. Some aspects of the material surveyed here confirm a binary view of the Mediterranean. The mystical poets discussed in this essay operated exclusively within the Arabic poetic tradition. Indeed, some of their references rely on the listeners' familiarity with the history and corpus of Arabic poetry. Then

---

[49] Wadud, *Qur'an and Woman*. For an introduction to Wadud's thought, see Barlas, "Amina Wadud's Hermeneutics of the Qur'an."

again, the contemporaneous tendencies in Persian mystical poetry suggest that the phenomena referred to here existed well beyond the Arabic-speaking world. Future comparative work may reveal to what extent similar developments existed in Romance literature as well.

As well connected as Christians were to areas in which Muslims were the majority, to our mystical poets they mostly seem to have constituted the Other, albeit a familiar Other. The poetic character of the female beloved/Beloved unfolds a similar dynamic as both Other and familiar, her Otherness and familiarity rooted in social as well as poetic contexts.

A stronger case against binary views of the Mediterranean emerges from the regional differences within the Muslim and Arabic-speaking world. Whatever distinguished the northern from the southern shores of the Mediterranean, they should not lead us to consider the respective realms homogeneous spheres.

Bibliography

Abou-Bakr, Omaima. "The Religious Other: Christian Images in Sufi Poetry." In *Images of the Other: Europe and the Muslim World before 1700*, ed. David R. Blanks, 96–108. Cairo: American University in Cairo Press, 1997.

Addas, Claude. *Quest for the Red Sulphur: The Life of Ibn 'Arabī*. Cambridge: The Islamic Texts Society, 1993.

Akasoy, Anna. "Niffarī: A Sufi Mahdi of the Fourth/Tenth Century?" In *Antichrist. Konstruktionen von Feindbildern*, ed. Wolfram Brandes and Felicitas Schmieder, 39–67. Berlin: Akademie-Verlag, 2010.

———. "Andalusi Exceptionalism: The Example of 'Philosophical Sufism' and the Significance of 1212." *Journal of Medieval Iberian Studies* 4, no. 1 (2012): 113–17.

Bachmann, Peter. "Manifestations of the Divine as Represented in Poems by Ibn al-'Arabī." In *Representations of the Divine in Arabic Poetry*, ed. Gert Borg and Ed de Moor, 71–83. Amsterdam: Rodopi, 2001.

Baldick, Julian. "The Legend of Rābi'a of Basra: Christian Antecedents, Muslim Counterparts." *Religion* 20 (1990): 233–47.

Barlas, Asma. "Amina Wadud's Hermeneutics of the Qur'an: Women Rereading Sacred Texts." In *Modern Muslim Intellectuals and the Qur'an*, ed. Suha Taji-Farouki, 97–123. Oxford: Oxford University Press, 2004.

Behloul, Martin-Samuel. "The Testimony of Reason and the Historical Reality: Ibn Ḥazm's Refutation of Christianity." In *Ibn Ḥazm of Cordoba: The Life and Works of a Controversial Thinker*, ed. Camilla Adang, Maribel Fierro, and Sabine Schmidtke, 457–83. Leiden: Brill, 2013.

Böwering, Gerhard. *The Mystical Vision of Existence in Classical Islam: The Qur'anic Hermeneutics of Sahl at-Tustarī (d. 283/896)*. Berlin: Walter de Gruyter, 1979.

———. "God and his Attributes." In *Encyclopaedia of the Qur'ān*, ed. Jane Dammen McAuliffe. 6 vols., 2:316–31. Leiden: Brill, 2001–2006.

Chittick, William. "Love in Islamic Thought." *Religion Compass* 8, no. 7 (2014): 229–38.

Ebstein, Michael. *Mysticism and Philosophy in al-Andalus. Ibn Masarra, Ibn al-'Arabī and the Ismā'īlī Tradition*. Leiden: Brill, 2014.

Homerin, Th. Emil. *From Arab Poet to Muslim Saint: Ibn al-Farid, his Verse, and his Shrine*. Cairo: American University in Cairo Press, 2001.

———. *Passion before Me, My Fate behind: Ibn al-Fāriḍ and the Poetry of Recollection*. Albany: State University of New York Press, 2011.

Ibn 'Arabī. *The Tarjumán al-Ashwáq: A Collection of Mystical Odes by Muḥyi'ddín Ibn al-'Arabí*. Edited and translated by Reynold A. Nicholson. London: Royal Asiatic Society, 1911.

Khairallah, As'ad E. *Love, Madness, and Poetry: An Interpretation of the Maǧnūn Legend*. Beirut: Orient Institut der Deutschen Morgenländischen Gesellschaft, 1980.

Knysh, Alexander D. *Ibn 'Arabi in the Later Islamic Tradition: The Making of a Polemical Image in Medieval Islam*. Albany: State University of New York Press, 1990.

Kuntze, Simon. "Love and God: The Influence of Ghazal on Mystic Poetry." In *Ghazal as World Literature*, vol. 1 *Transformations of a Literary Genre*, ed. Thomas Bauer and Angelika Neuwirth, 157–79. Beirut: Ergon, 2005.

Little, Donald P. "Did Ibn Taymiyya Have a Screw Loose?" *Studia Islamica* 41 (1975): 93–111.

Massignon, Louis. "Ibn Sab'īn et la 'conspiration Ḥallāgienne' en Andalousie et en Orient au XIIe siècle." In *Études d'orientalisme dédiées à la mémoire de Lévi-Provençal*. 2 vols., 2:661–81. Paris: Maisonneuve et Larose, 1962.

Sells, Michael. "Ibn 'Arabi's Polished Mirror: Perspective Shift and Meaning Event." *Studia Islamica* 67 (1988): 121–49.

Seyed-Gohrab, Ali Asghar. *Laylī and Majnūn: Love, Madness and Mystic Longing*. Leiden: Brill, 2003.

Shaikh, Sa'diyya. *Sufi Narratives of Intimacy: Ibn 'Arabī, Gender, and Sexuality*. Chapel Hill: University of North Carolina Press, 2012.

Sharma, Sunil. "Love: Premodern Discourses." In *Encyclopedia of Women and Islamic Cultures*, ed. Suad Joseph, 3:236–41. Leiden: Brill, 2003.

al-Shushtarī, Abū 'l-Ḥasan. *Dīwān*, ed. 'Alī Sāmī al-Nashshār. Cairo: al-Ma'ārif, 1960.

———. *Songs of Love and Devotion*. Translated by Lourdes María Alvarez. New York: Paulist Press, 2009.

Stetkevych, Jaroslav. *The Zephyrs of Najd: The Poetics of Nostalgia in the Classical Arabic Nasīb*. Chicago: University of Chicago Press, 1993.

Stroumsa, Sarah. *Maimonides in his World: Portrait of a Mediterranean Thinker*. Princeton: Princeton University Press, 2009.

Sviri, Sara. "Between Fear and Hope: On the Coincidence of Opposites in Islamic Mysticism." *Jerusalem Studies in Arabic and Islam* 9 (1987): 316–49.

van Gelder, Geert Jan. "Rābiʿa's Poem on the Two Kinds of Love: A Mystification?" In *Verse and the Fair Sex: Studies in Arabic Poetry and the Representation of Women in Arabic Literature*, 66–76. Utrecht: M. Th. Houtsma Stichting, 1993.

Wadud, Amina. *Qur'an and Woman: Rereading the Sacred Text from a Woman's Perspective*. New York: Oxford University Press, 1999.

Williams, Wesley. "Aspects of the Creed of Imam Ahmad ibn Hanbal: A Study of Anthropomorphism in Early Islamic Discourse." *International Journal of Middle East Studies* 34, no. 3 (2002): 441–63.

Zargar, Cyrus Ali. *Sufi Aesthetics: Beauty, Love, and the Human Form in the Writings of Ibn ʿArabi and ʿIraqi*. Columbia: University of South Carolina Press, 2011.

Chapter 6
NAVIGATING GENDER IN THE MEDITERRANEAN: EXPLORING HYBRID IDENTITIES IN
AUCASSIN ET NICOLETE

MERIEM PAGÈS,
KEENE STATE COLLEGE

Although much attention has been paid to the unique thirteenth-century Old French *chantefable Aucassin et Nicolete*, few have examined the narrative from the perspective of Mediterranean Studies. Yet looking at *Aucassin et Nicolete* in this light raises critical questions about gender, genre, ethnicity, and identity. In addition to the crucial fact that travel, and especially travel across the Mediterranean, plays an important role in narrative and character development, hybridity and cultural exchange are also essential to the tale. Both title characters evolve in ways that problematize the separation between Self and Other/Christian West and Muslim East and suggest a need to embrace rather than reject difference. At the heart of these concerns lies the issue of Nicolete's Saracen parentage: toward the end of *Aucassin et Nicolete*, the heroine, who is traditionally understood throughout the tale to be Christian, discovers that she is in fact the daughter of the Saracen king of Cartagena. The revelation that Nicolete is a Saracen princess seems almost an afterthought on the author's part, and the newly found princess hastens to leave her long-lost home and family to return to Latin Christendom. Perhaps because of the arbitrariness with which her origins are made known, Nicolete is usually not included in studies focusing on the medieval literary motif of the Saracen princess, the Muslim woman who falls in love with a Christian knight and betrays faith and kin to rescue him.[1] After all, the motif seems to owe its presence in *Aucassin et Nicolete* to the author's need to render Nicolete worthy of marrying Aucassin, future count of Beaucaire and the text's

---

[1] The first to identify and explore the literary motif of the Saracen princess was Metlitzki in her 1977 monograph *The Matter of Araby in Medieval England*. However, the motif did not garner much critical attention until the 1990s. Several important studies, such as de Weever's *Sheba's Daughters* and Ramey's *Christian, Saracen and Genre in Medieval French Literature*, have since examined the topic.

hero. However, I would like to argue that Nicolete's Saracen identity is essential to the development of the story and the success of the author's didactic approach. Nicolete's identification as a Saracen plays a crucial role in transforming the text from one ostensibly steeped in the medieval European literary tradition to a prime example of what Sharon Kinoshita has called "medieval Mediterranean literature."[2] The heroine's Mediterranean-Saracen identity permits her to act in a manner not befitting more conventional Christian heroines of high and late medieval texts, in turn allowing for a profound, though often comical, exploration of conventional gender roles.

The charming tale of two young lovers struggling to be with each other, *Aucassin et Nicolete* is unique, for it is the only surviving medieval *chantefable*, a genre in which the story is divided equally between passages in prose meant to be recited or read out loud and lyrical sections to be sung. Because *Aucassin et Nicolete* represents the only example of the genre and the text itself has survived in a single manuscript, it is difficult to draw larger conclusions about the *chantefable*'s generic conventions. The fact that the narrative dates to the thirteenth century, however, allows us to make certain inferences about it. *Aucassin et Nicolete* was composed in a society that had become both well versed and a little wary of the art of courtly love. Unlike twelfth-century writers such as Chrétien de Troyes, the anonymous author of the *chantefable* feels no need to conceal his misgivings about courtly love. By the thirteenth century, the relationship between Europe and the Muslim world had also become more complicated. While enthusiasm for crusading remained high well into the fourteenth century and beyond, the loss of most of the Crusader holdings, including Jerusalem itself, by the end of the twelfth century led to an increased need for negotiation with Muslim rulers in order to retain a foothold in the Holy Land — at least until the fall of Acre in 1291. Finally, but perhaps most important, the thirteenth century saw the rise and growth of the merchant class. As such, *Aucassin et Nicolete* was produced during a period of great transition and flux, one marked precisely by the kind of cultural exchange and interaction so important to the work. *Aucassin et Nicolete* was written at a time when Europe's relationship to the Mediterranean changed dramatically, again emphasizing the need for the text to be investigated through the lens of Mediterranean Studies.

Despite standing out in so many ways from other medieval European narratives, *Aucassin et Nicolete* at first seems to follow the rather predictable plotline of young love at odds with society. Aucassin, the son of Count Garin of Beaucaire, is desperately in love with Nicolete. She returns Aucassin's feelings, but Aucassin's parents will not allow their son to marry her. In an effort to secure a higher-born marriage partner for Aucassin, Garin and his wife have Nicolete imprisoned. The resourceful heroine escapes, finds Aucassin, who has by then

---

[2] Kinoshita, "Medieval Mediterranean Literature," 601.

also been locked away by his father, then runs away to a nearby forest. As soon as his father releases him from prison, Aucassin makes his way to the forest and his Nicolete. Finally reunited, the two lovers hop onto a merchant ship that takes them to Torelore, a land where gender roles are reversed and where our two heroes remain for three years. The two are then captured by Saracens attacking Torelore and separated. Here Aucassin's adventures come to an end, for his ship washes up on the shores of Beaucaire, where he learns he has become the new count. Nicolete, however, is taken to Cartagena, which she recognizes as her native city. Her father, the king, welcomes her home, but Nicolete leaves when she finds out that he intends to marry her to a fellow Saracen prince. She dyes her hair and face black and disguises herself as a black male minstrel before leaving for Beaucaire. Once there, Nicolete tests her lover one last time. When Aucassin makes it clear that he still loves her, Nicolete returns to the house of her foster-father, changes out of her disguise, and washes her face. Reunited for the last time, Aucassin and Nicolete marry and rule Beaucaire together.

In his preface to Edward Francis Moyer and Carey DeWitt Eldridge's translation of the work, Urban T. Holmes proposed that *Aucassin et Nicolete* should be read as a parody.[3] Since then, much scholarly attention has been directed at this particular aspect of the text, with much contention over what constitutes the anonymous author's primary target.[4] Only recently have scholars begun to turn from an examination of the larger question of parody—and the implications for Aucassin—to that of Nicolete's function within the text.[5] Those critics primarily concerned with Nicolete explore not only the manner in which she crosses and transgresses gender boundaries but also her identity as a Saracen woman converted to Christianity. For example, SunHee Kim Gertz and Paul S. Ropp mention Nicolete's Saracen identity to support their theory that Nicolete uses her imagination to transform her reality—exhibiting both male and female traits as

---

[3] Holmes, "Preface," v–viii.

[4] A brief summary of a few of the theories concerned with this question will suffice to show the variety of opinion on the subject: in *"Aucassin et Nicolette* as Parody," Harden suggests that the *chantefable* parodies the idyllic novel. Expanding Harden's argument, Sargent ("Parody in *Aucassin et Nicolette*," 605) has argued that "the creator of *Aucassin* was indulging in a light-handed and good-natured mockery of the whole art of fiction as practiced at the time, packing into a few dozen pages an astonishing number of 'mistakes,' i.e. deliberate infractions of the rules of composition both as expounded by the theorists and as put into practice by writers of fiction." Going even further than Sargent, Spraycar ("Genre and Convention in *Aucassin et Nicolette*") proposes that it is conventionality itself that the anonymous author of the *chantefable* wishes to render humorous. For a comprehensive survey of the work done on the use of parody in *Aucassin et Nicolette*, see Spraycar, "Genre and Convention"; see also Jodogne, "La parodie et le pastiche dans *Aucassin et Nicolette*," for the multiple ways in which the author uses parody.

[5] Smith was the first to raise the issue of Nicolete's role in the *chantefable* in 1977 in his "The Uncourtliness of Nicolette."

she does so—while Jane Gilbert claims that Nicolete displays a different kind of femininity precisely because she is a Saracen woman.[6]

Likewise captivated by Nicolete's Saracen background, Marla Segol has linked *Aucassin et Nicolete* with *Floire et Blancheflor*, proposing that both texts rejoice in the existence of hybrid Christian-Muslim identity in medieval Europe. Segol connects the need for Nicolete to be a Saracen with the probable Occitanian background of the text's anonymous author. Looking at *Aucassin et Nicolete* in juxtaposition with the late twelfth-century romance *Floire et Blancheflor*, Segol argues that both texts embrace and celebrate the presence of a hybrid Christian-Saracen identity, using what she calls the "hybrid self" to differentiate themselves from communities in northern and western France less directly influenced by the Muslim world. According to Segol, this hybridity is found both in the Christian-Saracen alliances formed in each of these texts as well as in subtle references to Muslim culture.[7]

In contrast to Segol, Lynn Ramey argues that Latin Christians progressively lose interest in the Muslim world and that this change is reflected in the diminishing importance of Saracen characters in popular medieval French literature. To Ramey, *Aucassin et Nicolete* constitutes a transitional step in this process. Juxtaposing the *chantefable* with *Floire et Blancheflor* as does Segol, Ramey claims that

> whereas in *Floire et Blancheflor* the entire community of Niebla and Hungary is converted to Christianity because of the exemplary love of the two young lovers, in *Aucassin et Nicolette*, the focus is on rejection of Islam and the Arab culture rather than on the conversion and continued positive interaction of two different peoples.[8]

Ramey suggests that *Aucassin et Nicolete* marks the beginning of an attitude of growing indifference to the Muslim world, a development that will end in the fifteenth century with the Saracen world merely serving as a place where the Christian protagonists resolve their problems. To a certain extent, this even seems the case for Nicolete in the *chantefable*: the Saracen world provides a background against which the work's heroine finds an answer to the question of her birth, gaining in value as a result of her encounter with the East.

If most recent critical studies of *Aucassin et Nicolete* have made Nicolete their focal point, few investigate the tools the author employs in order to craft his piece. In fact, those elements which make *Aucassin et Nicolete* a parody belong mostly, if not exclusively, to the tradition of western European texts dealing with

---

[6] Gertz and Ropp, "Literary Women, Fiction and Marginalization"; Gilbert, "The Practice of Gender in *Aucassin et Nicolette*."

[7] Segol, "Medieval Cosmopolitanism and the Saracen-Christian Ethos."

[8] Ramey, *Christian, Saracen and Genre*, 80.

the Muslim Other—and especially with those narratives set against the background, real or imaginary, of the Mediterranean.[9]

That *Aucassin et Nicolete* is a Mediterranean text essentially concerned with Mediterranean paradigms is concealed by the work's unique genre, one that both emphasizes its relationship to its Mediterranean context and complicates it. Indeed, the *chantefable*'s author presents us with a tale about love that leads his audience to entertain certain expectations about the piece. We assume, for example, that the narrative will belong to the genre of romance and that the main characters will act according to prescribed roles. Aucassin will strive to prove his prowess while Nicolete will display her virtue and nobility of heart. Our introduction to these characters confirms these expectations. Yet it quickly becomes obvious that Aucassin, though handsome and accomplished, is anything but heroic and that it is Nicolete who will function as the work's true hero. While the Mediterranean context of the text's landscape naturalizes much cross-cultural interaction, it simultaneously highlights the alterity of its gender politics.

How does the anonymous author set about rectifying our mistaken assumptions about the narrative and its characters? *Aucassin et Nicolete*'s unusual genre serves as the first important marker of the text's difference. Rather than a verse romance or a *chanson de geste* with romance elements, the *chantefable*'s constant shift from verse to prose signals its inability to settle on any one particular form. Perhaps this also intimates that *Aucassin et Nicolete* inhabits two distinct worlds, those of the Latin Christian Mediterranean and the Muslim Mediterranean, equally well.

Yet another important hint of the text's alterity lies in Aucassin's unconventional masculinity, a factor intricately linked to the *chantefable*'s exceptional genre. As mentioned above, the author initially portrays Aucassin in a manner that evokes the typical romance hero of high and late medieval works. However, Aucassin does not act the part of the hero. In fact, he acts very little, preferring to lament his fate for most of the narrative. Aucassin's atypical behavior indicates that the genre of *Aucassin et Nicolete* resists easy classification at the same time that its unique status makes it possible for the story's putative hero to be described in such unflattering terms. If Aucassin's deviant masculinity recalls the problematic behavior of such romance heroes as Erec in Chrétien de Troyes's *Erec et Enide*, it is explored in far more depth than in the earlier text. The ambiguity of the *chantefable*, itself a hybrid marrying prose with verse, is reflected in the treatment of its male protagonist: where *Erec and Enide* ends with a re-masculinized Erec, Aucassin remains passive throughout the tale. Like the form of the narrative to

---

[9] Medieval texts focusing on Latin Christian interaction with the Muslim world include *La chanson de Roland*, *Le cycle de Guillaume d'Orange*, *Floire et Blancheflor*, and the thirteenth-century Middle High German *Willehalm*. Other less well-known works such as the late Middle English romances *The King of Tars*, *Sir Bevis of Hampton*, and *The Sultan of Babylon* also belong to this widespread and highly popular medieval tradition.

which he belongs, Aucassin is two things at once: he is introduced as a paragon of male excellence but acts like a romance heroine.[10] This duality is reminiscent of the Mediterranean itself, which encompasses both Christian Self and Muslim Other. Aucassin's alternate masculinity, then, provides us with a good starting point for a discussion of *Aucassin et Nicolete* as a "Mediterranean" text.

Two particular scenes best illustrate Aucassin's unorthodox gender positioning. One such moment occurs when Aucassin, searching for Nicolete after her escape into the woods and his release from prison, encounters a hideously ugly herdsman, himself in hiding. The two decide to exchange stories, and Aucassin, who has just heard Nicolete's message referring to her as a marvelous and priceless beast, tells the man that he is looking for a valuable white greyhound he has lost. To this the peasant responds:

> Os! fait cil, por le cuer que cil Sires eut en sen ventre! Que vos plorastes por un cien puant? Mal dehait ait qui ja mais vos prisera, quant il n'a si rice home en ceste terre, se vos peres l'en mandoit dis u quinse u vint, qu'il ne les eust trop volentiers et s'en esteroit trop liés. Mais je doi plorer et dol faire.[11]

> ["What!" said he, "By the heart that Christ had in His stomach! You are crying for a stinking dog? Damn whoever praises you, when there is no man in this land so powerful, if your father asked him for ten or fifteen or twenty, that he would not give them very willingly, and he would be all too happy to do so. But I must cry and lament."][12]

The man then goes on to explain his own troubles: he cannot find the prize ox of the rich peasant for whom he works and has no money to make up for the loss. In the end, Aucassin solves the herdsman's problem by giving him the twenty *sous* he needs to pay for the lost animal, and the two part ways.

What purpose does this episode serve in the narrative? First and foremost, Aucassin's encounter with the peasant adds an element of surprise to the story. As many have noted, the figure of the hideous herdsman is hardly unique to *Aucassin et Nicolete*. As such, the *chantefable*'s medieval audience may have expected the encounter to develop in a specific fashion: the hideous herdsman is supposed to inquire about Aucassin's problem, then help him pursue his quest. Indeed, the episode seems at first to unfold along these lines. Only when the villain responds that Aucassin can expect no sympathy or respect if losing a white greyhound is his only trouble does the emphasis shift. By the end of the episode, the author has once again turned convention upside down, for it is Aucassin who ultimately

---

[10] Such examples of deviant masculinity as Aucassin and Erec are far less likely to occur in *chansons de geste* than in romances.

[11] *Aucassin et Nicolete*, trans. Walter, 112–14. Throughout this essay I use Walter's edition of the work.

[12] All translations are mine.

provides assistance to the hapless herdsman, rather than the other way around. Moreover, the character's description itself serves as a source of comic reversal—albeit one based on class rather than gender—for his ugliness suggests that he will prove to be dangerous, perhaps even evil.[13] But the peasant develops into a profoundly human character, one who is given a voice and depth usually absent in commoners.

The unusual depiction of the hideous herdsman is connected with the development of Aucassin as a character, for the nameless peasant provides a positive foil to our hero.[14] This is done in several ways. On the one hand, the herdsman renders any quest for love trivial by referring to the very basic and tangible need for food, shelter, and money. On the other, the peasant also makes Aucassin's particular quest for love look ridiculous by reminding us of how inferior Aucassin is to Nicolete. What provokes the man's tirade against Aucassin is the latter's allusion to his lost greyhound. The herdsman cannot understand why someone as rich as Aucassin would cry over a lost dog. Here it is important to note that Aucassin's invention of a lost white greyhound constitutes one of the very few moments in the piece when he acts according to his own impulse.

As SunHee Kim Gertz and Paul S. Ropp have suggested, Aucassin tries to show that he too can create an image capable of communicating to others the depth of his love for Nicolete, this in response to his beloved's own imaginative transformation of herself into a wondrous beast.[15] Aucassin fails miserably in this endeavor—the best he can come up with when trying to think of a marvelous creature is a white greyhound—and it is the herdsman who emphasizes the inadequacy of his substitution of a dog for a unique, mythical beast. On this rare occasion when Aucassin is alone and able to demonstrate his abilities as a lover and a courtly hero, the peasant he encounters reminds us of Nicolete's infinite superiority in both domains. The episode featuring the hideous herdsman thus stresses that the young man's masculinity is impaired. Although Aucassin possesses attributes that typically epitomize normative Christian noble masculinity, the text denounces him as a failed hero. Simply put, the parts that usually point to an idealized whole do not come together in any meaningful way in *Aucassin et Nicolete*, setting Aucassin further apart from other medieval heroes and masculinities.

The *chantefable*'s author again forces us to question his hero when he describes Aucassin's behavior in the imaginary land of Torelore. In the kingdom of Torelore—to which Aucassin and Nicolete are taken after their flight from Beaucaire—gender roles as well as the most fundamental rules of warfare are turned upside down. Thus the king of Torelore lies in bed after the birth of his

---

[13] Payen, *Le Moyen Age I*, 173.

[14] For two articles belonging to this school of thought, see DuBruck, "The Audience of *Aucassin et Nicolete*"; and Clark and Wasserman, "Wisdom Buildeth A Hut," 251.

[15] Gertz and Ropp, "Literary Women," 243.

son while the queen leads the army in battle. War is further perverted in this episode, for the Torelorians fight not with real weapons but with mushrooms, fresh
cheeses, and rotten apples. Aucassin attempts to teach the kingdom's ruler and
people to adhere to a more conventional understanding of gender and warfare,
first by beating the king until the latter has promised never to lie in childbed
again, then by throwing himself on the enemy with his sword.

The majority of scholars who have looked at this episode in the *chantefable*—and there have been many—have seen Torelore as an inversion of the "normal" world, one where Aucassin finally learns to act as a man and a knight.[16]
According to this analysis of the episode, Torelore and its people serve to emphasize the danger of Aucassin's earlier passive behavior and lack of interest in
knightly pursuits. The encounter with the king and queen of Torelore highlights
the abnormality of Aucassin and Nicolete's conduct up to this point by revealing
the ridiculous extremes to which male passivity and female activity lead: a king
lying in bed after the delivery of a child and a queen leading the army.[17] Here
Aucassin learns by negation how to behave, a lesson that will prove useful when
he succeeds his father as count of Beaucaire.

However, there are at least two problems with this received reading of the
episode. First of all, Aucassin does not seem to develop as a character as a result
of his stay in Torelore.[18] It is true that he becomes count of Beaucaire immediately upon his return from this strange land. One might therefore argue that his
experiences in this realm of fantasy provide him with the skills necessary to act
as a good and just ruler to his people. But we are never given the chance to judge
what kind of a count Aucassin makes; in fact, the emphasis shifts even more
noticeably towards Nicolete after the Torelore episode.[19] The only time we do see
Aucassin in action after his return to Beaucaire—when Nicolete comes to him
disguised as a black minstrel—he once again relegates all decision-making to
her, leaving her to ensure that their marriage finally take place. Thus, although

---

[16] Amongst others who have subscribed to this interpretation of the Torelore episode, McKean ("Torelore and Courtoisie," 64), has argued that "in the much-maligned
Torelore episode . . . the reversal of roles [is] so obvious that even the courtly lover had to
realize its foolishness." Here is a small sample of the theories that have sprung from this
reading of the Torelore episode: Harden (*"Aucassin et Nicolette* as Parody," 6–7) and Spraycar ("Genre and Convention," 110) see Torelore as emphasizing the danger of Aucassin's
earlier behavior while Brownlee ("Discourse as *Proueces* in *Aucassin et Nicolette*," 171) con-
tends that Torelore underscores Aucassin's inadequacy as the text's *locus* of *proueces* and
Szabics ("Amour et prouesse dans *Aucassin et Nicolette*," 1348) proposes that the episode
constitutes the author's response to Garin of Beaucaire's earlier exhortation to his son to
fight.

[17] Clevenger, "Torelore in *Aucassin et Nicolette*," 661; Gilbert, "The Practice of Gender," 218.

[18] Hunt, "La parodie médiévale," 370; Gertz and Ropp, "Literary Women," 229.

[19] Brownlee, "Discourse as Proueces."

one might expect Aucassin to have learned the importance of behaving in an active and knightly fashion in Torelore, the opposite seems to be the case: at the end of the *chantefable*, the main male character is no more dynamic than he was at the beginning. This conclusion compels us to take another look at the Torelore episode and reconsider its interpretation as a didactic moment when hero and audience alike realize the need for Aucassin to play the part of the aggressive warrior.

There exists a second difficulty with this traditional reading of the Torelore episode, namely that it does not end with a celebration of feudal life as represented by Aucassin. One might expect the episode to conclude in a resounding affirmation of the way of life embodied by our hero, with the king joyfully swearing to break with the land's abnormal traditions. Yet such is not the case. Although the king does promise never to lie in childbed again when Aucassin beats him for doing so, the emphasis is on the hero's violent behavior. As for the king, it remains unclear whether he is truly convinced of the need to get up from his *couvade*, especially when he asks, "Ha! biax sire, fait li rois, que me demandés vos? Avés vos le sens dervé, qui en me maison me batés?" ["Ah! Dear lord," said the king, "What do you want from me? Have you lost your mind, you who beat me in my house?"].[20] With these words, the ruler of Torelore himself calls attention to the lack of judgment and moderation displayed by the young man.[21]

If affirmation of Aucassin and the way of life he stands for seems to be missing upon his first encounter with the king of Torelore, it is even more so when he attempts to rectify what he sees as the Torelorians' inappropriate understanding of war. Once again, one might expect the inhabitants of this outlandish kingdom to show admiration for Aucassin's aggressive martial behavior, for he kills several of the enemy before they run away. Instead, the king forces him to stop and tells him, "trop en avés vos fait: il n'est mie costume que nos entrocions li uns l'autre" [you have done too much: it is not our custom to kill one another].[22] In this the king is supported by his people, who demand that Nicolete stay in the land and marry the heir to the throne but that Aucassin be banished.

Should the king's exhortation not to kill be taken seriously or as yet another comic moment? I would argue that we should heed the king's words; it is he who plays the part of the wise man, tolerantly and patiently explaining the laws of the land to Aucassin in spite of the young man's wild and destructive behavior.[23]

---

[20] *Aucassin et Nicolete*, 132.

[21] Clark and Wasserman ("Wisdom Buildeth a Hut," 261) claim that Aucassin reveals his lack of moderation and judgment when he kills several of the mock combatants attacking Torelore with cheese, mushrooms, and rotten apples. I would argue that the same can be said for his earlier assault on the king of Torelore.

[22] *Aucassin et Nicolete*, 136.

[23] I disagree with Jodogne's depiction ("La parodie et le pastiche," 61) of Aucassin as a wise man among fools in Torelore.

Moreover, despite—or perhaps because of—Aucassin's conservative approach to warfare, the episode provides yet another opportunity for our hero to appear foolish. Indeed, when Aucassin faces imminent expulsion from Torelore, it is Nicolete who must come to her lover's rescue. She refuses the king's son and reasserts her loyalty to Aucassin. The Torelore episode, one that initially focuses on Aucassin, presenting him as the embodiment of a normative feudal lifestyle, concludes once again with Nicolete taking charge and saving her lover. What is most interesting about this passage is that it presents the text's audience with an alternative masculinity far more flexible than the conventional western idea about manliness with which Aucassin struggles so much. Yet when confronted with a performance of gender that is both more comfortable and more successful than his own, Aucassin rejects it.

The gender reversal in practice in Torelore not only replicates the dynamic between Aucassin and Nicolete prior to and following their adventures in this strange land but also points to a broader focus on the concept of reversal in the *chantefable*, one inherently tied to its nature as a Mediterranean narrative. There exists no one cultural, political, class, or gender convention sacred enough to escape the text's irony and humor. For example, when Aucassin encounters the herdsman, his complaint about his missing Nicolete—and, one might argue, the nobility's obsession with courtly love—is ridiculed by the peasant. Likewise, when Aucassin arrives in Torelore, he reacts to the unfamiliar culture he confronts by asserting his own understanding of gender and warfare. The resulting tension between the king of Torelore and his guest poses unsettling questions about normative medieval constructions of chivalry and gender. After all, what makes killing people more honorable than throwing cheese and mushrooms at them? What makes Aucassin's idea of masculinity, at least as he describes it to the king, the correct one? Far from affirming the violence endemic in thirteenth-century Europe, the Torelore episode strips the aggressive chivalric behavior displayed by Aucassin of its customary value. At the end of Aucassin's Torelorian adventures, we—and perhaps even the titular character himself—can no longer act as if Beaucaire holds the truth about how to conduct oneself in the world.

If *Aucassin et Nicolete* serves to instruct about Mediterranean fluidity and Latin Christian rigidity, it places special emphasis on differing gender systems. I have argued against reading the Torelore episode as a didactic moment for Aucassin, but Aucassin does learn several important lessons in Torelore: for example, he realizes that there exist other cultures with diverse approaches to life, gender, and identity. The exchange with the king of Torelore also teaches Aucassin that masculinity—and especially Mediterranean masculinity—depends upon femininity and that the two must complement each other. When the king's behavior first suggests this to Aucassin, our protagonist reacts with the aggression expected of a product of noble chivalric society. This initial response is met first with shock, then with condemnation as the outraged people of Torelore prepare to banish their ungracious guest. Only Nicolete's intercession saves Aucassin, and when we next come across him, he asks her to make the final decision that will allow them to marry and rule Beaucaire together. In the end, Aucassin leaves Torelore a little bit wiser: while he has followed Nicolete's lead since the beginning of the work, only then does he accept and appreciate the ability to rely on his female partner. His encounter with the Other in Torelore has finally made it possible for him to embrace his ambiguous Mediterranean masculinity.

Any attempt to discuss Aucassin's alternate masculinity invariably leads us back to Nicolete. Nicolete goes beyond transgressing traditional gender roles; and if she does not simply celebrate the encounter between Muslims and Christians, she also presents the Mediterranean world as intrinsically valuable. Nicolete's character epitomizes the duality of the Mediterranean itself: she is both the Self, the familiar lady of courtly love literature, and the Other, the active, crafty Saracen princess of later medieval romance. She reveals her many talents not only in her ability to compensate for Aucassin's lack of heroic behavior but also in her capacity to adopt different, at times contradictory, roles. Thus she is at the same time beautiful heroine and active hero, white and black, Christian slave and Saracen princess, loyal sweetheart and trickster testing her lover. Even more unsettling perhaps, Nicolete shows an equal aptitude for each of these guises, displaying as much skill at playing music as she does at assessing her lover's worth.[24]

In addition to this chameleon-like potential to change and adapt to new surroundings—one that echoes the text's own shifting between prose and verse and between a court in France and its Mediterranean *outremer*—Nicolete is a character in perpetual motion.[25] From the moment we are introduced to her, Nicolete is on the move. At the very beginning of the *chantefable*, we are told that Nicolete has already traveled extensively: she comes from a mysterious foreign land and converted to Christianity only after arriving in Beaucaire. This initial suggestion is reinforced when Nicolete runs away from Count Garin and her foster-father. Later on, she will continue the journey begun in her infancy, first with a trip to Torelore, then one to Cartagena, before finally coming back to Beaucaire. One might argue that she does not choose to travel to Torelore and Cartagena—just as she did not choose to be enslaved and brought to Beaucaire as a child—since these journeys result from chance encounters with pirates. However, a comparison with Aucassin highlights Nicolete's relative predilection for travel. Even accidentally, Aucassin leaves his ancestral domain only once. At stake here is Nicolete's Mediterranean identity: Nicolete's ability to cross the sea again and again, moving back and forth from Christendom to Muslim lands,

---

[24] This kind of duality is not restricted to Mediterranean heroines. In the early fourteenth-century Middle English romance *Sir Bevis of Hampton*, the Saracen princess Josian presents many of the same potentially duplicitous characteristics as Nicolete. Like Nicolete, for example, Josian disguises herself as a minstrel.

[25] In this respect as well, she stands in stark contrast to Aucassin, a character who prefers to weep and lament rather than take action.

hints at her strong connection with the world of the Mediterranean. She—and not Aucassin—serves as the text's primary representative of the Mediterranean. Yet both characters possess a bond with the Mediterranean, and both are ultimately enriched by this relationship. Nicolete must fully explore her Mediterranean identity so as to become the advisor Aucassin will need by his side once he inherits Beaucaire.[26] Both Aucassin and Nicolete have to shed their Christian French identity and become Other—doing so through the journeys they undertake—to increase their value in Latin Christian society. If the perspective through which the story is told remains Christian and French, the Mediterranean—and particularly the Saracen Mediterranean—invokes nothing but respect and admiration.

At this point, it may no longer seem so surprising to discover that Nicolete is the daughter of the Muslim king of Cartagena. By giving Nicolete a Saracen lineage, the anonymous author of *Aucassin et Nicolete* taps into the long-established tradition of the Saracen princess motif, one according to which a Saracen woman, usually beautiful and of high birth, is shown to betray her faith, culture, and family in order to join the Christian world through conversion and marriage to the hero. That Nicolete presents us with a character in which gender and ethnicity collide recalls the treatment of Saracen princesses in late medieval romances—for example, the fifteenth-century Middle English *Sowdone of Babylon*. Like other Saracen princesses, Nicolete can perform gender and ethnicity equally well. She can choose to pass as white or black just as she can act the part of the traditional heroine or adopt the role of the hero.[27] If anything, Nicolete seems to surpass her Saracen sisters in her ability to shape-shift, differing from her literary counterparts only in the reach of her talent.

That Nicolete possesses such a gift for performance could lead us to question her value as a character—as well as that of the Muslim world in general. When Nicolete disguises herself as a black male minstrel at the end of the story, her disguise allows her to pretend that she is the exact opposite of who she really is—black rather than white, male instead of female, and a commoner rather than a princess.[28] This ability to pass as the opposite of oneself initially seems to highlight the author's anxiety at the possibility of penetration by the Saracen Other.[29] Nicolete's disguise echoes that of William when he first enters the Saracen city

---

[26] That the work ends with Nicolete serving the dual function of Beaucarian ambassador to the Mediterranean and permanent Mediterranean presence in Beaucaire bears witness to the power of the Mediterranean as a political force as well as one that shapes individual performances of gender.

[27] For more on Nicolete's blackface performance at the end of the *chantefable*, see Menocal, "Signs of the Times"; and de Weever, "Nicolette's Blackness—Lost in Translation."

[28] Ramey, *Christian, Saracen and Genre*, 86.

[29] Ramey, *Christian, Saracen and Genre*, 86.

of Orange in *La prise d'Orange*, having taken the precaution of smearing his face with black dye so as to blend in with the dark-skinned Saracens. In *Aucassin et Nicolete*, however, it is not the Christian hero who possesses the power to assume a different identity and move fluidly across boundaries but the Saracen-born heroine, and the text conveys a very different message from *La prise d'Orange*. Here the emphasis lies on the fluidity and ambiguity of difference between the two halves of the medieval Mediterranean—especially when viewed from the class perspective of the nobility. The text shows the porousness of these boundaries, suggesting that class superseded religious difference in the Latin Christian Mediterranean.

The other Saracen characters in the work can also appear menacing. In addition to Nicolete herself, the Saracens are represented by three distinct groups: (1) the nameless Saracen merchants who sell Nicolete to her Christian foster-father; (2) the men who capture the castle of Torelore, thereby causing the lovers' second and final separation; and (3) Nicolete's Saracen family personified in the king of Cartagena. To begin with the Saracen merchants, those who kidnap and sell Nicolete to the vassal of Garin of Beaucaire are the direct cause of her predicament.[30] It is they who are responsible not only for Nicolete's loss of freedom but also for her loss, perhaps more important, of her own knowledge and understanding of her place in society. Unlike the merchants who are likewise accountable for the capture and enslavement of Rennewart in Wolfram von Eschenbach's *Willehalm*, the Saracen merchants in *Aucassin et Nicolete* compound their crime by failing to transmit the secret of her royal birth, thereby making it impossible for Garin to accept her as his future daughter-in-law. The men who assault and take the castle in Torelore, then capture the lovers and separate them, seem equally threatening.

Yet both sets of Saracens ultimately serve a positive function in the story. If the Saracen merchants who capture and sell Nicolete are responsible for her loss of freedom and status, they are also to be lauded for bringing her to Europe, enriching Garin's lands with a unique and highly valued commodity. The second group of Saracens likewise plays an important and constructive role in the narrative. These men return Nicolete to the Saracen world, enabling her to gain

---

[30] Merchants are mentioned twice in the *chantefable*. The first reference to trade occurs when Nicolete is described as having been purchased from merchants, designated twice as *Sarasins*. On another occasion, the man who sold Nicolete is labeled a *Saisne*, a term originally used for Saxons but later applied to non-Christians in general: *Aucassin et Nicolete*, 189. The second group of merchants encountered by Aucassin and Nicolete bring our hero and heroine to Torelore. Unlike the men who sold Nicolete to her foster-father, these are designated by the generic term *marceans*. This reinforces the impression that Saracens are presented as frightening and evil in the work, for only the least appealing of the merchants—those who engage in slavery—are clearly indicated to be Saracens.

crucial information about her birth and status.[31] Virginia M. Green has argued that commerce and financial exchanges are essential to the plot and meaning of the *chantefable*, and, throughout the text, it is the Saracens who are portrayed as the principal agents of such transactions.[32] Saracens—whether they be merchants or invaders—function as the link between East and West, Christians and Saracens, and, in doing so, they also act as agents of change, transmitting precious Saracen commodities and knowledge to the Christian world. That Latin Christendom and those who inhabit it continue to grow and develop depends in large part on the goods made accessible to them by the Saracens.

As for Nicolete's father, he is portrayed in even more unambiguously positive terms than the Saracen merchants and raiders. In addition to identifying Nicolete as a princess, the king of Cartagena serves as a positive foil to Aucassin's Christian father, Garin of Beaucaire. Here it is important to note what the king of Cartagena does and does *not* do upon recovering his long-lost daughter. Nicolete's royal father does try to arrange an alliance between Nicolete and a Saracen king. But when Nicolete runs away, he is not portrayed as stubbornly attempting to force her into this loveless match—something Garin might happily have done to Aucassin had an alliance with a princess or a count's daughter been possible. Nor is the king of Cartagena shown to use violence in trying to rein in his rebellious daughter, providing a positive contrast to Garin in this respect as well. Finally, the Saracen king's actions can be justified and explained in a way that Garin's cannot. Finding that his daughter is alive and now a marriageable young woman of about eighteen, it is his duty and obligation as her father to present her with a suitable match. Having been separated from Nicolete for most of her life, Nicolete's biological father cannot be expected to know of the depth of her feelings for Aucassin, and this ignorance exculpates him. In contrast, Garin of Beaucaire's knowledge of the lovers' feelings for each other makes him bear the full responsibility for dividing the two young people. The Saracen father thus appears much more understanding than his Christian counterpart.[33]

---

[31] This particular group epitomizes the ambiguous nature of the relationship with the Saracen world in *Aucassin et Nicolete*; while their purpose seems to be to cause pain and violence, their interference in fact leads to the permanent reunion of the two lovers: Pauphilet, *Le Legs du Moyen Age*, 244.

[32] Green (*"Aucassin et Nicolette,"* 197) also emphasizes that Nicolete is treated as a valuable commodity, but Segol ("Medieval Cosmopolitanism") points out that, when Nicolete disguises herself as a *jongleur* at the end of the text, she becomes both merchant and merchandise, assuming control of her own exchange to Aucassin and Latin Christendom.

[33] Of course, in reality, few, if any, fathers cared about the feelings of their noble daughters. Rather, noble parents sought to forge political alliances that would further their bloodlines. See Brundage, *Law, Sex, and Christian Society in Medieval Europe*; Duby, *Medieval Marriage*; Duby, *The Knight, the Lady and the Priest*; Duby, *Love and Marriage in the Middle Ages*; and Bloch, *Etymologies and Genealogies*.

A Saracen princess, pirates, multiple examples of international trade and commerce: *Aucassin et Nicolete* is filled with Mediterranean elements that, while initially perceived as a mere illustrative backdrop, are in fact crucial to the development of the story as a whole. Moreover, the text's Mediterranean features carry highly positive value, this even when they appear threatening at the outset. I have argued above that trade with the Muslim world ultimately serves a positive function for Latin Christendom. As for Nicolete herself, she continuously exerts a constructive influence on Aucassin, teaching him by example to become more active, leading him on adventures that he could never have undertaken on his own, and eventually returning to Beaucaire to rule his lands by his side.

That Nicolete can accomplish so much hinges almost entirely on her identification as a Mediterranean princess, the Saracen daughter of the king of Cartagena. The figure of the Saracen princess stands for a literary convention that has become both well established and highly popular by the beginning of the thirteenth century. Revealing that Nicolete is really a Saracen princess places our anonymous *chantefable* in company with such great and diverse medieval texts as, amongst others, *La chanson de Roland*, *Le cycle de Guillaume d'Orange*, and Wolfram von Eschenbach's *Parzival* and *Willehalm*. The author of *Aucassin et Nicolete* knows of his audience's exposure to the Saracen princess motif, and it is this familiarity that he intends to use not only to increase the appeal of his narrative but also to render Nicolete's active and independent behavior acceptable. As a Saracen princess—and especially one connected with the Mediterranean—she is allowed and even expected to go off on adventures alone, escape from prison, lure her lover back to her in the middle of the forest and so on and so forth. While the fact that Nicolete was born a Saracen makes it fully permissible for her to act in this fashion, her Mediterranean background grants her the ability to blend and pass between Christian and Muslim worlds.

Not only does Nicolete's Saracen birth make her the feisty heroine we know and love but it further allows the anonymous author of *Aucassin et Nicolete* to raise important questions about genre and gender, particularly by exploring Aucassin's alternative and unconventional masculinity. Although Aucassin is introduced as the embodiment of Latin Christian masculinity, the *chantefable*'s author makes it clear early on that his character is in fact the very opposite of the ideal medieval hero. From his lack of activity to his relegation of all major decision-making to Nicolete, Aucassin displays none of the features found in conventional heroes of high and late medieval narratives. Such a treatment of the text's hero could be read as simple parody, and, indeed, the work's reversal of its audience's expectations adds greatly to its comic effect. However, the inclusion of the Torelore episode illustrates that more is at stake than simple fun at Aucassin's expense. While Aucassin reveals his inability to embrace his unusual masculinity in Torelore, his exchange with Nicolete at the end of the work suggests that he has come to value rather than reject or deny it. Throughout this process, Nicolete's status as a Saracen woman plays a vital role, for it enables her to serve as Aucassin's positive foil and adopt the role of the hero prior to taking her rightful place as co-ruler of Beaucaire.

By investigating what it means to be a hero, the narrative thus poses deeper questions about popular genres such as romance, whose protagonists must display a certain number of required attributes and provide specific models for noble audiences. More important perhaps, the text presents its audience with the possibility that there exist multiple masculinities that need not always conform to the ideal found in romances and other contemporary narratives. *Aucassin et Nicolete* advocates for gender flexibility, stressing that it does not matter whether husband or wife assume the more active role as long as the two complement each other and work toward a common goal.

Through Nicolete and her capacity to take on multiple roles and guises, the *chantefable* further addresses issues of ethnicity and identity. In the end, how can we classify Nicolete? Is she a Christian countess or a Saracen princess? At what point does she become more Christian than Saracen? And where does the troubling episode about her disguise as a black minstrel fit in our attempts to understand who and what she really is? Perhaps these questions are not answered quite as satisfactorily as those about Aucassin, and Nicolete remains, to some extent, a mystery to the *chantefable*'s audience. What we *do* know at the end of *Aucassin et Nicolete* is that the tale's heroine, however we might want to label her, will remain by Aucassin's side and that Beaucaire will be the better off for her Mediterranean connections.

Bibliography

Aucassin et Nicolete. Translated by Philippe Walter. Paris: Folio, 1999.

Bloch, R. Howard. *Etymologies and Genealogies: A Literary Anthropology of the French Middle Ages*. Chicago: University of Chicago Press, 1983.

Brownlee, Kevin. "Discourse as Proueces in *Aucassin et Nicolette*." *Yale French Studies* 70 (1986): 167–82.

Brundage, James A. *Law, Sex, and Christian Society in Medieval Europe*. Chicago: University of Chicago Press, 1987.

Clark, S. L., and Julian Wasserman. "Wisdom Buildeth a Hut: *Aucassin et Nicolette* as Christian Comedy." *Allegorica* 1 (1976): 250–68.

Clevenger, Darnell H. "Torelore in *Aucassin et Nicolette*." *Romance Notes* 11 (1970): 656–65.

De Weever, Jacqueline. "Nicolette's Blackness—Lost in Translation." *Romance Notes* 34 (1994): 317–25.

———. *Sheba's Daughters: Whitening and Demonizing the Saracen Woman in Medieval French Epic*. New York: Garland, 1998.

DuBruck, Edelgard E. "The Audience of *Aucassin et Nicolete*: Confidant, Accomplice and Judge of Its Author." *Michigan Academician: Papers of the Michigan Academy of Science, Arts, and Letters* 5 (1972): 193–201.

Duby, Georges. *Medieval Marriage: Two Models from Twelfth-Century France*. Baltimore and London: Johns Hopkins University Press, 1978.

———. *The Knight, the Lady and the Priest: The Making of Modern Marriage in Medieval France*. Translated by Barbara Bray. Chicago: University of Chicago Press, 1983.

———. *Love and Marriage in the Middle Ages*. Translated by Jane Dunnett. Chicago: University of Chicago Press, 1994.

Gertz, SunHee Kim, and Paul S. Ropp. "Literary Women, Fiction and Marginalization: Nicolette and Shuangqing." *Comparative Literature Studies* 35 (1998): 219–54.

Gilbert, Jane. "The Practice of Gender in *Aucassin et Nicolette*." *Forum for Modern Language Studies* 33 (1997): 217–28.

Green, Virginia M. "*Aucassin et Nicolette*: The Economics of Desire." *Neophilologus* 79 (1995): 197–206.

Harden, Robert. "*Aucassin et Nicolette* as Parody." *Studies in Philology* 63 (1966): 1–9.

Holmes, Urban T. "Preface." In *Aucassin et Nicolete*, trans. Moyer and Eldridge, v–viii. Chapel Hill, NC: Robert Linker, 1937.

Hunt, Tony. "La parodie médiévale: le cas d'*Aucassin et Nicolette*." *Romania* 100 (1979): 341–81.

Jodogne, Omer. "La parodie et le pastiche dans *Aucassin et Nicolette*." *Cahiers de l'Association Internationale des Études Françaises* 12 (1960): 53–65.

Kinoshita, Sharon. "Medieval Mediterranean Literature." *PMLA* 124 (2009): 600–608.

McKean, Sister M. Faith. "Torelore and Courtoisie." *Romance Notes* 3 (1962): 64–68.

Menocal, Maria Rosa. "Signs of the Times: Self, Other and History in *Aucassin et Nicolette*." *Romanic Review* 80 (1989): 497–511.

Metlitzki, Dorothee. *The Matter of Araby in Medieval England*. New Haven: Yale University Press, 1977.

Pauphilet, Albert. *Le Legs du Moyen Age*. Melun: Librairie d'Argences, 1950.

Payen, Jean-Charles. *Le Moyen Age I: Des origines à 1300*. Paris: Arthaud, 1970.

Ramey, Lynn Tarte. *Christian, Saracen and Genre in Medieval French Literature*. New York: Routledge, 2001.

Sargent, Barbara Nelson. "Parody in *Aucassin et Nicolette*: Some Further Considerations." *French Review* 43 (1970): 597–605.

Segol, Marla. "Medieval Cosmopolitanism and the Saracen-Christian Ethos." *CLCWeb: Comparative Literature and Culture* 6 (2004): no pages.

Smith, Nathaniel B. "The Uncourtliness of Nicolette." In *Voices of Conscience: Essays on Medieval and Modern French Literature in Memory of James D. Powell and Rosemary Hodgins*, ed. Raymond J. Cormier, 169–82. Philadelphia: Temple University Press, 1977.

Spraycar, Rudy S. "Genre and Convention in *Aucassin et Nicolette*." *Romanic Review* 76 (1985): 94–115.

Szabics, Imre. "Amour et prouesse dans *Aucassin et Nicolette*." In *Et c'est la fin pour quoy sommes ensemble: Hommage à Jean Dufournet: Littérature, histoire et langue du Moyen Age*, ed. Jean-Claude Aubailly et al. 3 vols., 3: 1341–49. Paris: Champion, 1993.

Chapter 7
GENDER AND AUTHORITY:
THE PARTICULARITIES OF FEMALE RULE
IN THE PREMODERN MEDITERRANEAN

ELENA WOODACRE,
UNIVERSITY OF WINCHESTER

In a period when the exercise of power by women was generally limited and fairly unusual, the Mediterranean offers a wealth of intriguing examples of female rule in the premodern era. It could even be argued that the Mediterranean offered a more amenable climate for female rule than northern Europe. Certainly it offered unique opportunities for women, enabled in part by the distinctive features of the political landscape in the Mediterranean. This essay will analyze the prospects for women to exercise power and authority in the Mediterranean sphere through a survey of case studies from the Byzantine empresses of late antiquity to Aragonese queen-lieutenants in the fifteenth century. It will examine women who ruled in their own right, including the Neapolitan queens Giovanna I and II and the queens of Jerusalem, whose reigns preserved dynastic continuity while the selection of their spouse maintained the Crusader kingdom's tradition of elected or selected kings. It will also provide examples of women who rose to power in widowhood, as the consort of the previous ruler such as Sharjar al-Durr in thirteenth-century Egypt or as a regent for their son such as the Byzantine empresses Irene and Anna of Savoy. In addition to these more typical routes for women to access power, this survey will highlight more unusual positions of authority, including the office of queen-lieutenant, a role developed in large part to cope with the demands of ruling Aragón's far-flung Mediterranean empire, which allowed the queen to rule on her husband's behalf during his absence. Taken together, these regional case studies will highlight the distinctive environment with regard to gender and authority in the premodern Mediterranean and how this atmosphere created a singular climate for female rule.

The study of female rule and queenship in wider terms has been a thriving area of academic study in recent years. Examinations of queenship in the premodern period and in a European context has been a particular area of strength, however studies of female political agency in both modern and global contexts are continuing to emerge.[1] Although queenship studies arguably began with bio-graphical studies of particular figures, comparative studies and collections that highlight regional histories of female power and agency have become a trend in the field. While these collections and studies have greatly increased our under-standing of queenship in particular areas, such as medieval Iberia or early mod-ern England, the Mediterranean basin is an area that is only just beginning to be examined in the context of female authority and political influence.[2] Despite the fact that the Mediterranean region is incredibly diverse in terms of religious practice and political entities, these case studies of feminine agency, drawn from across seemingly disparate contexts, all highlight and reinforce key themes in queenship studies such as the importance of family connections, maternity, and marital relationships in framing female authority. These wide-ranging case stud-ies also serve to increase our understanding of how women were able to access and wield political power in the premodern period both in the unique context of the Mediterranean world and beyond.

Empresses of Byzantium

The history of the ancient Mediterranean left a distinctive imprint with regard to female rule. Legendary female rulers such as Dido of Carthage, the biblical queen of Sheba, Nefertiti, Hatsheput, and Cleopatra VII of Egypt are still at the forefront of the modern imagination, providing impetus for popular culture and academic research.[3] While prohibited from direct rule, empresses of Rome, such as Livia, Agrippina the Younger, and Julia Domna are excellent examples of female agency in the classical Mediterranean.[4] This foundation built by the women of imperial Rome was later leveraged by the empresses of Byzantium. The power wielded by Byzantine empresses has not always been fully appreciated

---

[1] An excellent work that brings together a range of studies from across medieval Europe is Earenfight, *Queenship in Medieval Europe*. Cambell Orr's imortant study of queenship (*Queenship in Europe 1660–1815*) bridges the gap between premodern and modern research on queens consort. Cutter and Crowell's translation of sections of Chen Shou's records of Imperial China (*Empresses and Consorts*) sheds light on female agency in the Chinese court in the 3rd century BCE and contains a helpful introduction to the study of Chinese empresses and the role of women in the Chinese court.

[2] Examples of collections with an Iberian or English focus include Earenfight, *Queenship and Political Power in Medieval and Early Modern Spain*; and Whitelock and Hunt, *Tudor Queenship*. With regard to the Mediterranean context, see Woodacre, *Queenship in the Mediterranean*.

[3] Lassner, *Demonizing the Queen of Sheba*; Roehrig, Dreyfus, and Keller, *Hatshepsut*; Roller, *Cleopatra*.

[4] For more on these figures, see Barratt, *Livia*; Ginsburg, *Representing Agrippina*; and Levick, *Julia Domna*.

in modern historiography; in order to do so, Liz James has argued that we need to step away from modern understandings of political agency and appreciate the significance of religious mediation during theological disputes and activities, such as church-building, as an expression of authority.[5] Kathryn Ringrose has argued that it is also necessary to understand the unique gendered mechanisms of the Byzantine court and the importance of eunuchs as a mediator between the male and female spheres and as an interlocutor for imperial authority.[6] Access to a team of eunuchs, experienced in court protocol and bureaucracy, was crucial, for they "acted as an extension of an empress's power, allowing her to govern despite the constraints of her gender and the traditionalism of an elaborate court bureaucracy."[7]

While it is important to understand the nuanced exercise of power and the complex structure of the Byzantine court to fully contexualize the agency of imperial women, there are multiple examples of empresses who clearly wielded power. These women include consorts such as the infamous Theodora, who ruled alongside Emperor Justinian in the sixth century, and the "forceful power-broker" Eirene Doukaina, mother of the chronicler Anna Kommene.[8] Women have also risen to power in the Byzantine empire as regents; seven women assumed the regency between 527–1204, and later examples include Anna of Savoy in the fourteenth century.[9] The most famous of these regents was Irene, consort of Leo IV, first regent for their son Constantine VI then sole ruler (797–802) after Constantine's death, who adopted the male and female titles of *basileus* and *basilissa*.[10]

While royal mothers were often advantageously placed to assume a regency, serving as a key dynastic link as the widow of the last ruler and the mother of the next, women often struggled to be accepted in this role, particularly if they were considered to be a foreigner. This can be seen not only in the context of the Byzantine empire and the Mediterranean but also in cases of female regency across Europe in the premodern era. Blanche of Castile, the mother of and regent for Louis IX of France, was able to overcome initial opposition to her rule as a woman and a foreigner to create a successful regency that set an important precedent for a long line of French queens regent.[11] However, while Irene is an excellent example of a successful empress regent in the Byzantine empire, Maria of Antioch, a near contemporary of Blanche of Castile, had a short and disastrous regency for her son, Alexios II, after the death of her husband Manuel

---

[5] James, "Goddess, Whore, Wife or Slave?" 135.

[6] Ringrose, "Women and Power at the Byzantine Court."

[7] Ringrose, "Women and Power," 79.

[8] Smythe, "Behind the Mask," 147.

[9] Garland, *Byzantine Empresses*, 7. For a study of Anna of Savoy, see Nicol, *The Byzantine Lady*, 82–95.

[10] Earenfight, *Queenship in Medieval Europe*, 87.

[11] See Poulet, "Capetian Women and the Regency."

I Komnenos in September 1180. Maria, who came from the Crusader States, was unpopular due to the perception that she was a westerner and the rumor that she was engaged in an illicit affair with her late husband's nephew, Alexios the *protosebastos*. Her decision to install her relatives in powerful positions and enact policies that were perceived to be "pro-Latin" also opened her up to criticism.[12] Opponents of her regency included several key members of the imperial dynasty, headed by her step-daughter, Maria Porphyrogenita. Maria of Antioch was eventually unseated in a coup d'état in 1182 by Andronikos Komnenos that claimed the lives of the regent, her son Alexios II, and even her step-daughter and her husband who had opposed Maria's regency.

However, women did not only come to power in the Byzantine empire through their husbands and sons. As Dion Smythe noted "the increasing significance attached to birth in the Porphyry Chamber of the imperial palace meant that the succession to the throne was not determined simply by primogeniture . . . [making] it possible for the supreme office to be filled by a woman."[13] A number of women were acknowledged as imperial heirs, including Anna Komnene and Maria Porphyrogenita, daughter of Manuel I. Maria was considered to be her father's heir for the majority of her youth; her father used her as a high-stakes piece in a European-wide effort in matrimonial diplomacy.[14] Maria was put forth as a prospective bride for Bela of Hungary, William II of Sicily, John Lackland of England, and Henry, heir of Fredrick Barbarossa, before she was finally wed to Ranier of Montferrat in 1180. Anna Komnene was keenly aware of the importance of her birth in the Porphry Chamber, which gave her the right to use the sobriquet *"porphyrogenita,"* and Smythe argues that "her goal in life [was] to ascend the imperial throne as empress-regnant."[15] While it has to be acknowledged that these women were later displaced in the line of succession by the birth of brothers, despite Anna Komnene's vociferous attempts to prevent what she saw as the usurpation of her rightful place, the fact that women were accepted as potential heirs and viable claimants is important.

An excellent example of women who were able to rule in their own right are the sisters Zoe and Theodora, who were considered the rightful heirs of their father Constantine VIII. Zoe Porphyrogenita (r. 1028–1050) was married three times; her husbands became emperor through their marriage to her. Although her birthright as her father's heir, born in the Porphry Chamber, was acknowledged, she had to combat men who sought to prevent her from fully exercising the imperial office. Zoe's opponents included the powerful eunuch John the Orphanotrophos, who thwarted her attempt to appropriate her father's experienced staff of eunuchs into her service and replaced them with women

---

[12] Garland, *Byzantine Empresses*, 205.

[13] Smythe, "Behind the Mask," 152.

[14] Kinnamos, *Deeds of John and Manuel Comnenus*, 94.

[15] Smythe, "Middle Byzantine Family Values and Anna Komnene's *Alexiad*," 125.

from his own family.[16] However, her position as empress was supported by her subjects, who rose up in violent opposition when Zoe's adopted heir, Michael V, attempted to remove her from power by exiling her to a nunnery. According to the chronicler Michael Psellos, the mob, which included a considerable number of women and even children, cried out in indignation:

> Where can she be, she who alone is free, the mistress of all the imperial family, the rightful heir to the Empire, whose father was emperor, whose grandfather was monarch before him-yes and great-grandfather too? How was it this low-born fellow dared to raise a hand against a woman of such lineage?[17]

Michael was dethroned and Zoe restored to her position, ruling alongside her sister, Theodora.[18] Garland notes that although Theodora was initially reluctant to leave the convent and embrace her imperial role, once installed as empress she was authoritative and far more determined than her sister Zoe to ensure that Michael and his supporters were adequately punished and removed from the center of political power.[19] Zoe and Theodora minted coins during their joint rule with images of both sisters and performed all duties and functions that were considered part of the emperor's prerogative. Although the chronicler Michael Psellos was often critical of their rule, he notes that "both the civilian population and the military caste were working in harmony under [the] empresses, and more obedient to them than to any proud overlord issuing arrogant orders."[20] Theodora was temporarily set aside after Zoe's remarriage to Constantine IX Monomachos, but on Zoe's death in 1050, Theodora ruled alongside her brother-in-law for five years and on her own until her own death in 1056.

Although, as Lynda Garland notes, the role of empress lacked a clear constitutional definition, the framework of the Byzantine empire allowed women to exercise power in a number of ways.[21] While female rule was permitted, imperial women had to negotiate the complex court protocols and bureaucracy, leveraging the knowledge and position of their eunuchs and crafting alliances at court to support their authority and enable them to exercise power. Empresses consort were active rulers alongside their husbands, at times overtly engaged in the political arena, while at other moments expressing their agency by more subtle means through their patronage of the Church and connection to theological disputes. Empresses possessed even more authority as regents for their sons and were rec-

---

[16] Ringrose, "Women and Power," 78.

[17] Psellos, *Chronographia*, Bk. 5, 99. See also Garland's comments on the riot in *Byzantine Empresses*, 142–44.

[18] Karagianni, "Female Monarchs in the Medieval Byzantine Court," 23.

[19] Garland, *Byzantine Empresses*, 143–44.

[20] Psellos, *Chronographia*, Bk. 6, 113.

[21] Garland, *Byzantine Empresses*, 2.

ognized as imperial heiresses and rulers in their own right, as the examples of
Irene, Zoe, and her sister Theodora aptly demonstrate. Thus, the empresses of
Byzantium are a critical case study for female agency in the Mediterranean, providing a link to the classical heritage of the region and key examples of a legal
and social framework that enabled women to exercise political authority as influential consorts, powerful regents, and as sovereigns in their own right.

The Queens of Jerusalem

The inception of the Crusader kingdom of Jerusalem in the eastern Mediterranean created a truly unique environment for female rule. Although the new
lords of the realm brought with them feudal ideals and legal traditions from
their homes of origin across Europe, the laws of the new kingdom were arguably progressive in terms of female inheritance. It was completely permissible for
a daughter to inherit property from her father, including a fief or even a throne,
in the absence of a male heir. Joshua Prawer notes that the *assise* that allowed
females to inherit their father's holdings was an early one, possibly dating back to
the time of Godfrey de Bouillon, immediately after the First Crusade, ca. 1100.[22]
Prawer remarks that this *assise* was not necessarily in line with current practices
in Europe, and Sylvia Schein concurs, remarking that the inheritance laws of
the kingdom were more favorable to women than those in the West.[23] Prawer
claims that female inheritance was permitted in order to reassure knights "that
their family, even their distant family, might enjoy the fruits of their bravery."[24]
This legislation paved the way for many heiresses in the kingdom of Jerusalem,
such as Helvis of Ramle and Stephanie of Milly, who inherited important fiefs in
their own right, and also made it possible for the kingdom itself to be inherited
by a woman.

The succession to Baldwin II became the test case for female succession to
the throne of the kingdom of Jerusalem in the twelfth century. Initially the Crusader kingdom was founded on the principle of an elected or selected ruler, but
the first three kings of Jerusalem were all closely linked by blood, and a tendency
toward dynastic continuity quickly set in. Baldwin II, in contrast to his uncles
Godfrey and Baldwin, had several children with his wife Morphia of Melitene
and hoped to place a child of his own on the throne. Morphia died in 1126 or
1127, leaving four surviving girls but no son. Baldwin had the option to marry
again in the hopes of siring a son, but he may have decided that it was better to
secure the succession through the marriages of his nearly grown daughters than
risk lengthy regency for an infant son. The succession to Baldwin II would be a

---

[22] Prawer, *Crusader Institutions*, 25.

[23] Schein, "Women in Medieval Colonial Society," 141.

[24] Prawer, *Institutions*, 25.

new test of the principles of succession for the still fledgling kingdom. In theory there were three options: (1) the throne could go to Melisende as Baldwin's eldest child; (2) the throne could go to Baldwin's nearest male relative; or (3) it could go to another unrelated man who was chosen by the assembly. The end result was a hybrid of the first and third options; Baldwin decided to marry his eldest daughter to a man chosen by the assembly, and together they would succeed him on the throne. In this way both the elective and hereditary principles would be satisfied and a precedent for an heiress was created, providing the dynastic continuity that was critical for the fledgling and vulnerable kingdom.[25]

Baldwin's eldest daughter Melisende married Fulk, Count of Anjou, a man known to and approved by the barons of the kingdom in 1129.[26] Melisende and Fulk came to the throne upon the death of Baldwin II in 1131 and initially struggled to rule together. Fulk appears to have conceived of himself as the sole ruler of the kingdom, while Melisende saw herself as the rightful heiress to the kingdom and a co-ruler, not a consort. Moreover, she had the support of both the Church and many of the barons who felt that Fulk was disregarding Melisende's rights as set out in the will of Baldwin II and who resented his appointment of Angevins to key posts in the realm.[27] In order to placate the barons who supported Melisende, Fulk had to acknowledge the rights of his wife as the rightful heiress to the kingdom, and, according to the chronicler William of Tyre, "not even in unimportant cases did he take any measures without her knowledge and assistance."[28]

After Fulk's death in 1143, William of Tyre declared that "The royal power passed to Lady Melisend, a queen beloved of God, to whom it belonged by hereditary right" although her son Baldwin III was elevated to the throne on his father's death as Melisende and Fulk's mutual heir.[29] Jaroslav Folda and Sarah Lambert have both analyzed images of Melisende in manuscript images and note two examples that give Melisende a key role her son's coronation, demonstrating her position and authority.[30] In one of these images, Melisende is clearly pictured being crowned again alongside her son Baldwin III at his coronation, perhaps to

---

[25] A recent study on this topic is Hayley Bassett, "Regnant Queenship and Royal Marriage."

[26] Fulk was well known to the nobility of the kingdom after a successful visit to Jerusalem in 1120, when William claims that Fulk "gained, as he well deserved, the favour of all the people as well as that of the king": William, Archbishop of Tyre, *A History of Deeds done beyond the Sea* (*Volume Two*), Bk. 14, chap. 2, 50.

[27] Mayer, "Studies in the History of Queen Melisende of Jerusalem," 108. See also Mayer, "Angevins versus Normans"; and *The Ecclesiastical History of Orderic Vitalis*, VI, 390–92.

[28] William of Tyre, *History of Deeds*, Bk. 14, chap. 18, 76

[29] William of Tyre, *History of Deeds*, Bk. 15, chap. 27, 135.

[30] Folda, "Images of Queen Melisende"; Lambert, "Images of Queen Melisende."

emphasize that she was a queen regnant and co-ruler, not regent.[31] In another example, Melisende, already wearing her own crown as queen, crowns her son in tandem with the bishop.[32]

After nearly ten years on the throne of Jerusalem, Baldwin was firmly into his majority and he wanted his mother to step aside and leave him as sole ruler of the kingdom. Melisende refused to do so and had the support of a large faction of the nobility for her continued rule. However, Baldwin had the advantage of being able to lead the army and wisely pressed this advantage in his struggle for control. Ultimately, Melisende lost her struggle with her son and was forced to give up control of the kingdom and assume the place of Queen Mother. However, she set a precedent in the kingdom of Jerusalem for female succession and left the example of a strong queen who "ruled the kingdom and administered the government with such skillful care."[33]

This precedent enabled the succession of two of Melisende's granddaughters, Sibylla and Isabella; however, while their right to the throne was accepted and acknowledged, both women struggled to rule the kingdom.[34] The difficulty stemmed from both the extremely turbulent political situation within the kingdom and the aggressive expansion of Saladin, which culminated in the loss of Jerusalem after the Battle of Hattin in 1187. Both women were also hampered by husbands who did not have the support of the kingdom as their king consort, unlike Fulk of Anjou, whose selection had been ratified by an assembly of the barons. While Sibylla crowned her unpopular husband, Guy de Lusignan, at her own coronation, against the will of the majority of the barony, Isabella was forced to end her marriage to Humphrey of Toron, who was felt to be an inadequate king consort. Moreover, Isabella's second husband, Conrad de Montferrat was assassinated and possibly her third husband, Henri de Champagne as well, given his untimely death in fall from a window.[35] However, her marriage to her fourth husband, Amaury de Lusignan, King of Cyprus, did have the support of the majority of the barons as well as the influential Archbishop of Tyre. A contemporary chronicle noted that only with this more widely accepted fourth marriage

---

[31] Paris, Bibliothèque Nationale, MS fr. 779, fol. 145v. (French, 1270–1279).

[32] Paris, Bibliothèque Nationale, MS fr. 2824, fol. 102v (Flemish, ca. 1300).

[33] William of Tyre, *History of Deeds*, Bk. 16, chap. 3, 140.

[34] Sibylla was crowned in 1186 and died in 1190. Isabella's reign is difficult to date, due to her disputed marriages and the political maelstrom in the kingdom after the loss of Jerusalem. Theoretically, however, she would have succeeded her elder half-sister Sibylla in 1190. Isabella died in 1205.

[35] For more detail on Sibylla, Isabella, and their controversial consorts, see Woodacre, "Questionable Authority." Isabella's husbands were (in order) Humphrey of Toron, Conrad of Montferrat, Henry of Champagne, and Amaury de Lusignan, king of Cyprus.

did she finally settle into her queenship, noting *"Lors a primes fu ele royne"*.[36] These examples demonstrate that although female rule and inheritance may have been accepted in principle, it was nearly impossible for a queen to assert her right to the crown if her consort was not accepted by her subjects.

While the reigns of Melisende, Sibylla, and Isabella set an important precedent for queens regnant in the kingdom, the legal right of female successors to the throne of Jerusalem was firmly established by the *Livre au Roi*. This important piece of legislation, believed to have been drafted in the early thirteenth century during the reign of Isabella and her fourth husband Amaury de Lusignan, clearly sets out in writing the procedures for succession to the throne of Jerusalem. This legislation also ensured that Isabella's daughter Maria of Montferrat had smooth ascent to the throne and also enabled the succession of Maria's daughter Yolande (sometimes referred to as Isabella II).[37]

The queens of Jerusalem are a controversial group of female rulers; both Sarah Lambert and Bernard Hamilton have argued for their diminishing power and influence, particularly after the fall of Jerusalem itself.[38] While it cannot be contested that these women all struggled to fully implement their rule in an increasingly difficult political situation in the Latin East, the fact that female succession was permitted in the kingdom and their hereditary right as queen was acknowledged, makes their situation an important case study for female rule in the Mediterranean region. There is also a key link between these Crusader queens and the Byzantine empresses of the first case study with regard to female succession, as both realms allowed women to inherit the throne in their own right.

Women and Power in the Islamic Mediterranean

It is interesting to note that during eleventh to the thirteenth centuries, the same period that saw the creation and high point of the Crusader States, there were a number of women in positions of power in the Islamic Mediterranean, including areas in close proximity to the kingdom of Jerusalem. There is often a presumption that women had no access to political power in Muslim territories; this misunderstanding stems from a general omission of female political figures in western histories and a misconstruction of the workings and composition of the

---

[36] Morgan (ed.), *La Continuation de Guillaume de Tyr* 199, roughly translated as "For the first time she was queen".

[37] Anon., "Le Livre au Roi." For more on the *Livre au Roi*, see Greilsammer, "Structure and Aims of the Livre au Roi." Maria of Montferrat's reign was 1205–1212, and that of her daughter Yolande or Isabella II was 1212–1228.

[38] Lambert, "Queen or Consort"; Hamilton, "Women in the Crusader States"; Hamilton, "King Consorts of Jerusalem and their Entourages from the West," 13.

harem.[39] Another difficulty in recognizing female agency in the Islamic Mediterranean is the lack of an analogous term to the western counterpart of "queen" or, indeed, consistent terminology for a female ruler in the Maghreb and Levant. Fatima Mernissi explores the range of honorifics used in the Islamic world for women with high status and access to power, including *sultana* (the female equivalent of sultan), *khatun* (lady or noblewoman), *malika* (the closest equivalent word to "queen"), *sitt* (lady), and *al-hurra*—literally a free woman, although Mernissi argues that as an honorific it stresses that the woman was "a sovereign woman who obeyed no superior authority."[40] There were two key criteria for recognized sovereignty in the Islamic world: the ability to issue coinage in a ruler's name and the inclusion of the ruler's name in the *khutba* or Friday prayers. Mernissi cites fifteen female Muslim rulers who meet these criteria, in addition to numerous examples of politically influential women who visibly exercised authority in spite of failing to meet the criteria of sovereignty.[41]

The eleventh century was a particularly active period for female agency in the Islamic Mediterranean, with women in powerful positions in Morocco, al-Andalus, Egypt, and Yemen. The first of these women to come to power was Sitt al-Mulk, the beloved daughter of the Fatimid sultan of Egypt al-Aziz (r. 975–996). On the death of her father, her brother al-Hakim (r. 996–1021) came to power and began an increasingly stormy reign during which his relationship with his sister deteriorated to such a degree that she feared for her safety.[42] When al-Hakim disappeared in February 1021, Sitt al-Mulk took power, ruling alone for six weeks. While her aggressive actions after her brother's death led some chroniclers, such as Hilal al-Sabi, to view her as the likely murderer, other chroniclers, such as Ibn al-Athir, argued that, given the widespread hatred al-Hakim had incurred through his violent rule, there were many potential assassins.[43]

Sitt al-Mulk ensured a smooth transition of power to her nephew al-Zahir by eliminating any potential rivals. Yaacov Lev argued that her willingness to be completely ruthless in order to ensure her nephew's accession gave her "a much-needed and much-appreciated quality in a ruler, that of *hayba*, i.e. she

---

[39] See an excellent discussion of "the myth of the harem" in Peirce, "Beyond Harem Walls."

[40] Mernissi, *The Forgotten Queens of Islam*, particularly the chapter "How does one say 'Queen' in Islam?" 9–25; this quotation at 140.

[41] Mernissi, *The Forgotten Queens of Islam*, chap. 5, "The Criteria of Sovereignty in Islam", 71–87. However, Chaves Hernández ("Mujeres y poder en el Islam II," 11) argues that coinage is not necessarily a marker for sovereignty, noting that even some male rulers did not issue coinage in their name.

[42] Lev, "The Fatimid Princess Sitt al-Mulk," 321–25.

[43] Mernissi, *Forgotten Queens*, 166; Rustow "A Petition to a Woman at the Fatimid Court," 10.

who inspired awe, and was accordingly obeyed."[44] She remained as the linchpin in her nephew's government for a further two years until her death; working to stabilize the finances of the state, which had been poorly managed under the rule of al-Hakim, and lifting an edict that confined women to the home.[45] Although Sitt al-Mulk's rise to power and political agency were certainly atypical, it is important to note that many women of the Fatimid dynasty played an important part in the family's activities and were active patrons who possessed considerable wealth.[46]

Sitt al-Mulk possessed undeniable political authority in Egypt during her lifetime as an important and influential member of the reigning dynasty, rather than ruling alone in her own right. In the mid-thirteenth century, Sharjar (also known as Sharajarat or Sharjara) al-Durr went one step further to become the acknowledged sole ruler of Egypt. Again, Sharjar's rule was enabled by a period of crisis following the death of a sultan, Sharjar's husband Aiyub. Sharjar worked to temporarily conceal the death of her husband while she built alliances with the leader of the army, Fakhr al-Din, and the chief eunuch, Jamal al-Din.[47] The Crusaders, led by Louis IX of France, aimed to take advantage of the death of the sultan and killed Fakhr in a skirmish; however, Sharjar was able to rally the army under the command of her husband's heir Turanshah, and they were able to secure victory over the Crusader army. Turanshah was later murdered by the Mamluks, who then appointed Sharjar as sultana, no longer to rule behind the scenes but alone as the official sovereign. The chronicler ibn Wasil commented:

> From that time she became titular head of the whole state; a royal stamp was issued in her name with the formula "mother of Khatil" and the *khutba* was pronounced in her name as Sultana of Cairo and all Egypt. This was an event without precedent throughout the Muslim world: [although] that a woman should hold the effective power and govern a kingdom was indeed known . . .[48]

Sharjar managed to achieve the key criteria of sovereignty mentioned by Mernissi: the ability to issue coins in her name and the proclamation of the *khutba*. The *khutba* for Sharjar was "May Allah protect the Beneficent One, Queen of the Muslims, the Blessed of the Earthly World and of the Faith, the Mother of Khalil

---

[44] Lev, "Sitt al-Mulk," 326.

[45] Lev, "Sitt al-Mulk," 327.

[46] Lev, "Sitt al-Mulk," 320–21; Rustow "A Petition," 14–16, for detail on the architectural patronage of Fatimid women. For more detailed coverage on the women of the Fatimid dynasty, see Cortese and Calderini, *Women and the Fatimids in the World of Islam*.

[47] For an effective biographical summary of her career, see Duncan, "Scholarly views of Shajarat al-Durr," 52–53. Duncan's article contains an interesting discussion of different historiographical studies and opinions of Sharjar's rule and political career.

[48] Ibn Wasil, cited in Gabrieli, *Arab Historians of the Crusades*, 298.

al-Mustasimiyya, the Companion of Sultan al-Malik al-Salih."[49] Although her *khutba* does emphasize her role as mother and wife, it is important that she was acknowledged as the ruler and that her own sovereign titles came before her familial and marital ties. She was forced to take a second husband by the caliph to legitimize her position but continued to reign and "maintained *de facto* control to the end."[50] However, her second husband proved to be her undoing; fearing that he meant to replace her with a more pliable wife, Sharjar arranged his murder. Her involvement with the crime led to her own execution, ironically ending her period in power.

Returning to the eleventh century, two important examples of women exercising power and authority can be found in nearby Yemen, which was also in the orbit and influence of the Fatimid dynasty in Egypt. The first of these women was Asma Bint Shihab al-Sulayhiyya, who ruled Yemen as an active queen consort and co-ruler with her husband Ali Ibn Muhammad al-Sulayhi from 1047 to 1067. Eva Chaves Hernández noted that Asma was already a distinguished woman of high rank before her marriage; this may have been a factor in why she was readily accepted as a co-ruler with her husband.[51] Asma's status as a co-ruler was affirmed by the inclusion of her name alongside her husband's in the *khutba*, and Asma's presence in councils of governance, unveiled, was recorded by contemporaries.[52]

Asma's co-rule with her husband was an enabling factor for her daughter-in-law, Arwa Bint Ahmad al-Sulayhiyya (also known as al-Sayyida al-Hurra or Sayyida Hurra), who ruled from 1091 to 1138, first alongside her husband al-Mukarram and later independently. During her period of sole rule, the *khutba* was proclaimed in her name: "May Allah prolong the days of al-Hurra the perfect, the sovereign who carefully manages the affairs of the faithful."[53] Arwa was an active ruler during her lengthy reign; she was a successful politician and military strategist as well as a prolific patron who renovated and constructed secular and religious buildings and improved the infrastructure of her realm with road building and agricultural projects.[54] She made the decision to relocate the capital from San'a to Dhu Jibla and built a palace in the new capital. Another indication of her abilities as a ruler was her appointment as *hujja* or head of the *da'wa* or missionary unit that oversaw expansion of the faith into Oman and western India.[55]

---

49 Mernissi, *Forgotten Queens*, 90.
50 Duncan, "Shajarat al-Durr," 53.
51 Chaves Hernández, "Mujeres y poder I," 14.
52 Mernissi, *Forgotten Queens*, 115.
53 Quoted in Mernissi, *Forgotten Queens*, 115–16.
54 Mernissi, *Forgotten Queens*, 148; Chaves Hernández, "Mujeres y poder II," 31–44.
55 Chaves Hernández, "Mujeres y poder II," 26–29. Arwa's anointment as *hujja* is also discussed in Daftary, "Sayyida Hurra."

In the western end of the Islamic Mediterranean, several female contemporaries of Sitt al-Mulk and the Yemeni queens also wielded power, influence, and
authority. These women included Zaynab al-Nafazawiyya, consort of a powerful
Berber ruler, and Yusuf ibn Tashfin, whose domains were spread across North
Africa and the Iberian Peninsula. Zaynab was, like Asma Bint Shihab al-Sulayhiyya, an active co-ruler with her husband Tashfin between 1061 and his death
in 1107.[56] Again, during the eleventh century, other women were actively sharing
power with husbands and sons in al-Andalus, including Subh, wife of al-Hakim
II al-Mustansir bi-llah and mother of Hisam II al-Mu'ayyad, and I'timad al-
Rumaykiyya, wife of Mu'tamid, king of Seville, and the mother of 'Abd Allah,
king of Grenada.[57]

Subh's rise to power was remarkable. Beginning as a Christian prisoner of
war from the Basque country in Navarre, she built her influence until she dominated the caliph al-Hakim and his chief secretary Ibn 'Amir; she later became
effective regent for her son Hisam. However, though her power was undeniable, Mourtada-Sabbah and Gully argue that Subh's period of influence had a
detrimental effect on the authority of the caliph and the stability of the realm,
leading to a period of civil war.[58] Mernissi has noted that many medieval chronicles and modern historians have emphasized her non-Islamic origins in their
critique of her reign, which evokes an interesting comparison to the Byzantine empress Maria of Antioch's unpopularity as a foreign consort and regent.[59]
I'timad al-Rumaykiyya was another woman who entered the harem as a slave but
was able to wield enormous influence as the favorite wife of the king of Seville,
al Mu'tamid.[60] Mernissi argues that women like Subh and Rumakiyya, who
accessed power as the favorite of a caliph or sultan, cannot be considered true
heads of state like Sharjar al-Durr or the Yemeni queen Arwa, as "they failed to
cross the threshold that separated women's territory from that of men."[61]

While these examples of female power and influence in the western half of
the Islamic Mediterranean suggest a potential high-water mark in the eleventh

---

[56] Mernissi, *Forgotten Queens*, 14; Mourtada-Sabbah and Gully, "'I am, by God, Fit
for High Positions,'" 197–98.

[57] Mourtada-Sabbah and Gully, "I am, by God, Fit for High Positions," 186.

[58] For a summary of the effects of Subh's rule, see Mourtada-Sabbah and Gully, "I
am, by God, Fit for High Positions," 195.

[59] Mernissi, *Forgotten Queens*, 48–49. For example, "In the words of Ahmad Amin,
Subh is neither *malika* (queen) nor *sayyida* (Madame); she has no title. She is Subh, the
Christian" (49).

[60] Mourtada-Sabbah and Gully, "I am, by God, Fit for High Positions," 195–96.

[61] Mernissi, *Forgotten Queens*, 50. Mernissi also examines the career of Khayzuran,
who in the eighth century also began as a slave but ultimately ruled through her influence with three successive caliphs of Baghdad: her husband al-Mahdi and her two sons
al-Hadi and al-Rashid.

century, it is important to note that there were other women who exercised significant influence and agency in the premodern period. Examples include Tarub and Al-Zahra, the wives and favorites of 'Abd al-Rahman II and III respectively in the ninth and tenth centuries; A'isha al-Hurra, the mother of the last Muslim king of Grenada in the fifteenth century, Boabdil; and Sayyida al-Hurra, who wielded extensive authority in North Africa in the sixteenth century as a "pirate queen" and the ally of the infamous Barbarossa of Algiers.[62] Sayyida herself forms an interesting link between the Iberian Peninsula and North Africa, as she hailed from Andalucía and came to Morocco as a refugee from Granada after it fell to the *Reyes Catolicos* in 1492. Sayyida leveraged connections from her natal family and multiple advantageous marriages to wield power in the Tétouan region of Morocco, on the southern side of the strait of Gibraltar, for thirty years from approximately 1510 until 1542, when she was unseated by her son-in-law.[63] She began by co-ruling the region with her first husband and after his death took on sole governance of this strategic area, using her fleet and her alliance with Barbarossa to harass Spanish and Portuguese shipping in the Mediterranean. Her power and talent for governance attracted the sultan of Morocco, who journeyed to Tétouan to wed her, but after their marriage he allowed her to continue her effective rule of the area.[64]

These women are only a few examples of female authority in the Islamic world, but they demonstrate that, although the political systems of the Islamic Mediterranean differed from that of their northern neighbors, Muslim women could access power both as co-rulers with husbands and sons and as independent rulers, just as Christian queens and empresses did.[65] Although the legal framework of the Islamic areas of the Mediterranean did not permit females to inherit the throne in their own right, as the women of Byzantium and the Crusader States could, this did not preclude Muslim women from becoming sole rulers, as the examples of Sharjar al-Durr and Arwa of Yemen demonstrate.

---

[62] For A'isha, see Mourtada-Sabbah and Gully, "I am, by God, Fit for High Positions," 198–99; and for Sayyida, see Mernissi, *Forgotten Queens*, 18–19.

[63] Gil Gramau, "Sayyida al-Hurra, Mujer Marroquí de Origen Andulusí," 318.

[64] Sadiqi et al., *Des femmes écrivent l'Afrique*, 52.

[65] Additional case studies of women wielding power and influence in the Islamic Mediterranean can be found in *Global Queenship*, see especially Miranda "al-Dalfa and the Political Role of the umm al-walad," Lourinho, "Queen Zaynab al-Nafzawiyya" and Echevarria and Lluch "The 'Honourable Ladies' of Nasrid Grenada."

Female Rulers (and Proxy Rulers) in Iberia

The Iberian Peninsula was once part of the Muslim hegemony of the southern and eastern Mediterranean; the Christian kingdoms that expanded south in the process of the *Reconquista* developed unique traditions with regard to female agency and rule. The Pyrenean kingdom of Navarre cemented the ability of women to inherit their family lands and recognized their place in the line of succession to the throne in their *Fueros* or code of law and custom. This enabled the accession of five women to rule the kingdom as regnant queens between 1274 and 1512.[66] While this was the same number of female monarchs as seen in the kingdom of Jerusalem in the twelfth and thirteenth centuries, the Navarrese queens were able to exercise power and authority as sovereign monarchs in a way that the beleaguered Jerusalemite queens struggled to do in their ever-threatened and fast disappearing realm. In addition to these female sovereigns, Navarre possessed powerful queens regent, queens consort, and female lieutenants, such as Leonor de Trastámara and Magdalena of France, who were either closely involved with or, in some cases, solely responsible for governing the realm.

Navarre was not the only Iberian realm that permitted female rule: indeed, all of the kingdoms of Iberia—including Navarre, Castile, Aragón, and Portugal—experienced female rule at some point in the premodern era. Castile also permitted regnant queens, including Urraca of Leon-Castile (r. 1109–1126) and the famous Isabel *la Católica* (r. 1474–1504).[67] Another often omitted example is Berenguela, who ruled in tandem with her son Ferdinand III from 1217 until her death in 1246. Janna Bianchini has argued firmly in her recent monograph that this was not an abdication or abjuration of Berenguela's own right to the throne, as her position as the hereditary heiress was firmly acknowledged.[68] Portugal also permitted female rule, although the accession of Beatriz in 1383 was contested and ultimately unsuccessful, primarily due to opposition to her mother, Leonor Teles as regent and to her husband, Juan I of Castile.[69] However, in Aragón the reign of Petronilla (r. 1137–1164) proved to be an exception to succession practices that ultimately barred regnant queens, although succession through the female line continued to be permitted.[70]

---

[66] These rulers were Juana I (1274–1305), Juana II (1328–1349), Blanca I (1425–1441), Leonor (Lieutenant from 1455–1479, queen 1479), and Catalina (1483–1517, kingdom annexed by Castile 1512). For more, see Woodacre, *The Queens Regnant of Navarre*.

[67] Works on these queens include Reilly, *The Kingdom of León-Castilla under Queen Urraca*; and Weissburger, *Isabel Rules*.

[68] Bianchini, *The Queen's Hand*.

[69] Olivera Serrano, *Beatriz de Portugal*.

[70] For more on Petronilla, see Stalls, "Queenship and the Royal Patrimony in Twelfth-Century Iberia." On the development of the succession practices in Aragón, see Garcia Gallo, "El Derecho de Sucesion del Trono en la Corona de Aragón."

Although Aragón moved to bar reigning queens, royal women were enfranchised through the Aragónese tradition of lieutenancy, which was developed as a means of administering Aragón's expanding Mediterranean empire. On the mainland, the Crown of Aragón consisted of three major realms: Aragón, Catalonia, and Valencia; while in the Mediterranean their empire included (at various points) the Balearic Isles, Corsica, Sardinia, Sicily, the kingdom of Naples, bases in North Africa, and part of the Grecian mainland. After the accession of Charles V, this empire continued to expand to include the greater part of Italy, the Holy Roman Empire, the Low Countries in Europe, and an emerging global empire as well.

The premise of the lieutenancy was to deputize a close family member with the responsibility to govern a particular region of Aragón's Mediterranean empire, as it was impossible for the king to be everywhere at once, and it was crucial to maintain the physical presence of the dynasty in as many places as possible.[71] This also fits with the premise of corporate monarchy, which was central to the Iberian practice of rule, drawing in the skill set of various members of the dynasty to administer and govern the realm as a unit represented by the ruler. The deputy or lieutenant could theoretically be any member of the family, but it was most often the heir or the queen consort. The heir needed to learn how to govern, and lieutenancy was an ideal opportunity to do so; as the next ruler, an heir could be theoretically relied upon to protect the best interests of the realm. The queen consort was also a logical choice, as the king's helpmeet and partner and the guarantor of dynastic continuity, she too could be trusted to work in the best interests of the empire.[72]

The Middle Ages saw a series of able queens lieutenant in the fourteenth and fifteenth centuries, including Maria de Luna (wife of Martín *el Humano*), Maria of Castile (wife of Alfonso V), and Juana Enríquez (second wife of Juan II).[73] While these women all ruled mainland provinces in the heartland of Aragón, Blanca of Navarre became queen lieutenant for her husband Martí, king of Sicily and heir of Aragón, during his absences to visit his father in Iberia or fight rebels in Sardinia. When he died in 1409, Blanca continued to rule Sicily as viceroy for the king of Aragón, retaining Sicily for the Aragónese in spite of a rebellion on the island and a period of dynastic transition in Iberia between the death of Martín *el Humano* in 1410 and the Compromise of Caspe in 1412.[74]

---

[71] For more background on the practice of lieutenancy in Aragón, see Lalinde Abadia, "Virreyes y lugartentientes medievales en la corona de Aragón."

[72] Earenfight, "Absent Kings."

[73] Silleras-Fernández, *Power, Piety and Patronage in Late Medieval Queenship*. Earenfight, *The King's Other Body*.

[74] For more on Blanca, see Woodacre, "Blanca, Queen of Sicily and Queen of Navarre."

Spanish royal women continued to be deputized to rule portions of their expanding European and global empire in the early modern period. The Hapsburg rulers Charles V and Philip II continued the practice of female lieutenancy, relying on wives, sisters, aunts, and daughters to be their proxy rulers, particularly in Iberia and the Low Countries.[75] However, Theresa Earenfight has noted that after Philip II's succession in 1555, the increasing dominance of Castilian practices and the centralization of power led to the rise of male bureaucrats who served as viceroys across the empire, leading to the ultimate demise of the Aragonese tradition of queen lieutenancy.[76]

Although the institution of queen lieutenancy and proxy rulers is somewhat unique to this region, in other ways female agency in the Iberian Peninsula demonstrates clear similarities to the previous case studies in the Mediterranean. The ability for women to inherit the throne in their own right, particularly in Castile and Navarre, mirrors that of the Crusader queens and the empresses of Byzantium. There is also a strong connection to both the Byzantine and Muslim territories in examples of women exercising authority on behalf of or alongside sons and husbands, such as the powerful regent Maria de Molina in Castile and the politically able consort Juana Enríquez, second wife of Juan II of Aragón and mother of Ferdinand II.[77]

Female Power, Authority, and Influence in the Italian Peninsula

The Italian Peninsula, linked with Aragón through its Mediterranean and later pan-European empire, also possessed a tradition of formidable female rulers. In the kingdoms of Naples and Sicily, women could inherit the crown, as did Constance and Maria of Sicily and the two Giovannas of Naples. Although both Giovanna I and II exercised sovereign power in the realm, they each struggled with difficult consorts who sought to completely usurp their position rather than rule alongside them. Giovanna I faced the most difficult challenge from the first of her four husbands, Andrew of Hungary, due to the fact that as a member of her own Angevin dynasty, he also possessed a viable claim to the throne. His murder in September 1345 removed the threat he posed in the short-term but

---

[75] Examples include Isabel of Portugal, Margaret of Austria, and Mary of Hungary (respectively the wife, aunt, and sister of Charles V) and Juana of Castile and Isabella Clara Eugenia (the sister and daughter of Philip II).

[76] Earenfight, *Queenship in Medieval Europe*, 254–55.

[77] The most recent English language biography is Pepin, *María de Molina* but there are also biographies in Spanish on this important regent, such as Carmona Ruiz, *Maria de Molina*. For Juana Enríquez, see the classic biography by Coll Julia, *Doña Juana Enríquez*; or, more recently, Earenfight, "Absent Kings," 47–51.

led to the invasion of Naples by Giovanna's brother-in-law, Louis of Hungary, who blamed Giovanna for Andrew's death.[78] Giovanna's rights were supported by the pope, who affirmed her as the rightful ruler of the kingdom and negotiated a peace settlement with Louis of Hungary. In the terms of this settlement, the pope also protected Giovanna's authority against her ambitious second husband, Louis of Taranto; Machiavelli noted in his Italian chronicle that the pope "effected her (Giovanna's) restoration to the sovereignty, on the condition that her husband, contenting himself with the title of prince of Tarento, should not be called king."[79] Giovanna remained on the throne until 1382, exercising sovereign authority in her realm and surviving all three of her children and three of her four husbands.

Her namesake Giovanna II also faced a challenge from her second husband, Jacques de Bourbon, who sought to rule as king rather than remain as a consort after their wedding in 1415. Machiavelli analyzed the couple's relationship in his chronicle of Italian history; "between the husband and the wife wars ensued; and although they contended with varying success, the queen at length obtained the superiority."[80] The Giovannas of Naples represent the dichotomy of female rule; it may be permitted, but reigning queens often had to defend their right to rule from uncles, sons, and husbands who sought to usurp their authority and position. In a patriarchal society, where the understanding of marriage made man the dominant figure in the partnership, Jacques de Bourbon's assumption that he would wield power in Naples was understandable. Indeed, the Aragonese chronicler Zurita felt it was entirely "improper . . . [that] the Giovannas of Naples . . . excluded some of their husbands from the title and regiment of the realm."[81]

In addition to these reigning queens in the South, the northern and central Italian peninsula saw a number of politically and culturally influential women across the courts of the Renaissance. While opportunities for women to rule in their own right were limited by the perception that "rulership was a specifically masculine activity," women did exercise authority as regents for sons and absent husbands—particularly in times of political turbulence such as the "Italian Wars" of 1494–1559.[82] Perhaps the most well known of these women was

---

[78] Giovanna's struggles to reign and her long term reputation as a ruler are very effectively analyzed in Casteen, *From She-Wolf to Martyr*.

[79] Machiavelli, *History of Florence*, Bk. I, chap. VI, https://ebooks.adelaide.edu. au/m/machiavelli/niccolo/m149h/. For Giovanna I's reign, one of the best biographies continues to be Léonard, *La jeunesse de Jeanne I*, given both Léonard's excellent scholarship and access to the Neopolitan archives before the damage suffered by bombing in WWII.

[80] Machiavelli, *History of Florence*, Bk. I, chap. 7. For more on both Giovannas, see Woodacre "Questionable Authority," 390–93.

[81] Zurita, *Anales de la Corona de Aragón*, 8:74.

[82] De Vries, "Caterina Sforza's Portrait Medals," 23.

Isabella d'Este, who was politically savvy, an able administrator of Mantua during the absences of her Gonzaga husband, and a collector par excellence whose impressive patronage has been intensively studied.[83] Indeed, cultural patronage was a means through which many elite women in Renaissance Italy demonstrated considerable agency. Their wealth gave them the ability to control and mediate expressions of dynasty, emphasizing their own position, authority, and lineage, as McIver demonstrates in her study of Silvia Santivale and Laura Pallavicina.[84] For example, in addition to her well-known military exploits, Caterina Sforza made her wealth and agency visible through her wide-ranging patronage supporting religious institutions, refurbishing palaces, and funding improvements in the territories that she governed as regent for her son. She also used the medium of portrait medals to communicate her authority; this medium was both appropriate and effective, as Joyce de Vries notes: "portraits were central to the Renaissance ruler's strategy for maintaining power . . . [and] an especially potent method of this self-presentation."[85]

Although the Italian Peninsula was incredibly diverse in terms of the variety and number of political entities present in the premodern period, the key typologies of female agency are present here, just as in the earlier case studies. Once again there are female rulers who have inherited the throne in their own right, as the two queens regnant of Naples demonstrate. Politically active and culturally influential consorts and regents can be seen in the examples of Isabella d'Este and Caterina Sforza, among others, reflecting the experiences of their Muslim, Iberian, and Byzantine counterparts across the Mediterranean in exercising authority.

Conclusions: Connecting Threads

This study has highlighted many examples from across the premodern period and all sides of the Mediterranean basin. It has demonstrated that women were able to access authority and power in kingdoms, caliphates, empires, and marquisates—as Sunni and Shi'ite Muslims, Roman Catholics, and Greek Orthodox Christians. Regardless of whether these women were called by the title of Empress, Queen, Marquessa, *Malika*, or Sultana, they all demonstrated a high degree of agency and influence. Most frequently, these women came to power through marital and familial links, ruling beside or on behalf of a husband or a

---

[83] Recent studies on Isabella's life and patronage include Hickson, *Women, Art and Architectural Patronage in Renaissance Mantua* ; and Cockram, *Isabella d'Este, and Francisco Gonzaga*. The extent of focus on Isabella d'Este's career has also triggered an interest in exploring other female patrons in more depth; see Reiss and Wilkins, *Beyond Isabella*.

[84] McIver, "Matrons as Patrons."

[85] De Vries, "Portrait Medals," 24.

son. While some of the examples in this study were elite women from noble and royal families whose standing was enhanced through the alliance that their marriage brought, other women successfully rose from slavery through the harem and into an impressive position of power and influence. However, many Mediterranean realms—such as the kingdoms of Castile, Navarre, Jerusalem, Naples, Sicily, and the Byzantine empire—allowed women to inherit the throne in their own right as legitimate successors. Even in territories that did not normally permit female rule, women such as Sitt al-Mulk and Arwa bint Ahmad successfully governed alone.

The political, ethnic, and religious diversity of the Mediterranean and its core function as a meeting point between cultures and religions and as a conduit of exchange throughout millennia has made it a fruitful area for the study of civilizations.[86] In a similar way, it makes an excellent comparative study for female rule, due to the number and diversity of political systems and cultural norms. These case studies, which highlight only a sample of the women who wielded significant power, authority, and influence in the premodern era, raise the possibility that the Mediterranean area offered an enhanced climate for women to exercise power and authority. While some of the roles and positions of authority mirrored those in northern Europe and the wider Islamic world, many of these political systems were atypical and offered unique opportunities for women. The pan-Mediterranean empires of the Byzantines, Aragonese, and the Cordoba caliphate offered women the opportunity to rule as empress regnant or regent, as a queen lieutenant, or as the favored consort of a caliph or sultan. The Crusader States, with their unusual mix of elected and hereditary monarchy, gave rise to an impressive number of female sovereigns in a relatively short history. The wealthy courts of the Italian Renaissance gave women the opportunity to wield not only political authority but also cultural influence as important patrons.

Ultimately, all of the women in this study, no matter their religion, era, or domicile, lived in patriarchal societies where men were expected to wield political power and authority. However, this study has demonstrated that women were able to exploit either the possibility for female rule in the political framework of their society or opportunities for influence that arose through accidents of fate or personal relationships and were able to exercise power and authority. While some of these female monarchs struggled to assert their authority, such as the beleaguered queens of the kingdom of Jerusalem, others, such as Arwa bint Ahmad, Irene of Byzantium, and Isabel *la Católica*, enjoyed lengthy reigns and are excellent examples of successful female rulers, both in the Mediterranean and beyond.

---

[86] For an interesting discussion of this concept, see Abulafia, "Mediterranean History as Global History."

Bibliography

Published Primary Sources

Anon. "*Le Livre au Roi.*" In *Assises de Jérusalem, ou, Recueil des ouvrages de jurisprudence composés pendant le XIIIe siècle dans les royaumes de Jérusalem et de Chypre; Assises de la Haute Cour (Lois I), Tome I.* Paris: Imprimerie Royale, 1841.

Arab Historians of the Crusades. Edited by Francisco Gabrieli. London: Routledge, 1969.

La Continuation de Guillaume de Tyr (1184–1197). Edited by M.R. Morgan. Paris: Librarie Orientaliste Paul Geutner, 1982.

The Ecclesiastical History of Orderic Vitalis. Edited by Marjorie Chibnall. 6 vols. Oxford: Oxford University Press, 1978.

Kinnamos, John. *Deeds of John and Manuel Comnenus.* Edited and translated by Charles M. Brand. New York: Columbia University Press, 1976.

Machiavelli, Niccolo. *History of Florence and the Affairs of Italy from the Earliest Times to the Death of Lorenzo the Magnificent.* Adelaide: University of Adelaide, 2010, unpaginated electronic edition, https://ebooks.adelaide.edu. au/m/machiavelli/niccolo/m149h/.

Psellos, Michael. *Chronographia.* Edited and translated by E. R. A. Sewter. New Haven: Yale University Press, 1953.

William, Archbishop of Tyre. *A History of Deeds done beyond the Sea (Volume Two).* Edited and translated by E. Babcock and A. C. Krey. New York: Octagon Books, 1976.

Zurita, Jerónimo, *Anales de la Corona de Aragón.* Edited by Ángel Canellas López. 9 vols. Zaragoza: Instituto Fernando el Católico, 1980–190.

Secondary Sources

Abulafia, David. "Mediterranean History as Global History." *History and Theory* 50 (May 2011): 220–28.

Barratt, Anthony. *Livia; First Lady of Imperial Rome.* New Haven: Yale University Press, 2004.

Bassett, Hayley. "Regnant Queenship and Royal Marriage between the Latin Kingdom of Jerusalem and the Nobility of Western Europe" in *A Companion to Global Queenship*, ed. Elena Woodacre, 39–52. Bradford: ARC Humanities Press, 2018.

Bianchini, Janna. *The Queen's Hand; Power and Authority in the Reign of Berenguela of Castile.* Philadelphia: University of Pennsylvania Press, 2012.

Campbell Orr, Clarissa, ed. *Queenship in Europe 1660–1815: The Role of the Consort.* Cambridge: Cambridge University Press, 2004.

Carmona Ruiz, Maria Antonia. *María de Molina.* Madrid: Plaza y Janes, 2005.

Casteen, Elizabeth. *From She-Wolf to Martyr: The Reign and Disputed Reputation of Johanna I of Naples.* Ithaca, NY: Cornell University Press, 2015.

Chaves Hernández, Eva. "Mujeres y poder en el Islam I: La reina Asma bint Sihib de Yemen (m. 479/1086–7)." *MEAH* 56 (2007): 3–20.

———. "Mujeres y poder en el Islam II: La Reina Libre sulayhí al-Sayyida (Arwa) bint Ahmad (440–532/1048–9–1138)." *MEAH* 57 (2008): 3–50.

Chen, Shou. *Empresses and Consorts: Selections from Chen Shou's Records of the Three States with Pei Songzhi's Commentary.* Translated and annotated by Robert Joe Cutter and William Gordon Crowell. Honolulu: University of Hawaii Press, 1999.

Cockram, Sarah D. P. *Isabella d'Este and Francisco Gonzaga: Power Sharing at the Italian Renaissance Court.* Farnham: Ashgate, 2013.

Coll Julia, Nuria. *Doña Juana Enríquez, lugarteniente real en Cataluña (1461–1468).* 2 vols. Madrid: CSIC, 1953.

Cortese, Delia, and Simonetta Calderini. *Women and the Fatmids in the World of Islam.* Edinburgh: University of Edinburgh Press, 2006.

Daftary, Farhad. "Sayyida Hurra: The Isma'ili Sulayhid Queen of Yemen." In *Women in the Medieval Islamic World: Power, Patronage and Piety*, ed. Gavin R. G. Hambly, 117–30. New York: Palgrave Macmillan, 1998.

de Vries, Joyce. "Caterina Sforza's Portrait Medals: Power, Gender and Representation in the Italian Renaissance Court." *Woman's Art Journal* 24, no. 1 (2003): 23–28.

Duncan, David J. "Scholarly Views of Shajarat al-Durr: A Need for Consensus." *Arab Studies Quarterly* 22, no. 1 (2000): 51–69.

Earenfight, Theresa. *Queenship in Medieval Europe.* New York: Palgrave Macmillan, 2013.

———. "Absent Kings: Queens as Political Partners in the Medieval Crown of Aragón." In *Queenship and Political Power in Medieval and Early Modern Spain*, ed. Theresa Earenfight, 33–54. Aldershot: Ashgate, 2005.

———, ed. *Queenship and Political Power in Medieval and Early Modern Spain.* Aldershot: Ashgate, 2005.

———. *The King's Other Body: Maria of Castile and the Crown of Aragón.* Philadelphia: University of Pennsylvania Press, 2010.

Echavarria, Ana and Roser Salicru I Lluch. "The 'Honourable Ladies' of Nasrid Grenada: Female Power and Agency in the Alhambra (1400–1450)" in *A Companion to Global Queenship*, ed. Elena Woodacre, 255–70. Bradford: ARC Humanities Press, 2018.

Folda, Jaroslav. "Images of Queen Melisende in Manuscripts of William of Tyre's History of Outremer: 1250–1300." *Gesta* 32, no. 2 (1993): 97–112.

Garcia Gallo, Alfonso. "El Derecho de Sucesion del Trono en la Corona de Aragón." *Anuario de Historia del Derecho Español* 36, no. 5 (1966): 5–188.

Garland, Lynda. *Byzantine Empresses; Women and Power in Byzantium AD 527–1204.* New York: Routledge, 1999.

Gil Gramau, Rodolfo, "Sayyida al-Hurra, Mujer Marroquí de Origen Andu-lusí." *Anaquel de Estudios Árabes* 11 (2000): 311–20.

Ginsburg, Judith. *Representing Agrippina: Constructions of Female Power in the Early Roman Empire.* Oxford: Oxford University Press, 2005.

Greilsammer, Miriam. "Structure and Aims of the *Livre au Roi.*" In *Outremer: Studies in the History of the Crusading Kingdom of Jerusalem Presented to Joshua Prawer*, ed. B. Z. Kedar, H. E Mayer, and R. C. Smail, 218–26. Jerusalem: Yad Izhak Ben-Zvi Institute, 1982.

Hamilton, Bernard. "Women in the Crusader States: The Queens of Jerusalem (1100–1190)." In *Medieval Women*, ed. D. Baker, 143–74. Oxford: The Ecclesiastical History Society, 1978.

———. "King Consorts of Jerusalem and their Entourages from the West from 1186–1250." In *Crusaders, Cathars and Holy Places*, ed. Bernard Hamilton, 12–24. Aldershot: Ashgate, 1999.

Hickson, Sally. *Women, Art and Architectural Patronage in Renaissance Mantua.* Farnham: Ashgate, 2012.

James, Liz. "Goddess, Whore, Wife or Slave? Will the Real Byzantine Empress Please Stand Up?" In *Queens and Queenship in Medieval Europe*, ed. Anne Duggan, 123–40. Woodbridge: Boydell, 1997.

Karagianni, Alexandra. "Female Monarchs in the Medieval Byzantine Court: Prejudice, Disbelief and Calumnities." In *Queenship in the Mediterranean: Negotiating the Role of the Queen in the Medieval and Early Modern Eras*, ed. Elena Woodacre, 9–26. New York: Palgrave Macmillan, 2013.

Lalinde Abadia, Jésus. "Virreyes y lugartentientes medievales en la corona de Aragón." *Cuadernos de Historia de España* 31–32 (1960): 98–172.

Lambert, Sarah. "Queen or Consort: Rulership and Politics in the Latin East: 1118–1228." In *Queens and Queenship in Medieval Europe. Proceedings of a Conference at Kings College London, April 1995*, ed. Anne J. Duggan, 153–69. Woodbridge: Boydell, 1997.

———. "Images of Queen Melisende." In *Authority and Gender in Medieval and Renaissance Chronicles*, ed. Juliana Dresvina and Nicholas Sparks, 140–65. Newcastle: Cambridge Scholars Publishing, 2012.

Lassner, Jacob. *Demonizing the Queen of Sheba: Boundaries of Gender and Culture in Postbiblical Judaism and Medieval Islam.* Chicago: University of Chicago Press, 1993.

Léonard, Emile G. *La jeunesse de Jeanne I, Reine de Naples, Comtesse de Provence.* Paris: Librarie Auguste Renard, 1932.

Lev, Yaacov. "The Fatimid Princess Sitt al-Mulk." *Journal of Semitic Studies* 32, no. 2 (1987): 319–28.

Levick, Barbara. *Julia Domna; Syrian Empress.* London: Routledge, 2007.

Lourniho, Ines. "Queen Zaynab al-Nafzawiyya and the Building of a Medi-terranean Empire in Eleventh-Century Magreb" in *A Companion to Global*

Queenship, ed. Elena Woodacre, 159–170. Bradford: ARC Humanities Press, 2018.

Mayer, Hans Everard. "Angevins versus Normans: The New Men of King Fulk of Jerusalem." *Proceedings of the American Philosophical Society* 133 (1989): 1–25.

———. "Studies in the History of Queen Melisende of Jerusalem." *Dumbarton Oaks Papers* 26 (1972): 95–182.

McIver, Katherine A. "Matrons as Patrons: Power and Influence in the Courts of Northern Italy in the Renaissance." *Artibus et Historiae* 22, no. 43 (2001): 75–89.

Mernissi, Fatima. *The Forgotten Queens of Islam*. Cambridge: Polity, 1993.

Miranda, Ana. "Al-Dalfa' and the Political Role of the umm al-walad in the Late Umayyad Caliphate of al-Andalus" in *A Companion to Global Queenship*, ed. Elena Woodacre, 171–82. Bradford: ARC Humanities Press, 2018.

Mourtada-Sabbah, Nada, and Adrian Gully. "'I am, by God, Fit for High Positions': On the Political Role of Women in al-Andalus." *British Journal of Middle Eastern Studies* 30, no. 2 (2003): 183–209.

Nicol, Donald M. *The Byzantine Lady: Ten Portraits 1250–1500*. Cambridge: Cambridge University Press, 1994.

Olivera Serrano, César. *Beatriz de Portugal: la pugna dinastica Avís-Trastámara*. Santiago de Compostela: Instituto de Estudios Gallegos, 2005.

Peirce, Leslie. "Beyond Harem Walls; Ottoman Women and the Exercise of Power." In *Servants of the Dynasty: Palace Women in World History*, ed Anne Wathall, 81–95. Berkeley: University of California Press, 2008.

Pepin, Paulette Lynn. *María de Molina, Queen and Regent: Life and Rule in Castile-León, 1259–1321*. London: Lexington Books, 2016.

Poulet, Andre. "Capetian Women and the Regency: The Genesis of a Vocation." In *Medieval Queenship*, ed. John Carmi Parsons, 93–116. Stroud: Alan Sutton, 1998.

Prawer, Joshua. *Crusader Institutions*. Oxford: Clarendon, 1980.

Reilly, Bernard F. *The Kingdom of León-Castilla under Queen Urraca, 1109–1126*. Princeton: Princeton University Press, 1982.

Reiss, S. E., and D. G. Wilkins, eds. *Beyond Isabella: Secular Women Patrons of Art in Renaissance Italy*. Kirksville, MO: Truman State University Press, 2001.

Ringrose, Kathryn. "Women and Power at the Byzantine Court." In *Servants of the Dynasty: Palace Women in World History*, ed Anne Wathall, 65–80. Berkeley: University of California Press, 2008.

Roehrig, Catharine H., Renée Dreyfus, and Cathleen A. Keller. *Hatshepsut: From Queen to Pharaoh*. New York: Metropolitan Museum of Art, 2005.

Roller, Duane W. *Cleopatra: A Biography*. Oxford: Oxford University Press, 2010.

Rustow, Marina. "A Petition to a Woman at the Fatimid Court." *Bulletin of the SOAS* 73, no. 1 (2010): 1–27.

Sadiqi, Fatima, Amira Nowaira, Azzi el Kholy, and Moha Ennaji, eds. *Des femmes écrivent l'Afrique: L'Afrique du Nord*. Paris: Kathala, 2013.

Schein, Sylvia. "Women in Medieval Colonial Society: The Latin Kingdom of Jerusalem in the 12th Century." In *Gendering the Crusades*, ed. Susan B. Edgington and Sarah Lambert, 140–53. Cardiff: University of Wales Press, 2001.

Silleras-Fernández, Nuria. *Power, Piety and Patronage in Late Medieval Queenship: Maria de Luna*. New York: Palgrave Macmillan, 2008.

Smythe, Dion C. "Behind the Mask: Empresses and Empire in Middle Byzantium." In *Queens and Queenship in Medieval Europe. Proceedings of a Conference at Kings College London, April 1995*, ed. Anne J. Duggan, 141–52. Woodbridge: Boydell, 1997.

———. "Middle Byzantine Family Values and Anna Komnene's *Alexiad*." In *Byzantine Women: Varieties of Experience 800–1200*, ed. Lynda Garland, 125–39. Aldershot: Ashgate, 2006.

Stalls, William Clay. "Queenship and the Royal Patrimony in Twelfth-Century Iberia: The Example of Petronilla of Aragón." In *Queens, Regents and Potentates*, ed. Theresa M. Vann, 49–62. Dallas: Academia, 1993.

Weissburger, Barbara F. *Isabel Rules: Constructing Queenship, Wielding Power*. Minneapolis: University of Minnesota Press, 2004.

Whitelock, Anna, and Alice Hunt, eds. *Tudor Queenship*. New York: Palgrave Macmillan, 2012.

Woodacre, Elena. "Questionable Authority: Female Sovereigns and their Consorts in Medieval and Early Modern Chronicles." In *Authority and Gender in Medieval and Renaissance Chronicles*, ed. Juliana Dresvina and Nicholas Sparks, 377–407. Newcastle: Cambridge Scholars, 2012.

———. *The Queens Regnant of Navarre 1274–1512: Succession, Politics and Partnership*. New York: Palgrave Macmillan, 2013.

———. "Blanca, Queen of Sicily and Queen of Navarre—Connecting the Pyrenees and the Mediterranean via an Aragónese Alliance." In *Queenship in the Mediterranean: Negotiating the Role of the Queen in the Medieval and Early Modern Eras*, ed. Elena Woodacre, 207–28. New York: Palgrave Macmillan, 2013.

———, ed. *Queenship in the Mediterranean: Negotiating the Role of the Queen in the Medieval and Early Modern Eras*, ed. Elena Woodacre. New York: Palgrave Macmillan, 2013.

Chapter 8
RELIGIOUS PATRONAGE IN BYZANTIUM: THE CASE OF KOMNENIAN IMPERIAL WOMEN

VASSILIKI DIMITROPOULOU

Throughout the history of the Byzantine empire, which flourished for more than ten centuries in the region of the eastern Mediterranean, women played an important role as patrons.* In the God-dominated society of Byzantium, the majority of patronage had God as its point of reference. The purpose of this study is to discuss the practice of gift-giving to God by the women of the Komnenian dynasty.[1] Komnenian imperial women were actively involved in religious patronage: they were not only great founders, refounders, and benefactors of monasteries and holy men but they also commissioned objects of religious art that they offered as gifts to churches. On the basis of the surviving textual and archaeological material, I will seek to establish the role played by imperial women in patronage. What sort of patterns can we identify in their activities? What did those women value in spending their money on commissions? What were the implications of those acts of imperial patronage for the relationship between Byzantine and Mediterranean women, on the one hand, and power, on the other? Additionally, by broadening the perspective on Mediterranean gender practices, I will indicate the extent to which the patronage activities of Komnenian women conformed to or differed from those of other noble women across the Mediterranean.

---

* I would like to express my gratitude to Professor Liz James for her invaluable help with bibliographical material I have used in this essay.

[1] The period under study will cover the years from the accession of Alexios I Komnenos in 1081 to 1185, which marks the end of the Komnenian dynasty.

Large-Scale Monastic Patronage

The revival of monastic building in the capital of the Byzantine empire, Constantinople, during the Komnenian period owed much to imperial women—after all, the foundation and refoundation of monasteries such as Kecharitomene, Pantokrator, Pantepoptes, Pammakaristos, and Chora are all attributed to the patronage of these women. The textual and material evidence about their activities, although limited and sometimes misleading, can reveal the patterns of Komnenian female patronage, showing us that, despite the often limited sphere in which medieval women operated, many women were devoted to the support of religious institutions by using their material wealth to express their piety in an era when spiritual and worldly matters were closely intertwined.

First, Komnenian female patrons of monasteries belonged to the top of the social hierarchy, and the activities in which they were involved were not at all representative of women of other social levels. Most of the female patrons involved in monastic foundation and refoundation projects were empresses. For instance, the empress Eirene Doukaina, wife of Emperor Alexios I Komnenos, was a great religious patron involved in the highly visible work of founding monasteries. She was responsible for the founding of a double monastery located in the northern section of Constantinople in the early years of the twelfth century. Although no buildings survive today either from the convent of Kecharitomene ("full of grace")[2] or from the adjacent male monastery of Christ Philanthropos,[3] the *typikon* [foundation charter][4] of the convent, dated between 1110 and 1116, does survive. This reveals that the monastic complex of Kecharitomene was of considerable size, as it included, apart from the religious buildings, two courtyards, two bath-houses, and the luxurious imperial apartments where Eirene withdrew after her husband's death. The existence of mosaics, icons, and furnishings is documented in the *typikon* and in an inventory. All these suggest that Eirene's convent was a large, richly decorated imperial foundation and a conspicuous one in every sense of the word. Apart from scale, its physical location contributed to its visibility, which, in turn, meant that Eirene's act of patronage had not only a personal but also a public dimension.

---

[2] Janin, *La géographie ecclésiastique de l'empire byzantin*, 3:188–91; Gautier, "Le typikon de la Théotokos Kécharitoméné."

[3] Janin, *La géographie ecclésiastique*, 3:525–27; Janin, "Les monastères du Christ Philanthrope à Constantinople."

[4] A *typikon* is a prescriptive rather than a narrative text that includes various provisions and rules according to which the convent should be governed. For *typika*, see *Byzantine Monastic Foundation Documents*; Galatariotou, "Byzantine Women's Monastic Communities"; Thomas, *Private Religious Foundations in the Byzantine Empire*; and Barber, "The Monastic Typikon for Art Historians."

Another empress, Eirene Piroska-Xene, whose representation still exists on the mosaic on the east wall of the south gallery in Hagia Sophia, is also known as the co-founder—together with her husband, the emperor John Komnenos—of the Pantokrator Monastery in Constantinople according to contemporary sources.[5] The Pantokrator complex consists of two churches: the south church, dedicated to St. Saviour Pantokrator (Christ the Almighty), and the north church, dedicated to the Virgin Eleousa (Virgin of Tenderness), with a mausoleum chapel dedicated to the Archangel Michael between them. The three interconnected sanctuaries, which formed the focal point of the monastery, are still preserved under their Turkish name, Zeyrek Kilisse Camii, in the north central part of the modern city of Istanbul.[6] The fact that the monastery was built on the top of the hill made the whole foundation extremely conspicuous. The *typikon* along with the surviving three churches of the complex give us an adequate picture of what the whole foundation looked like. The monastery

---

[5] What Eirene's role exactly was is not clear in the sources. The historian John Kinnamos wrote that "she established a monastery in the name of the Pantokrator, which is among the most outstanding in beauty and size"; see Kinnamos, *Epitomi ton katorthomaton*, 10. The *Synaxarium* of Constantinople also emphasizes Eirene's exclusive contribution to Pantokrator's foundation, and a fourteenth-century *ekphrasis* of the monastery repeats this; see *Synaxarium ecclesiae Constantinopolitane*, 887–90. See also Kampouroglou, Μνημεῖα τῆς Ἱστορίας τῶν Ἀθηναίων, 127. In contrast to these accounts acknowledging Eirene Piroska's foundation, her contribution to the building of Pantokrator is an act of female patronage that remains unacknowledged by the historical account of Niketas Choniates and of another anonymous historian who relies on Choniates; see Choniates, Χρονικὴ Διήγησις, 49; and Sathas, Μεσαιωνικὴ Βιβλιοθήκη, 7:216. Both claim that it was John who founded Pantokrator. The *typikon* says that Eirene, who was John's helper in its planning and construction, left this world before the completion of the task; see Gautier, "Le typikon du Christ Sauveur Pantocrator." It is quite possible that Eirene may have played a significant part in the foundation of the monastery if we take into consideration that she did not die until 1134 and that Pantokrator was fully operational in 1136. The fourteenth-century *ekphrasis* of the Pantokrator claims that it was Eirene who supervised the building of the monastery, advising the architect Nikephoros Beseleil, while John was preoccupied with military campaigning and foreign affairs most of the time and was away from the capital; see Kampouroglou, Μνημεῖα τῆς Ἱστορίας τῶν Ἀθηναίων, 127. In this source, Eirene was glorified because she glorified God by co-founding Pantokrator. Moreover, Eirene was the only Byzantine woman of the twelfth century to become a saint, and her memory was celebrated on 13 August in the Pantokrator; see Dimitropoulou, "Imperial Women Founders and Refounders in Komnenian Constantinople." Her reputation for holiness and piety is plausibly related to her contribution to the foundation of the monastery; see *Synaxarium ecclesiae Constantinopolitane*, 887–90.

[6] Megaw, "Notes on the Recent Work of the Byzantine Institute in Istanbul"; Magdalino, *The Empire of Manuel Komnenos: 1143–1180*, 117; Ousterhout, "Architecture, Art and Komnenian Ideology at the Pantokrator Monastery"; Congdon, "Imperial Commemoration and Ritual."

was an extensive institution, incorporating a big monastic community of eighty monks, a hospital, a hospice for old men, an asylum for the insane, and a bath.[7] Built between 1118 and 1136, the Pantokrator monastery combined charity with traditional imperial opulence. Without doubt this was a high-class Byzantine church, a highly prestigious religious foundation built and decorated by the best artisans in the city and co-founded by an emperor and his empress. We do know that the empress Eirene endowed the monastery with a list of properties, but there is no evidence about the possible provenance of her economic resources.[8] Yet what she chose to do with her wealth is made clear in the building program, as Eirene surely expressed imperial status in material terms. Because of her sudden death, however, she missed the chance to enjoy the prestige and status that patrons normally gained from such magnificent foundations.

A certain tradition and continuity in the foundation of monasteries by imperial women is evident. Eirene Piroska's influential and ambitious building plans surely influenced her daughter-in-law, the empress Maria of Antioch, who undertook the project of transforming Ioannitzes' house into the convent of Pantanassa after her husband's death.[9] Yet beyond this bare fact, there is no further evidence about Maria's monastic building. Nevertheless, mothers, daughters-in-law, and other relatives of the imperial couple were also involved in founding and refounding richly decorated monasteries at the heart of the imperial capital.

One of the most visible female patrons was Anna Dalassene, the mother of Emperor Alexios I Komnenos. Anna Dalassene founded the monastery of Saviour Pantepoptes (Christ the All-Seeing) dedicated to Christ.[10] The Pantepoptes, built before 1087, was a conspicuous building located on the fourth hill of Constantinople and overlooking the Golden Horn.[11] Shortly before her death, Anna retired to the apartments she had prepared within the monastery.[12] What survives today from that religious foundation is the church of the monastery, now the mosque Eski Imaret Camii.[13] It is the most carefully built of the later churches of Constantinople, and both the exterior and interior of the church point to the fact that Pantepoptes must have been a rich foundation.

The list of imperial female founders of monasteries goes on. Maria Doukaina, the empress Eirene Doukaina's mother, was responsible for refounding and reconstructing the ancient monastery of St. Saviour in Chora (now known

---

[7] Gautier, "Le typikon du Christ Sauveur Pantocrator."

[8] Gautier, "Le typikon du Christ Sauveur Pantocrator," lines 1559–1573, p. 123–25.

[9] Choniates, Χρονικὴ Διήγησις, 419.

[10] Zonaras, *Epitomae Historiarum*, 3:XVIII, 24.

[11] Miklosich and Müller, *Acta*, 6:26–27, 32–33.

[12] Zonaras, *Epitomae Historiarum*, 3:XVIII, 24.

[13] Mango, "Where at Constantinople Was the Monastery of Christos Pantepoptes?"

as Kariye Camii) at the end of the eleventh century.[14] Some fragments of Maria's church, dated between 1077 and 1081, still remain in the surviving church.[15] Other more distant members of the imperial family also undertook building projects. Anna Doukaina co-founded with her husband John the monastery of Pammakaristos (now known as Fethiye Camii) in Constantinople during the second half of the twelfth century.[16] The evidence for their patronage is provided by an inscription that was once visible on the cornice of the bema in the church.[17] The original church, which commanded a fine view of the Golden Horn, was intended to serve as a family mausoleum. The founders' children and grandchildren together with their spouses were buried in tombs arranged along the north and south aisles. Although today only some remains from the original foundation survive, evidence suggests that the Komnenian church must have been richly decorated with mosaics, marbles, *opus sectile*, and icons. This is another example of a well-built religious foundation co-founded by a female member of the imperial family and her husband.

What is more, apart from founding and refounding monastic houses, Komnenian imperial women were also involved in the benefaction of monasteries and monastic figures. Written sources indicate that these women patronized monastic houses, either directly, in the form of money or property for their maintenance, or indirectly, through the patronage of holy men who founded or refounded monasteries with their help. For example, Anna Dalassene's daughter, the *kouropalatissa* Theodora Komnene, offered immovable property to the monastery of Panoiktirmon:

> It should be known that the property of the Monokellion donated by the patriarch of Theoupolis, the great Antioch, which was taken by force from him, belonged to the nun Xene Komnene, the most noble *kouropalatissa*, and was later given by her to the monastery of the All-Merciful, with the

---

[14] Gregoras, *Byzantina Historia* IX.13, 1:458–59; Migne, *Patrologiae cursus completes, Series graeca* 148, 653 C.

[15] Van Millingen, *Byzantine Churches in Constantinople*, 288–331; Oates, "A Summary Report on the Excavations of the Byzantine Institute in the Kariye Camii: 1957 and 1958"; Underwood, *The Kariye Djami*, 1:8–10; Janin, *La géographie ecclésiastique*, 531–38; Mathews, *The Byzantine Churches of Istanbul*, 40–58; Ousterhout, *The Architecture of the Kariye Camii in Istanbul.*

[16] Van Millingen, *Byzantine Churches*, 138; Ebersolt and Thiers, *Les églises de Constantinople*, 225–47; Underwood, "Notes on the Work of the Byzantine Institute in Istanbul: 1954"; Underwood, "Notes on the Work of the Byzantine Institute in Istanbul: 1957–59," 215–19; Mango and Hawkins, "Report on Field Work in Istanbul and Cyprus, 1962–1963"; Janin, *La géographie ecclésiastique*, 208–13; Mathews, *The Byzantine Churches*, 346–65; Belting, Mango, and Mouriki, *The Mosaics and Frescoes of St. Mary Pammakaristos.*

[17] Belting, Mango and Mouriki, *The Mosaics.*

approval of her holy mother, lady Anna; and they should be commemorated both during their lifetime and after their death, together with Constantine, the late husband of the nun, lady Xene, and their memorial rites should be celebrated in perpetuity in accordance with the text of their donation.[18]

Another imperial female figure, Eudokia Komnene, niece of the emperor Alexios Komnenos, also made offerings to the monastery of St. John Prodromos of Phoberos. In the *typikon* of the monastery, Eudokia, who became a nun under the popular monastic name Xene, is hailed as the monastery's beloved "second founder" out of consideration for her many gifts to the foundation, including a very large sum of money for the purchase of landed property:

> But then a second founder after God appeared for us, lady Eudokia Kom-
> nene, *sebaste* among *sebastai* and nun among nuns, the daughter of the glo-
> rious *sebastokrator* lord Isaakios, who changed her name to Xene and often
> bestowed many gifts and acts of kindness on us and our monastery.[19]

Also, Anna Dalassene was patron of the holy man John the Faster, who refounded the monastery of the St. John the Baptist in Petra. She was recorded as a benefac-tor of this monastery in the unpublished testament of the monastery's founder preserved in the Codex Ambrosianus E 9 Sup.[20] Thanks to imperial benefaction, this monastery was flourishing throughout the Komnenian period.[21]

And it was Anna who interceded with Emperor Alexios I on St. Christ-odoulos' behalf, so that Christodoulos—an important monastic figure of the eleventh century—would be granted the island of Patmos in the Aegean Sea, where he founded the still-surviving Monastery of St. John the Theologian.[22] In his *diataxis* of 1091, Christodoulos clearly states that the donations to Patmos were due to the benevolence of Anna Dalassene and that she was instrumental in getting her son to accede to his request:[23]

> When it became clear, even to the emperor, that these monks were com-
> pletely unacceptable for my purpose, I again begged and beseeched his
> imperial majesty to accede to my wish concerning Patmos. This time, with
> the empress of blessed memory, the emperor's mother, also interceding for

---

[18] Translation taken from *Byzantine Monastic Foundation Documents*, 360.

[19] Translation taken from *Byzantine Monastic Foundation Documents*, 927–28.

[20] See Darrouzès, "Le mouvement des foundations monastiques," 161, footnote 2; Magdalino, "The Byzantine Holy Man," 52.

[21] Darrouzès, "Le mouvement des foundations monastiques," 161, footnote 2; Mag-dalino, "The Byzantine Holy Man in the Twelfth Century," 52; Angold, *Church and Society in Byzantium*, 275; Majeska, *Russian Travellers to Constantinople*, 339–45.

[22] Miklosich and Müller, *Acta*, 6:44–53, 55–59, 65; Hill, *Imperial Women in Byzan-tium 1025–1204*, 161–65.

[23] Miklosich and Müller, *Acta*, 6:65.

me and urging this course, the most powerful emperor granted the request of our miserable self.[24]

Without these women's imperial grants and privileges, it would have been impossible for monasteries to survive for more than a short period of time.

What is interesting is that imperial women tended to engage in founding and refounding mostly after their husbands' death. Widowhood appears to have motivated them to take this step in order to provide themselves with a monastic refuge and spiritual comfort after they had taken the veil.[25] Anna Dalassene, Maria Doukaina, and Maria of Antioch were all widows when they were engaged in monastic patronage. The empress Bertha-Eirene, who did not appear as a monastic patron at all, died before her husband Manuel Komnenos, so she missed the opportunity to develop her own building program according with the practices of other imperial widows.

The fact that most Komnenian female founders were widows suggests that they were financially empowered by widowhood. Widows who retained the right of ownership and administration of family property had more chance to operate in economic life without much hindrance.[26] As long as they did not remarry, widows had full control of the whole property as opposed to nominal ownership, and they were closely involved in managing their property as transmitters of money. This is why many women took full advantage of the widow's status. As Barbara Hill has suggested in the context of literary patronage, "the patronage of imperial women seems to corroborate what one might suspect about the place of women in Byzantium. It was an excellent thing to be a widow and a bad thing to be a wife."[27]

Also, few married women appear to have been involved in monastery patronage without the assistance of their husbands, which suggests that they rarely had the large resources required for founding a monastery. Such commissions were attributed to both parties, as is the case with Anna Doukaina and her husband, but sometimes they were attributed to the husband alone, even though as a co-

---

[24] Translation taken from *Byzantine Monastic Foundation Documents*, 583.

[25] On widowhood, see Runciman, "The Widow Danelis"; Kazhdan, "Widows Lost and Regained," 509; McNamara, "Wives and Widows in Early Christian Thought"; Verdon, "Virgins and Widows"; Thurston, *The Widows*; Bremmer, "Pauper or Patroness"; McGinn, "Widows, Orphans, and Social History"; Grubbs, "Virgins and Widows, Show-Girls and Whores"; and Grubbs, *Women and the Law in the Roman Empire*.

[26] Aristocratic widows were transmitters of not only money but also lineage. They could ensure the proper ancestry to the offspring of aristocratic families. There were strong family links between the members of the dominant families in the Komnenian period, and much of politics was run by these closely related families. See Laiou, "The Role of Women in Byzantine Society," 251.

[27] Hill, *Imperial Women*, 179.

founder the wife was the driving force behind them, as is the case with Eirene-Piroska-Xene and the monastery of Pantokrator.[28]

Moreover, the evidence suggests that almost all Komnenian imperial women tended to found, rather than refound, monastic houses, even though both founding and refounding required new endowments and resources and carried the same ideological weight. By restoring a holy site from destruction, by dedicating it to God, and by making it ready to offer once again its services to the community, the refounder acted in a similar way as the founder of a monastery. Both the construction of a new monastery and the restoration of an old one resulted in something equally praiseworthy.

Almost all women built or rebuilt within the walls of the city of Constantinople. There was no better place to display the patron's God-like philanthropic nature. Constantinople was considered to be a safe and secure site for a monastery.[29] In many ways, Constantinople was the only socially and ideologically acceptable place for women patrons to locate their monasteries. The location of the monasteries sponsored by imperial women indicates that almost all the monasteries were situated in the northern part of the city of Constantinople, the area of Blachernai, which had become the new imperial center.

The significant role of female agency in the founding and refounding of monasteries means that such public activities were open to imperial women and most probably indicates that they saw monastic investments as an opportunity to expand their influence and personal agenda through patronage. Spending time and money on building monasteries was expected not only of imperial women but also of emperors, aristocrats, military commanders, diplomats, and ecclesiastics. In the male-dominated society of Byzantium, women could not become military commanders or occupy positions in the Church or the bureaucracy, owing to restrictive patterns of behavior imposed on them; as a result, they had no access to those particular areas of public life and influence.[30] Yet the building of monasteries appears to have been an open area in which imperial women could freely operate. Such actions conformed to the cultural norms of Byzantine society, so they were considered to be appropriate for women and were even expected of them. As Anthony Cutler maintains, the "great" are those who can least afford to take liberties with the official norms.[31] The ability of aristocratic women to negotiate alternative spaces for influence was at least as circumscribed by the power of the men around them as that of peasants and women involved in retail trade. However, the economic function of an aristocratic woman was

---

[28] Dimitropoulou, "Imperial Women Founders."

[29] Talbot, "A Comparison of the Monastic Experiences of Byzantine Men and Women," 3.

[30] James and Hill, "Women and Politics in the Byzantine Empire," 158.

[31] Cutler, "Uses of Luxury," 302.

fundamentally different from that of other classes. Building in glorification of religion offered them the possibility of personal expression through patronage.

Monastic patronage gave Byzantine women the chance to create and claim a geo-cultural space for exerting their influence. The monastic spaces of Byzantium afforded imperial women alternative ways of constructing their public image, which was the case in the wider Mediterranean too, but they were exceptional because they were so numerous. The monastery comes to represent not only religious piety and zeal but also a space that itself represents alternative gender practices.

The Motivation behind Patronage

Let us now examine more closely what prompted women to dedicate so much of their time and resources to such extensive projects. A consideration of their motives provides significant insights into the religious and secular lives of Komnenian imperial women, insights that appear to be applicable to female patronage across the Mediterranean.[32] The best place to look at is the *typika* of the monasteries.[33] Eirene Doukaina's *typikon* of the Kecharitomene convent, for instance, is a valuable source written for an empress founder, bearing her signature and shedding light on the practices and motivations shared by most of the founders.[34] To begin with, religious feeling provided a significant motive for founders. Monastery and church building was associated with the patrons' concerns about the salvation of their soul after death. The metaphysical anxieties of the Byzantines were concentrated on the question of salvation and the inheritance of the eternal Kingdom of God. By building a religious foundation, and by dedicating it to a divine being, donors manifested their piety and love towards God so that the deity in His turn would be better disposed towards the founder on the Day of Judgment.[35] Founders hoped that, after their death, heavenly beings—such as the Virgin or Christ, to whom the monastery was dedicated—would appear before God on their behalf. This form of intercession appears to be the ultimate hope of the patron. Evidence for such hopes is provided by the *typikon* of Kecharitomene, in which Eirene Doukaina invokes the help of the Virgin. A monastery was the donor's investment in eternal life:

---

[32] Schaus, *Women and Gender in Medieval Europe*; McCash, *The Cultural Patronage of Medieval Women*; Ward, *English Noblewomen in the Later Middle Ages*; Ward, *Women in Medieval Europe 1200–1500*; Bennett and Karras, *The Oxford Handbook of Women and Gender in Medieval Europe*; Wood, *Studying Late Medieval History*.

[33] Galatariotou, "Byzantine Ktetorika Typika."

[34] Gautier, "Le typikon de la Théotokos."

[35] Morris, *Monks and Laymen in Byzantium, 843–1118*, chap. 5; Galatariotou, "Byzantine Ktetorika," 91–95.

Since it is impossible for human beings who still live and move in this world to show the ardour of their faith in you in a human way by more divine and immaterial offerings, imitating and copying the condescension and humility of the Word, I myself have built for you, the mother of the Word, a holy temple . . . Since you have gently tasted the faith of my heart, receive my offering with favour and do not thrust away my oblation, nor "turn away your face from" your child but add a happy ending to an auspicious beginning.[36]

Imperial women founders expressed not only their piety but also their philanthropy in material terms, for, as Demetrios Constantelos points out, the classical virtue of philanthropy was seen as a mark of proper imperial behavior.[37] Philanthropy was not only a policy through which the empress endeared herself to her people but also a means that was expected to have a positive impact on her soul after death: forgiveness of her sins and salvation of her soul. The philanthropist would not be left without satisfaction from God, for the monasteries were centers of hospitality, almsgiving, and care for the sick, the poor, the orphans, the pilgrims, and the wayfarers. One of the provisions of monasteries was that distribution of food should be made not only on certain holidays but also on every single day at the gate of the monastery. For example, the various *mnemosyna* (memorial services) held for the benefit of the souls of the relatives of the founder Eirene Doukaina — as they are described in the *typikon*—were also to be accompanied by the distribution to the poor of bread, wine, and money.[38] With such provisions, the founder must have believed that she pleased God and that God in turn would favor and reward her in paradise.

In that context, monastic foundation exemplified the common Byzantine belief that the salvation of the soul would be better achieved through the efficacious prayers of nuns or monks, who were spiritual people. Therefore, their prayers for the founder's soul would be more effective and the sins of the founder would be more successfully erased. In the *typikon* of the Kecharitomene convent, Eirene Doukaina asked the Virgin to protect and keep safe the foundation on her behalf so that the nuns of the convent could achieve purity and their supplications for Eirene's salvation might reach the ears of the Lord more easily.[39] The fact that the longest chapter in the Kecharitomene *typikon* is the one including directions for the commemorative services suggests how significant this was. Eirene laid down precise directions for prayers for the salvation of her own and her family's souls. Their names were not only to be commemorated while they were alive but also to be written in the diptychs and commemorated after death.

---

[36] Translation taken from *Byzantine Monastic Foundation Documents*, 665–66.

[37] Constantelos, *Byzantine Philanthropy and Social Welfare*.

[38] Gautier, "Le typikon de la Théotokos," lines 1760–1877, p. 119–25.

[39] Gautier, "Le typikon de la Théotokos," lines 713–715, p.59.

This chapter even contains details about the frequency of the commemorative services to be held, the lighting, the liturgy, and even the diet to be followed on the day of each commemoration service.[40] This type of motivation behind monastic foundation apparently characterizes female piety in the western Mediterranean too. It seems that noble women across the Mediterranean world used very similar strategies to secure the salvation of their souls.[41]

Alongside the founders' expression of religious feeling, kinship, and allegiance to the family was another motivating factor for the foundation. The monastery served as a material and eternal bond between the founder and her kin, as provisions make explicit in the *typikon* of Kecharitomene. Eirene provided for the emotional needs of her relatives by offering a home, a place for retirement to be used not only for religious comfort but also in times of old age, misfortune, and political danger. She provided for members of the immediate family who may have wanted to join the monastery during their lifetime.[42] She made it clear that her relatives who chose to enter the monastic life would not have to lead the life of an ordinary monk or nun. Any descendant of hers was to be admitted freely and to be given extensive privileges. Eirene ensured that her family would retain the privileges they had before entering the monastic life.[43] The patron was also concerned with providing for her relatives' financial needs by tying up huge amounts of property and by ensuring, through specific provisions in the *typikon*, that members of her family would be financially provided for, for life.[44] Maria Doukaina's refoundation also demonstrated family concern. Her grandson Isaac Komnenos appears to have inherited proprietary rights to the monastery of St. Saviour in Chora after Maria's death, since it was he who restored Maria's church a few years later.

In addition, the founder provided not only a home for her kin while alive but also an eternal home in the form of burial ground. The emotional desire of members of the same family to be buried together is illustrated in the Kecharitomene *typikon*'s provisions for the burial of Eirene's children and descendants.[45] The common burial ground offers the possibility to maintain the bond not only among the dead but also between the dead and the living members of the family. Anna Doukaina also provides a burial ground for her family within the church of Pammakaristos.

---

[40] Gautier, "Le typikon de la Théotokos,"lines 289–290, p. 35, lines 1165–1186, p. 83–85, lines 1759–1877, p. 119–25, lines 1984–2000, p. 131–33.

[41] Ward, *Women in Medieval Europe 1200–1500*; Bennett and Karras, *The Oxford Handbook of Women and Gender*; Wood, *Studying Late Medieval History*.

[42] Gautier, "Le typikon de la Théotokos," lines 299–358, p. 37–39.

[43] Gautier, "Le typikon de la Théotokos," lines 299–339. p. 37–39, lines 2088–2226, p. 137–43.

[44] Gautier, "Le typikon de la Théotokos," lines 460–484, p. 47.

[45] Gautier, "Le typikon de la Théotokos," lines 1984–2006, p. 131–33.

Economic reasons must have played a role in the founding of monasteries, as the evidence reveals. The patrons put their money in trust for all future generations, and the monasteries were endowed with large amounts of property.[46] The inventories of Kecharitomene and Pantokrator give us an idea by revealing the founders' financial contribution to the monastic complexes. Founders were aware of the fact that the huge amounts of money and property that they swept under the monastic habit would be by law inalienable and would enjoy tax and judicial immunities.[47] This was achieved by the appointment of an *ephoros*, a curator, who was a layperson, not surprisingly a member of the family of the founder, and in whom the use and possession of the monastery was legally vested.[48] In the Kecharitomene *typikon*, there are provisions so that the curatorship would be passed on to other family members in perpetuity.[49] The property with which the monastery was endowed would be vested in the monastery only if the entire family died out, something which reveals that the women's considerations were not only spiritual but also in the best economic interests of their families.

Other considerations, such as the desire to express gratitude for a successful period in office, might well have been motives for founding or refounding, as we see in Kecharitomene's *typikon*, which begins with an invocation to the Mother of God. Eirene refers to her good fortune during her earthly life, praising her pious family. Her foundation was to be a thanks-offering to God for having good, pious parents, for the educational opportunities that she had, and for the material comforts of a successful career. Throughout her life she saw signs of supernatural protection at the hand of the Mother of God.[50] The preface of her *typikon* serves as a "panegyric to its dedicatee," who was a guardian not only of Eirene but also of the city of Constantinople and its people.[51] Eirene underlines the fact that, with the help of the Theotokos and through her family and her husband, she was led to the summit of human good fortune, to the position of an empress.[52]

However, these public acts of patronage had a political dimension as well. At first sight, founding or refounding monasteries may seem a pious act practiced under the influence of Christian ideals. Yet serious and determined political goals sometimes accompanied and complicated the apparently religious promotion of monastic establishments. By founding or refounding a monastery, the patron imitated God in beneficent works, and it is particularly through this imitation that the founders demonstrated their special relationship with God and

---

[46] Galatariotou, "Uses of Religion in Byzantium," 34.
[47] Galatariotou, "Uses of Religion in Byzantium," 35.
[48] Galatariotou, "Byzantine Ktetorika Typika," 101.
[49] Gautier, "Le typikon de la Théotokos," lines 2243–2247, p. 145.
[50] Gautier, "Le typikon de la Théotokos," 19–29.
[51] Morris, *Monks and Laymen*, 126.
[52] Gautier, " Le typikon de la Théotokos," 19–29.

God's favor to them.[53] It was a good thing for an individual and, particularly, for a member of the ruling elite to have God on their side. The monasteries that were built or rebuilt were public witnesses of the women's offering to God and, consequently, of their piety and virtue. By founding a monastery, women gained a reputation for piety and holiness, which was instrumental in the enhancement of their power, prestige, and social standing. Anna Dalassene and Eirene Doukaina were much praised for their piety in the *Alexiad*.[54] It is claimed that when the latter died, myrrh (μύρον) flowed out of her coffin.[55] Eirene-Piroska-Xene became the only Byzantine female saint in the twelfth century. The relationship between the founder and God is such that it indicates power and promotes the patron's significance in society. Thus in Byzantium, "any individual in making an offering to God was making a claim for his or her status in relation to God, an indication of accession to God."[56] Such a reputation constituted a form of symbolic capital that could consolidate the patron's prestige and standing.

The size and location of the foundations constitute two significant factors that contributed to the public and political character of a monastic house. Building was a large-scale activity, and its products thereby were highly visible; the size of the monasteries, for example, was an explicit object of admiration for the Russian pilgrims.[57] Equally important was the location. Many of these female-sponsored religious establishments were built within the very heart of the Byzantine capital, the urban and political center of the empire. Most of the monasteries were situated in the northern side of the city, where the new urban settlement had been developed. No one could have missed such a magnificent and wealthy foundation as the Pantokrator, which dominated the city skyline. Even today its buildings can be seen from everywhere within the modern city of Istanbul. Similarly, Pantepoptes was situated on a conspicuous location, which justified its name Pant-epoptes (the All-Seeing). The central location of these monasteries on the hills of Constantinople meant that they occupied a "panopticon,"[58] which

---

[53] James, *Empresses and Power in Early Byzantium*, 156–59.

[54] Anna Comnena *Alexiade*, 3.8.3 (Leib 1. 126), 3.6.2 (Leib 1. 119–20), 12.6.4 (Leib 3. 72), 12.3.9 (Leib 3. 63).

[55] "μύρου σαφῶς ὑποβλυστάνοντος ἐν τῷ τάφῳ τῆς γεννητρίας μου"; see Papazoglou, *Τυπικόν Ἰσαακίου Ἀλεξίου Κομνηνοῦ τῆς μονῆς Θεοτόκου τῆς Κοσμοσώτειρας*, 130.1779. The same information is reported by the twelfth-century historian Konstantinos Manasses in a monody: Kurtz, "Die Monodien des Eustathios von Thessalonike," 306.

[56] James' remarks (*Empresses and Power*, 157) on the founders' claim for their relationship with God refer to the period the fourth century to the eighth; however, they continue to be valid for the twelfth century as well, as the evidence suggests, because Byzantine society was a God-dominated society both in early Byzantium and in the Komnenian era.

[57] Majeska, *Russian Travellers to Constantinople*.

[58] See Foucault, *Discipline and Punish*, 202.

reflected the hierarchies of the Komnenian society, as it symbolically enabled the monasteries and, consequently, their founders to have a full view of their subjects and the city. Such a location simultaneously ensured that their subjects continuously gazed upwardly to the founders, thereby reinforcing the latter's power over their people, and made a statement about the ruling class and its authority. The patrons of Constantinopolitan foundations used space to reinforce this hierarchy and to assert their power. Thanks to their size and location, those religious foundations were public monuments deliberately designed to provoke memories and to serve as the sites of commemorative rituals.[59] Instead of referring the spectator to a past historical or political event, which is usually the case with public monuments, religious buildings constitute stable public spaces that serve to remind one of the ubiquity of God, of one's duty to glorify Him, of the founders' piety and philanthropy, and, finally, of the founder's public status and prestige.

The monasteries built by imperial women ensured that the Komnenian family became part of the spiritual scenery of Constantinople, reifying these imperial women as both spiritually important and politically essential.[60] The founders made not only a statement about themselves but also a dynastic statement about their family and lineage. The provision of burial places for themselves and members of their families would remind everybody, viewers and relatives alike, of the elements of their lineage, family structure, and power. Through a strengthened and empowered family, the patron's reputation and prestige would benefit as well. In glorifying their family, Komnenian women made a political statement about themselves. These statements about power were addressed to the community, which would have been aware of the patron because the founders took steps so that their monasteries would provide specific community services to the city of Constantinople. The frequent readings of the *typikon* and especially the elaborate commemoration services carried out weekly for the founder and her family would also have contributed to making the patron known to the community.[61]

Furthermore, the act of founding can be regarded as compliant with the significant maternal role of women in Komnenian society. The woman founder can be seen as symbolizing the mother not only of the foundation but also of the nuns or monks, because she is the one who provides for them emotionally, financially, and socially. The nuclear family was at the center of the Komnenian society and also the locus of sanctity for women who unquestionably played an important part in the maintenance of family life.[62] The mother's role was openly acknowledged as significant during that period. Thus women patrons, by work-

---

[59] See Alcock, "The Recollection of Memory in the Eastern Roman Empire," 327.

[60] Morris, "The Byzantine Aristocracy and the Monasteries," 121–23.

[61] Kecharitomene's *typikon* was read on the first day of each month by the members of the monastic house; see Gautier, "Le typikon de la Théotokos," lines 1645–1655, p. 113.

[62] Kazhdan and Constable, *People and Power in Byzantium*, 33.

ing within this ideological framework and by conforming to the gender roles into which they were expected to fit, gained prestige and power.[63]

What is more, the foundation of monasteries indicates that imperial women had the financial means required to be involved in such expensive activities. Even though the question of the origin of their economic resources cannot be answered satisfactorily, we can draw interesting conclusions by studying the ways in which they chose to spend their money.[64] The monastic *typika* show patterns of property management by female founders and indicate that there was certainly property in the hands of women. Some of the imperial women who belonged to the upper echelon had their own property, while others used and acquired full ownership of their husband's property upon widowhood. Anna Dalassene must have invested a lot of money in her foundation of Pantepoptes. Similarly, Maria Doukaina's Monastery of St. Saviour in Chora required money in order to be rebuilt. Eirene Doukaina and Eirene-Piroska-Xene endowed Kecharitomene and Pantokrator respectively with a list of properties. The source of Komnenian imperial patrons' economic power was landed property, which was a corollary of their higher class. As the aristocracy was becoming more solid and dominant after the end of the eleventh century, aristocratic women were financially more active and had more important economic functions.[65]

This issue of wealth is crucial in the context of patronage. A woman with economic resources and control over them for religious reasons would have been in a stronger position than a woman who depended on someone else. Access to and control over financial sources could certainly be translated into power, because wealth could be used to generate ideological power in order to say how great and pious an individual was.[66] Insofar as control over resources was one meaning and measure of power,[67] Komnenian imperial women held it in differing degrees. Anna Dalassene, for instance, had great resources: she was the head of the Komnenoi family, she possessed power as the mother of the emperor Alexios, and she also had imperial authority invested in her by her son.[68]

In addition, founding monasteries highlights one way in which these women were able to take decisions, to act, and to pursue their will. According to Pauline Stafford's definition of power as the ability to act, to take part in events, to have a strategy and to pursue it, without necessarily succeeding, to be in a position to

---

[63] Hill, *Imperial Women*, 78–83; Hill, "Imperial Women and the Ideology of Womanhood," 93–94.

[64] However, the fact of spending money by women patrons is not necessarily evidence for their economic independence; see Cormack, "Patronage and New Programs of Byzantine Iconography"; Van Bremen, "Women and Wealth."

[65] Laiou, "The Role of Women," 241–49.

[66] James, *Empresses and Power*, 159; Hill, *Imperial Women*, 178.

[67] Weingrod, "Patronage and Power," 43.

[68] Hill, *Imperial Women*, 178.

influence others, and to use one's labors for one's own prestige, the female patron had power because she had the authority to act and to pursue her strategies; she was in a position to command others too.[69] This was a type of power that operated and manifested differently from that of men, who could lead an army to war, for instance.[70] The founder of monasteries was already in a somewhat powerful position before embarking on patronage activities, and this power offered him/her the chance to get involved in patronage. Throughout the *typikon* of Kecharitomene, Eirene Doukaina refers to herself as "my majesty," and she very often uses the verb *want* (βούλομαι) as well as emphatic phrases such as "this is what I want and I want it very much" (ὅ γάρ βούλομαι, σφόδρα βούλομαι). Phrases such as these stress the empress's high social status. Eirene was aware of her unique position, and she emphasized that in the *typikon* of her convent. She was able to command and demand that her orders be fulfilled.

At the same time, their patronage contributed to the enhancement of their visibility and social status. In the first place, the social system of patronage plays a strategic role in the maintenance and reproduction of power relations in society.[71] One of the properties of patronage is the dominance of vertical over horizontal relations of solidarity.[72] The term *patron* itself necessarily implies a notion of social subservience insofar as it presupposes an exchange between a superior and an employee rewarded or protected for his efforts, artistic or otherwise.[73] As Gellner has maintained, patronage involves inequality of power, for there is always an element of submission on the part of the client.[74] In the second place, patronage confers status and prestige on the patron, both of which values are associated with power. Patronage contributes to one's social prestige and is also governed by it.[75] The public character of the products of patronage studied above increased the prestige that female patrons gained. Patronage not only reflects power but also can be used to cultivate and consolidate power. Thus Komnenian women patrons were in a powerful position to commission monastic foundations, which, in turn, made them visible in society and enhanced their status and prestige.

The involvement of aristocratic women in religious patronage appears to be a common strategy in the Mediterranean world. The patronage activities of noble women across the Mediterranean, including North Africa, did not differ

---

[69] Stafford, "Emma," 11.
[70] James, *Empresses and Power*, 157.
[71] Weingrod, "Patronage and Power," 41–52.
[72] Johnson and Dandeker, "Patronage: Relation and System."
[73] Hanna, "Some Norfolk Women and Their Books," 289.
[74] Gellner, "Patrons and Clients," 4.
[75] See Campbell, *Honour, Family and Patronage*, 263–316.

substantially from those of Byzantine aristocratic women.[76] However, the latter are arguably exceptional by virtue of the significant financial resources they could access and spend with a view to expressing their devotion and philanthropy. In addition, the number of projects in which Komnenian women were involved and the large scale of these projects meant that they set a very high standard that women from other Mediterranean cultures strove to emulate. Some historians point out the competitive spirit in which Fatimid court women tried to match their Byzantine counterparts.[77] A study investigating the phenomenon of female religious patronage from a trans-religious perspective would throw new light onto women's history in the medieval Mediterranean.[78]

Small-Scale Patronage

In addition to large-scale commissions, Komnenian imperial women were involved in patronage of objects smaller in scale. A range of religious objects such as richly woven altar cloths, icon coverings of silk set with gold or gems, decorated crosses with fragments of the True Cross, and icons were commissioned by Komnenian women and offered as gifts to churches. The patronage of such items, most of which no longer exist, is well documented in the surviving epigrams. Insofar as these gifts were accompanied by epigrams, the donor was involved in a "double" commission. Some of the epigrams are inscribed upon commissioned items that still survive, while others, which are likely to have been written on works of art that are now lost, have reached us through Byzantine poetry collections. The epigrams were usually composed by well-known court poets such as Theodoros Prodromos, Nikolaos Kallikles, and Manuel Straboromanos, but sometimes they were written by anonymous poets, as is the case with the verses that survive in Venice, Biblioteca Marciana, Codex Gr. 524. Despite their limitations, the epigrams constitute a valuable source of information that can shed light on the patronage of Komnenian female donors and on the relationship between gift-giving and their personal expectations.

The study of the epigrams allows us to discern some recurring patterns of patronage. The basic pattern observed in monastery patronage is evident in smaller-scale patronage too. There is a tradition and a continuity in this kind of patronage for the wives of the emperors, their daughters, daughters-in-law, and other female members of the imperial family engaged in similar activities.

---

[76] Cortese and Calderini, *Women and the Fatimids in the World of Islam*; Al-Harithy, "Female Patronage of Mamluk Architecture in Cairo 1260–1517"; Ward, *Women in Medieval Europe 1200–1500*; Bennett and Karras, *The Oxford Handbook of Women and Gender*; Wood, *Studying Late Medieval History*.

[77] Cortese and Calderini, *Women and the Fatimids*, 179.

[78] Sperling and Wray, *Across the Religious Divide*.

A mother who had offered gifts to the holy provided a strong motivation for the daughter to do the same. However, the same tradition could be passed on from mother to son or from wife to husband. It was as common for imperial women as it was for imperial men to offer sumptuous items as gifts to the Church. Anthony Cutler has suggested that such offerings were cognate expressions of a culturally sanctioned norm. He maintains that the conversion of wealth into "symbolic capital," which Pierre Bourdieu identified as a phenomenon of Kabyle society, can be shown to be a habit of aristocracies wherever and whenever they existed.[79] Offering gifts to God was a truly appropriate act for the Byzantine aristocracy and something socially acceptable for women.

Moreover, it becomes evident from the epigrams that Komnenian women tended to deploy titles that identified them as wives or daughters of high-ranking court officials. For instance, on a surviving Latin cross that contained a piece of the True Cross and was commissioned by Maria Komnene to be offered to the Virgin Mary,[80] one cannot miss the relationship of the female donor to the emperor: the dedicatory inscription identifies her as the one who was born in the *porphyra*,[81] as the daughter of the emperor. The Komnenian system of titles, as set up by Alexios I Komnenos, was based on male privilege; therefore, the rank of women was a consequence of the rank of their male relations. The same form of identification can be found in those women's seals, where the titles used identified them through their family connections. Maria Komnene's identification on her seal as "the daughter of Andronikos Sevastokrator" is reproduced in an epigram accompanying a gift of hers, an *encheirion* to the Virgin Mary.[82] By identifying herself as the daughter of a Sevastokrator, she showed off her imperial family connections, by virtue of which her social status and prestige was enhanced. Female donors became visible through their titles in epigrams and seals, but this visibility was to a great extent due to their relationship to their husbands and fathers. This phenomenon, documented both in textual and visual material, suggests that family was indeed of great importance in the Komnenian era and that imperial women could become publicly visible by promoting their roles as wives, daughters, or mothers.

Also, several epigrams celebrated the same event or requested the same favor, most probably due to the belief that the more one offered, the more effectively one's request would be heard. Eirene Sevastokratorissa, the sister-in-law of the Manuel I Komnenos, donated two *encheiria*[83] to two different churches

---

[79] Cutler, "Uses of Luxury," 295.

[80] Frolow, *La relique de la vraie croix*, 283–84.

[81] *Porphyra* is the purple chamber of the imperial palace in Constantinople that was reserved for the wife of the emperor.

[82] Miller, "Poésies inédites de Théodore Prodrome," 38–40.

[83] *Encheirion* is a woven cloth embroidered with gold thread used for the covering of icons.

dedicated to the Virgin, the Theotokos of Pege and the Theotokos at ta Kyrou, asking for the same favors.[84] Eirene's daughter-in-law dedicated a *peplon*[85] to Christ as a thanks-offering on behalf of her husband, Alexios Komnenos, who was claimed to have been cured of a terrible illness by touching a veil of the icon of Christ at the church in the Chalke.[86] This gift is paralleled by a similar ex-voto offering, on behalf of the same Alexios, by his mother Eirene Sevastokratorissa to the Virgin Hodegetria.[87]

The epigrams explain why Komnenian women used their resources in order to offer gifts to churches, echoing, to a certain extent, the motivating factors of monastic foundation already discussed. The gift was inscribed within a pattern of exchange whereby either it was hoped that God would reciprocate with a future favor, or the donor intended to offer thanks for a favor already granted according to the evidence presented below.

In the first place, the donors, far from disguising the fact that they were looking forward to receiving something from God, specified in the epigrams what they were after in return for their gifts. Piety and concerns about the salvation of their soul motivated the offering of those small but expensive gifts to churches. The eternal joy that the donor could secure on the Day of Judgment was their ultimate hope. They specifically asked for forgiveness of their sins, entry into heaven, and everlasting life. In the case of an *encheirion* donated to be hung on an icon of the Virgin Hagiosoritissa during the feast of the Holy of the Holies, the supplication of the female donor is clear: Eirene Sevastokratorissa donated this *encheirion* in exchange for the salvation of her soul on the Day of Judgment.[88] In addition, donors sought to ensure, through generosity to God, not only their own salvation but also that of their beloved ones. The salvation of her late husband's soul was requested in return for an icon of St. Stephen commissioned by Anna Komnene and offered to the eponymous church.[89]

Gifts were also offered with the aim of receiving other personal and familial favors: the patrons wished themselves or their family to be cured or recover from health problems, they requested the protection of their husbands in battle, they desired to become mothers and give birth successfully, and they hoped for the well-being of their children. There are examples illustrating these motives: Eirene Doukaina offered an icon of St. Demetrios asking for the protection of her husband Alexios in battle;[90] Eirene Sevastokratorissa donated an *enchei-*

---

[84] Miller, "Poésies inédites," 36–37.

[85] *Peplon* is a woven cloth embroidered with gold thread used for the covering of icons.

[86] Marcianus Codex 524, 123–92, 35–36, no. 70.

[87] *Recueil des historiens des croisades, Historiens grecs*, 2:692.

[88] Miller, "Poésies inédites," 33–34.

[89] Prodromos, *Theodoros Prodromos: Historische Gedichte*, LI.

[90] Gautier, "Le dossier d'un haut fonctionnaire," 201.

rion to the Virgin Hodegetria asking for the healing of her ill child;[91] Theodora Komnene offered an icon to the Virgin asking for help in order to become a mother and give birth.[92] Each object is given in explicit expectation of something in return. The same seems to have been the case in the twelfth century. In her writings about early Byzantium, Marlia Mango has suggested that

> the gift offered was a "ticket" bought in advance to receive the desired favour, even if the favour was not delivered until later . . . if so, such a practice directed towards the Almighty and his Saints in a sense paralleled the widespread contemporary bribery of state officials in order to obtain favours.[93]

In the second place, many gifts were offered as thanks-offerings for a successful life, a happy marriage, or for having been healed of sickness; in other words, the donors sought to return a favor that God was believed to have already granted them. This is apparent in an epigram written on behalf of Eirene Sevastokratorissa which accompanied an *encheirion* offered to the Virgin at Pege as a thanksgiving token for a miraculous cure. Eirene thanks the Virgin, who is described as a source of favors, for being her companion and defender and for keeping misfortune at bay, as was the case when the Virgin healed her son of an eye injury. The donor also emphasized that she was very fortunate with respect to her marriage to the noble Andronikos.[94] Similarly, Eudokia Komnene offered an *encheirion* to the Virgin Hodegetria, whereby she addressed a prayer to the Virgin thanking her for the favors she enjoyed under her protection, and especially for her son's protection from a near-death experience.[95]

Interestingly, the majority of these gifts were small but sumptuous and costly, as their descriptions in the epigrams indicate. The verses accompanying *pepla* and *encheiria* often describe deluxe creations of heavy purple twill, embroidered with gold and silver thread and sprinkled with pearls. They were luxury and expensive items, beyond the reach of ordinary people, made of fine fabric, most probably silk, and intended to enhance the icon's mystery by obscuring its presence. Some female patrons even commissioned more than one gift. Wealth and class appear to have been the essential prerequisites for the patronage of such sumptuous religious objects. Many imperial women patrons involved in this type of patronage also undertook, thanks to their financial resources, projects

---

[91] *Recueil des historiens des croisades, Historiens grecs*, 2:692.

[92] Marcianus Codex 524, 177, no. 334.

[93] Mundell Mango, *Silver from Early Byzantium*, 5. On the gift economy in Byzantium, see also Hilsdale, "The Social Life of the Byzantine Gift"; Hilsdale, "Gift"; and Hilsdale, *Byzantine Art and Diplomacy in an Age of Decline*.

[94] Miller, "Poésies inédites," 36–37.

[95] *Theodoros Prodromos: Historische Gedichte*, LXXIII.

of monastic foundation. Therefore, they were active in more than one type of patronage.

By putting resources and effort into dedicating small but costly gifts to churches, imperial women patrons gained visibility and prestige. Once dedicated, the offerings were no longer in the donor's possession but became public property. Those gifts were placed in the public space of a church and were inscribed with dedication verses. The details about the donor's identity included in the epigrams, together with the luxurious items that contributed to the splendor of the church, underscored their patron's wealth and, insofar as they would remind all of the piety and patronage of their donors, enhanced the respectability and public image of the donors. Female donors must have become highly visible through their offerings to the holy.

Compared to the number of imperial women involved in the foundation and refoundation of monasteries, more women are visible as patrons of religious art objects. Although these gifts were expensive, they were certainly more affordable than founding a monastery. It is empresses who were involved in large-scale patronage, whereas it is other imperial women, not necessarily empresses, who were engaged in small-scale patronage of religious art objects. This suggests a hierarchy in patronage, which might simply reflect the financial resources of the patrons. Still, small-scale patronage could not express the same power as large-scale patronage. Small religious gifts offered to the Church were not as visible as monastery buildings. Different sorts of patronage had different effects on viewers and, in some cases, different audiences. The bigger and more expensive the medium, the more visible its patron.

In the Byzantine world, aristocratic women played an important and distinctive role as religious patrons. High social standing and economic resources made it possible for them to be involved in patronage. Religious patronage was an area that offered more opportunities and less constraint for women, who were able to manipulate the limitations of their gendered roles in order to sponsor large- and small-scale projects, thereby consolidating their standing and wielding influence. Offering gifts to God was an appropriate act for the Byzantine aristocracy and a socially acceptable gesture as far as women were concerned. Although the scale of their projects and the degree of their involvement was exceptionally high, their patronage pursuits conformed to a strategy shared with other aristocratic women across the Mediterranean who deployed their resources to negotiate power and enhance their status.

Bibliography

Alcock, Susan. "The Recollection of Memory in the Eastern Roman Empire." In *Empires: Perspectives from Archaeology and History*, ed. Susan Alcock, Terence N. D'Altroy, Kathleen D. Morrison, and Carla M. Sinopoli, 323–50. Cambridge: Cambridge University Press, 2000.

Al-Harithy, Howayda. "Female Patronage of Mamluk Architecture in Cairo." In *Beyond the Exotic: Women's Histories in Islamic Societies*, ed. Amira El Azhary Sonbol, 321–35. Syracuse, NY: Syracuse University Press, 2005.

Angold, Michael. *Church and Society in Byzantium under Comneni, 1081–1261*. Cambridge: Cambridge University Press, 1995.

Barber, Charles. "The Monastic Typikon for Art Historians." In *The Theotokos Evergetis and Eleventh-Century Monasticism*, ed. Margaret Mullett and Anthony Kirby, 198–214. Belfast Byzantine Texts and Translations 6.1. Belfast: Belfast Byzantine Enterprises, 1994.

Beaucamp, Joëlle, and Gilbert Dagron, eds. *La transmission du patrimoine: Byzance et l'aire méditerranéenne*. Paris: De Boccard, 1998.

Belting, Hans, Cyril Mango, and Doula Mouriki. *The Mosaics and Frescoes of St. Mary Pammakaristos (Fethiye Camii) at Istanbul*. Washington DC: Dumbarton Oaks, 1978.

Bennett, Judith M., and Ruth M. Karras, eds. *The Oxford Handbook of Women and Gender in Medieval Europe*. Oxford: Oxford University Press, 2013.

Bremmer, Jan. "Pauper or Patroness: The Widow in the Early Christian Church." In *Between Poverty and Pyre: Moments in the History of Widowhood*, ed. Jan Bremmer and Lourens van den Bosch, 31–57. London and New York: Routledge, 1995.

Byzantine Monastic Foundation Documents. Edited by John P. Thomas and Angela Constantinides Hero. Vol. 1, *Dumbarton Oaks Studies* 35. Washington, DC: Dumbarton Oaks Research Library and Collection, 2000.

Campbell, John K. *Honour, Family and Patronage*. Oxford: Clarendon, 1964.

Choniates, Niketas, Χρονικὴ Διήγησις. *Nicetae Choniatae historia*. Edited by Jan Louis van Dieten. *Corpus fontium historiae byzantinae*. Berlin and New York: de Gruyter, 1975; English translation by Harry J. Magoulias as *O City of Byzantium: Annals of Niketas Choniates*. Detroit: Wayne State University Press, 1984.

Comnena, Anna, *Alexiade: Règne D L'empereur Alexis I Comnène, 1081–1118*. Edited and translated by Bernard Leib. 3 vols. Paris: Budé, 1937–1945, repr. 1967; English translation by E. R. A. Sewter, *The Alexiad of Anna Comnena*. Harmondsworth: Penguin, 1979. References are by book and chapter, and by volume and page.

Congdon, Eleanor. "Imperial Commemoration and Ritual in the Typikon of the Monastery of Christ Pantokrator." *Revue des études byzantines* 54 (1996): 161–99.

Constantelos, Demetrios. *Byzantine Philanthropy and Social Welfare.* New Brunswick: Rutgers University Press, 1968.

Cormack, Robin. "Interpreting the Mosaics of S. Sophia at Istanbul."*Art History* 4, no. 2 (1981): 131–46.

———. *Writing in Gold: Byzantine Society and Its Icons.* London: George Philip, 1985.

———. "Patronage and New Programs of Byzantine Iconography." *Seventeenth International Byzantine Studies Conference: Major Papers (Washington, DC, August, 1986),* 609–38. New Rochelle: Caratzas, 1987.

Cortese, Delia, and Simonetta Calderini. *Women and the Fatimids in the World of Islam.* Edinburgh: Edinburgh University Press, 2006.

Cutler, Anthony. "Uses of Luxury: On the Function of Consumption and Symbolic Capital in Byzantine Culture." In *Byzance et les images: cycle de conférences organisé au musée du Louvre par le service culturel du 5 octobre au 7 décembre 1992,* ed. André Guillou and Jannic Durand, 287–327. Paris: La Documentation française, 1994.

Darrouzès, J. "Le mouvement des fondations monastiques au XIe siècle." *Travaux et Mémoires* 6 (1976): 159–76.

Dimitropoulou, Vassiliki. "Imperial Women Founders and Refounders in Komnenian Constantinople." In *Founders and Refounders of Byzantine Monasteries,* ed. Margaret Mullett. Belfast Byzantine Texts and Translations 6.3, 87–106. Belfast: Belfast Byzantine Enterprises, Institute of Byzantine Studies, Queen's University of Belfast, 2007.

———. "Giving Gifts to God: Aspects of Patronage in Byzantine Art." In *A Companion to Byzantium,* ed. Liz James, 161–70. Malden, MA: Wiley-Blackwell, 2010.

Ebersolt, Jean, and Adolphe Thiers. *Les églises de Constantinople.* Paris: Leroux, 1913.

El Azhary Sonbol, Amira, ed. *Beyond the Exotic: Women's Histories in Islamic Societies.* Syracuse, NY: Syracuse University Press, 2005.

Foucault, Michel. *Discipline and Punish: The Birth of the Prison.* London: Penguin, 1977.

Frolow, A. *La relique de la vraie croix: recherches sur le développement d'un culte.* Paris: Institut français d'études byzantines, 1961.

Galatariotou, Catia. "Byzantine Ktetorika Typika: A Comparative Study." *Revue des études byzantines* 45 (1987): 77–138.

———. "Byzantine Women's Monastic Communities: The Evidence of the Typika." *Jahrbuch der* österreichischen *Byzantinistik* 38 (1988): 263–90.

———. "Uses of Religion in Byzantium."*Sophia* 1 (1991): 31–43.

Gautier, Paul. "Le dossier d'un haut fonctionnaire d'Alexis Ier Comnène, Manuel Straboromanos." *Revue des* études *byzantines* 23 (1965): 168–204.

———. "Le typikon du Christ Sauveur Pantocrator." *Revue des* études *byzantines* 32 (1974): 1–145.

——. "Le typikon de la Théotokos Kécharitoméné." *Revue des études byzantines* 43 (1985): 5–165.

Gellner, Ernest. "Patrons and Clients." In *Patrons and Clients in Mediterranean Societies*, ed. Ernest Gellner and John Waterbury, 1–6. London: Duckworth, 1977.

Gregoras, Nikephoros. *Byzantina Historia*. Edited by Ludwig Schopen. 3 vols. Corpus scriptorium historiae byzantinae. Bonn: Weber, 1829.

Grubbs, Judith E. "Virgins and Widows, Show-Girls and Whores: Late Roman Legislation on Women and Christianity." In *Law, Society and Authority in Late Antiquity*, ed. Ralph W. Mathieson, 220–41. Oxford and New York: Oxford University Press, 2001.

——. *Women and the Law in the Roman Empire: A Sourcebook on Marriage, Divorce and Widowhood*. London and New York: Routledge, 2002.

Hanna, Ralph. "Some Norfolk Women and Their Books, ca. 1390–1440." In *The Cultural Patronage of Medieval Women*, ed. June H. McCash, 288–305. Athens: University of Georgia Press, 1996.

Hill, Barbara. "Imperial Women and the Ideology of Womanhood in the Eleventh and Twelfth Centuries." In *Women, Men and Eunuchs: Gender in Byzantium*, ed. Liz James, 76–99. London: Routledge, 1997.

——. *Imperial Women in Byzantium 1025–1204: Power, Patronage and Ideology*. London: Longman, 1999.

Hilsdale, Cecily. "The Social Life of the Byzantine Gift: The Royal Crown of Hungary Re-Invented." *Art History* 31, no. 5 (November 2008): 602–31.

——. "Gift." *Studies in Iconography* 33 (2012): 171–82.

——. *Byzantine Art and Diplomacy in an Age of Decline*. Cambridge: Cambridge University Press, 2014.

James, Liz, and Barbara Hill. "Women and Politics in the Byzantine Empire: Imperial Women." In *Women in Medieval Western European Culture*, ed. Linda E. Mitchell, 157–78. New York: Garland, 1999.

James, Liz. *Empresses and Power in Early Byzantium*. London: Leicester University Press, 2001.

Janin, R. "Les monastères du Christ Philanthrope à Constantinople." *Revue des études byzantines* 4 (1946): 135–50.

——. *La géographie ecclésiastique de l'empire byzantin*, vol. 3: *Les églises et les monastères*. Paris: Institut français d'études byzantines, 1969.

Johnson, Terry, and Chris Dandeker. "Patronage: Relation and System. "In *Patronage in Ancient Society*, ed. Andrew Wallace-Hadrill, 219–42. London: Routledge, 1989.

Kampouroglou, D. Μνημεῖα τῆς Ἱστορίας τῶν Ἀθηναίων. Athens, 1889–1892.

Kazhdan, Alexander. "Widows Lost and Regained." *Byzantion* 43 (1973): 509.

——, and G. Constable. *People and Power in Byzantium: An Introduction to Modern Byzantine Studies*. Washington DC: Dumbarton Oaks, 1982.

Kinnamos, Ioannis. *Epitomi ton katorthomaton. Ioannis Cinnami Epitome Rerum ab Ioanne et Manuele Comnenis Gestarum.* Edited by A. Meineke. Corpus scriptorium historiae byzantinae. Bonn: Weber, 1836; English translation by Charles M. Brand as *Deeds of John and Manuel Comnenus.* New York: Columbia University Press, 1976.

Kurtz, E. "Die Monodien des Eustathios von Thessalonike und des Konstantino Manasses auf den Toddes Nikephoros Komnenos." *Vizantiiskii vremennik* 17 (1910): 306.

Laiou, Angeliki E. *Gender, Society and Economic Life in Byzantium.* Aldershot: Variorum, 1992.

———. "Addendum to the Report on the Role of Women in Byzantine Society." *Jahrbuch der Österreichischen Byzantinistik* 32, no. 2 (1982): 98–103.

———. "Observations on the Life and Ideology of Byzantine Women." *Byzantinische Forschungen* 9 (1985): 59–102.

———. "The Evolution of the Status of Women in Marriage and Family Law." In Kongress der Gesellschaft für das Recht der Ostkirchen, *Mutter, Nonne, Diakonin: Frauenbilder im Recht der Ostkirchen,* 71–85. Egling an der Paar: Kovar, 2000.

———. "The Role of Women in Byzantine Society." *Jahrbuch der Österreichischen Byzantinistik* 31, no. 1 (1981): 233–60.

———. "Women in Byzantine Society." In *Women in Medieval Western European Culture,* ed. L. E. Mitchell, 81–94. New York: Garland, 1999.

Magdalino, Paul. "The Byzantine Holy Man in the Twelfth Century." In *The Byzantine Saint,* ed. Sergei Hackel, 51–66. London: Fellowship of St. Alban and St. Sergius, 1981.

———. *The Empire of Manuel Komnenos, 1143–1180.* Cambridge: Cambridge University Press, 1993.

Maguire, Henry. *Image and Imagination: The Byzantine Epigram as Evidence for Viewer Response.* Toronto: Canadian Institute of Balkan Studies, 1996.

Majeska, George. *Russian Travellers to Constantinople in the Fourteenth and Fifteenth Centuries.* Washington DC: Dumbarton Oaks, 1984.

Mango, Cyril, and Hawkins, Ernest. "Report on Field Work in Istanbul and Cyprus, 1962–1963." *Dumbarton Oaks Papers* 18 (1964): 319–33.

———. "Where at Constantinople was the Monastery of Christos Pantepoptes?" Δελτίον της Χριστιανικής Αρχαιολογικής Εταιρείας (1998): 87–88.

Marcianus Codex 524, "Ὁ Μαρκιανός Κῶδιξ 524." Edited by Sp. P. Lampros. Νέος Ἑλληνομνήμων 8 (1911): 1–59, 123–92.

Mathews, Thomas. *The Byzantine Churches of Istanbul: A Photographic Survey.* University Park: Pennsylvania State University Press, 1976.

McCash, June Hall, ed. *The Cultural Patronage of Medieval Women.* Athens: University of Georgia Press, 1996.

McGinn, Thomas A. "Widows, Orphans, and Social History." *Journal of Roman Archaeology* 12 (1999): 617–32.

McNamara, Jo Ann. "Wives and Widows in Early Christian Thought." *International Journal of Women's Studies* 2 (1978): 575–92.

Megaw, A. H. S. "Notes on the Recent Work of the Byzantine Institute in Istanbul." *Dumbarton Oaks Papers* 17 (1963): 335–64.

Migne, J.-P., ed. *Patrologiae cursus completes, Series graeca.* 161 vols. Paris, 1857–1866.

Miklosich, Franciscus, and Joseph Müller. *Acta et diplomata graeca medii aevi sacra et profana.* 6 vols. Vienna, 1860–1890.

Miller, E. "Poésies inedites de Théodore Prodrome." *Annuaire de l'Association pour l'encouragement des etudes greques en France* 17 (1883): 18–64.

Morris, Rosemary. *Monks and Laymen in Byzantium, 843–1118.* Cambridge: Cambridge University Press, 1995.

——. "The Byzantine Aristocracy and the Monasteries. " In *The Byzantine Aristocracy IX to XIII Centuries,* ed. Michael Angold, 112–29. Oxford: British Archaeological Reports, 1984.

Mullett, Margaret. "The Missing Jezebel: Saints' Lives and Imperial Women in Twelfth-Century Byzantium." In *The Modern Traveller to Our Past: Festschrift in Honour of Ann Hamlin,* ed. Marion Meek, 192–201. Belfast: DPK, 2006.

Mundell Mango, Marlia. *Silver from Early Byzantium: The Kaper Koraon and Related Treasures.* Baltimore: Trustees of the Walters Art Gallery, 1986.

Nunn, Valerie. "The Encheirion as Adjunct to the Icon in the Middle Byzantine Period." *Byzantine and Modern Greek Studies* 10 (1986): 73–102.

Oates, David. "A Summary Report on the Excavations of the Byzantine Institute in the Kariye Camii: 1957 and 1958." *Dumbarton Oaks Papers* 14 (1960): 223–31.

Oikonomides, Nicolas. "The Mosaic Panel of Constantine IX and Zoe in St. Sophia." *Revue des* études *byzantines* 36 (1978): 219–32.

Ousterhout, Robert. *The Architecture of the Kariye Camii in Istanbul.* Washington, DC: Dumbarton Oaks Research Library and Collection, 1987.

——. "Architecture, Art and Komnenian Ideology at the Pantokrator Monastery." In *Byzantine Constantinople: Monuments, Topography and Everyday Life,* ed. Nevra Necipoglu, 133–50. Leiden: Brill, 2001.

Papazoglou, George. Κ. *Τυπικόν Ισαακίου Αλεξίου Κομνηνού της μονής Θεοτόκου της Κοσμοσώτειρας.* Komotini: Ziti, 1994.

Prodromos, Theodoros, *Theodoros Prodromos: Historische Gedichte.* Edited by Wolfram Hörandner in *Wiener Byzantinische Studien* 11. Vienna: Akademie der Wissenschaften, 1974.

Recueil des historiens des croisades, Historiens grecs. 2 vols. Paris: Imprimerie royale, 1875–1881.

Runciman, Steven. "The Widow Danelis." In *Études dédiées à la mémoire d'André M. Andréadès,* ed. K. Varvaressos, 425–31. Athens: Pyrsos, 1940.

Sathas, K. N., ed. *Μεσαιωνική Βιβλιοθήκη.* 7 vols. Venice and Paris, 1872–94.

Schaus, Margaret. *Women and Gender in Medieval Europe: An Encyclopedia*. London: Routledge, 2006.

Sperling, Jutta G., and Shona K. Wray, eds. *Across the Religious Divide: Women, Property and Law in the Wider Mediterranean (ca. 1300–1800)*. New York and London: Routledge, 2010.

Stafford, Pauline. "Emma: The Powers of the Queen in the Eleventh Century. "In *Queens and Queenship in Medieval Europe*, ed. Anne Duggan, 3–26. Woodbridge: Boydell, 1997.

Synaxarium ecclesiae Constantinopolitanae. Propylaeum ad Acta sanctorum Novembris. Edited by H. Delehaye. Brussels: Sociéte des Bollandistes, 1902

Talbot, Alice-Mary. "A Comparison of the Monastic Experiences of Byzantine Men and Women." *Greek Orthodox Theological Reveiw* 30, no. 1 (1985): 10–20.

———. "Epigrams in Context: Metrical Inscriptions on Art and Architecture of the Palaiologan Era."*Dumbarton Oaks Papers* 53 (1999): 75–90.

Theis, Lioba, Margaret Mullett, and Michael Grünbart, eds. *Female Founders in Byzantium and Beyond: An International Colloquium. September 23–25, 2008*. Vienna: Institüt Kunstgeschichte, 2008.

Thomas, John P. *Private Religious Foundations in the Byzantine Empire*. Washington, DC: Dumbarton Oaks, 1987.

Thurston, Bonnie B. *The Widows: A Women's Ministry in the Early Church*. Minneapolis, MN: Fortress, 1989.

Underwood, Paul. "Notes on the Work of the Byzantine Institute in Istanbul: 1954." *Dumbarton Oaks Papers* 9–10 (1956): 291–300.

———. "Notes on the Work of the Byzantine Institute in Istanbul: 1957–59." *Dumbarton Oaks Papers* 14 (1960): 205–23.

———. *The Kariye Djami*. 3 vols. New York: Pantheon, 1966.

Van Bremen, Riet. "Women and Wealth." In *Images of Women in Antiquity*, ed. Averil Cameron and Amélie Kuhrt, 223–41. Detroit: Wayne State University Press, 1983.

Van Millingen, Alexander. *Byzantine Churches in Constantinople*. London: Macmillan, 1912.

Verdon, Michel. "Virgins and Widows: European Kinship and Early Christianity." *Man* 23 (1988): 488–50.

Ward, Jennifer. *English Noblewomen in the Later Middle Ages*. London: Longman, 1992.

———. *Women in Medieval Europe 1200–1500*. New York: Routledge, 2016.

Weingrod, A. "Patronage and Power." In *Patrons and Clients in Mediterranean Societies*, ed. Ernest Gellner and John Waterbury, 41–52. London: Duckworth, 1977.

Whittemore, Thomas. *The Mosaics of Haghia Sophia at Istanbul: Third Preliminary Report. The Imperial Portraits of the South Gallery*. Boston: John Johnson at the Oxford University Press for the Byzantine Institute, 1942.

————. "A Portrait of the Empress Zoe and of Constantine IX." *Byzantion* 18 (1946/1948): 223–27.

Wood, Cindy. *Studying Late Medieval History: A Thematic Approach.* New York: Routledge, 2016.

Zonaras, Ioannis. *Epitomae Historiarum.* Edited by M. Pinder and Th. Büttner-Wobst. 3 vols. Corpus scriptorium historiae byzantinae. Bonn: Weber, 1897.

Chapter 9

JEWISH WOMEN AND PERFORMANCE IN EARLY MODERN MANTUA

ERITH JAFFE-BERG,
UNIVERSITY OF CALIFORNIA, RIVERSIDE

Scholars working in the archives are always aware of the paradox that the more one looks for answers, the more one becomes aware of the omissions, *lacunae*, and silence of the archives. Claire Sponsler writes persuasively about the need for informed speculation in the archives: "[t]he history of performance scholarship is in some ways a history of the trying-on of various narratives that aim to make sense of evidence from the archive."[1] Carol Symes poignantly considers the leads that she is likely missing in the archives: "how many times have I been caught out while browsing in the archives, unable to pick up signals that once were plain to everyone? How many times have I been left staring in bewilderment, my eyes fixed on the page, while something of significance passed by?"[2] I aim to write this essay with the same humility expressed by these two important scholars, a humility borne of the fact that I am very much aware of my own limitations at approaching an incomplete archive. The archive in question is that left to us by the Jewish community of Mantua. It is an important and rich collection of traces of a long-lived community's life, not least of all because the Jewish community was so active in developing the performing arts for which early modern Mantua is famous. Under Gonzaga rule, beginning in the early sixteenth century and continuing well into the seventeenth, the small city of Mantua played host to a number of noted artists ranging from musicians to visual artist and actors. At the same time, Mantua generated art forms that reflected its own character and the tastes and proclivities of its most famous patrons, the Gonzaga. A combination of factors led the Jewish community to settle in this southern part of Lombardia, seeking safe haven in Mantua many centuries before the Spanish edict of expulsion in the late fifteenth century.

---

[1] Sponsler, "Writing the Unwritten," 98. An earlier version of this essay appeared as "Writing the Unwritten: Morris Dance and the Study of Medieval Theatre," *Theatre Survey* 38, no. 1 (May 1997): 73–95.

[2] Symes, "Out in the Open, in Arras."

By the late fifteenth century, perhaps in imitation of the professional artists around it, the Jewish community was producing musicians, dance masters,
playwrights, and performers for the active theater scene in Mantua.[3] In another
publication, I detail the ways in which the performances evolved from an act of
tribute to the Gonzaga in the early sixteenth century to a compulsory "tax" that
was expensive and punitive in the early seventeenth century.[4] I also allude to the
fact that the performances in Mantua ended in the middle of the seventeenth
century, after they had been forcibly stopped during the 1628–1630 War of Mantuan Succession, in which the sack of Mantua and the expulsion of its Jews for
the first time since they had resided there sent convulsive shock waves through
both Jewish and Christian residents of the city. While the performances resumed
and continued sporadically after the return of the Jews to the city in 1630, they
were never quite the same, and their annual regularity ended in 1649, apparently
by consensus of both the Gonzaga and the Jews.

What I have not yet detailed are the wisps of an idea still embryonic and
fragile that nevertheless is very telling in terms of the Jewish community of
Mantua and the functioning of minority artistic communities in the Italian peninsula at the time. It is to that archival whisper which I now turn. What appears
dim in passing belies a historical fact that is far more prominent than its barely
existent archival trace lets on. Here I am guided by Sponsler and Symes' attentiveness to the silences in the archives and to the importance of persisting to
ponder on the faint echoes of traces left to me, as they attune my archival ear to
important facts that call into question our thinking about the Jewish community
and its relationship to theater at the time. The archival trace in the Jewish community archives of Mantua and in the State Archives of the Gonzaga in Mantua
suggests that women, who are never mentioned in relation to the performances
of the Jewish community of Mantua, played a role in theater when it has been
assumed they did not. This evidence, which I will explore in greater detail in
this essay, is relevant to our understanding of the theater produced by the Jewish community and to the ways in which the Jewish and Christian communities
used theater as a means of exchange and a basis for interaction in a period in
which restrictions on contact between the communities were becoming more and
more palpable. If Jewish women participated in the theatrical performances — as
audience members and also as collaborators in the creative process — then their
involvement paralleled in part the ways in which women were becoming increasingly central in Mantua and other northern Italian cities as producers, performers, and consumers of theater. Therefore, theater must be considered as one more
cultural form in which the Jewish community was influenced by the mainstream

---

[3] For more on the vast amount of theatrical activities happening in Italy see Henke,
Performance and Literature in the Commedia dell'arte.

[4] See Jaffe-Berg, "Performance as Exchange."

Christian cultural context, and the Jewish community was one more venue in which women taking an active role.[5]

Much of what we know about the Jewish theatrical output in Mantua comes to us from studies of its most important exponent: Leone de' Sommi, also known as Leone Ebreo (Leone the Jew). De' Sommi was prolific, leaving an immense footprint as community leader, playwright, and producer or director of numerous musical productions and plays. A century before the full flowering of the Baroque, he was very much the image Gianlorenzo Bernini would conjure in *The Impresario* (1642). Among his important ventures and publications is a document so ahead of its time that it serves as a touchstone for scholars of "directing" even though the concept of a director was many centuries in the making. *Four Dialogues on the Art of Plays* (*Quattro dialoghi in materia di rappresentazioni sceniche*) (ca. 1565) presents de Sommi's ideas about how to stage, costume, and cast a play.[6] It also includes ideas about the progress of rehearsals and incorporating *intermedi* or musical interludes within the productions. In short, it is a rich source of information about how plays were staged in his day and how theater practitioners thought about the dilemmas of putting on a production. Because of its prominence, this document has been translated several times over the last century and has been reprinted in part or whole by English, American, and Italian scholars. Among the many issues de' Sommi discusses is the place of women in terms of staging plays, the possibility of women as actors, and the limitations and permissions that should be granted to female actors on the stage.

The focus on women's role in the theater is a recurrent question the *dialoghi* returns to, probably because sixteenth-century Italy witnessed a revolution in theater production signaled by the inclusion of female actresses for the first time in theater history.[7] The *commedia dell' arte* (the profession of improvised theater), the most popular theater of the late sixteenth century to the early seventeenth, changed the course of theater history forever with its introduction of female actresses in 1565. Women were now able to act on stage, collaborate in

---

[5] The mutual influences between the communities have been studied by Bonfil, *Jewish Life in Renaissance Italy*; and Amnon Raz-Krakotzkin, *The Censor, the Editor, and the Text*. Recently, scholarship by Stefano Patuzzi has focused on the ways in which Jewish culture has left a lasting influence on Mantuan cultural life. See, for example, Patuzzi, *Una Tavola Apparecchiata*.

[6] De'Sommi, *Quattro dialoghi in materia di rappresentazioni sceniche*; De'Sommi, *Four Dialogues on Stage Affairs* (English trans. Nicoll, "The Dialogues of Leone di Somi"). Nicoll notes that parts of the *Dialogues* were published by Luigi Rasi in *I Comici italiani* (1905) and in Alessandro D'Ancona's magisterial *Origini del teatro italiano* (1891). In English, portions were translated by Winifred Smith in *The Commedia dell' Arte* (1912) and Kathleen M. Lea in *Italian Popular Comedy* (1934).

[7] For work about women in the *commedia dell' arte*, see Kerr, *The Rise of the Diva*. Also see Scott, "La Virtu et la volupté." Foundational work on the actresses was done by MacNeil in *Music and Women of the Commedia dell' Arte*.

the creation of plays, and even lead as heads of troupes or *capocomici*. At a time when professional options for women were limited, the new opportunity offered considerable economic benefits and even the hope of a degree of upward mobility.[8] De' Sommi himself was vocal about the non-participation of women while at the same time admitting that it was a female actress who came closest to achieving an ideal performance. For de' Sommi, that was the Roman *commedia dell' arte* actress known as Flaminia, who performed in Mantua in 1567.[9] He wrote about her in the *Dialogues*:

> I have always thought and still think that the acting of a young Roman girl called Flaminia is the most extraordinary. Besides being gifted with many beauteous qualities, she is judged so unique in her profession that I do not believe the ancients ever saw or the moderns are likely to see a more brilliant actress. When she is on the stage the audience gets the impression not of a play composed and finished by an author, but rather of a series of real events taking shape before them. She so varies her gestures, tones, and moods in accordance with the diverse nature of her scenes that every one who sees her is moved to wonder and delighted admiration.[10]

What strikes de' Sommi most, along with her beauty and grace, is Flaminia's capacity to realistically portray a character and embody her writer's words naturally. He notes her capacity to transport her audience, making them believe and be moved. Given this exhilaration about Flaminia, it is surprising to find in the same text that de' Sommi is less than enthusiastic about the participation of women in theater, especially if they are "virgins," which we can take to mean unmarried young women.

> The ancients, therefore, did well in accepting the law that a virgin should not be permitted to appear in comedies lest by such an example citizens' daughters, who ought to be bashful and retiring, might be induced to gad abroad and engage in public gossip. On the other hand, a prince's daughter might be allowed to appear in public, for the reason that few would be so bold as to dare attack the honour of such a woman—where there is no hope love clearly can take no root. Love is universally recognized as arising from a certain equality between lover and object—equality in blood

---

[8] Many important works have been dedicated to the contribution of women as professional actors in the *commedia dell' arte*. As examples, see Barasch, "Italian Actresses in Shakespeare's World: Vittoria and Isabella"; Barasch, "Italian Actresses in Shakespeare's World: Flaminia and Vicenza"; Detenbeck, "Women and the Management of Dramaturgy in La Calandria"; MacNeil, *Music and Women of the Commedia dell' Arte*; Henke, *Performance and Literature in the Commedia dell' Arte*; Katritzky, "Reading the Actress in Commedia Imagery"; and McGill, "Women and Performance."

[9] De' Sommi, *Dialogues*, trans. Nicoll, 252.

[10] De' Sommi, *Dialogues*, trans. Nicoll, 268.

or constellation or position; speaking generally, where there is inequality there can be no love. Daughters of princes, therefore, may go out and speak to others in the streets, both because their position makes them freer and, more particularly, because it is presumed that no one will violate their honour, there being few persons (and those far distant) of an equality with them. Such procedure is not allowed to citizens' daughters because in the city there are thousands of their own class; going out of doors, therefore, brings to them much danger of evil happening. She who values her honour must avoid the chance of scandal, even if that be purely baseless. Comedy, therefore, which is designed to present good examples, ought not to permit anyone to say a word or to indulge in an action contrary to that person's position and quality.[11]

The daughter of a prince, de' Sommi argues, is so far above the average citizen that even if she speaks in public, there is no doubt that she is far above and beyond contact of an average male citizen. Being "off limits," so to speak, the princess is safe in a way that an average female is not. A citizen's daughter, differently from a prince's daughter, is vulnerable because she is tangible, and therefore she must be protected even more than a prince's daughter ought to be. That citizen's daughter cannot perform publicly or speak within the public domain because male citizens watching may be lured by her performance and the suggestiveness of her words and may fall in love or lust with her, making it possible for her to fall prey to them. Acting is prohibited because it is a form of public speech and because public speech is dangerous for a woman to undertake. De' Sommi's argumentation is different from the usual anti-female polemic characteristic of the time and studied by feminist scholars over the last two decades.[12] His objection to women actors is rooted more in his mistrust of men than in his mistrust of women. In fact, within the *querelle des femmes* (the debate about women) he is a defender of women, as evidenced at least by the fact that he authored a bilingual poetic defense of women in Hebrew and Italian named "Magen Nashim, in difesa delle donne" [Protector of Women, A Defense of Women].[13]

Notwithstanding de' Sommi's defense of women, for reasons that he explains in his *Dialogues*, as we see, he does not advocate for female actresses in comedies. Therefore, based on de' Sommi's influence within his community and on the fact that there is no evidence to the contrary, it could be assumed that no Jewish women participated in theater. Considering that de' Sommi was a leader within the Jewish community (known as a *massaro*) and repeatedly advocated on its behalf to Dukes Guglielmo and later Vincenzo, his opinions were

---

[11] De' Sommi, *Dialogues*, trans. Nicoll, 258.

[12] See the work of Joan Kelly and Margaret King. See also Günsberg, *Gender and the Italian Stage.*

[13] See my publication and explication of this poem in Italian: Jaffe-Berg, "Leone De' Sommi, 'Magen Nashim, In difesa delle donne." In English, see my "'Magen Nashim,'"

respected and, one assumes, accepted. In addition, Jewish female performers are rarely publicly known to us. The one big exception is Mme. Europa, a singer and sister of the famous composer Salamone de' Rossi, who was active in Mantua at the same time as the *commedia dell' arte* was in its golden age.[14] Another smaller exception is an archival trace of a singer known as Rachel, who apparently disobeyed the Venetian laws and sang for money in Venice. "Rachel hebrea cantarina," along with her father and brother, was given permission to leave the Venetian ghetto at night in order to visit the homes of Christians. "Subsequently, secret reports from allegedly reliable persons had revealed that, under pretext of going to sing in homes of 'nobles, citizens, and other honorable persons,' they were staying in homes of common persons, eating, drinking, and behaving dishonestly with Christians."[15] We do not know if the accusations were founded, but either possibility—that she performed for the nobility or that she performed for plebeians—reveals the Jewish singer's attractiveness to the broader Christian community. This beckons Ravid's questions: "Why were the services of Jewish entertainers so sought after in Venice at the time? Did Christian Venice not have enough singers and musicians of its own? Did the Jews have different musical traditions or styles of performance that the Christians might have found attractive? Were the Jews held to be better singers or instrumentalists?"[16] Perhaps it was just a curiosity or a novelty to have Jews sing and dance and perform as entertainers? Other than these women, the record is silent. No female Jewish actresses, no female Jewish playwrights, no female audience members, no female interaction with the lively theater world of Mantua.

Except that, in recent visits to two important archives in Mantua—the State Archives (Archivio di Stato di Mantova, ASM), which hold the Gonzaga Archives (Archivio Gonzaga, AG), and the Jewish community archives (Archivi della communita ebraica a Mantova, ADCEM)—the evidence suggest a more complicated reality. Several notes found in the Jewish community archives indicate that women were active participants in the comedies that were staged by the Jews within the ghetto. The Jews of Mantua were forced to live in a ghetto in 1612, a relatively late date considering that the Venetian ghetto had been established a century earlier. A note from the ducal secretary Annibale Chieppo from 7 January 1641 forbade Jews from gambling (*giochi*) in the ghetto. The same document also prohibited Jewish women from going to comedies at night ("Come anche d'andar donne hebree di note a comedia").[17]

---

[14] Harrán, *Salamone Rossi*; Harrán, "Madama Europa."

[15] Ravid, "Curfew Time in the Ghetto of Venice," 247.

[16] Ravid, "Curfew Time in the Ghetto of Venice," 214.

[17] ADCEM filza 26 doc. 33. The document is found on the digital archive of the Jewish community of Mantua ("communita ebraica Mantova" under the "sezione Antica"). I was fortunate to have the privilege of visiting the Jewish community of Mantua's archives, currently under the supervision of Dottore Emanuele Colorni. Dottore

Another piece of evidence in the Jewish archives details a similar prohibition only briefly mentioned by historian Shlomo Simonsohn and never studied by theater scholars.[18] The prohibition was issued during Carnival of 1649, which just happened to be the year of the last annual performance by the Università. It prohibited Jews from playing games or gambling ("divieto gli ebrei di dedicarsi al gioco"), and it specifically prohibited Jewish women from helping with comedies at night: "Jewish women are forbidden from attending comedies at night" ("Divieto [. . .] alle donne ebree di assitere alle commedie di notte").[19] We have countless receipts for costumes and props bought and borrowed to be used in performances by the Jews of Mantua. Among these, we have a receipt for payment to a seamstress for her work on a performance.[20] This is the first time, other than the well-documented participation of Salamone de Rossi's sister, Madama Europa, that we hear of women's explicit connection to the plays performed by the Jews of Mantua. This "whisper" from the archive is clamorous in what it suggests: Jewish women took an active part in making the comedies for Carnival. Natasha Korda has reframed the ways in which we consider theatrical production and made visible the presence of female contributors to theatre making through costume and prop making for Shakespeare's stage. These arguments are equally compelling for Jewish theatre in Mantua.[21]

Furthermore, we have evidence of another restriction that comes from a later date, 1651, and is found in a more formal document called a *pragmatica*. Jewish and Christian communities were regulated by ecclesiastical and secular authorities alike, especially in matters related to dress, gambling, games, and performances; the regulations were published as ordinances and called *pompe* or *pragmatica*.[22] The Jewish community exercised its own form of self-governance in the Middle Ages, and similar forms of governance continued in the early modern period. Jewish communities in Forlì in 1418 issued a prohibition on gambling, and a series of *pragmatiche* were issued in Mantua in 1599, 1619, 1635, and 1651.[23] The *pragmatiche* would be drafted in Hebrew within the Jewish community, the draft would be translated into Italian and shown and approved

---

Colorni was kind enough to show me the original copy of this document and allow me to view the entire archive, which is a wealth of information. It was under the supervision of Prof. Vittore Colorni, Emanuele Colorni's father, that Shlomo Simonsohn pursued his research at the archive several decades ago.

[18] Much research on Mantua is indebted to the meticulous work of Shlomo Simonsohn in his *History of the Jews in the Duchy of Mantua*; see 536. However, in his interpretation, he writes of women attending, rather than assisting at the events.

[19] ADCEM Filza (file) 29 Cartella (document) 37.

[20] Simonsohn, 665, f.n. 311.

[21] Korda, "Women's Theatrical Properties," 22.

[22] Simonsohn, *History of the Jews*, 530.

[23] Simonsohn, *History of the Jews*, 530–36.

by the duke, and it would be published in Hebrew.²⁴ According to the *pragmatica* of 1651 and 1652, women are "forbidden to attend theatrical performances."²⁵ The recurrent mention of this prohibition suggests, of course, that even though it was not permitted, women did, in fact, attend the theater, and for that reason needed to be reminded that it was forbidden to do so. The recurrence of ordinances and *pragmatiche* forbidding women from participating in or attending comedies reveals that by the seventeenth century, and increasingly by the middle of that century, women were active participants—audience members and perhaps collaborators—in the producing of plays. While these productions were internal to the Jewish community and took place within the ghetto, the active role of women should not be separated from the restrictions on theatrical performances that were soon to follow.

Writing about this period, Simonsohn reflects a prevailing attitude about the environment occasioned by the Counter Reformation and ghettoization. From his point of view, ghettoization was synonymous with an oppressive restrictiveness.

> From the mid-seventeenth century, the publication of bans against gambling, and various kinds of *pragmatiche* became more and more frequent. They forbade the wearing of masks during the carnival and the Feast of Purim, as well as the use of fireworks and rattles. These last prohibitions testify to a fundamental change in Jewish customs as they had existed in previous years [. . .] The influence of the ghetto spirit can be felt here, as it conquered and repressed the simple joys of life.²⁶

Simonsohn views the ghettos as repressing festivities and altering the "centuries old" habits of Jews in Mantua. His viewpoint is common in historians writing after the Second World War, when the horrors of Nazi ghettoization and extermination camps were too present in the minds of those writing about early modern ghettos. David Nirenberg has written about this historiographical tendency, and contemporary historians such as David Bonfil and Amnon Raz-Krakotzkin are seeking to nuance the way in which we look at the Counter Reformation period and even ghettoization.²⁷ In the theatrical context as well, Simonsohn's reading of the middle of the seventeenth century as a repressive one for Jewish

---

²⁴ Simonsohn, *History of the Jews*, 531.

²⁵ Filza 30 document 34 for the 24 Dec 1651 *pragmatica*. Filza 30 Cartella 54 for the 29 Dec, 1652 *pragmatica*.

²⁶ Filza 30 document 34, 537.

²⁷ David Nirenberg (*Communities of Violence*, 4–5) writes: "Regardless of their different periodizations, all these quests for the origins of European intolerance have much in common. All take the long view, seeking to establish a continuity between the hatreds of long ago and those of the here and now. This focus on the long durée means that events are read less within their local contexts than according to a teleological leading, more or

theatrical activities does not take into account the fact that, at least for Jewish women, this period was one of relative permissiveness in undertaking theatrical activities. Furthermore, it may have been the very exposure to Christian society (paradoxical because of the creation of the separation barrier of the ghetto) that encouraged among Jews more activities common to Christian society, including female participation in theater. For the Jewish community, as Raz-Krakotzkin has persuasively argued, contact with Hebraists and other Christians interested in exchange and study with members of the Jewish community may have meant that the rabbis and other community leaders were losing their influence over the very community they were charged with protecting.[28] A fact even Simonsohn concedes in part when he writes: "As for the frequency of the publication of bans and *pragmatiche*—it is hard to know whether this demonstrates the multiplicity of offences, or the increasing concern of the community's leaders and rabbis."[29] Consequently, it may have been the openness and contact with Christian ways (including theater), rather than the repressive hand of Christian rulers, which eventually led to the internal clamp-down on these very activities. Indeed, when the theatrical activities of the Jews ended, they ended by mutual consensus and after repeated attempts by Duke Carlo II to persuade the Jews to stage yet one more play.

The cessation of the performances was consonant with the Jewish community's state. Simonsohn writes that from the sources it appears that the performance had become a burden (נטל) for the community and no longer something done willingly.[30] Soon after, Jews stopped performing at all in Mantua, and the function of staging became forbidden for Jews in the community, who were forbidden from attending theater or performing at the Jewish holiday of Purim, during which Jews traditionally were encouraged to put on plays.[31] Thus the cessation of theater appears to be reciprocal. The community communicated to the ruler that they no longer wanted to perform for him, and at the same time they prohibited performances within the community itself. The separateness from which Jews had emerged returned by the middle of the seventeenth century, ushering in again an insularity for the community. Even when rebellious younger

---

less explicitly to the Holocaust." See Raz-Krakotzkin, *The Censor, the Editor, and the Text*, 2–3, 183–84; and Bonfil, *Jewish Life in Renaissance Italy*.

[28] Raz-Krakotzkin, *The Censor, the Editor, and the Text*, 2–3.

[29] Raz-Krakotzkin, *The Censor, the Editor, and the Text*, 2–3.

[30] Simonsohn, "Lehakat ha-Teatron Shel Yehudei Mantova," 16. Simonsohn takes this information again from the Jewish archival sources in Mantua. Also noted in Simonsohn, *History of the Jews*, 667–68.

[31] Simonson, "Lehakat ha-Teatron Shel Yehudei Mantova," 16.

members of the community petitioned their community elders to be allowed to produce plays, their desire was quickly and absolutely thwarted.[32]

During the War of Mantuan Succession (1628–1630), the siege, plague, and exile of the Jews and their diminished state upon being permitted to return in 1630 had made the financial burden of the performances impossible. Furthermore, internal tensions within the community meant the increasing enforcements of restrictions on the performances. As restrictions grew, and when the performance was a mere imposition, it ended. However, in the period of waning public performances by the Jews for the Christian community, and paradoxically under ghettoization, a new participant population was added to the performances for the brief time that they still took place: that of Jewish women. Precisely in the years of Jewish ghettoization, and even in the period following the traumatic expulsion of the Jews from Mantua during the War of Mantuan Succession, Jewish women participated in and attended Jewish theatrical events within the ghetto, asserting their own place within the long chapter of Jewish theatrical activity in Mantua.

Bibliography

Primary Documents

ADCEM Filza (file) 26 and Cartella (document) 33. The document is found on the digital archive of the Jewish community of Mantua ("communita ebraica Mantova" under the "sezione Antica").
ADCEM Filza (file) 29 Cartella (document) 37.
Pragmatica. 24 December 1651. Filza 30 Document 34.
Pragmatica. 29 December, 1652. Filza 30 Document 54.

Secondary Works

Barasch, Frances K. "Italian Actresses in Shakespeare's World: Vittoria and Isabella," *Shakespeare Bulletin* 19, no. 3 (Summer 2001): 5–9.
———. "Italian Actresses in Shakespeare's World: Flaminia and Vicenza." *Shakespeare Bulletin* 18, no. 4 (Fall 2000): 17–21.
Bonfil, Robert. *Jewish Life in Renaissance Italy.* Translated by Anthony Oldcorn ([Italian original, *Gli Ebrei in Italia nell' epoca del Rinascimento* (Florence: Sansoni, 1991)]. Berkeley: University of California Press, 1994.

---

[32] Simonsohn ("Lehakat ha-Teatron Shel Yehudei Mantova," 16) recounts attempts to perform plays in 1729, 1757, and 1779. The community resisted these petitions but was forced to perform them in 1729 and 1757. However, the 1757 performance was allowed on condition that only Jewish community members be allowed to see it.

De' Sommi, Leone. *Four Dialogues on Stage Affairs* Translated by Allardyce Nicoll, "The Dialogues of Leone di Somi." Appendix B in *The Development of the Theatre: A Study of Theatrical Art from the Beginning to the Present Day*, 252–78. 5th ed. New York: Harcourt, Brace and Company, 1966.

———. *Quattro dialoghi in material di rappresentazioni sceniche.* Edited by Ferruccio Marotti. Milan: Il Polifilo, 1968.

Detenbeck, Laurie. "Women and the Management of Dramaturgy in *La Calandria*." In *Donna: Women in Italian Culture*, ed. Ada Testaferri, 245–62. University of Toronto Italian Studies 7. Toronto: Dovehouse, 1989.

Günsberg, Maggie. *Gender and the Italian Stage: From the Renaissance to the Present Day* (Cambridge: Cambridge University Press, 1997).

Harrán, Don. "Madama Europa, Jewish Singer in Late Renaissance Mantua." In *Festa Musicologica: Essays in Honor of George J. Buelow*, ed. Thomas J. Mathiesen and Benito V. Rivera, 197–231. New York: Pendragon, 1995.

———. *Salamone Rossi: Jewish Musician in the Late Renaissance Mantua.* Oxford: Oxford University Press, 2003.

Henke, Robert. *Performance and Literature in the Commedia dell' Arte.* Cambridge: Cambridge University Press, 2002.

Jaffe-Berg, Erith. "Leone De' Sommi, 'Magen Nashim, In difesa delle donne.'" *Testuale: critica della poesia contemporanea* 42 (2007): 40–50.

———. "'Magen Nashim': An Early-Modern Defense of Women." *Metamorphoses* 16, no. 2 (Fall 2008): 105–28.

———. "Performance as Exchange: Taxation and Jewish Theatre in Early Modern Italy." *Theatre Survey* 54, no. 3 (September 2013): 389–418.

Katritzky, M. A. "Reading the Actress in Commedia Imagery." In *Women Players in England, 1500–1660: Beyond the All-Male Stage*, ed. Pamela Allen Brown and Peter Parolin, 109–44. Aldershot: Ashgate, 2005.

Kerr, Rosalind. *The Rise of the Diva on the Sixteenth-Century Commedia dell' Arte Stage.* Toronto: University of Toronto Press, 2015.

Korda, Natasha. "Women's Theatrical Properties." In *Staged Properties in Early Modern English Drama*, eds. Jonathan Gil Harris and Natasha Korda. 202–29. Cambridge: Cambridge UP: 2002.

MacNeil, Anne. *Music and Women of the Commedia dell' Arte in the Late Sixteenth Century.* Oxford: Oxford University Press, 2003.

McGill, Kathleen. "Women and Performance: The Development of Improvisation by the Sixteenth-Century Commedia dell' Arte." *Theatre Journal* 43 (1991): 59–69.

Nirenberg, David. *Communities of Violence: Persecution of Minorities in the Middle Ages.* Princeton: Princeton University Press, 1996.

Patuzzi, Stefano. *Una Tavola Apparecchiata: Il 'mangiare degli ebrei' e il caso di Mantova.* Mantua: Publi Paolini, 2013.

Ravid, Benjamin. "Curfew Time in the Ghetto of Venice." In *Medieval and Renaissance Venice*, ed. Ellen E. Kittell and Thomas F. Madden, 237–75. Urbana: University of Illinois Press, 1999.

Raz-Krakotzkin, Amnon. *The Censor, the Editor, and the Text: The Catholic Church and the Shaping of the Jewish Canon in the Sixteenth Century*. Translated by Jackie Feldman [Hebrew original, *Ha-Tsensor, ha-orech, vehatext* (Jerusalem: Magnes Press, 2005)]. Philadelphia: University of Pennsylvania Press, 2007.

Scott, Virginia. "La Virtu et la volupté: Models for the Actress in Early Modern Italy and France." *Theatre Research International* 23, no. 2 (1998): 152–58.

Simonsohn, Shlomo. "Lehakat ha-Teatron Shel Yehudei Mantova" [The Theatre Troupe of the Jews of Mantua]. In *Pargod: Bamah Le-Enyane Sifrut ve-Tiatron* [*Pargod: Theatre Art and Literature*], ed. Arieh Mark, 13–17. Jerusalem: Halakah Ha-Deramatit Misrad Dikan Ha-Studentim Ha-Universitah Ha-Ivrit Be-Yerushalayim, 1963.

———. *History of the Jews in the Duchy of Mantua*. Jerusalem: Kiryath Sepher, 1977.

Sponsler, Claire. "Writing the Unwritten: Morris Dance and Theatre History." In *Representing the Past: Essays in Performance Historiography*, ed. Charlotte M. Canning and Thomas Postlewait, 84–113. Iowa City: University of Iowa Press, 2010.

Symes, Carol. "Out in the Open, in Arras: Sightlines, Soundscapes, and the Shaping of a Medieval Public Space." In *Cities, Texts and Social Networks, 400–1500 Experiences and Perceptions of Medieval Urban Space*, ed. Caroline Goodson, Anne E. Lester, and Carol Symes, 279–302. Surrey, UK, and Burlington, VT: Ashgate, 2010.

Chapter 10
THE POLITICS OF MEDITERRANEAN MARRIAGE
IN CHAUCER, SHAKESPEARE, AND MILTON

KAT LECKY,
BUCKNELL UNIVERSITY

A long-running legend recounts how a sultan's daughter boarded a merchant ship to pursue the English crusader Gilbert Becket after his release from an eastern Mediterranean prison. Accounts paint her as the quintessential romance heroine:

> O wonderful beyond measure both the courage and the love of this woman in undertaking such difficulties and hardships! She did not hesitate, though she was of such noble birth and possessed such great wealth, irrevocably to forsake all; she did not fear, though frail and delicate, to undergo the dangers of poverty; nor did she hesitate to face alone the innumerable perils of a vast extent of country and of a stormy sea, so long as she might seek for one man . . . though she had no assurance of his being alive or of her being able to find him, and still less assurance of his marrying her.[1]

The Saracen princess is the feminine agent shaping this Mediterranean romance, which is staged in terms of economic risk.[2] Her gamble pays off: she marries her knight and gives birth to a child who would grow up to be Thomas Becket, one of the most famous saints in English history.

This legend appeared in five different sources within 100 years of Becket's death and circulated steadily in both manuscript and print through the nineteenth century.[3] The myth about Becket's Saracen mother proliferated in an

---

[1] From the Later Quadrilogus, the earliest known source of this legend. Cited in and translated by Paul Brown, *The Development of the Legend of Thomas Becket*, 30.

[2] Crewe ("Believing the Impossible," 12) defines "the chaste, charismatic, patient heroine as the central, animating figure of romance."

[3] The first accounts are found in the Later Quadrilogus, Brompton's chronicle, Grim's Life, London, British Library Harley MS 978, and London, British Library Cotton MS Julius D 6. It emerges in texts such as the *South English Legendary*, Mirk's *Festial*, the *Legenda Aurea* and Caxton's *Golden Legend*, Capgrave's and Tynemouth's Nova *Legenda Angliae*, Challoner's *Briannia Sancta*, and Dickens' *A Child's History of England*. For

English nation whose economy relied heavily upon this sea.[4] Becket's cross-cultural parentage fashioned him into an incarnation of England's intimate encounters with this foreign world.[5] His cosmopolitan body proved that the English could enter into productive unions with Mediterranean trading partners despite their geographical estrangement. At a time when England's financial viability depended on its tenuous ties to this maritime economy—and when its denizens' economic adventures could easily lead to violence and enslavement—the romance of cross-cultural marriage offered a manageable metaphor for thinking through the complex diplomacies of trans-Mediterranean relations.

Helen Cooper explains, "almost all romances are narratives either of courtship leading to marriage, or of the trials that part a loving married couple."[6] This essay explores how some representative English authors used romance to negotiate their nation's dependence on (and alienation from) the Mediterranean culture that dominated the premodern western world. Chaucer's *Man of Law's Tale*, Shakespeare's *Othello*, and Milton's *Samson Agonistes* all use romantic marriage to make sense of a fluid Mediterranean economy that blended mercantilism with piracy, slavery, and imperialism. In each text the marriage performs in microcosm the dramas of trade and conquest playing out between the yoked societies of the Christian West and the Muslim East. In each text the wife embodies the ambiguity of these cross-cultural contacts: she is the open vessel that drifts between the poles of equity and subjugation, transnationalism and imperialism, profit and loss. She is the agent of the *oikos*, the household economy that is the foundation of the political.[7] In this way the wife is also the ship of state, the embodiment of a nation that in its relationship to foreign states oscillates between a merchant vessel and a slave ship.[8] Despite their generic and contextual

---

the transmission history, see Paul Brown, *The Development of the Legend of Thomas Becket*, 28–50; bibliography on 278–87.

[4] On the Mediterranean's cultural, economic, and literary impact on England, see Lavezzo, *Angels on the Edge of the World*; Robinson, *Islam and Early Modern English Literature*; and Stanivukovic, *Remapping the Mediterranean World*.

[5] Abulafia, *Mediterranean Encounters*; Fuchs, *Mimesis and Empire*; W. Harris, *Rethinking the Mediterranean*; Finucci, "Special issue: Mapping the Mediterranean"; Horden and Purcell, *The Corrupting Sea*. The seminal study remains Braudel, *The Mediterranean and the Mediterranean World in the Age of Philip II* (vols. 1–2). See also Piterberg, Ruiz, and Symcox, *Braudel Revisited*.

[6] Cooper, *The English Romance in Time*, 28. See also Winkler, "The Invention of Romance."

[7] Jordan, "The Household and the State"; Kahn, "Margaret Cavendish and the Romance of Contract"; Lupton, "Rights, Commandments, and the Literature of Citizenship"; Thompson, *The Ship of State*.

[8] Keyt ("Plato and the Ship of State," 201) explains that Plato "takes a normal merchant ship, steered and captained by a competent, or 'true,' steersman, to be an image of an ideal city . . . [T]he owner of a well-run ship . . . has not forgotten that his goal is to

differences, Chaucer's, Shakespeare's, and Milton's texts share one of the structuring tropes of English romance: its emphases on the subjective interiority and transformational agency of the desiring female protagonist.[9] The foreign bride has the power to erase geographical and economic difference, while the foreign husband widens cultural schisms. Productivity depends upon feminine mobility; masculine wanderings engender nothing but loss.

The texts of Chaucer, Shakespeare, and Milton are examples of an English literary tradition that seeks to understand England's place on this international stage.[10] Medieval and early modern romances often explore their nation's shifting role in Mediterranean power relations through the trope of the foreign bride. The literary progression from Chaucer's text to those of Shakespeare and Milton mirrors England's historical progression. In Chaucer's day, the late medieval nation was dependent upon but marginal to the Mediterranean economy; in Shakespeare's time, post-Elizabethan England emerged as a naval power in its own right after its defeat of the Spanish Armada; and by Milton's era, the seventeenth-century empire aggressively dominated the sea. As historical England transforms its Mediterranean role from subservient to domineering, it ceases to identify with the wife to align with the husband. Consequently, the fecund potential of cross-cultural romance in Chaucer's *Tale* is reduced to a lost possibility in Shakespeare's *Othello*, while in Milton's *Samson* it is no more than a barren cipher. Chaucer's romance turns tragic in Shakespeare's before becoming irrelevant in Milton's, as England hardens against its neighbors.

Shakespeare's and Milton's devaluation of romance is itself part of a greater shift marking the difference between English literature of the Middle Ages and that of the Renaissance. Cooper notes the labile quality of romance, which presents itself through a set of "family resemblances" with the capacity to adapt to the genre's changing times and places, while Barbara Fuchs emphasizes romance's voracious opportunism, in its ability to adapt to and even cannibalize other genres.[11] These traits enabled romance to dominate English literature for more

---

make a profit by transporting goods from one port to another." Niccoli ("Images of Society," 112) recounts that the "long history" of the metaphor of the ship of state also has ties to the Christian Church as the "ship of salvation."

[9] Cooper, *The English Romance in Time*, 19. Cooper explains that the romance genre is at base about "women's sexuality," which "is centrally regarded as positive, to the point where it is one of the key factors that enables the restoration of social and providential order" (220).

[10] Salvatore ("From Tension to Dialogue?" 221) explains that all of Europe defined itself in relation to the Mediterranean while "find[ing] itself outside of the civilizational 'axis' that supports the fundamentals of its purported politico-cultural legacy" located in Greece and Jerusalem. England was, of course, at the far margins of a European world negotiating the strategic space of the Mediterranean.

[11] Cooper, *The English Romance in Time*, 9; Fuchs, *Romance*.

than 500 years.[12] Part of this genre's power derived from its talents for simultaneously reflecting and reshaping the world outside its readers' horizons. Robert Rouse traces in the later English Middle Ages a romance geography within
which a nation's churches and cities are connected by international trade routes.[13]
As protagonists move through this multifaceted landscape, they mesh religious
and political affiliations with mercantile interests. In this way, late medieval
romance stages an economy that undermines even as it reinforces state- and
faith-generated boundaries. Romance's hold over the English imagination less-
ened in tandem with the post-Reformation rise of an epic literature that celebrated national and religious separatism. Claire Jowitt points out that although
romances fueled by "the desire for material wealth" continued to be popular in
early modernity, they were "clearly secondary to the patriotic motive and desire
for glory" that molded epics.[14] Rather than remaining the primary way in which
English authors and audiences mapped their nation's imaginary and pragmatic
links to the world, romance became in early modernity the mercantile-minded
relation of the noble epic form.

Chaucer's Boat:
Constance as Open Mediterranean Vessel

Chaucer's *The Man of Law's Tale* is an example of medieval English romance at
the height of its generic supremacy, and the text stages its transnational Mediterranean romance by recounting the story of a seafaring Roman princess's two
cross-cultural weddings.[15] David Wallace states that Chaucer's explorations of
marriage take place in conjunction with the author's interrogations into other
social and political institutions, and Custance's alliances play out within a framework yoking international mercantile trade with religious difference and imperial violence.[16] In his prologue, the Man of Law foregrounds the importance of

---

[12] For the generic distinctions of medieval and early modern romance, see Chism,
Alliterative Revivals; Doody, *The True Story of the Novel*; Field, Hardman, and Sweeney,
Christianity and Romance in Medieval England; Frye, *Anatomy of Criticism*; Hardman,
The Matter of Identity in Medieval Romance; Heng, *Empire of Magic*; P. Parker, *Inescapable
Romance*; and C. Saunders, *A Companion to Romance*.

[13] Rouse, "Walking (between) the Lines."

[14] Jowitt, *The Culture of Piracy*, 82.

[15] Chaucer, *The Man of Law's Tale*, in *The Riverside Chaucer*, ed. Robinson, 87–104.
Line citations follow in the text.

[16] Wallace, *Chaucerian Polity*. Hendrix links religious and economic profit in "'Pennance profytable.'"

the Tale's economic element by attributing his story to a traveling merchant.[17] He contrasts his condemnation of the failed dynastic marriages of the scheming Aeneas, Theseus, and Jason with his encomium on "riche marchauntz" whose sea travels have granted them the knowledge of "al th'estaat / Of regnes" (ll. 122–129).[18] Susan Phillips notes that Chaucer's romance "celebrates merchants rather than magic," and this is true in the Tale's favoring of the pragmatics of conjugal economies over dynastic mystifications: Custance's first marriage fails because of its inherent imperialism and hierarchical structure, while her second succeeds as a result of the partners' equity and desire for common profit.[19]

Over the past few decades, critics have read Custance as a vessel rather than an agent: for instance, Geraldine Heng notes that Custance's "very emptiness and availability" invite the author and his audience to look past her at broader questions of nation and empire.[20] Carolyn Dinshaw argues that Custance's marriages dictate "the dynamics of *The Man of Law's Tale*" and are themselves dictated by Gayle Rubin's theory of marriage as the traffic in women.[21] The ideology of the dynastic, masculinist model of marriage is indeed at work in this text; however, this version coexists with the presence of its romance double, which hinges upon the woman's active choice of her spouse.[22] Chaucer places the two in tension within Custance's marriages, setting them against each other in order to draw out the dialectic of coverture and consent, endogamy and exogamy, and enslavement and equity. Her first marriage to the sultan is beset by imperialism, endogamy, and hierarchy, while her second marriage is at base a microcosm of the system of Mediterranean trade.[23] Throughout the tale Custance is a vessel; but as the boat of romance towing the ship of state, she is not passive. Her romance adventures—consisting in part of five sea crossings that total more

---

[17] In response to the critical view that the narrator is suspect, Barlow ("A Thrifty Tale," 339) argues that the Man of Law's unreliability opens a liminal space "in which alternative forms of value and authority can interact and come into conflict, bearing with them the potential to change the balance of power." The cultural bias of Chaucer's pilgrim sets a critical distance between the legal-minded speaker and his romance-loving audience, and it allows a hermeneutics of suspicion to flourish in the gap. See also Dinshaw, *Chaucer's Sexual Poetics*, 88–112; Nolan, "'Aquiteth yow now'"; Robertson, "The 'Elvyssh' Power of Constance"; and Schibanoff, "Worlds Apart."

[18] Delaney (*The Naked Text*, esp. 165–71) recounts how Chaucer developed firsthand knowledge of Mediterranean politics in his role for the English court.

[19] Phillips, "Chaucer's Language Lessons," 52.

[20] K. Davis, "Time Behind the Veil"; Heng, *Empire of Magic*, 191; Schibanoff, "Worlds Apart."

[21] Dinshaw, "New Approaches to Chaucer," 278.

[22] Cooper, *The English Romance in Time*, 218–68.

[23] As Honig points out (*Democracy and the Foreigner*, 89–90), "marriage in general [is] . . . always a site at which all sorts of goods and services are exchanged, including citizenship, legal residence status, money, companionship, and sex."

than eight years in duration—juxtapose drift with choice, and openness with agency.

At the core of Chaucer's romance are Custance's marriages, which reflect the contradictory nature of the late medieval English marriage contract.[24] It was a feudal system that subjected the wife to her spouse; as a metaphor of the social contract, it promoted the ruler's subjugation of those he ruled. At the same time, consent was considered crucial to marriage, and the law privileged the woman's choice.[25] This feminine-oriented mode of "companionate" marriage ensured that wives were not mere commodities subsumed under the legal fiction of coverture.[26] Martha Howell explains that companionate marriage rose to prominence with the rise in movable wealth in the later Middle Ages.[27] The economic advantages of this equitable union appealed to a mercantile class whose wealth was easily gained or lost: in a companionate marriage, husband and wife were "partners in life" who would "combine energies to preserve what they had and secure what they did not."[28] This transactional union "appropriated the language of love and sexual desire and . . . attached to it friendship, cooperation, mutuality, and morality" to define the companionate ideal.[29]

Simon Gaunt notes the "strict exogamy" promoted by this model, in contrast with the "feudal" model of marriage that relied on "endogamy . . . and family control of the choice of marriage partner."[30] In other words, miscegenation promised lucrative rewards: Valerie Forman points out that in some early modern tragicomedies incest is a "localized and insular economy" overcome through exogamy, which is "an idealized fantasy of the abundance that comes with incorporating others into a world of economic exchange."[31] In companionate marriage, the personal becomes the political through an embrace of the foreign. Furthermore, the couple's interest in accumulating goods in common translates into the social macrocosm as a drive towards the common good. What is "common" in this system is not divided along cultural or national lines; rather, companionate marriage gathers alien and native together under a shared purpose. Of course,

---

[24] Pamela Brown, *Better a Shrew Than a Sheep*; Cressy, *Birth, Marriage, and Death*; Dolan, *Marriage and Violence*; Fletcher, *Gender, Sex, and Subordination in England*; Hume, "The Medieval Marriage Market and Human Suffering"; Wall, "For Love, Money, or Politics?"; Wrightson, *English Society*.

[25] Donahue, *Law, Marriage, and Society in the Later Middle Ages*; McCarthy, *Marriage in Medieval England*.

[26] Kennedy, *Maintenance, Meed, and Marriage in Medieval English Literature*.

[27] Howell, *Commerce Before Capitalism in Europe*; B. Harris, *English Aristocratic Women*.

[28] Howell, "The Properties of Marriage in Late Medieval Europe," 61.

[29] Howell, "The Properties of Marriage in Late Medieval Europe," 61.

[30] Gaunt, *Gender and Genre in Medieval French Literature*, 74.

[31] Forman, *Tragicomic Redemptions*, 66–67.

this cosmopolitan model of wedded bliss, which played out in innumerable late medieval romances that centered on the feminine protagonist's desires, existed in tandem with the earlier model that reinforced patriarchal hierarchies and social stasis. In romance, this feudal model emerges as a microcosm of imperial lust that vies for supremacy over its amiable mercantile counterpart.

Custance's first marriage places the imperial and companionate models in dialogue but ultimately falls on the side of domination and enslavement. Her father, the emperor of Rome, arranges her match to the Muslim sultan of Syria. He negotiates this marriage

> by tretys and embassadrie,
> And by the popes mediacioun,
> And al the chirche, and al the chivalrie,
> That in destruccioun of mawmettrie,
> And in encrees of Cristes lawe deere,
> They been acorded. (233–238)

The terms are simple: the sultan will convert himself and his people, and in return he will receive Custance along with a quantity of gold. Economics and faith work hand in hand to cement the terms of the marriage contract.[32] The fantasy of equity dominates the language of this treaty, in which "This same accord was sworn on eyther syde" (244). Nevertheless, this union grounds itself in imperial claims on the part of the Roman church and state, which seeks to expand its influence in the East. Although the match furthers the financial and spiritual interests of both parties, it is not companionate: the emperor's motives are imperialist while the sultan's are selfish; Custance has no choice but to follow her father's bidding; and the Tale's analogues begin with incest.[33] Although this marriage appropriates the discourse of the free trade agreements circulating among various nations doing business in the Mediterranean, it exemplifies the law of dynastic exchange.

Chaucer reveals the feudal, imperialist underpinnings of this cross-cultural union by highlighting women's reactions against it. As Custance sails across the Mediterranean to meet her betrothed, she rails against the unfairness of being sent "unto the Barbre nacioun" (281). Susan Nakley notices that the image Custance paints of Syrian barbarity belies the sophisticated arguments the sultaness forwards to persuade her lieges to kill the converts.[34] Nakley notes that the sultan's mother calls for a "newly reformed and redeemed Islamic community" that will emerge when the sultan's mother, the sultaness, reverses her son's "deca-

---

[32] Heffernan, "Mercantilism and Faith in the Eastern Mediterranean."
[33] Dinshaw, *Chaucer's Sexual Poetics*; Heng, *Empire of Magic*, 400–401 n. 35.
[34] Nakley, "Sovereignty Matters," 383–87.

dent abandonment of his nation's faith for private satisfaction."[35] The sultan's precipitous conversion to Christianity in return for personal gratification, paired with the emperor's trade of his daughter for land in the eastern Mediterranean, creates within this marriage a dynamic fueled by the desire for private gain rather than common good. Custance's cultural bias against the Syrians reveals that she too participates in this system of endogamy and violent empire. Although the sultaness advocates the common good rather than the interests of a few, it is a good that includes only her native community and not its immigrants. The sultaness chooses social endogamy: she slaughters her son to keep out foreign influence. This marriage is personal, and so are the feminine rejections of it.

As a result of its exclusivity, the union of Custance and the sultan borrows from the discourse of the Mediterranean slave trade—an antagonistic economy that traded in prisoners of international wars or religious conflicts such as the Crusades.[36] The narrator claims that Custance is "bounden under subjeccioun" to her new spouse—a view to which she herself subscribes when she mourns that "Wommen are born to thraldom and penance, / And to been under mannes governance" (270; 286–287). The images of enslavement that stem from this vertical model of marriage dominate the sultaness' discourse as well. When she appeals to her subjects to help overthrow her son, she paints his decision to marry as an act of abasement. The sultaness explains that if the Syrians accept the "newe lawe" of Custance's Rome, they are agreeing to a life of "thraldom to oure bodies and penance" (337–338). The sultan's enforced conversion of his people to Christianity is essentially the imposition of foreign imperium. With his tyrannical act, the Islamic leader exposes himself as a slave of the Roman emperor. The political and religious aspects of this conversion are inseparable and contribute equally to the enthrallment of the Muslim nation by a Christian aggressor. The sultaness stages her usurpation of Syria as a democratic act: she asks if her people will support her, and "They sworen and assenten, every man" (344). Nonetheless, the sultaness' version of common good excludes transnational accommodation: its rejection of miscegenation places Syria in conflict with a large portion of the Mediterranean world.

Custance's second marriage stands in sharp contrast to the first. Set adrift by her mother-in-law after her husband's death, for over five years she follows a major shipping route between the Middle East and western Europe as she drifts from the coast of Syria through the Strait of Gibraltar, up the Atlantic to the North Sea. Finally she lands on the shores of Northumberland, where she naturalizes willingly into the community. Custance's change in attitude is striking: rather than continuing to lament her personal losses, she "thanketh Goddes

---

[35] Nakley, "Sovereignty Matters," 388.

[36] Fleet, *European and Islamic Trade in the Early Ottoman State*, 37–58; Constable, "Muslim Spain and Mediterranean Slavery"; Rotman, *Byzantine Slavery and the Mediterranean World*, 57–68.

sonde" and refuses to divulge her past to her new compatriots (523). Like Gilbert Becket's Saracen princess, she puts aside her former claims to wealth and gambles on her new romance adventure. Nationless and without official status as either the daughter of a Roman emperor or the widow of a Syrian sultan, Custance makes a fresh start on English soil. She retains her Christian and Roman identity (she communicates with the natives in a "maner Latyn corrupt") but blends into her adoptive body politic to "serve and plese" her townspeople, who accept the foreign woman as one of their own (519; 531). Custance's performance of cultural accommodation leads to her companionate marriage to Alla, the king of Northumberland, who marries her and converts to Christianity for her sake.

Of course this marriage also contains elements of its hierarchical counterpart, again exemplified in the response of Custance's mother-in-law Donegild, who denounces her son's spouse and tries to cleanse her body politic of foreignness by placing her son's alien bride and their child in the same rudderless boat that brought her to England's shores.[37] This time Custance and her son are adrift in the Mediterranean for another five years before being rescued by Romans returning home from killing the sultaness. Meanwhile, Alla counters his mother's attempt at social endogamy with matricide — a definitive, if disturbing, rejection of the feudal model of marriage — and finds his wife and son safe in Rome. Their reunion spurs Custance's final two Mediterranean journeys: she returns to England with Alla, and after his death a year later she sails back to Rome.[38]

The nexus of adaptation and accommodation that defines the union of Custance and Alla engenders a cosmopolitan model of a transnational social contract that connects England with Rome on equal terms and also invokes the would-be Muslim conversion of her first spouse through her second husband's strikingly Islamic name. Their union thus embodies companionate marriage while mimicking the medieval Mediterranean's thriving mercantile economy. In the Middle Ages, English merchants participated in a transnational system so complex that it required intense and sustained collaboration among numerous trading companies spanning the sea.[39] For instance, the textile industry brought together merchants from the Brabant, Egypt, England, Flanders, France, Italy, the Levant, and the Magreb: a length of wool or silk was usually the result of the transfer of "industrial raw materials, half-finished and finished products . . . over long distances."[40] Cities throughout the Mediterranean hosted branches of international mercantile companies, whose members often lived in "virtual

---

[37] Unlike the democratically minded sultaness, Donegild is "ful of tirannye" and makes no claims to act for the common good (696).

[38] Dinshaw (*Chaucer's Sexual Poetics*, 101–02) points out that Custance's return to Rome after Alla's death places her back into an endogamous relationship with her father.

[39] Abulafia, "The Role of Trade in Muslim-Christian Contact during the Middle Ages."

[40] Jacoby, "The Migration of Merchants and Craftsmen," 545.

free-trade areas" while enjoying a degree of "individual or collective privileges" that governments granted to stimulate the economy.[41] This system promoted exogamy in addition to economic gain: in England these business incentives for foreign merchants "consisted primarily in tax reductions or exemptions and in citizenship or burgess rights in cities or the status of denizens."[42] The accommodative nature of this maritime trade produced international goods for an international clientele, while producing cosmopolitan Mediterranean citizens with affiliations in multiple states.[43]

The marriage of Custance and Alla participates in this equitable, adaptive economy, and its consummation produces Mauricius, who becomes the half-English emperor of Rome. He is the cosmopolitan product of Custance's willingness to sexually accommodate Alla:

> For though that wives been ful holy thinges,
> They moste take in pacience at night
> Swich maner necessaries as been plesinges
> To folk that han ywedded hem with ringes,
> And leye a lite hir holinesse aside
> As for the time — it may no bet bitide. (709–714)

Chaucer explains that Custance, like all wives, is a "ful holy thinge." Her integrity is marked by her adherence to that ideal of self-sufficiency which allows her to be a vessel brimming with virtue, which opens for the common good. Custance, like a vase full of the wine of divine grace, needs to remove her stopper — to "leye a lite hir holinesse aside" — so that she may pour out some of her sacramental libation for her conjoined bodies politic. Custance's accommodation is not a breach but a reinforcement: her liquidity, represented in her son Mauricius, joins England with Christianity and Rome with Englishness.

As Custance adapts to her transnational union, she creates with her husband an individual in whom the bloodlines of Rome and England mingle seamlessly in equitable proportion.[44] This mingling is significant not least because of England's own status as "other" within the international Mediterranean economy.[45] Custance's and Alla's marriage exemplifies the societal ideal of an equal union between distinct nations all invested in the flourishing system of intellectual, religious, political, and economic exchange that characterizes the medieval Mediterranean. Meanwhile, Custance's decisions, pivotal to this couple's success, reflect Chaucer's England's newly established House of Commons, which granted

---

[41] Jacoby, "The Migration of Merchants and Craftsmen," 547.

[42] Jacoby, "The Migration of Merchants and Craftsmen," 549.

[43] Kelly, "Jews and Saracens in Chaucer's England."

[44] Lavezzo, *Angels on the Edge of the World*, 102.

[45] Lavezzo, "Complex Identities," 450. Lavezzo also stresses the essential role that England's "others" play in the formation of medieval Englishness (453).

representative agency to the burghers who ruled over local affairs. This extension of governmental power to the merchant class granted legitimacy to those traditionally marginalized by the feudal system.[46] In Chaucer's day, those formerly excluded from political influence could now help steer their nation's course. In his *Tale*, the author translates this mercantile figure of governance—who is eccentric to the Crown and invested in a commonwealth fueled by economic prosperity—into the seafaring Custance, the abandoned woman who forges a valuable new history for a Christian England shaped by the exchange of cultures, faiths, and communitarian ideals throughout the Mediterranean.

Reforming English Romance: Early Modern Mediterranean Mutations

But what happens when these medieval emphases on individual and marginal agency come into contact with an ever more centralized state vying for supremacy in the Mediterranean? Shakespeare and Milton each explore the increasing futility of viewing the space of the sea as the ground of cross-cultural romance in an early modern English nation that, over the course of the sixteenth and seventeenth centuries, comes to define itself as an empire. This ideological shift necessitates a rejection of companionate models of cross-cultural unions in favor of an imperial system that subjugates the foreign into colonial service. As epic becomes the overriding literary and ontological mode of England's relationship to the world, the once-potent romance genre fissures into a vehicle of lost promise. Like Chaucer, Shakespeare and Milton fix this medieval possibility of Mediterranean relations in the microcosm of cross-cultural marriage; but for Shakespeare the promise is fleeting, and Milton forecloses its possibilities.

Nevertheless, the seafaring bride is one of the major medieval tropes retained by Renaissance romances. David Quint explains that "the boat of romance," which emphasizes mercantile exploration, signals a "romance adventure" that is "an individualistic alternative to the collective epic mission" that Quint identifies with militant nationalism.[47] Laura Doyle connects this individualism with community: the boat signifies at once a freedom from national boundaries and the shelter for a transnational intersubjectivity.[48] "Open-ended and potentially

[46] Backman, *Worlds of Medieval Europe*, 288.

[47] Quint, "Tasso, Milton, and the Boat of Romance," 252. See also Quint, "The Boat of Romance and Renaissance Epic."

[48] Doyle ("Toward a Philosophy of Transnationalism," 3) notes how "the transnational and the intersubjective [work] together" to stage an interconnectedness that resists hegemonic boundaries. She explains, "Nations do exist, but as transnations or internations; they share a 'tilted' structure of orientation to other nations that is dialectical and dyadic yet also multiple and circumferential or horizontal" (12).

endless," the boat's journey disrupts the teleological force of epic imperialism and charts new possibilities of a culture's relationship to others.[49] The tension between singularity and collectivity resonates in a Mediterranean world in which, as Molly Greene explains, "territorial identity—that is, the claims of sovereigns over their subjects—had come to coexist uneasily with an older tradition of personal law that followed an individual across the sea."[50] The boat of romance plays into the ambiguities of the Mediterranean's inherently transnational economy: for instance, Quint explains that in early modern England the merchant could be read as a romance adventurer who "shows as much if not more valor, courage, and patriotism" as the soldier, which suggests that "trading exploits, rather than martial ones, are the source of England's national glory."[51] Literary representations of this unstable financial system that simultaneously effaced and reinforced national boundaries turned to the genre of romance to perform the economics of this superfluid identity.

For these writers and others, the foreign bride adrift on the sea is seductive because her meanderings offer an alternative course to the imperial maneuvering dominating the early modern Mediterranean. Although Levant trade continued to foster cosmopolitanism by bringing immigrants to England while inspiring English merchants to convert to Islam or "turn Turk," piracy and slavery dominated the basin.[52] Human trafficking was part of the cost of doing business in the Mediterranean: legions of merchants were captured by pirates at sea and sold as slaves.[53] During the seventeenth century, the numbers of those captured reached such epidemic proportions that their captivity narratives offer the most complete picture of England's early modern Muslim encounters.[54] Slavers and pirates regularly "pillaged the coasts of France, Flanders, England, Ireland, and even Iceland."[55] Accounts of savage English raids on Muslim-held territories circulated in the eastern Mediterranean.[56] Nabil Matar explains, "slave trading, privateering, and piracy were carried out by Christians against Muslims, Muslims against Christians, and Christians against their Protestant or Catholic adversaries and even, among the undiscriminating English, against Orthodox Christians

---

[49] Quint, "Tasso," 249.

[50] Greene, *Catholic Pirates and Greek Merchants*, 10. Her evocation of the Mediterranean as a "friendly sea" relies on Goitein, *A Mediterranean Society*.

[51] Quint, "Tasso," 266.

[52] Vitkus, *Turning Turk*.

[53] Greene, *Catholic Pirates and Greek Merchants*. Burton ("Emplotting the Early Modern Mediterranean," 21–40) highlights the multiple power structures driving this economy.

[54] Matar, "Introduction," 6.

[55] R. Davis, "The Geography of Slaving in the Early Modern Mediterranean," 67. Also see R. Davis, *Christian Slaves, Muslim Masters*.

[56] Matar, "Introduction," 1–52.

as well."[57] Jewish slaves and slavers were also involved.[58] Salvatore Bono estimates that "from the sixteenth through the nineteenth century . . . a total of five million" slaves were sold in the Mediterranean.[59] England had a share in this industry: Fuchs observes that the seventeenth-century nation turned to "piracy as a central strategy for negotiating its imperial, military, and cultural belatedness."[60] English slavers sold "Turks" and "Moors," and English pirates plundered Mediterranean cargoes and crews.[61] This xenophobic counterpoint to the system of collaborative transnational trade operated via enslavement and imperialism, and like its equitable counterpart bled into the literature of the times.

Shakespeare's Ships: Mediterranean Marriage and the Intercultural Macrocosm

In his portrayal of Othello's and Desdemona's Mediterranean marriage, Shakespeare highlights this cosmopolitan model of equitable trade relations that connects personal accommodation with transnational growth, before drowning it in the darker undercurrents of slavery and violence.[62] Shakespeare also explores the superfluidity of identity that derives from the transnational Mediterranean economy: Dennis Austin Britton points out that when reading Shakespeare's *Othello* "we need to consider not only Othello's difference but also his belonging" in Venice.[63] As Eric Griffin notes, *Othello* speaks to an English nation that defines itself fundamentally not by its insularity but by its intersections with other Mediterranean cultures.[64] Shakespeare, like Chaucer, dramatizes those intersections as a cross-cultural romance.[65] Like Chaucer's Custance, Desdemona is also a seafaring vessel: Iago describes her as "a land carrack," or rich galleon, that

---

[57] Matar, "Introduction," 7.

[58] Kizilov, "Slave Trade in the Early Modern Crimea."

[59] Bono, "Slave Histories and Memoirs in the Mediterranean."

[60] Fuchs, *The Poetics of Piracy*, 8. See also Fuchs, "Faithless Empires."

[61] Heywood, "The English in the Mediterranean"; Matar, *Turks, Moors, and Englishmen in the Age of Discovery*.

[62] For Shakespeare and citizenship, see Archer, *Citizen Shakespeare*; Arnold, *The Third Citizen*; and Lupton, *Citizen-Saints*, whose reading of *Othello* inspires mine. See also Collinson, "The Monarchical Republic of Queen Elizabeth I"; and Peltonen, "Rhetoric and Citizenship in the Monarchical Republic of Queen Elizabeth I."

[63] Britton, "Re-Turning *Othello*," 27.

[64] Griffin, *English Renaissance Drama and the Specter of Spain*, 168–206. See also Bartels, *Speaking of the Moor*.

[65] Recent studies focusing on Shakespeare's works within a Mediterranean context are Boerth, "The Mediterranean and the Mediterranean World on the Stage of Marlowe and Shakespeare"; Cantor, "The Shores of Hybridity"; Clayton, Brock, and Forés, *Shakespeare and the Mediterranean*; and Stanivukovic, *Remapping the Mediterranean World*. For

Othello has pirated away from her father, Brabantio.[66] Desdemona's value lies in her status as a noble Venetian citizen, and their secret wedding allows Othello to naturalize himself forcibly, if incompletely, into the body politic. Othello's covert seizure parallels the impending Turkish invasion of the Venetian colony of Cyprus and also mirrors the anxieties about enslavement that were a real concern for Elizabethan merchants who traded in the Mediterranean during Shakespeare's time. The microcosm of their marriage reveals the troubled relationship between the Venetians and the Turks. Although Desdemona initiates this union, their companionate marriage is on shaky ground: Iago wonders if Desdemona will "prove lawful prize" for Othello (I.ii.61). The ambiguity of Venetian law reflects a society with isolationist tendencies: Othello and Desdemona face a community that at once depends upon and excludes foreigners. When xenophobia wars with cosmopolitanism, personal and societal relations suffer alike.

The general conflates with the particular through Othello's perceived act of piracy. Desdemona's father protests against his daughter's marriage with the assertion,

> The Duke himself,
> Or any of my brothers of the state,
> Cannot but feel this wrong as 'twere their own.
> For if such actions may have passage free,
> Bondslaves and pagans shall our statesmen be. (I.ii.119–123)

Brabantio describes this unauthorized match as a microcosm of the mutual aggression between the Venetians and the Turks.[67] The course of the relationship between these antagonistic states flows in accord with the dynamics of this marriage, which is defined by the Venetians as an instance of piracy leading to slavery. Here Brabantio frames his protest with the metaphor of sea travel: if Othello's seizure of the feminine "sea carrack" has "passage free," then the Venetians will become slaves rather than masters within the international Mediterranean economy. This sentiment echoes that of Chaucer's sultaness: as Brabantio splits native and foreign into a binary division ruled by imbalances of power, he denounces miscegenation while sanctioning cultural endogamy.

Othello and Desdemona's marriage stands in the crosshairs of this cross-cultural antagonism. Shakespeare emphasizes this point with the Ottoman invasion

---

Shakespeare's indebtedness to late medieval English literature and culture, see Perry and Watkins, *Shakespeare and the Middle Ages.*

[66] William Shakespeare, *Othello*, I.ii.60. Citations follow in the text. See also Orlin, *Othello: New Casebooks*, especially the essays by Lynda Boose, Alan Sinfield, Michael Bristol, Harry Berger, Jr., and Elizabeth Hanson.

[67] Greene (*Catholic Pirates and Greek Merchants*) highlights the aggression and atrocities against Muslims as well as Orthodox Christians by Catholic pirates in the eastern Mediterranean during the seventeenth century.

of Venetian-held Cyprus, which never actually comes to fruition. Instead, the battle for cultural supremacy plays out within the parameters of their union and ends in their marriage bed. Shakespeare yokes the macrocosm with the microcosm by placing Othello and Desdemona at the site of the would-be invasion. The author also defines their marriage as an example of Mediterranean romance by foregrounding Desdemona's agency and influence. She insists on accompanying Othello to Cyprus, despite his wish that she remain behind. She avows,

> That I [did] love the Moor to live with him
> My downright violence and storm of fortunes
> May trumpet to the world . . .
> And to his honors and his valiant parts
> Did I my soul and fortunes consecrate. (I.iii. 283–285; 288–289)

Cooper explains that the trope of "the woman who focuses all her newly awakened desire on the man she chooses to be her husband" is the crucial element in situating a Shakespearean work as a romance.[68] It is also the essential aspect of a companionate marriage. Desdemona chooses Othello of her own volition and stakes herself and her "fortunes" on her new partner. However, she also paints her love with the colors of war, while referring to her spouse as "the Moor." Desdemona internalizes the vexed relationship between her society and its outsiders by adopting its combativeness along with its descriptor of Othello's difference. Desdemona's native diet of Venetian imperialism tilts the scales of her marriage towards its hierarchical counterpart and sets the tragic course of their union.

Nevertheless, during Othello's and Desdemona's journey to Cyprus, romance derails the tragic narrative to reveal alternate possibilities for the cross-cultural couple and their conjoined societies. This intrusion takes the form of the romance trope of a storm so powerful that it destroys the Turkish fleet and throws the Venetians' ships into confusion. Cassio's story of Desdemona's sea voyage casts her as the heroine: he exclaims that the

> Tempests themselves, high seas, and howling winds
> The guttered rocks and congregated sands . . .
> As having sense of beauty, do omit
> Their mortal natures, letting go safely by
> The divine Desdemona. (II.i.75–76; 78–80)

The Mediterranean itself ensures the heroine's safety, caring for Desdemona as it did for Custance when she was in danger. The seascape offers itself as a model of pacifism and accommodation, as the storm renounces its typically deadly nature to allow the romance adventurer's safe passage. This peaceful interlude in the midst of the rush to war causes Othello to exclaim that "If after every tempest

---

[68] Cooper, *The English Romance in Time*, 218.

come such calms / May the winds blow till they have wakened death" (II.i.201–202). Othello welcomes the stasis of death at this moment because he recognizes that now he is "most happy" (II.i.206). This episode uses the generic qualities of romance to slow down the tragedy and make a space within which to contemplate a different ending. Nonetheless, the moment's openness closes when the Venetians in Cyprus return to the business of creating strife.

Shakespeare describes this inimical power structure with terms borrowed from the Mediterranean slave trade. Othello explains that he is himself a victim of this economic system: he was "sold to slavery" and later ransomed in order to fight as a Venetian mercenary (I.iii.160).[69] Othello's freedom from enslavement is therefore illusory and ultimately short-lived: after he murders Desdemona, he reviles himself as a "cursed, cursed slave" (V.ii.327). Othello's admissions of thralldom, which come at the beginning and again at the end of the tragedy, frame Shakespeare's narrative. They reveal that, in effect, the Moor has been the victim of the Mediterranean slave trade throughout the course of the play, not least because of his indenture to the Venetian state. Othello's status as a hired hand who snatches the valuable commodity of Venetian citizenship through his seizure of Desdemona also reveals the indiscernible line separating the self-interested acts of a renegade pirate from the imperialist acts of a state-sponsored privateer. The personal is indistinguishable from the general, and the drama of servitude unfolds simultaneously on individual and collective levels to highlight their symbiotic, intersubjective nature.

Othello's enslavement derives in part from his religious affiliations. Although racism is a driving force in this tragedy—Ben Saunders argues that *Othello* is early proof of the fact that "the central metaphors of racist discourse make waste of humanity"—Julia Reinhard Lupton points out that Othello is also "a Muslim-turned-Christian" who is more threatening to Elizabethans because he is "more likely to go renegade" than a "barbarian" would.[70] Lupton suggests that for Shakespeare's audiences, "religious difference is more powerfully felt, or at least more deeply theorized, than racial difference" due to Elizabethans' familiarity with Mediterranean slavery.[71] These audiences could not have failed to notice the evocation of an array of Mediterranean locales—Florence, Verona, and Venice in Italy; the Barbary coast of North Africa; Cyprus, Rhodes, and Turkey to

---

[69] Slights ("Slaves and Subjects in Othello," 388) argues that "the early modern English fascination with and occlusion of slavery register the fear that a developing concept of individual autonomy could lead to isolation, that an ideal of freedom . . . could lead to its opposite."

[70] B. Saunders, "Iago's Clyster"; Lupton, *Citizen-Saints*, 106. For racism in *Othello*, see Little, *Shakespeare Jungle Fever*; Neill, "Unproper Beds; Newman, "'And wash the Ethiop white'"; Orkin, "*Othello* and the 'plain face' of Racism"; and Skura, "Reading Othello's Skin." See also Boyarin, "Othello's Penis."

[71] Lupton, *Citizen-Saints*, 106.

the east—joined by Iago's praise of England over its neighboring trading centers of Denmark, Germany, and Holland.[72] Text reflects reality: all of these places come together in the play's discursive structure, as they did within the early modern Mediterranean economic system. They all condense in Othello, who is, in Roderigo's words, the "extravagant and wheeling stranger / Of here and everywhere" (I.i.151–152). As the companionate marriage erodes, Othello transforms from an exemplar of cosmopolitanism to the metonym of the Ottoman empire's imperial aggression.[73]

The dissolution of Othello's and Desdemona's cross-cultural union evokes the breakdown of their conjoined bodies politic and stages a concurrent decomposition of their social stature. In the latter stages of Othello's transformation into the stereotypical "Turk," Lodovico sees him and wonders, "Is this the noble Moor, whom our full senate / Call all in all sufficient?" (IV.i.296–297).[74] His loss of integrity is so profound that it is physically apparent. Othello has become unrecognizable, and his changed body betrays his dissolution from cosmopolitan citizen to imperial caricature. This corporal decay is antithetical to the accumulative process embodied in Thomas Becket and Chaucer's Mauricius: they accrue transcultural value, while Othello loses cultural value to the extent that he reviles himself as a "dog" as he commits suicide (V.ii.416). Othello's double extinction of their wedded bodies marks the extinguishing of their union's potential to engender their own cosmopolitan son—a promise evoked in Othello's vow to Desdemona that "The profit's yet to come 'twixt me and you'" (II.iii.10). Desdemona's body similarly loses its worth as a vehicle of cosmopolitanism: although she maintains that she has "preserve[d] this vessel" for Othello with her chastity, its value has depreciated within the imperialist system (IV.ii.96). Unlike Custance, the chaste "vessel" who engenders cross-cultural connections with her procreative body, Desdemona's generative potential is turned to dust. These are the consequences of empire: the imperial mode smothers the possibility of transnational miscegenation.

Othello's imperialist turn reveals itself most fully when he resolves to kill Desdemona: at this moment, he divulges that

> . . . Like to the Pontic Sea,
> Whose icy current and compulsive course
> Ne'er feels retiring ebb, but keeps due on
> To the Propontic and the Hellespont,

---

[72] Mediterranean references are found in I.i.21, I.i.30, I.i.119, I.i.125, II.i.29, and II.iii.79–91.

[73] Robinson (*Islam and Early Modern English Literature*) traces this early modern anxiety about Ottoman aggression in numerous English texts written during the sixteenth and seventeenth centuries.

[74] Lezra, "Translated Turks on the Early Modern Stage," esp. 166–69.

> Even so my bloody thoughts, with violent pace,
> Shall ne'er look back, ne'er ebb to humble love. (III.iii.514–519)

Othello defines himself as the current that runs from the Black Sea, which borders Turkey to the north, through the Dardanelles and into the Aegean Sea, which is a part of the Mediterranean. In his mission to destroy Desdemona, the rich Venetian vessel whom he has captured at the beginning of the play, Othello's course follows the likely route of an Ottoman invasion of western Europe. His plan is a microcosmic version of the Muslim conquest of Christian Mediterranean lands — a prospect feared by Elizabethans. When this drama of the religious antagonism between economically interdependent nations draws to its inevitable conclusion — when, in short, Othello murders Desdemona in their marriage bed — he declares, "Here is my journey's end, here is my butt / And very sea-mark of my utmost sail" (V.ii.318–319). Throughout this tragedy, Shakespeare describes their union by using the seafaring metaphors of this complex transnational culture. The will to power driving both partners in this marriage dramatizes the frequently antagonistic relationship among early modern Christians and Muslims profiting from their cross-cultural encounters. Here the tragic outcome is also an economic failure: rather than profiting from their adherence to imperialism, the Venetians suffer the catastrophic loss of both Desdemona (one of their most prominent citizens) and Othello (their best general).[75]

Milton's Wreck: Marital Differences and Anglo-Mediterranean Incompatibility

In *Samson Agonistes* Milton also taps into this long-running discourse on the profits and pitfalls that stem from England's reliance on Mediterranean trade, painting a grim picture of the consequences of its failure as cosmopolitanism degrades into imperialism. Like Chaucer and Shakespeare, he explores this transnational economic system through the metaphor of the cross-cultural marriage between Samson and Dalila. In Milton's text, their debate centers on the nature of their marriage: Samson defines it in masculinist, power-centered terms while Dalila argues that the hero should embrace their union as companionate.[76] Their wedded status is a Miltonic creation found neither in the biblical Judges

---

[75] Marcus ("Provincializing the Reformation," 436) emphasizes the ambiguity of Othello's position within his adoptive state even at the end of the tragedy: "With Othello's suicide, Venice is saved from internal contamination by Islam, but the city-state is hugely diminished in the process, having lost its most talented military leader."

[76] For analyses of the tension between patriarchal and companionate visions of marriage in Milton's divorce tracts and *Paradise Lost*, see Chaplin, "'One Flesh, One Heart, One Soul'"; Fish, "Wanting a Supplement"; Hausknecht, "The Gender of Civic Virtue";

account nor in other versions of this story, and Milton's revision of the tale high-lights the continued importance during this time of the marriage contract as a synecdoche of transnational social contracts.[77] Critics have often noted the intersections of private and common concerns in this text: for example, Derek Wood and Stella Revard see Dalila as a political leader who works actively to further the interests of her Philistine body politic.[78] Meanwhile, scholars read Samson variously as either a Christian or Hebraic hero or as a Middle Eastern terrorist.[79] Victoria Kahn explains that Milton redefines Dalila as Samson's wife rather than his concubine to highlight the overtly political nature of their mar-riage as a microcosm of the problematics of nationhood vis-à-vis international law.[80] Holly Sypniewski and Anne MacMaster assert that the dialogue between Samson and Dalila highlights their identical yet antithetical beliefs that their actions are divinely sanctioned, and they assert that at the end the reader is left to decide which "individual or state acts in accordance with the will of God."[81] For Sypniewski and MacMaster, Milton's Dalila is "the foreign wife" who is "a sympathetic character with compelling arguments of her own," and their article foregrounds Milton's "cultural relativism."[82] This essay augments these views by suggesting that Milton situates that relativism within the early modern Med-iterranean, where competing cultural systems circulated along with economic trade. As these interrelated yet distinct communities negotiated fiscally with each other, their concurrent negotiations about faith and nationhood informed one another intimately, often towards different and even inconsistent ends. In *Samson*, these cultural divergences clash within Samson's and Dalila's argument about her motives for betraying her spouse. In Milton's text, Dalila, as the ship of

---

Nyquist, "The Genesis of Gendered Subjectivity in the Divorce Tracts and in *Paradise Lost*"; and Rosenblatt, "Milton, Natural Law, and Toleration."

[77] Labreche ("Espousing Liberty," 970) finds that Milton defines "the private house-hold as a source of authority distinct from—and potentially in competition with—that of the state" in the divorce tracts, *Areopagitica*, and *The Tenure of Kings and Magistrates*. Labreche explains that although Milton believed in marriage hierarchies, he proposed that this relationship be inverted when the wife's "wisdom" exceeded that of her spouse (982).

[78] Revard, "Dalila as a Euripidean Heroine"; Wood, *Exiled from Light*.

[79] Cox ("Neo-Roman Terms of Slavery in *Samson Agonistes*," 1) adds yet another Mediterranean dimension to these identifiers: she sees Samson working through a "neo-Roman understanding of . . . citizenship." She notes that Samson "employs the same discourses of marriage and divorce and slavery and liberty that Milton was using in the divorce tracts and his other prose works" (2).

[80] Kahn, "Disappointed Nationalism."

[81] Sypniewski and MacMaster, "Double Motivation and the Ambiguity of 'Ungodly Deeds,'" 147.

[82] Sypniewski and MacMaster, "Double Motivation and the Ambiguity of 'Ungodly Deeds,'" 154.

the Philistine state, is simultaneously merchant vessel and slaver: she welcomes her alien husband into her body politic before chaining him to the service of her people and their god.

Milton's text begins after Dalila's betrayal and delves into the social repercussions of a failed cross-cultural marriage. *Samson* concentrates on the consequences of Dalila's decree that "to the public good / Private respects must yield."[83] Rather than viewing personal and political interests as identical—a basic principle of companionate marriage—here the individual is antithetical to the communal. As in Chaucer's and Shakespeare's texts, this dissolution of a trans-Mediterranean body politic marks itself upon the bodies of Samson and Dalila. Samson brings together East and West, Occident and Orient, and Hebrew, proto-Christian and Muslim/pagan worlds: his identity reflects the hybrid cosmopolitan identity of the early modern Mediterranean citizen. However, the hero who, like Becket, once embodied cosmopolitanism is degraded into "a common workhorse" ("Argument"). We find him "Eyeless in Gaza at the Mill with slaves," and hear about his exploits in Chalybean Pontus, Ascalon, Hebron, Ramath-lechi, Timna, Eshtaol, and Zora in quick succession (41). These place names constitute a catalogue of international port cities along the shores of the Pontic and eastern Mediterranean seas that Samson navigated as the Israelites' champion. Now his physical transformation is so profound that his father does not recognize him: when Manoa approaches, he muses, "O miserable change! is this the man, / That invincible Samson, far renown'd?" (340–341). Like Othello, the degradation imprints itself on Samson after this once free-wheeling stranger has foundered upon his foreign marriage. He mourns that he, "like a foolish Pilot have shipwreck't / My Vessel trusted to me from above, / Gloriously rigg'd" (198–200). Samson's maritime metaphor foregrounds the tenuous nature of this Mediterranean seascape: Samson's imprudent guidance of his body as the microcosm of the Israelite ship of state has made him a slave in foreign lands.

Whereas Samson is a pilot, Dalila (like Custance and Desdemona) is described as a Mediterranean merchant ship. When the Chorus sees her approaching, they wonder

> But who is this, what thing of Sea or Land?
> Female of sex it seems,
> That so bedeckt, ornate, and gay,
> Comes this way sailing
> Like a stately Ship
> Of Tarsus, bound for th' Isles
> Of Javan or Gadire
> With all her bravery on, and tackle trim,
> Sails fill'd, and streamers waving,

---

[83] Milton, *Samson Agonistes*, ll. 867–868. Line numbers follow in the text.

> Courted by all the winds that hold them play,
> An Amber scent of odorous perfume
> Her harbinger, a damsel train behind. (710–721)

This passage, redolent of Shakespeare's description of Cleopatra in another of his Mediterranean romances, clusters nautical and economic signifiers to describe Dalila. Adorned with the trappings of a prosperous merchant vessel of an ambiguously Spanish, Turkish, or Lebanese provenance sailing for either the Greek islands or Spanish Cadiz, Dalila embodies the entwined elements of "Sea" and "Land" that comprise the topography of Mediterranean trade relations. Her deliberate course charts the separate yet interconnected states within this cultural geography. Definitively and richly feminine, Dalila heads a caravan of exotic women while being courted by the tradewinds fueling transnational exchange. She is the personification of the lucrative promise of this Mediterranean economic system.

Their ensuing argument reveals Dalila's complicity in Samson's enslavement. She admits that she was the agent of his capture and confinement, and her discourse glides quickly from requests for Samson's forgiveness to conflicting justifications of her deed. First she claims that she enslaved him out of "the jealousy of love," before abruptly changing course to assert that she was influenced by "all the bonds of civil Duty" to her nation (791; 853). Her rhetorical fluidity highlights her ambiguous role. As the embodiment of the boat of romance and the Philistine ship of state, Dalila drifts between the opposing poles of equity and imperialism in her relationship to her foreign husband. Her shifting characteristics follow her fluctuating allegiances to her spouse and her nation.

Nevertheless, now Dalila claims she is visiting Samson out of "conjugal affection" (739). She asks him for a second chance and invites him back into their nuptial home:

> I to the Lords will intercede, not doubting
> Thir favourable ear, that I may fetch thee
> From forth this loathsom prison-house, to abide
> With me, where my redoubl'd love and care
> With nursing diligence, to me glad office,
> May ever tend about thee to old age. (920–925)

However, Samson reads her offer to reconcile their loving bond as another grab for sovereignty, in which he would live "in perfect thralldom" to her (946). Once Dalila despairs of any reunion between herself and her spouse, she exclaims,

> I see thou art implacable, more deaf
> To prayers, than winds and seas, yet winds to seas
> Are reconcil'd at length, and Sea to Shore:

Thy anger, unappeasable, still rages,
Eternal tempest never to be calm'd. (960–964)

Dalila defines their marriage as an unfit model of Mediterranean romance, and
she abandons her efforts to reunite with him in companionate marriage. The
Mediterranean offers a conciliatory model of accommodation—one in which
storms rage occasionally, but ultimately ebb and leave in their place a living,
adaptive ecosystem in which the elements of wind, sea, land, and sky exist in
symbiosis. Though the marriage of Samson and Dalila appears throughout Milton's text as a seafaring metaphor of this transnational ecosystem, the falsehood
of these comparisons emerges in Samson's refusal to naturalize into his adoptive
home. Cosmopolitanism fails in both its microcosmic and macrocosmic forms,
and the tragedy runs its inevitable course towards the general destruction of Phi-
listines and Danites alike in the temple of Dagon, the Mediterranean sea-god.
When peaceful negotiations break down, everyone suffers the consequent violence.

The message remains consistent in Chaucer's, Shakespeare's, and Milton's
texts: cross-cultural unions have the potential to engender citizens with multinational interests, who maintain their former alliances while embracing their
new community. The historical circumstances dictating cross-cultural exchange
shift, of course. For instance, the Rome of Shakespeare and Milton is no longer
the sympathetic second home it can be for Chaucer, and the Reformation throws
another divisive element into the already vexed relationship among Christians,
Jews, and Muslims.[84] Despite these contextual differences, the romances of *The
Man of Law's Tale*, *Othello*, and *Samson Agonistes* all stage the possibilities of a
cosmopolitan model of citizenship that re-energizes national identities while
forging productive cross-cultural connections.[85] Companionate marriages, like
successful multinational trade relationships, stage a horizontal politics of shared
agency that respects difference and allows diversity to thrive. These unions contrast the asymmetrical divisions of imperialism with transnationalism, miscegenation, and naturalization. Chaucer, Shakespeare, and Milton all tap into
romance as the business model of Mediterranean trade—a system of exchange
that is mutually lucrative when it privileges the equity of the cultures enmeshed
in these cross-cultural encounters, rather than fighting for individual or national
supremacy.

---

[84] For a qualification, see Netzloff, "The English Colleges and the English Nation."
[85] Balibar, *We, The People of Europe?*

Bibliography

Abulafia, David. "Gli italiani fuori d'Italia." In *Commerce and Conquest in the Mediterranean, 1100–1500,* ed. David Abulafia, 261–86. Brookfield, VT: Ashgate Variorum, 1993.

———. *Mediterranean Encounters: Economic, Religious, Political, 100–1550.* Surrey, UK: Ashgate Variorum, 2000.

———. "The Role of Trade in Muslim-Christian Contact during the Middle Ages." In *The Arab Influence in Medieval Europe,* ed. Dionisius A. Agius and Richard Hitchcock, 1–24. Reading, UK: Ithaca Press, 1994.

Archer, John Michael. *Citizen Shakespeare: Freemen and Aliens in the Language of the Plays.* New York: Palgrave, 2005.

Arnold, Oliver. *The Third Citizen: Shakespeare's Theater and the Early Modern House of Commons.* Baltimore: Johns Hopkins University Press, 2007.

Backman, Clifford. *Worlds of Medieval Europe.* Oxford: Oxford University Press, 2002.

Balibar, Étienne. *We, The People of Europe? Reflections on Transnational Citizenship.* Translated by James Swenson. Princeton: Princeton University Press, 2004.

Barlow, Gania. "A Thrifty Tale: Narrative Authority and Competing Values of the *Man of Law's Tale." The Chaucer Review* 44, no. 4 (2010): 397–420.

Bartels, Emily. *Speaking of the Moor: From Alcazar to Othello.* Philadelphia: University of Pennsylvania Press, 2008.

Blake, John. *The Sea Chart: The Illustrated History of Nautical Maps and Navigational Charts.* London: Conway Maritime Press, 2004.

Boerth, Robert. "The Mediterranean and the Mediterranean World on the Stage of Marlowe and Shakespeare." *Journal of Theater and Drama* 2 (1996): 35–58.

Bono, Salvatore. "Slave Histories and Memoirs in the Mediterranean: A Study of the Sources (Sixteenth–Eighteenth Centuries)." Translated by Sarah Barrett. In *Trade and Cultural Exchange in the Early Modern Mediterranean: Braudel's Maritime Legacy,* ed. Maria Fusaro, Colin Heywood, and Mohamed Salah Omri, 97–116. London: Taurus, 2010.

Boyarin, Daniel. "Othello's Penis: Or, Islam in the Closet." In *Shakesqueer: A Queer Companion to the Complete Works of Shakespeare,* ed. Madhavi Menon, 254–62. Durham, NC: Duke University Press, 2011.

Braudel, Fernand. *The Mediterranean and the Mediterranean World in the Age of Philip II,* vols. 1–2. Translated by Siân Reynolds. Berkeley: University of California Press, 1995.

Britton, Dennis Austin. "Re-Turning *Othello*: Transformative and Restorative Romance." *ELH* 78 (Spring 2011): 27–50.

Brown, Pamela Allen. *Better a Shrew than a Sheep: Women, Drama, and the Culture of Jest in Early Modern England.* Ithaca: Cornell University Press, 2003.

Brown, Paul Alonzo. *The Development of the Legend of Thomas Becket*. Philadelphia: University of Pennsylvania Press, 1930.

Burrow, Colin. *Epic Romance: Homer to Milton*. Oxford: Oxford University Press, 1993.

Burton, Jonathan. "Emplotting the Early Modern Mediterranean." In *Remapping the Mediterranean World in Early Modern English Writings*, ed. Goran V. Stanivukovic, 21–40. New York: Palgrave Macmillan, 2007.

Calkin, Siobhain Bly. *Saracens and the Making of English Identity: The Auchinleck Manuscript*. New York: Routledge, 2005.

Cantor, Paul A. "The Shores of Hybridity: Shakespeare and the Mediterranean." *Literature Compass* 3, no. 4 (July 2006): 896–913.

Chaucer, Geoffrey. "The Man of Law's Tale." In *The Riverside Chaucer*, ed. F. N. Robinson. Boston: Houghton Mifflin, 1987.

Chaplin, Gregory. "'One Flesh, One Heart, One Soul': Renaissance Friendship and Miltonic Marriage." *Modern Philology* 99 (2001): 266–92.

Chiat, Marilyn J., and Kathryn L. Reyerson, eds. *The Medieval Mediterranean: Cross-Cultural Contacts*. St. Cloud, MN: North Star Press, 1988.

Chism, Christine. *Alliterative Revivals*. Philadelphia: University of Pennsylvania Press, 2002.

Clayton, Tom, Susan Brock, and Vicente Forés, eds. *Shakespeare and the Mediterranean: The Selected Proceedings of the International Shakespeare Association World Congress, Valencia 2001*. Newark: University of Delaware Press, 2004.

Collinson, Patrick. "The Monarchical Republic of Queen Elizabeth I." *Bulletin of the John Rylands Library* 69, no. 2 (1987): 394–424.

Constable, Olivia R. "Muslim Spain and Mediterranean Slavery: The Medieval Slave Trade as an Aspect of Muslim-Christian Relations." In *Christendom and Its Discontents: Exclusion, Persecution, and Rebellion, 1000–1500*, ed. Scott L. Waugh and Peter D. Diehl, 264–84. Cambridge: Cambridge University Press, 1996.

Cooper, Helen. *The English Romance in Time: Transforming Motifs from Geoffrey of Monmouth to the Death of Shakespeare*. Oxford: Oxford University Press, 2004.

Cox, Rosanna. "Neo-Roman Terms of Slavery in *Samson Agonistes*." *Milton Quarterly* 44, no. 1 (March 2010): 1–22.

Cressy, David. *Birth, Marriage, and Death: Ritual, Religion, and the Life Cycle in Tudor and Stuart England*. New York: Oxford University Press, 1997.

Crewe, Jonathan. "Believing the Impossible: *Aethiopika* and Critical Romance." *Modern Philology* 106, no. 4 (May 2009): 601–16.

Daileader, Celia. *Racism, Misogyny, and the Othello Myth: Inter-Racial Couples from Shakespeare to Spike Lee*. Cambridge: Cambridge University Press, 2005.

Davis, Kathleen. "Time Behind the Veil: The Media, the Middle Ages, and Orientalism Now." In *The Postcolonial Middle Ages*, ed. Jeffrey Jerome Cohen, 105–22. New York: Palgrave Macmillan, 2000.

Davis, Robert. *Christian Slaves, Muslim Masters: White Slavery in the Mediterranean, the Barbary Coast, and Italy, 1500–1800.* Basingstoke, Hampshire: Palgrave Macmillan, 2003.

———. "The Geography of Slaving in the Early Modern Mediterranean, 1500–1800." *JMEMS* 37, no. 1 (Winter 2007): 57–74.

Delany, Sheila. *The Naked Text: Chaucer's Legend of Good Women.* Berkeley: University of California Press, 1994.

Dinshaw, Carolyn. *Chaucer's Sexual Poetics.* Madison: University of Wisconsin Press, 1990.

———. "New Approaches to Chaucer." In *The Cambridge Companion to Chaucer,* ed. Piero Boitani and Jill Mann, 270–89. Cambridge: Cambridge University Press, 2003.

Dolan, Frances. *Marriage and Violence: The Early Modern Legacy.* Philadelphia: University of Pennsylvania Press, 2008.

Donahue, Charles. *Law, Marriage, and Society in the Later Middle Ages: Arguments About Marriage in Five Courts.* New York: Cambridge University Press, 2007.

Doody, Margaret Anne. *The True Story of the Novel.* New Brunswick: Rutgers University Press, 1996.

Doyle, Laura. "Toward a Philosophy of Transnationalism." *Journal of Transnational American Studies* 1, no. 1 (2009): 1–30.

Field, Rosalind, Philippa Hardman, and Michelle Sweeney, eds. *Christianity and Romance in Medieval England.* Cambridge: Cambridge University Press, 2010.

Finucci, Valeria, ed. Special issue: "Mapping the Mediterranean." *JMEMS* 37, no. 1 (Winter 2007).

Fish, Stanley. "Wanting a Supplement: The Question of Interpretation in Milton's Early Prose," In *Politics, Poetics, and Hermeneutics in Milton's Prose,* ed. David Loewenstein and James Grantham Turner, 41–68. Cambridge: Cambridge University Press, 1990.

Fleet, Kate. *European and Islamic Trade in the Early Ottoman State: The Merchants of Genoa and Turkey.* Cambridge: Cambridge University Press, 1999.

Fletcher, Anthony. *Gender, Sex, and Subordination in England 1500–1800.* New Haven: Yale University Press, 1995.

Forman, Valerie. *Tragicomic Redemptions: Global Economics and the Early Modern English Stage.* Philadelphia: University of Pennsylvania Press, 2008.

Frye, Northrop. *Anatomy of Criticism.* Princeton: Princeton University Press, 1957.

Fuchs, Barbara. "Faithless Empires: Pirates, Renegadoes, and the English Nation," *ELH* 67, no. 1 (Spring 2000): 45–69.

———. *Mimesis and Empire: The New World, Islam, and European Identities.* Cambridge: Cambridge University Press, 2001.

————. *The Poetics of Piracy: Emulating Spain in English Literature*. Philadelphia: University of Pennsylvania Press, 2013.

————. *Romance*. New York: Routledge, 2004.

Gaunt, Simon. *Gender and Genre in Medieval French Literature*. Cambridge: Cambridge University Press, 1995.

Goitein, S. D. A. *A Mediterranean Society: The Jewish Communities of the Arab World as Portrayed in the Documents of the Cairo Geniza*. 6 vols. Berkeley and Los Angeles: University of California Press, 1967–1993.

Greene, Molly. *Catholic Pirates and Greek Merchants: A Maritime History of the Mediterranean*. Princeton: Princeton University Press, 2010.

Griffin, Eric. *English Renaissance Drama and the Specter of Spain: Ethnopoetics and Empire*. Philadelphia: University of Pennsylvania Press, 2009.

Hardman, Phillipa, ed. *The Matter of Identity in Medieval Romance*. Woodbridge, Suffolk: Brewer, 2003.

Harris, Barbara J. *English Aristocratic Women, 1450–1550: Marriage and Family, Property and Careers*. Oxford: Oxford University Press, 2002.

Harris, William, ed. *Rethinking the Mediterranean*. London: Oxford University Press, 2005.

Hausknecht, Gina. "The Gender of Civic Virtue." In *Milton and Gender*, ed. Catherine Gimelli Martin, 19–33. Cambridge: Cambridge University Press, 2005.

Heffernan, Carol F. "Mercantilism and Faith in the Eastern Mediterranean: Chaucer's *Man of Law's Tale*, Boccaccio's *Decameron* 5,2, and Gower's *Tale of Constance*." In *The Orient in Chaucer and Medieval Romance*, ed. Carol Falvo Heffernan, 23–44. Cambridge: Brewer, 2003.

Hendrix, Laurel L. "'Pennance profytable': The Currency of Custance in Chaucer's *Man of Law's Tale*." *Exemplaria* 6 (1994): 141–66.

Heng, Geraldine. *Empire of Magic: Medieval Romance and the Politics of Cultural Fantasy*. New York: Columbia University Press, 2003.

Heywood, Colin. "The English in the Mediterranean, 1600–1630: A Post-Braudelian Perspective on the 'Northern Invasion.'" In *Trade and Cultural Exchange in the Early Modern Mediterranean: Braudel's Maritime Legacy*, ed. Maria Fusaro, Colin Heywood, and Mohamed-Salah Omri, 23–44. London: Tauris, 2010.

Honig, Bonnie. *Democracy and the Foreigner*. Princeton: Princeton University Press, 2001.

Horden, Peregrine, and Nicholas Purcell, eds. *The Corrupting Sea: A Study of Mediterranean History*. Oxford: Blackwell, 2000.

Howell, Martha C. *Commerce before Capitalism in Europe, 1300–1600*. Cambridge: Cambridge University Press, 2010.

————. "The Properties of Marriage in Late Medieval Europe: Commercial Wealth and the Creation of Modern Marriage." In *Love, Marriage, and*

Family Ties in the Later Middle Ages, ed. Isabel Davis, Miriam Muller, and Sarah Rees Jones, 17–61. Turnhout: Brepols, 2003.

Hume, Cathy. "The Medieval Marriage Market and Human Suffering: *The Man of Law's Tale*." In *Chaucer and the Cultures of Love and Marriage*, ed. Cathy Hume, 107–26. Cambridge: Brewer, 2012.

Jacoby, David. "The Migration of Merchants and Craftsmen: A Mediterranean Perspective." In *Trade, Commodities and Shipping in the Medieval Mediterranean*, ed. David Jacoby, 533–60. Brookfield, VT: Ashgate Variorum, 1997.

Jordan, Constance. "The Household and the State: Transformations in the Representation of an Analogy from Aristotle to James I." *Modern Language Quarterly* 54, no. 3 (September 1993): 307–26.

Jowitt, Claire. *The Culture of Piracy, 1580–1630: English Literature and Seaborne Crime*. Farnham, Surrey: Ashgate, 2010.

Kahn, Victoria. "Disappointed Nationalism: Milton in the Context of Seventeenth-Century Debates about the Nation-State." In *Early Modern Nationalism and Milton's England*, ed. David Loewenstein and Paul Stevens, 249–72. Toronto and London: University of Toronto Press, 2008.

———. "Margaret Cavendish and the Romance of Contract." *Renaissance Quarterly* 50, no. 2 (Summer 1997): 526–66.

Kelly, Henry Ansgar. "Jews and Saracens in Chaucer's England: A Review of the Evidence." *Studies in the Age of Chaucer* 27 (2005): 129–69.

Kennedy, Kathleen E. *Maintenance, Meed, and Marriage in Medieval English Literature*. New York: Palgrave Macmillan, 2009.

Keyt, David. "Plato and the Ship of State." In *The Blackwell Guide to Plato's Republic*, ed. Gerasimos Santas, 189–213. Malden, MA: Blackwell, 2006.

Kipling, Gordon. *Enter the King: Theatre, Liturgy, and Ritual in the Medieval Civic Triumph*. Oxford: Clarendon, 1998.

Kizilov, Mikhail. "Slave Trade in the Early Modern Crimea from the Perspective of Christian, Muslim, and Jewish Sources." *Journal of Early Modern History* 11 (2007): 1–31.

Labreche, Ben. "Espousing Liberty: The Gender of Liberalism and the Politics of Miltonic Divorce." *ELH* 77, no. 4 (Winter 2010): 969–94.

Lavezzo, Kathy. *Angels on the Edge of the World: Geography, Literature and English Community, 1000–1534*. Ithaca: Cornell University Press, 2006.

———. "Complex Identities: Selves and Others." In *The Oxford Handbook of Medieval Literature in England*, ed. Elaine Treharne and Greg Walker, 434–56. New York: Oxford University Press, 2010.

———, ed. *Imagining a Medieval English Nation*. Minneapolis: University of Minnesota Press, 2004.

Lezra, Jacques. "Translated Turks on the Early Modern Stage." In *Transnational Exchange in Early Modern Theater*, ed. Robert Henke and Eric Nicholson, 159–80. Burlington, VT: Ashgate, 2008.

Little, Arthur. *Shakespeare Jungle Fever: National-Imperial Re-Visions of Race, Rape, and Sacrifice*. Stanford: Stanford University Press, 2000.

Lupton, Julia Reinhard. *Citizen-Saints: Shakespeare and Political Theology*. Chicago: University of Chicago Press, 2005.

———. "Rights, Commandments, and the Literature of Citizenship." *Modern Language Quarterly* 66, no. 1 (March 2005): 21–54.

Marcus, Leah. "Provincializing the Reformation." *PMLA* 126, no. 2 (March 2011): 432–39.

Martin, Catherine Gimelli. "Dalila, Misogyny, and Milton's Christian Liberty of Divorce." In *Milton and Gender*, ed. Catherine Gimelli Martin, 53–76. Cambridge: Cambridge University Press, 2005.

Matar, Nabil. "Introduction: England and Mediterranean Captivity, 1577–1704." In *Piracy, Slavery, and Redemption: Barbary Captivity Narratives from Early Modern England*, ed. Daniel J. Vitkus, 1–52. New York: Columbia University Press, 2001.

———. *Turks, Moors, and Englishmen in the Age of Discovery*. New York: Columbia University Press, 1999.

McCarthy, Conor. *Marriage in Medieval England: Law, Literature and Practice*. Woodbridge: Boydell, 2004.

Milton, John. *Samson Agonistes. John Milton: Complete Poems and Major Prose*. Edited by Merritt Y. Hughes. New York: Macmillan, 1957.

Nakley, Susan. "Sovereignty Matters: Anachronism, Chaucer's Britain, and England's Future's Past." *Chaucer Review* 44, no. 4 (2010): 368–96.

Neill, Michael. "Unproper Beds: Race, Adultery, and the Hideous in *Othello*." *Shakespeare Quarterly* 40 (1989): 383–412.

Netzloff, Mark. "The English Colleges and the English Nation: Allen, Persons, Verstegan, and Diasporic Nationalism." In *Catholic Culture in Early Modern England*, ed. Ronald Corthell, Frances E. Dolan, Christopher Highley, and Arthur Marotti, 236–60. Notre Dame: University of Notre Dame Press, 2007.

Newman, Karen. "'And wash the Ethiop white': Femininity and the Monstrous in *Othello*." In *Shakespeare Reproduced: The Text in History and Ideology*, ed. Jean E. Howard and Marion F. O'Connor, 143–62. London: Methuen, 1987.

Niccoli, Ottavia. "Images of Society." In *Early Modern History and the Social Sciences: Testing the Limits of Braudel's Mediterranean*, ed. John A. Marino, 101–22. Kirksville, MO: Truman State University Press, 2002.

Nolan, Maura. "'Aquiteth yow now': The Man of Law's Introduction." In *The Letter of the Law: Legal Practice and Literary Production in Medieval England*, ed. Emily Steiner and Candace Barrington, 136–53. Ithaca: Cornell University Press, 2002.

Nyquist, Mary. "The Genesis of Gendered Subjectivity in the Divorce Tracts and in *Paradise Lost*." In *Re-Membering Milton*, ed. Mary Nyquist and Margaret W. Ferguson, 99–127. New York: Methuen, 1987.

Orkin, Martin. "*Othello* and the 'plain face' of Racism," *Shakespeare Quarterly* 38 (1987): 166–88.

Orlin, Lena Cowen, ed. *Othello: New Casebooks*. New York: Palgrave Macmillan, 2004.

Parker, Grant. "Mapping the Mediterranean." *JMEMS* 37, no. 1 (Winter 2007): 1–8.

Parker, Patricia. *Inescapable Romance: Studies in the Poetics of a Mode*. Princeton: Princeton University Press, 1979.

Peltonen, Markku. "Rhetoric and Citizenship in the Monarchical Republic of Queen Elizabeth I." In *The Monarchical Republic of Early Modern England: Essays in Response to Patrick Collinson*, ed. John F. McDiarmid, 109–28. Burlington, VT: Ashgate, 2007.

Perry, Curtis, and John Watkins, eds. *Shakespeare and the Middle Ages*. Oxford: Oxford University Press, 2009.

Phillips, Susan. "Chaucer's Language Lessons." *The Chaucer Review* 46, no. 1–2 (2011): 39–59.

Piterberg, Gabriel, Teofilo F. Ruiz, and Geoffrey Symcox, eds. *Braudel Revisited: The Mediterranean World, 1600–1800*. Toronto: University of Toronto Press, 2010.

Quint, David. "The Boat of Romance and Renaissance Epic." In *Romance: Generic Transformations from Chretien de Troyes to Cervantes*, ed. Kevin Brownlee and Maria Scordilis Brownlee, 178–202. Hanover and London: University Press of New England, 1985.

——. "Tasso, Milton, and the Boat of Romance." In *Epic and Empire: Politics and Generic Form from Virgil to Milton*, ed. David Quint, 248–67. Princeton: Princeton University Press, 1993.

——, ed. *Epic and Empire: Politics and Generic Form From Virgil to Milton*. Princeton: Princeton University Press, 1993.

Revard, Stella P. "Dalila as a Euripidean Heroine." *Papers on Language and Literature* 23 (1987): 291–302.

Robertson, Elizabeth. "The 'Elvyssh' Power of Constance: Christian Feminism in Geoffrey Chaucer's *The Man of Law's Tale*." *Studies in the Age of Chaucer* 23 (2001): 143–80.

Robinson, Benedict. *Islam and Early Modern English Literature: The Politics of Romance from Spenser to Milton*. New York: Palgrave Macmillan, 2007.

Rosenblatt, Jason P. "Milton, Natural Law, and Toleration." In *Milton and Toleration*, ed. Sharon Achinstein and Elizabeth Sauer, 126–43. Oxford: Oxford University Press, 2007.

Rotman, Youval. *Byzantine Slavery and the Mediterranean World*. Translated by Jane Marie Todd. Cambridge, MA: Harvard University Press, 2009.

Rouse, Robert. "Walking (between) the Lines: Romance as Itinerary/Map." In *Medieval Romance, Medieval Contexts*, ed. Rhiannon Purdie and Michael Cichon, 135–47. Cambridge: Brewer, 2011.

Rubin, Gayle. "The Traffic in Women: Notes on the 'Political Economy' of Sex." In *Toward an Anthropology of Women*, ed. Rayna Reiter, 157–210. New York: Monthly Review Press, 1975.

Salvatore, Armando. "From Tension to Dialogue? The Mediterranean between European Civilization and the Muslim World." In *Civilizational Dialogue and World Order: The Other Politics of Cultures, Religions, and Civilizations in International Relations*, ed. Michális S. Michael and Fabio Petito, 217–38. New York: Palgrave Macmillan, 2009.

Saunders, Ben. "Iago's Clyster: Purgation, Anality, and the Civilizing Process." *Shakespeare Quarterly* 55, no. 2 (Summer 2004): 148–76.

Saunders, Corinne, ed. *A Companion to Romance: From Classical to Contemporary*. Oxford: Blackwell, 2004.

Schibanoff, Susan. "Worlds Apart: Orientalism, Antifeminism, and Heresy in Chaucer's *Man of Law's Tale*." *Exemplaria* 8, no. 1 (1996): 59–96.

Shakespeare, William. *Othello*. Edited by Barbara A. Mowat and Paul Werstine. New York: Washington Square Press, 1993.

Skura, Meredith Anne. "Reading Othello's Skin: Contexts and Pretexts." *Philological Quarterly* 87, no. 3/4 (Summer 2008): 299–335.

Slights, Camille Wells. "Slaves and Subjects in Othello." *Shakespeare Quarterly* 48, no. 4 (Winter 1997): 377–90.

Stanivukovic, Goran V. *Remapping the Mediterranean World in Early Modern English Writings*. New York: Palgrave Macmillan, 2007.

Sypniewski, Holly M., and Anne MacMaster. "Double Motivation and the Ambiguity of 'Ungodly Deeds': Euripides's *Medea* and Milton's *Samson Agonistes*." *Milton Quarterly* 44, no. 3 (October 2010): 145–67.

Tinniswood, Adrian. *Pirates of Barbary: Corsairs, Conquests and Captivity in the Seventeenth-Century Mediterranean*. New York: Riverhead, 2010.

Thompson, Norma. *The Ship of State: Statecraft and Politics from Ancient Greece to Democratic America*. New Haven: Yale University Press, 2001.

Vitkus, Daniel. "Adventuring Heroes in the Mediterranean: Mapping the Boundaries of Anglo-Islamic Exchange on the Early Modern Stage." *JMEMS* 37, no. 1 (Winter 2007): 75–96.

———. *Turning Turk: English Theater and the Multicultural Mediterranean, 1570–1630*. New York: Palgrave Macmillan, 2003.

Wall, Alison. "For Love, Money, or Politics? A Clandestine Marriage and the Elizabethan Court of Arches." *Historical Journal* 38, no. 3 (1995): 511–33.

Wallace, David. *Chaucerian Polity: Absolutist Lineages and Associational Forms in England and Italy*. Stanford: Stanford University Press, 1997.

Winkler, John. "The Invention of Romance." In *The Search for the Ancient Novel*, ed. James Tatum, 23–37. Baltimore: Johns Hopkins University Press, 1994.

Wood, Derek N. C. *Exiled from Light: Divine Law, Morality, and Violence in Milton's Samson Agonistes.* Toronto: University of Toronto Press, 2001.

Wrightson, Keith. *English Society, 1580–1680.* New Brunswick: Rutgers University Press, 2003.